Monty and Patton

Two Paths to Victory

MONTY AND PATTON

TWO PATHS TO VICTORY

by

Michael Reynolds

SPELLMOUNT
Staplehurst

British Library Cataloguing in Publication Data:
A catalogue record for this book is available
from the British Library

Copyright © Michael Reynolds 2005
Maps © Jay Karamales 2005

ISBN 1-86227-257-3

First published in the UK in 2005 by
Spellmount Limited
The Village Centre
Staplehurst
Kent TN12 0BJ

Tel: 01580 893730
Fax: 01580 893731
E-mail: enquiries@spellmount.com
Website: www.spellmount.com

1 3 5 7 9 8 6 4 2

The right of Michael Reynolds to be identified
as the author of this work has been asserted by him
in accordance with the Copyright, Designs
and Patents Act 1988

Typeset in Palatino by MATS, Southend-on-Sea, Essex
Printed in Great Britain by
T.J. International Ltd
Padstow, Cornwall

Contents

CONTENTS

List of Maps

(The maps can be found on pages 325–340)

Publisher's Note

It is regretted that for commercial reasons it has not been possible to include coloured or pull-out maps in the book; however, for those purists who enjoying knowing the exact location of the places mentioned and their relationship to each other, it is suggested that they photocopy and enlarge the maps provided and have them to hand when reading. This will also enable them to insert the thrust and defensive lines etc. that particularly interest them.

Introduction and Acknowledgements

Of all the Allied generals who caught the headlines in the Middle East and Europe in WWII, two prevail. Neither held supreme command, but both had a magnetism and flair that set them apart from their contemporaries. Both achieved outstanding successes on the battlefield, both went out of their way to court the headlines and both made serious mistakes that attracted adverse publicity. Their names were Bernard Montgomery and George Patton.

Scores of books and articles have already been written about these men as individuals, but none, to the best of my knowledge, have made a direct comparison between their lives as men and soldiers. There were numerous similarities in their early years. They were born in the same month just two years apart, had chequered careers at military academy, were commissioned within a year of each other and they were both wounded in France in WWI. However, there were important differences – one was born into the family of a Victorian churchman, the other into that of a wealthy American landowner; one became an infantryman, the other a cavalryman. But despite these different backgrounds, Monty and Patton demonstrated similar traits in their later lives – their total dedication to their careers, their professionalism, selfishness, arrogance, their desire for the limelight and their unhesitating use of friends in high places to further their careers or achieve their aims. All these traits and characteristics will become clear as their stories unfold.

No attempt, however, is made in this book to present a definitive biography of either Monty or Patton; nor does it try to analyse their psychological, sexual or religious orientations. Readers interested in these aspects are recommended to read the detailed biographies listed in the Bibliography. On the contrary, this book has a quite simple aim: to summarize and compare their lives and careers; furthermore, there is no attempt to prove that one was a greater man or commander than the other – they were both great generals and they both made essential contributions to the final victory in Europe in WWII.

In the course of writing this book I have been quite surprised to find that my own path sometimes came quite close to those trodden by Monty and

Patton. During the war the former was of course a hero to all British schoolboys and in 1944 I wrote to him for, and received, his autograph. At Sandhurst I lived on the same floor in the same wing of the same College and much later on I lived for eighteen months (without knowing it) fairly near the location of his Tac HQ in Holland. I trained many times on Lüneburg Heath where Monty took the German surrender in May 1945 and thirty years later as a Brigade commander, I lived and worked within fifteen miles of his post-war Headquarters in Schloss Ostenwalde. Finally, like him, I spent the last years of my military career serving in NATO Headquarters. I heard Monty lecture only once – at Sandhurst in 1950, and I met him only once – at a private dinner at the Staff College in 1960.

In the case of George Patton there were obviously far fewer connections. I did, however, live for three years in Mannheim within five miles of the site of the car crash that led to his early death, and almost every day I was driven to my Headquarters in Heidelberg along the exact route taken by the ambulance conveying him to the hospital where he died. In fact I used to attend that same hospital for dental treatment. Sadly, during my three years in Mannheim and Heidelberg, 1980–1983, no one even *mentioned* George Patton and no one in the US Army seemed to have any interest in military history. When I told an American Corps commander that I had organized a number of battlefield tours in the Ardennes so that my officers could study the lessons of the Battle of the Bulge, he replied: 'I'm too busy planning for the next war to waste my time looking at the past'.

There is very little that is new in this book – almost every fact in it has already appeared in print somewhere before. Nevertheless, I hope that the way in which it has been compiled will bring out the most interesting aspects of the lives of these two very controversial characters and enable readers to make their own comparisons and judgements.

I am greatly indebted to Nigel Hamilton, Alistair Horne, Lord Montgomery and Carlo D'Este. Without their detailed biographies of Montgomery and Patton I would never have attempted to write this book and I have relied heavily on their meticulous research. It was *they*, not I, who initially read and published the relevant diary extracts and letters I have quoted, and it is only through *their* dedication, integrity and scholarship that I have been able to put this book together. I am also very grateful to David Montgomery for allowing me to quote from his father's letters, diaries and books, to Alistair Horne and again David Montgomery for permission to quote from their book *The Lonely Leader*, to the Montgomery Collections Committee of the Trustees of the Imperial War Museum (IWM) in London for permission to quote from the Montgomery Papers, and to Carlo D'Este for permission to quote from his magnificent work *A Genius for War*.

I would also like to thank Brigadier Brian Burditt and the Curatorial Officer of the Royal Regiment of Fusiliers Museum (Royal Warwickshire), at St John's House, Warwick, Miss Stephanie Bennett, for their help in discovering what really happened to Montgomery on 13 October 1914, my great friend Brigadier Tony Baxter for his initial proof reading and many useful suggestions, and my American friend and cartographer, Jay Karamales, for again turning my hand-produced maps into finished products.

Finally, I must once more thank my publisher, Jamie Wilson, and his wife Beverly, for their friendship and support and of course my own wife, Anne, for all her patience and encouragement, for listening to me 'trying out' various ideas and chapters and indeed, once again, for a number of very useful ideas.

MFR
Sussex, England
July 2004

CHAPTER I

The Early Years

Bernard Law Montgomery and George Smith Patton Jr were both born, appropriately enough, under the eighth sign of the zodiac, the scorpion – Montgomery on 17 November 1887 in Kennington Oval, London and Patton on 11 November 1885 in Pasadena, California. Their childhoods could not have been more different.

Montgomery

Monty's parents both came from distinguished Victorian families. His paternal grandfather, Sir Robert Montgomery, had played a prominent role in dealing with part of the Indian Mutiny in 1857 and had risen to be the Lieutenant Governor of the Punjab; his mother's father, Dean Frederic Farrar, was a recognized writer and scholar and had been a housemaster at Harrow School for sixteen years and Headmaster of Marlborough College for six years. His most famous book, *Eric, or Little by Little*, about English school life in the nineteenth century, was a bestseller and ran to over fifty editions. He subsequently became a Canon and Archdeacon of Westminster Abbey, Rector of St Margaret's Westminster, and an Honorary Chaplain to Queen Victoria, the House of Commons and the Dean of Canterbury. Monty's father, Henry, was also a churchman. He was 32 and the vicar of St Mark's Church, Kennington, when he married his 16-year-old bride, Maud. She had never been to school and was sexually uneducated. St Mark's parish was a large one of some 14,000 people and although it was clearly unreasonable to expect a teenager to play a full part as a vicar's wife, Monty's father is said to have burdened her with awesome responsibilities, as well as five children in the first eight years – Monty was the fourth. Furthermore, he left his children's up-bringing almost entirely to his wife. Perhaps not altogether surprisingly she, badly missing her own nine brothers and sisters, felt alone and imposed upon and she soon turned into a tyrannical mother. In Monty's own words:

> Certainly I can say that my own childhood was unhappy. This was due to a clash of wills between my mother and myself. My early life was a series of fierce battles from which my mother invariably emerged the victor.[1]

1

He is also wrote later: ' I do not care for the Farrar blood' and is said to have described any male near relative he disliked as: 'a Farrar, not a Montgomery'.[2]

In 1889 Monty's father was appointed first Bishop of Tasmania and the family moved to Hobart. Once again the mother was left to bring up the children while the Bishop threw himself into his evangelical work in the outback of Tasmania and its many outlying islands. His wife, in order to cope with her duties as a senior churchman's wife and a mother, became even more dictatorial and hard on her children, imposing a rigid discipline and swiftly punishing any disobedience with a cane. Part of the reason for his mother's behaviour was a shortage of money caused by the low salaries of the clergy and in particular the economic crash of the early 1890s. Maud soon became known as the worst dressed woman in Hobart. Although a male tutor was brought over from England for the older brothers and three other local children, Monty was deemed too young for this group and was sent instead to a girls' infant school with his younger sister. This did little for his self-confidence and his rebellious nature soon landed him in trouble. He was 'the bad boy of the family' and suffered the most – 'I was a dreadful little boy. I don't suppose anyone would put up with my sort of behaviour these days. I had a dreadful childhood'.[3] But despite the harsh treatment he received he held no long-term grudge against his mother: 'she brought up her family in her own way . . . the time came when her authority could no longer be exercised. Fear then disappeared, and respect took its place.'[4] Some idea of the way the children were treated in Hobart can be gauged from the following description:

> [They] rose at dawn, tidied their rooms, cleaned their shoes and chopped wood for the fires. Lessons began at 7.30, followed by an inspection of the bedrooms (the children standing on parade at the doorways), and then chapel. After chapel, breakfast and then lessons again all morning . . . [there were games in the afternoon while mother rested]. Supper, the children prepared themselves and ate in the schoolroom. And finally the day closed at the appointed hour with family prayers.[5]

Three more children were born into the Montgomery family in Tasmania.

At the end of 1900 Monty's father was called home to take up the appointment of Secretary of the Society for the Propagation of the Gospel, the organization responsible for Anglican missionary work throughout the world, and in November 1901 the family returned to London. Henry rented a large house in Chiswick and once again threw himself into his work – and again he left the running of the family to Maud. Despite the lack of attention from his father, Monty adored him:

All my childish love and affection was given to my father. I worshipped him. He was always a friend. If ever there was a saint on this earth, it was my father. He got bullied a good deal by my mother and she could always make him do what she wanted. She ran all the family finances and gave my father ten shillings a week; this sum to include his daily lunch at the Athenaeum.[6]

In January 1902 Monty, now 14 years old, was sent to one of the country's lesser 'public' (private) schools, St Paul's, in Hammersmith. Unusually for such a school, St Paul's was predominantly a day school; this however made it less expensive and, most importantly for Maud, it meant she was better able to keep control of a 'difficult' son. Monty passed the entrance examination but, unlike his elder brother Donald, he failed to win a scholarship. This was bad enough but when he came home at the end of his first day at St Paul's he shocked his mother, who by now had given birth to a ninth child, and father by announcing that he had chosen 'the Army class'. This did not mean he *had* to join the Army but it was the class designed for those more interested in physical rather than academic pursuits. His father had hoped Monty would follow him into the church but did not argue; though his mother inevitably tried to dissuade him by telling him he was totally unsuited to a military career. Nevertheless, he won this particular battle with his mother and was allowed to stay in the class. Maud had some revenge later that year when he was caught smoking and she was able to administer a severe thrashing.[7]

Although Monty did not excel academically at St Paul's, it was a relatively happy time in his life. 'I must admit that I did practically no work at school. My main preoccupation was games and I thought of little else'.[8] This paid off in that he rose to be a member of the school swimming VIII and captain of the rugby-football and cricket teams – a surprising achievement in view of the fact that he had never played football or cricket before he went to St Paul's and, although physically strong, he was always thin and of slight build. Monty had no close friends, no hobbies and no interest in art or music, but he was not unpopular. His time at school was also a relatively good period in his family relationships. The summers were always spent at the Montgomery house,[9] New Park, near the village of Moville on the shores of Lough Foyle in Ireland; most of the time was spent out of doors, swimming, walking in the mountains and playing games. And despite the fact that he was a moody and silent boy, Monty even made friends with some of the local people. The years between 1902 and 1906 have been described as the Indian summer of his family life. After he left school at the age of 18, Monty gradually lost most of his connections with his family, the only real exception being his father. It is noteworthy, however, that he wrote a total of sixty, often quite emotional, letters to his mother during his four years in France during WWI. He craved her affection, but she seemed incapable of being the loving mother he clearly needed. In later life he broke with her completely and when she died in 1949, he had not seen her for ten years. He did not even attend her funeral.

When Monty took the entrance examination and interview for the Royal Military College Sandhurst in the autumn of 1906, he said to have still been ill-educated, immature, 'rather backward for his age' and lacking in cultural and social graces – hardly the qualities required of a 'gentleman cadet'. Nevertheless he had earned something of a reputation as a natural leader and the following January he passed into Sandhurst, seventy-second in an intake of 170. He was five feet seven inches tall, weighed 138 pounds and his chest measurement was just thirty-four inches.

Patton

George Patton also came from a distinguished family. His father, George Smith Patton II, had married a Miss Ruth Wilson in 1884. She was the daughter of Benjamin Davis Wilson (known as Don Benito Wilson by the Mexicans and Indians of old California), one of southern California's founding fathers and the owner of some 14,000 acres in Los Angeles County including 4,000 acres of what is now the campus of the University of California (UCLA), and an estate called Lake Vineyard which by 1883 had become the largest winery (San Gabriel) in the world. It was at Lake Vineyard, in the south-west corner of the present day Pasadena, that George S Patton Jr, known as Georgie to the family, was born two years later. In the same year his father gave up his post as District Attorney in order to run the Wilson estate which was in serious trouble owing to mismanagement, drought and disease. Despite his efforts the mortgage was foreclosed in 1899 and the winery sold. Fortunately for the Pattons the new owner was a friend and Georgie's father became his manager; as such he became wealthy enough to ensure that his wife, son and daughter never wanted for anything.

The Patton home at Lake Vineyard was large and bustling. As well as Georgie, his mother, father and sister Nita, there were sometimes as many as eleven other relatives living under the same roof. The most important of these was Georgie's spinster aunt Annie, known as Nannie. She had been in love with Georgie's father but when he married her sister she gave up any further thoughts of marriage and moved in with the family. Following Georgie's birth Nannie devoted herself entirely to him and virtually became his surrogate mother. A woman of strong character and independent means, she soon came to dominate the household, doting on Georgie even to the point of trying to prevent him being punished for minor misdemeanours.

Georgie's boyhood was a happy one. He loved the wild, unsophisticated, frontier environment of Southern California where he was able to enjoy an outdoor life. Although Nannie spoiled him she was keen that he should have a good education and she spent hours reading to him from the Bible and major classics describing the exploits of heroes like Julius Caesar, Hannibal and Napoleon. Her readings were essential for his education because it soon became clear that he had a serious learning disability that made it difficult for him to read by himself – the family was of course unaware of it, but Georgie was dyslexic. Another result of this problem was that he did not begin to learn to write until he was 11. Fortunately Patton, who had an excellent memory, absorbed most of what he heard from Nannie, and the Bible became a major influence throughout his life. Another major influence on his thinking was the American Civil War. The Patton family had originally settled in Virginia and his grandfather and step-grandfather had fought with distinction in the Confederate army. He was thus able to hear first hand accounts of the fighting from the latter and other veterans who sometimes visited Lake Vineyard. His easygoing father, whom he adored, would also often describe the exploits of Robert E Lee, Stonewall Jackson and other heroes of the war. By the time he entered his teens therefore Georgie was not only thoroughly indoctrinated in his own national heritage but he was also well versed in the campaigns of many of Europe's great generals. At night in the privacy of his room he relived many of the actions he had heard about – even to the point of believing he was the incarnation of some of the heroes. This sense of reincarnation in this life of some of the great soldiers of the past was to stay with him throughout his army career.

Not surprisingly Georgie's main interests were soldiers, horses, guns and swords. His father gave him two horses and a shotgun when he was 10 and he soon became an accomplished horseman and an excellent shot and swordsman. The outdoors became part of his everyday life, helped by the fact that his parents owned a cottage on Catalina Island, a fashionable Southern Californian resort, where they holidayed every summer and where Georgie learned to sail, swim and hunt. Hunting later became one of his major interests.

George S Patton Jr believed passionately that the Pattons were one of the great families of America. They had always been staunch Episcopalian churchmen and as such were intolerant of people of mixed blood and Roman Catholics. Despite the fact that the lifestyle he enjoyed in his boyhood was due almost entirely to his maternal grandfather, Don Benito Wilson, Georgie rejected completely his Wilson heritage on the grounds that Don Benito had married the daughter of a rich Mexican landowner *before* his grandmother and had become a Catholic. He simply ignored the fact that he himself had Mexican/Catholic blood coursing through his veins. He was also ashamed that the Wilson grandfather was a self-made man rather than a 'Southern gentleman', completely ignoring the fact that he owed many of his traits as a potential warrior to this particular grand-father who had been a pioneer, trader, Indian fighter, trapper, rancher, politician and great landowner.

Up to the age of 11 Georgie Patton was tutored at home, principally because his parents and Nannie believed his learning difficulties would cause him embarrassment and even ridicule in school. In September 1897, however, just before he was 12, he was sent to the Stephen Cutter Clark's Classical School for Boys in Pasadena. Despite his dyslexia which gave rise to major problems in reading, spelling and punctuation, Patton did reasonably well during his six years at school. Fortunately he developed a photographic memory and this enabled him to overcome many of his problems. Needless to say his best subjects were ancient and modern history.

By the end of the summer of 1902, at the age of 16, Patton had decided on a career in the army. No one in the family was surprised and in September 1903 he was enrolled at the Virginia Military Institute (VMI) whence three previous generations of Pattons had graduated including his father. This was clearly a second best option to the US Military Academy at West Point since it did not guarantee a commission in the regular army but entrance to that illustrious establishment could only be secured by means of a presidential or Congressional appointment and the local Senator's first available appointment was not until 1904. Georgie's less than glowing academic record was another impediment and his father therefore chose the VMI, where his family connection guaranteed him a place, as the best place to prepare him for West Point. If Georgie failed to get a nomination for the Point he might still get into the regular army through the VMI. In the meantime his father continued to work on the Senator.

Patton spent the summer of 1903 studying hard and in the September of that year he travelled by train across the States to Lexington, Virginia, accompanied by his mother, father and sister – and the inevitable Aunt Nannie. When his parents waved him goodbye, she remained in Lexington. Georgie was one of a class of ninety cadets and he was thrilled when the VMI tailor recognized him as a Patton and told him his measurements were identical to those of his father and grandfather. He was also thrilled to find his fellow cadets were in the main 'Southern gentlemen'.

Despite his dyslexia and through sheer hard work, Patton excelled at the VMI. Six feet one inch in height, 167 pounds, ramrod straight, good-looking with blond hair, he revelled in the spit-and-polish and epitomized the perfect cadet. Nevertheless it was still his firm ambition to go to West Point and in February 1904, at the insistence of the local Senator, he sat an informal competitive examination to decide who would receive the nomination. Patton came first and on 4 March the Senator sent him a telegram confirming the nomination. On 1 June he resigned from the VMI and the following month arrived at West Point, anticipating 'Hell to come'.[10]

NOTES

1 Montgomery, *Memoirs*, p. 17.
2 Montgomery, Brian, *A Field Marshal in the Family*, p. 63.
3 Chalfont, *Montgomery of Alamein*, p. 29.
4 Montgomery, op. cit., p. 19.
5 Moorehead, *Montgomery*, p. 27.
6 Montgomery, op. cit. p. 19.
7 Montgomery, Brian, op.cit., p. 19.
8 Ibid, p. 129.
9 Built by Monty's great-great-grandfather in the second half of the 18th century.
10 All details of Patton's life before WWII have been taken from Carlo D'Este's excellent and meticulously researched book, *A Genius for War*.

CHAPTER II

Gentlemen Cadets

Montgomery

In 1907 one had to pay to go to Sandhurst – £150 for the year's training (approximately £8,000 or $12,000 at today's prices), but this included food, lodgings and all essential expenses. Nevertheless, a cadet still had to have some pocket money, and despite the problems of having to pay for the education of his other eight children and a mortgage, Monty's father agreed to give him a personal allowance of £24 a year (approximately £1,300 or $1,900 at today's prices).

The majority of the Gentlemen Cadets at the Royal Military College came from England's top Public Schools – Eton, Harrow, Wellington and so on – and from the upper classes. Many were the sons of army officers with only a few from the other professions, and although as a future military correspondent of *The Times* wrote later: 'there were some dreadful outsiders amongst us, as could hardly be prevented in an open examination',[1] there was a heavy atmosphere of social snobbery. Despite this Montgomery did quite well initially, revelling in his newly found freedom away from home. After six weeks he was promoted to cadet lance corporal and this meant that he could expect to become a cadet sergeant in his second term. This in turn gave him the prospect of becoming one of the top two cadets in his Company in his final term. He also had no difficulty in being selected for the College rugby-football team.

The training at Sandhurst in 1907 was not particularly difficult or extensive and it was in no sense a university. Half the time was taken up with academic studies such as Mathematics, French or German and History and there was plenty of sport, gymnastics, riding and fencing. The military training comprised drill, map reading, military engineering, administration and law. Only the lowest, platoon level, tactics were taught.

Cadets at Sandhurst were allowed to choose the regiment into which they wished to be commissioned; even so, acceptance depended on an interview with a senior officer in that regiment and, in some cases on achieving a high enough place in the final academic Order of Merit. Cadets were also able to apply to join the Indian Army. It had always been assumed by his parents that Monty would choose the Indian Army and follow the family tradition of service in India where his illustrious grandfather, Sir Robert, had made such a name for himself. And there were two other very relevant factors. One, the basic cost of living in an officers' mess in England in the early 1900s was about £120 a year (£6,400, $9,500) and a second lieutenant received only £118 per annum (£6,250, $9,400). 'It was generally considered that a private income or allowance of at least £100 a year [£5,300, $8,000] was necessary, even in one of the so-called less fashionable County regiments';[2] and two, promotion to major in the Indian Army was on an automatic time scale (thirteen years), whereas in the British Army it was governed by seniority and available vacancies. With no prospect of a private income, the choice for Monty was obvious. But there was one potential obstacle – in order to be accepted into the Indian Army he had to graduate in the top thirty.

Being a natural leader Monty became not only a cadet lance corporal but also the leader of a gang of cadets in 'Bloody B' (B Company was his Company in the College), noted for their toughness and frequent 'rags'. This gang indulged in rowdy behaviour and constant 'battles' with the other Companies accommodated in what is now called 'Old College' at Sandhurst. These 'battles' were often fought with hockey sticks and pokers and involved physical violence, and one such episode led to Monty being reduced in rank to Gentleman Cadet. 'During the ragging of an unpopular cadet I set fire to the tail of his shirt as he was undressing; he got badly burnt behind [and] retired to hospital.'[3] Monty had in fact not only set fire to the cadet's shirt but had led the gang involved and ensured that the unfortunate boy was pinioned hand and foot and menaced with a bayonet to prevent him escaping. Not surprisingly the College authorities took the matter very seriously and Monty's name was deleted from the list of cadets selected for graduation in December 1907. He chosen career lay in ruins. Rather surprisingly, however, his mother, not his father, came to the rescue. 'She was then forty-three and a very handsome woman with a great look of determination and resolve about her',[4] and she soon persuaded the Commandant to agree that Monty could stay at the College, but with the devastating, at least to Monty, proviso that he would have to undergo a further six months training. There is no known record of the conversation between Maud and the Commandant, but the fact that Monty's father was a bishop in the Church of England and had recently been made Prelate of the Most Honourable Order of St Michael and St George almost certainly influenced the latter's decision.

The shock of being 'relegated' shook Monty to the core and he applied himself much more diligently. 'I worked really hard during those [extra] six months and was determined to pass out high.' The fact that his meagre private income prevented him indulging in any real social life must have helped, as did Monty's clear preference for an ascetic life without drink or girls. Nevertheless, his final position of thirty-sixth out of 150 in the Order of Merit was insufficient to gain him a commission in the Indian Army.

Monty was forced to choose an English regiment, and although he had no family or geographical connections, he opted for the Royal Warwickshire Regiment – 'it had an attractive cap badge [an antelope] which I admired . . . it was a good, sound English County Regiment and not one of the more expensive ones'.[5] Fortunately for Monty the Regiment accepted him and he was commissioned on 19 September 1908. To his great relief he was posted to its 1st Battalion in Peshawar, south of the Kyber Pass on the North-West Frontier of India – hopefully he would be able to live on his pay. Nine months later, on the other side of the world, George Patton left West Point and was commissioned as a Second Lieutenant in the US Cavalry.

Patton

In 1904 the US Military Academy at West Point had little in common with Sandhurst. It offered a four-year course at the end of which the graduate received not only a commission in the US Army but also a Bachelor of Science degree. Discipline was extremely strict and for the first three months new cadets (plebes) were subjected not only to a regime of drill and ceremonial, but also to a process called 'hazing'. This was administered by upperclassmen and involved the torment and harassment of the plebes by subjection to strenuous, humiliating and even dangerous tasks. Patton knew all about hazing from his time at the VMI but this did little to lessen its unpleasantness. Nevertheless he enjoyed the pomp and ceremonial and even the tough routine that covered a 0530 to 2200 hours day, and being marched to every activity including classes, meals and even baths. Mathematics was a major subject and was taught every morning; it included geometry, algebra, trigonometry and surveying. The afternoons were taken up with French, history, artillery and infantry tactics, fencing, bayonet exercises and military gymnastics. Needless to say, Patton's dyslexia placed a heavy burden on his academic work.

'Georgie', as Patton was nicknamed by his classmates, was disappointed to find his fellow cadets at West Point were not of the same social status as those at the VMI. Most were 'nice fellows but very few indeed are born gentlemen . . . the only ones of that type are Southerners'.[6] He made no attempt to disguise his contempt and, with his rather patronising and aristocratic attitude he, perhaps not surprisingly, soon became very unpopular with his contemporaries. This unpopularity was fuelled by Patton's constant use of blasphemous and obscene language and an outright ruthlessness that he had unfortunately, and mistakenly, come to believe were important attributes in the makeup of a successful officer. Like Monty, he soon became somewhat of a loner.

Patton became an accomplished swordsman at West Point but he failed to get into the football team and although he took part in athletics he had little success, mainly due to injuries. Needless to say, he was closely supported in all his activities by his family – even to the point that his mother and the doting Aunt Nannie took up lodgings near West Point 'in case he needed anything'. And indeed Patton did need something – his dyslexia, which was of course an unknown disorder at the time, was causing him major problems in the academic field. On 12 June 1905 his father received a telegram: 'DID NOT PASS MATH. [mathematics] TURNED BACK TO THE NEXT CLASS'. Monty had taken eighteen months to obtain his commission; Patton was destined to spend a total, including the nine months at the VMI, of nearly six years in obtaining his!

Although Georgie was required to start his West Point career again from scratch, he was by definition not a plebe and was thus excused the indignity of a second period of hazing. Nevertheless, he knew he had to try even harder and was determined that 'destiny', as he called it, being unaware of his dyslexia, would not decree that he should fail again. The end of his second year at the Point saw him in the top third of his class of 152 cadets and promoted to second corporal. This meant he would be one of those in charge of the new cadets and be partly responsible for the hazing they would suffer at the coming summer camp. Sadly he was overzealous in his responsibilities and ran foul of not only his classmates, but also his superior officers – in the August of 1906 he was demoted to sixth corporal. But still his ambition was boundless; he wrote in his notebook: 'If you die not a soldier and having had the chance to be one I pray to God to dam [sic] you George Patton . . . Never Never Never stop being ambitious'.[7]

Patton's ambition and dedication to his chosen career paid off. Although he failed again to make the Academy football team, in March

1907 he regained his second corporal's stripes and went on to pass all his exams. He remained a borderline case in French and Spanish, but in mathematics he came in the middle of the remaining 114 cadets of his class. Further success came with promotion that summer to sergeant major, the highest cadet position in the second class.

In February 1908 Georgie Patton was promoted to Regimental Adjutant. As such he was always centre stage in front of the Corps of Cadets, read out the orders for the day and led the Corps wherever it marched. 'Impeccably dressed and a master of military posture, Patton was now the focus of attention.'[8] Needless to say such posturings did little for his popularity and he was thoroughly disliked by his classmates and superiors alike. He was seen as 'a young man on the make'. But his fifth and final year at the Point was also his most successful on the sports field. He set a new Academy record in the 220-yard hurdles, won the 120-yard hurdles and came runner-up in the 220-yard dash. He was also graded 'expert' in rifle shooting.

Patton had pondered long and hard on which branch of the Army he should apply to join. He was determined to get into the one promising him the best chance of rapid promotion, and after taking advice from an Academy officer who later became a close friend, he chose the cavalry. Still his ambition knew no bounds; hoping he would be assigned to the 15th Cavalry stationed in Fort Myer across the Potomac river from Washington, DC, he wrote to his father: 'If I have any capacity I might . . . get a boot lick on people of note'.[9]

On 11 June 1909 George Patton graduated forty-sixth out of 103 and obtained his commission in the US cavalry. Four of his classmates would also make four-star rank in the Second World War – William Simpson, Jacob Devers, Robert Eichelberger and Courtney Hodges,[10] but none would gain such fame and notoriety as George Patton.

Readers will have noticed the obvious differences in background, upbringing and character between our two subjects. But, by the time they were commissioned they had much in common: they adored their fathers rather than their mothers, they were natural leaders, they were already vain and clearly showmen, they never considered any career other than the army, they were highly ambitious, they were both good athletes, they both wished to excel in the military art, they were both 'back-squadded' at Officers' School (albeit for very different reasons), they were both 'loners' and they both had very high-pitched voices!

NOTES

1 Chalfont, *Montgomery of Alamein*, p. 52.
2 Montgomery, *Memoirs*, p. 23.
3 Ibid, p. 24.
4 Montgomery, Brian, *A Field Marshal in the Family*, p. 137.
5 Montgomery, op. cit., p. 26.
6 Letter to his father dated 24 Jul 04.
7 Entry in *1905 Notebook* dated 27 Nov 07.
8 D'Este, *A Genius for War*, p. 95.
9 Ibid, p. 107; letter to his father.
10 Hodges had been a classmate in Patton's first year at West Point.

CHAPTER III

Soldiering before WWI

Montgomery

Bernard Montgomery joined the 1st Battalion, the Royal Warwickshire Regiment in Peshawar on the North-West Frontier of India in December 1908. He was just 21.

> When I first entered the ante-room of the Officers' Mess . . . there was one other officer in the room. He immediately said 'Have a drink' and rang the bell for the waiter . . . I was not thirsty. But two whiskies and sodas arrived and there was no escape; I drank one and tasted alcohol for the first time in my life.[1]

Tradition dictated that a newly arrived officer should visit every Officers' Mess in the garrison and leave his visiting card. Monty spent an afternoon doing so, was required to drink a considerable quantity of whisky and disliked alcohol for the rest of his life.

Life for a young officer in a British Regiment in India before the First World War was bound by tradition, the social scene, sport and in particular the Officers' Mess. Military training was carried out at battalion level only and it was considered quite improper to show any enthusiasm for one's career or to study the art of war; indeed, such conduct was considered ungentlemanly. It was even forbidden to talk about military matters in the Mess.

Monty found life frustrating in Peshawar but 'was happy in the Battalion' and he became 'devoted to the British soldier'.[2] He actually enjoyed the constant routine of drill, ceremonial parades and musketry. Compared with his brother officers though, he lacked polish, had no 'connections' in the

Regiment or elsewhere in the Army, and showed no interest in the social scene; but his natural military and sporting abilities were self-evident and he was clearly a useful officer to have around. He soon became Assistant Adjutant and proved himself a great asset on the sports field, playing cricket and hockey for the Battalion. Monty was also a more than adequate horseman, having spent a lot of time riding in Tasmania in his early days and then continuing equitation at Sandhurst. Several writers claim that he owned a horse called *Probyn* on which he hunted with the Peshawar Vale Hounds and won a point-to-point race – despite falling off and remounting. On the other hand his brother wrote later that Monty never had enough money to own a horse until he was a senior officer.[3]

In 1910 the Battalion moved to Bombay to complete its tour in India. Monty was disappointed to find the training facilities there extremely limited and the daily military routine boring. There was, however, plenty of time and opportunity for athletic pursuits and he was made Battalion 'Sports Officer'. He also joined the Royal Bombay Sailing Club and was able to race, not very successfully, the Battalion yacht *Antelope*. Soon after arriving in Bombay Monty bought himself a motorcycle. This was frowned upon by his superiors since such vehicles were considered unsuitable for 'officers and gentlemen' – bicycles, yes, motorcycles, no! Some of the rebellious and unruly behaviour that had come to the fore at Sandhurst with such unfortunate results, again evidenced itself in Bombay. He was reported for 'uproarious proceedings' at the Royal Bombay Yacht Club after a dinner party with three other officers.[4] Monty failed to say if he was disciplined for this misdemeanour.

It seems that, despite his misgivings, Monty was able to live on his pay in India. It is unclear whether or not he received an allowance from his parents – according to Monty himself: 'From the time I joined the Army in 1908 . . . I never had any money except what I earned'. On the other hand, his brother claimed that he received: 'An allowance of £100 a year (£5,300 or $8,000) from our parents'.[5]

In 1911 Montgomery returned home for six months leave. He does not appear to have been short of money since he bought a motorcycle and sidecar and travelled extensively. In August and September he joined the family at New Park in Ireland but there are no other details of how he spent his time in the UK.

By 1913, when his Battalion returned to England, Monty was a lieutenant, had passed the examination for promotion to captain and had held the appointments of Quartermaster and Transport Officer – the transport being mule pack animals and mule carts! He was five feet nine inches tall, tough, wiry and sported the inevitable moustache of that period. His voice was high-pitched and rasping. His time in India had convinced him that his failure to get into the Indian Army had been a blessing in disguise.

My observations led me to think that a British officer [in the Indian Army] would need to be a man of strong character to spend, say, thirty years in the hot climate of India and yet retain his energy and vitality ... I was glad that fate had decided against my passing high enough out of Sandhurst.[6]

Monty's Battalion was stationed in Napier Barracks, Shorncliffe, in south-east England, not far from Dover. Also nearby was the Army's Musketry School at Hythe and Monty was sent on a course there designed to increase his expertise in the few weapons available to an infantry battalion at that time – pistol, rifle, machine-gun, grenades and bayonet. He came first.

Shortly afterwards a Captain Lefroy[7] joined the Battalion, having just completed the Staff College course. He was thus well versed in the Army's latest tactical doctrines and staff procedures – such as they were in 1913. Monty:

used to have long talks with him about the Army and what was wrong with it, and especially how one could get to grips with the military art. He was interested at once and helped me tremendously with advice about what books to read and how to study.[8]

He was by now the Assistant Adjutant of his Battalion but his duties were not onerous and there was plenty of time for sport and a good social life. The latter did not interest him but he was still a keen sportsman and gained a place in the Army hockey team. His financial situation at this time must have been fairly satisfactory because he bought a Ford motorcar – a luxury few other officers could afford to enjoy.

By early 1914 there was growing concern in England over deteriorating relations with Berlin and the possibility of a war. Monty kept himself up to date with international affairs but even as late as 30 July he wrote to his mother: 'I don't think myself that the war will involve us'. That evening, however, he got a nasty shock. He was playing tennis in a local town when an officer 'rushed down to summon us all back to barracks' and before he knew where he was he found himself on a train to a place called Sheerness and the Isle of Sheppey at the mouth of the river Thames. He had been appointed Adjutant of a composite infantry Battalion charged with guarding the important military facilities in the area. Monty returned to his own Battalion on 6 August. Following Germany's declaration of war on France on the 3rd and its invasion of Belgium on the 4th, Great Britain was at war and 1st Royal Warwicks, part of the 10th Infantry Brigade and the 4th Infantry Division, had been mobilized. 'No one knows when we shall go as everything is being kept very secret,' Monty wrote to his mother, 'we are working night and day to get ready.' Some of the preparations puzzled Monty – the Battalion armourer sharpened the officers' swords as well as the soldiers' bayonets and everyone was ordered to get his hair cut short. Furthermore the officers were told by the Commanding Officer that if they went to France there was no point in taking any money as 'money was useless in war as everything was provided . . . I was somewhat uncertain about this and decided to take ten pounds with me in gold. Later I was to find this invaluable'.[9]

During the next two days reservists rejoined the Battalion and then, on 8 August, to everyone's surprise, the Battalion moved by train to York in northern England. The 10th to 14th were spent route marching and the 15th to 17th marching and doing 'attack drills'. Why this training could not have been carried out in Shorncliffe remains a mystery. The unit then moved south to Harrow, near London, to a Brigade Assembly area and finally embarked on the SS *Caledonia* at Southampton on 22 August. The following day Monty's Battalion landed in France.

Patton

In September 1909, ten months after Monty had arrived in India, George Patton was ordered to report to Fort Sheridan, just outside Chicago, home of K Troop of the 15th Cavalry. Other elements of the Regiment were stationed at Fort Myer, Virginia and Fort Leavenworth, Kansas. It seemed Patton had drawn the worst posting, but his Troop was commanded by a Captain Francis Marshall who had been an officer in the Department of Tactics at West Point for four of the five years Patton had spent there and Georgie considered himself lucky to have such a capable man as his commanding officer.

Patton was one of 4,229 officers in an Army with a total strength of only 84,971. It was an Army starved of cash, with poor quarters and enlisted men who lacked education and ambition and who were despised by civilians. Patton was appalled by his personal quarters (room) which were on the third floor of a building described as little better than a slum. His only furniture was a desk, chair and an iron bed. Just as depressing were his duties, which comprised 'stable duty' and a responsibility for guarding a military prison, also located in Fort Sheridan. The only activities he was able to enjoy were practice marches and bivouacs on a horse 'who is not bad nor good'.[10] Life was not all bad though and Georgie was able to enjoy a fairly active social life both on post and in Chicago. He attended football games, dances and balls and dated a few girls even though he had been in love with one particular 'belle' since the age of 17. More of her shortly.

A portent of one of Patton's serious failings occurred shortly after his arrival at Fort Sheridan. Finding a horse untethered, he ordered a nearby soldier to run, tether the horse and run back. When the soldier walked instead of running Patton shouted, 'Run, damn you, run!'. He realised at once that he should not have sworn at the soldier and after assembling those who had witnessed the incident he apologised to the man. '[It] was one of the hardest things I ever did I think [,] but I am glad I did it now that it is done.'[11]

On 26 May 1910 Georgie married Beatrice Ayers in St John's Episcopal Church, in Beverly Farms, near the Ayers' summer home on the North Shore of Massachusetts. It was the first military wedding on the North Shore since the Civil War and the guests came from as far afield as New York, Virginia, Washington DC, Minnesota and California. Many were members of the Bostonian aristocracy.

Georgie had fallen in love with Beatrice when he was only 17 and he had wooed her throughout his time at the VMI and West Point. Her father was a multi-millionaire Bostonian businessman who had made his fortune through the sale of patent medicines, banking, real estate, printing and the textile industry.[12] She and Georgie met in 1902 on Catalina Island, the fashionable Southern Californian resort owned by Beatrice's mother's family and where the Pattons had a holiday home. Despite their differences, she a 'wealthy, well-educated, New England Yankee' and a highly talented musician, and he a 'dyslexic, rough-hewn son of . . . Confederate warriors who had grown up in the still untamed environment of frontier Southern California',[13] they fell in love at once.

Beatrice's father had severe misgivings about his daughter marrying a professional soldier but his objections were eventually overcome – not least by Beatrice locking herself in her bedroom and going on hunger strike – and he eventually capitulated in a letter saying he would earn the money and Georgie would earn the glory.[14]

Patton and his bride crossed the Atlantic on the SS *Deutschland* and spent their June honeymoon in south-west England and London before returning to the States and their tiny quarter at Fort Sheridan. When they had visited the Fort before the marriage Beatrice and both families had been appalled at its state and size – the dining room was only big enough for a table and just four chairs and the whole interior had been painted peacock blue with paint left over from the Garrison railway station. And there was more bad news – in early August K Troop was ordered on extended summer manoeuvres in Wisconsin with Georgie in charge of the horses and mules. Beatrice returned to her family's summer retreat in Massachusetts.

In March 1911 Beatrice gave birth to a girl. Patton was present at the birth and found it a shattering experience, with the result that he had little initial affection for the baby and resented Beatrice's switch of attention from himself to the child. He became depressed, not only by the baby whom he considered ugly, but also by the tedium of life in Fort Sheridan. Although, thanks to his wife's monthly allowance, Patton, unlike Monty, was never short of money, he had a problem. In April he wrote to his father, 'I wish I saw the chance of war. I get horribly bored doing nothing at all'.[15] Despite his appointment to command of K Troop during Captain Marshall's temporary absence at Fort Leavenworth, Patton could see no chance of achieving any of his immediate goals – an assignment in Washington, a posting to West Point as an instructor or even to South America as a military attaché.

Relief for both Georgie and Beatrice came in the autumn when Patton was ordered to report for duty with his Regiment in Fort Myer, Virginia. Beatrice, who had made no friends during her time at Fort Sheridan, would be returning to 'civilisation' and Georgie, now the proud owner of several horses and a motorcar, would be at the centre of Army power and have a chance of applying for a course at the French Cavalry School at Saumur – an essential prerequisite for a posting to West Point.

The Pattons were now in their element. The 15th Cavalry provided the ceremonial escorts on all state occasions, Fort Myer was the residence of the Army Chief of Staff and other senior officers stationed in the capital and the officers of the Regiment had automatic access to Washington society, including race meetings, foxhunting and polo matches. And it was not long before Georgie, on an early morning ride on one of the many equestrian trails south of the Fort, made an important new acquaintance – the Secretary of State for War, Henry Stimson.

The Pattons' new found status was reflected in their much larger and more comfortable quarters; Beatrice enjoyed the services of a full-time maid, Georgie employed a chauffeur and he quickly bought a thorough-bred to join his other six horses. After a short tour in A Troop, Patton was made Squadron quartermaster (recall Monty had been quartermaster of his Battalion in India).

The next major event in Patton's life was the Fifth Olympiad held in Stockholm in July 1912. Georgie, with his athletic record from West Point and proven horsemanship, was a natural choice for the Modern Pentathlon which in those days was only open to soldier-athletes; however, his nomination for the American Olympic team did not come through until 10 May and this left him precious little time for training. Beatrice, his father and most of the Patton 'clan' accompanied him to Sweden and in the event he finished a very creditable fifth in the overall placings. Forty-two others had started the competition; Patton did badly in the pistol shooting, coming twenty-first, but sixth out of thirty-seven in the swimming, third out of twenty-nine in fencing, third in the 5km steeplechase and third out of fifteen in the gruelling 4km cross-country run. In fact Patton had led the way into the stadium but collapsed and was overtaken by two Swedes. Two other runners also collapsed and one actually died in the intense heat and humidity. Patton remained un-conscious for a considerable time, not helped by a perfectly legal (in those days) shot of opium before the race and another after he collapsed, and there was concern that he also might not survive. Needless to say he did and the whole family was able to set off on a whirlwind tour of Germany. But Georgie and Beatrice did not finish the tour; while the rest of family continued their European tour, they journeyed to the French Cavalry School in Saumur where for two weeks Patton took instruction from the best fencing instructor in the French Army!

The Pattons returned to the States in August 1912, and while Beatrice went off to spend some time with her family, Georgie returned to duty. His new found fame had of course spread before him and he was soon invited to dinner by the Army Chief of Staff, Major General Leonard Wood. His new friend the Secretary of State for War was also present to hear about his exploits in Stockholm. Almost inevitably Patton was soon invited to join Wood's staff as a junior staff officer and aide. Although only a second lieutenant his name was now becoming widely known and furthermore, having by now almost completely overcome his dyslexia, in March 1913 the first of many articles by Georgie appeared in the prestigious *Cavalry Journal*. Patton was on his way!

In June he received new orders fulfilling his greatest ambition. In October he was to join the Mounted Service School at Fort Riley, Kansas, and in the meantime he was authorized to return to Saumur at his own expense, 'for the purpose of perfecting yourself in swordsmanship'. But Patton was to be more than just a student at Fort Riley – he was to be the Army's first instructor in swordsmanship.

Beatrice accompanied Georgie to Saumur and, thanks to father-in-law, they were able to take their car and enjoy the French countryside. Baby 'Bee' stayed with Beatrice's family and for the first time since their honeymoon the Pattons were able to enjoy some time on their own. Needless to say, though, Georgie spent virtually all his time with the fencing master and when he was not involved with him he attended classes at the Cavalry School! Even so they were able to tour the Loire valley before returning home in early September. On doing so Patton received the title 'Master of the Sword' – he was the first officer to hold this new US Army title.

Fort Riley was freezing cold in the winter and uncomfortably hot and humid in the summer. Beatrice hated the place, feeling as out of place as she had at Fort Sheridan but she stuck it out. Georgie, although only a student in the Mounted Service School, taught three classes in swordsmanship, often to students who were senior in rank. He graduated in May 1914, but his performance had earned him one of the ten coveted places on the Troop (company) commander's course and he was set to spend another year at Fort Riley. Then in June came three pieces of momentous news – Beatrice was pregnant again, Georgie learned that he had been unanimously selected for the US Olympic team (the Sixth

Olympiad was due to be held in Berlin in August), and on the 28th the Austrian Archduke Franz Ferdinand was assassinated in Sarajevo. The slide into the First World War had begun.

Patton followed the terrifying chain of events in Europe with a passion and, despite Beatrice's pregnancy, when Germany declared war on France on 3 August he wrote to his friend Leonard Wood, the Secretary of State for War, asking for a year's leave of absence so that he could join the French Army. Not surprisingly his request was turned down and Georgie, unlike Monty, was denied his chance of experiencing war. He was bitterly disappointed, but resigned himself to gaining a distinction on his current course which was due to end in June 1915.

NOTES

1   Montgomery, *Memoirs*, p. 27.
2   Ibid, p. 30.
3   Montgomery, Brian, *A Field Marshal in the Family*, p. 134.
4   Montgomery, op. cit., p. 31.
5   Montgomery, Brian, op.cit., p. 148.
6   Montgomery, op. cit., p. 29.
7   He was killed in WWI.
8   Montgomery, op. cit., p. 31.
9   Ibid, p. 32.
10 Letter to his future wife, 13 Sep 09.
11 Ibid.
12 D'Este, *Genius for War*, p. 51.
13 Ibid, p. 58.
14 Ibid, p. 114.
15 Letter to his father dated 23 Apr 11.

CHAPTER IV

Montgomery in WWI

(Map 1)

Monty was under direct fire[1] and in direct contact with the enemy for less than six weeks in the First World War. For the remaining four years of the 'War to end all Wars', he was a staff officer.

The 1st Battalion of the Royal Warwickshire Regiment arrived in Boulogne late on 23 August and immediately entrained for Le Cateau at 1000 hours the following day. In the meantime, the French Army on the right flank of the British Expeditionary Force (BEF) was in full retreat, and when one of the two British Corps was attacked at Mons, forty miles away to the north-east, the order was given to withdraw. Only some 1,600 casualties had been suffered, but there was no other option if the BEF was to be saved. On the 25th the Warwicks, as part of the 10th Infantry Brigade, marched north with the task of covering part of this British retreat; as it happened, no contact was made with either friendly or enemy forces. The Battalion War Diary for the day merely states: 'Sighted troops, evidently retiring, far to our right. No contact. Rained a good deal. No rations arrived'. At 1900 hours, after coming under artillery fire, the 10th Brigade was ordered to join the general retreat which was by now rapidly turning into a rout. Monty wrote in his diary: 'My first experience of shrapnel. It was not nice as we could not reply'.[2]

At 0430 hours the following morning, 26 August, Monty's Battalion (he was a platoon commander in C Company) and the rest of the Brigade:

> was bivouacked in the cornfields near the village of Haucourt after a long night march. One Battalion was forward on a hill, covering the remainder of the Brigade in the valley behind; we could see the soldiers having breakfast, their rifles being piled. That Battalion was suddenly surprised by the Germans . . . it withdrew rapidly down the hill towards us, in great disorder. Our Battalion was deployed in two lines; my Company and one other were forward, with the remaining two companies out of sight some hundred yards to the rear. The CO [commanding officer] galloped up to us forward companies and shouted to us to attack the enemy on the forward hill at once. This was the only order: there was no reconnaissance, no plan, no covering fire. We rushed up the hill, came under heavy fire, my Company commander was wounded and there were many casualties. Nobody knew what to do, so we returned to the original position from which we had begun the attack. If this was real war it struck me as most curious and did not seem to make any sense against the background of what I had been reading.[3]

Monty, according to his brother, later recalled:

> Waving my sword I ran forward in front of my platoon, but unfortunately I had only gone six paces when I tripped over my scabbard, the sword fell from my hand . . . and I fell flat on my face . . . By the time I had picked myself up and rushed after my men I found that most of them had been killed.[4]

The Battalion War Diary for 26 August recorded:

> Held our position under heavy fire for the remainder of the day. Ordered to retire south as night fell, but in the darkness the Battalion

got split up into three parts, each with no definite information as to the whereabouts of other troops.

Monty's version of the retreat was rather more scathing:

> the two forward companies which had made the attack . . . received no further orders; we were left behind when the retreat began and for three days we marched between the German cavalry screen and their main columns following behind, moving mostly by night and hiding by day. In command of our party was a first class regimental officer, Major A J Poole, and it was due entirely to him that we finally got back to the BEF and joined up with our Battalion. We then heard that our CO had been [court-martialled and] cashiered,[5] as also had another CO in the Brigade, and Poole took command.[6]

In a letter to his father written on 27 September, Monty went into more detail:

> Our men fell out by the dozens & we had to leave them; lots were probably captured by the Germans, some have since rejoined . . . Of course we had no rations all the time and there was no food in the villages. The villagers were all fleeing before the advancing Germans. All our kit was burnt to make room in the [liberated] wagons for the wounded etc, so we only had what we stood up in . . . We were in low spirits.

On 28 August Monty's group of about 300 'caught up our Division & they put us on the motor lorries of a supply column; they took us [across the Somme] to Compiègne which we reached at 3 pm on the 29th'. The Battalion then began to re-form under Major Poole's command and, due to a shortage of senior officers, Monty was given temporary command of a Company. In the meantime his parents had received a telegram from the War Office: 'Regret to inform you that Lieut B L Montgomery, Warwickshire Regiment, is reported missing. This does not necessarily mean that he is killed or wounded'.

'We left there [Compiègne] at 9 am on Sunday 30th by train & went to Le Mans & had a good rest; we were far away from the war there [some 200 miles behind the front] & we lunched and dined in restaurants daily'.[7]

By early September the German offensive had begun to run out of steam and seizing his opportunity, the French Marshal Joffre struck back. The British joined in the advance on 4 September with Monty's Battalion reaching Crécy-en-Brie on the 6th after an all-day march. On 15 September Monty wrote to his mother:

We ought all to have pneumonia as it rains hard most nights, but I suppose we are all too hard . . . I command my own Company . . . so I ride a horse, as all company commanders are mounted. I have a big beard. I have not washed my face or hands for 10 days; there is no means of washing & no time for it. The necessary things are sleep & food; washing is unnecessary. Don't forget the cigarettes, will you?

And to his father on the 27th:

From 5th to the 13th September we marched hard all day, generally starting at 4 am and not getting in till 7 or 8 pm . . . Every day we saw fresh signs of a retreating army, such as dead horses and men, discarded stores etc. We usually reached places in the evening which the Germans had left in the morning.[8]

By 13 September the Warwicks had reached the Aisne river, three miles east of Soissons, and found themselves up against a dug-in enemy. The German retreat was over and trench warfare had begun. In his letter of 27 September to his father Monty wrote: 'Our object is I think to hold them here while the French get round behind them, or there may be some other reason; we are not told much of the strategic plans'. In his personal diary for the following day he wrote: ' Went up to trenches with D Company at 2 p.m. under very heavy fire from enemy'.

His description of life in the trenches is typical of many written during WWI:

I had an awful night in the trenches last night. It poured with rain all night & the trenches became full of water . . . The advanced German trenches are only 700 yards from us . . . My clothes are in an awful state . . . I find that rum is a great standby; they give us some every day.

In early October the BEF was withdrawn from the Soissons sector and ordered north in what became known as the 'Race for the Sea'. In reality it was an attempt to outflank the German right flank. The Warwicks came out of the line on 6 October and, after an initial march of nearly fifty miles, were moved by train to St Omer in the Nord-Pas-de-Calais region. During this move Monty handed over command of C Company to a Captain Freeman, who had joined the Battalion from England, and reassumed command of his old platoon.

(Map 1A)

On 12 October the Warwicks were 'bussed' forward to Caestre which they reached at 0300 hours the following day. Monty wrote in his diary:

Company in empty house, officers in nice house opposite. Good breakfast, eggs, etc., at 5.30 a.m. Marched at 9 a.m. towards Fletre. A and C Companies vanguard. Deployed and attacked [Météren] village. Captured trenches and houses. About 3 p.m. got hit in lung; five minutes later in knee. Lay in rain for three hours. Carried back by four men.[9]

The Battalion War Diary for 13 October provides us with more detail:

0920 hours – Orders to move to Météren [from Caestre].

0930 hours – A and C Coys formed Advance Guard under Major A J Poole, with Divisional Cyclist Coy and Cavalry in front.

1000 hours – On reaching Fletre enemy were reported to be holding high ground along ridge in front of Météren. A and B Coys deployed . . . D Coy under Major Christie was sent up behind C Coy in support. Enemy retired into and just outside Météren, occupying trenches and houses.

1100 hours – Regiment ordered to push on and endeavour to push them out.

1300 hours – Gained outskirts of village, but were held up and great need of supports. C and D Coys again advanced and took several trenches, but suffered severely.

1330 hours – GOC [General Officer Commanding] ordered Regiment to halt and [said] he would attack with 10th Brigade to north of village and 12th Brigade . . . south of road.

1400 hours – 12th Brigade commence their attack.

1500 hours – Seaforths [another Battalion] attack on our left and through A Coy which withdrew at dusk to Planeboon [not identified on any map]. C and D Coys under Captain Freeman and Major Christie were unable to withdraw till much later owing to heavy fire, but about 2000 hours the King's Own [another Battalion] came up and passed through them.

2200 hours – C and D Coys join Battalion at Planeboon, the Regiment becoming reserve to the Brigade. Météren was taken during the night. Our casualties 42 killed, 85 wounded. Major C C Christie and Lieut C G P Gilliat (died of wounds), Lieut B L Montgomery (badly wounded) . . . Very wet all day – a perfect advance by Companies concerned, dash and spirit shown by all concerned.

In 1958 Monty gave a much fuller account of his part in the attack on Météren:

There was a plan and there were proper orders. Two companies were forward, my Company on the left being directed on a group of buildings on the outskirts of the village ... We charged forward towards the village; there was considerable fire directed at us and some of my men became casualties, but we continued on our way. As we neared the objective I suddenly saw in front of me a trench full of Germans, one of whom was aiming his rifle at me ... I hurled myself through the air at the German and kicked him as hard as I could in the lower part of the stomach ... He fell to the ground in great pain and I took my first prisoner! A lot of fighting went on during the remainder of the day, our task being to clear the Germans from the village. During these encounters amongst the houses I got wounded, being shot through the chest. But we did the job and turned the Germans out of the village [as readers are already aware, this was not true] ... My life was saved that day by a soldier of my platoon. I had fallen in the open and lay still hoping to avoid full attention from the Germans. But a soldier ran to me and began to put a field dressing on my wound; he was shot through the head by a sniper and collapsed on top of me. The sniper continued to fire at us and I got a second wound in the knee; the soldier received many bullets intended for me. No further attempt was made by my platoon to rescue us; indeed, it was presumed we were both dead. When it got dark the stretcher-bearers came to carry us in; the soldier was dead and I was in a bad way.[10]

Then in 1967 Monty allegedly gave another, very different account of how he was wounded on 13 October. It says that when the Warwicks' attack was called off at 1330 hours:

I made my platoon take up defensive positions behind a ditch and hedge about 100 yards from the village and went out myself in front to see what the positions looked like from the enemy point of view – in accordance with the book! It was then that I was shot by a sniper; the bullet entered at the back, which was towards the enemy, and came out in front, having gone through my right lung but broken no bones. I collapsed, bleeding profusely. A soldier from my platoon ran forward and plugged the wound with my field dressing; while doing so, the sniper shot him through the head and he collapsed on top of me. I managed to shout to my platoon that no more men were to come to me until it was dark. It was then 3 pm and raining. I lay there all the afternoon; the sniper kept firing at me and I received one more bullet in the left knee. The man lying on me took all the bullets and saved my life. I never learnt his name, or if I did, I cannot remember it. I must have known him. When dark a party from my platoon came to me; they had no stretcher, so four of them carried me in an overcoat to the road.[11]

Everyone makes mistakes, but if this latter account is true it seems incredible that a dedicated professional like Bernard Montgomery could have been so stupid as to go out into no-man's-land and turn his back on an enemy who was only 100 hundred yards away in order to look at his platoon's position. The 'book', as Monty described it, certainly never envisaged an officer looking at his own position from the enemy point of view when in close contact with that enemy. It is also surprising, at least to this author who had a very similar experience in the Korean war, that Monty either did not bother to find out the name of the soldier who saved his life, or if he did, that he should have forgotten it.

So who *was* the soldier who died in an attempt to help Monty? For a number of years it was thought that his name was Private Edward Darlow and that he had been awarded a posthumous Distinguished Conduct Medal (DCM) for his actions. This belief was the result of an article in the *Daily Mail* newspaper dated 27 November 1996, headed 'COURAGEOUS SECRET OF HERO WHO SAVED MONTGOMERY'. It carried photographs of Montgomery and said:

> It was a piece of gallantry that helped shape history. Not that Private Edward Darlow of the 1st Royal Warwickshire Regiment realised it at the time. He was merely obeying his instincts when he helped a fallen comrade wounded by a bayonet charge. The young lieutenant he helped save at Météren at the start of World War I went on to become Viscount Montgomery of Alamein . . . On Friday, the Distinguished Conduct Medal [DCM] awarded to 21-year old Pte Darlow in 1914 for 'great gallantry' is being sold anonymously at . . . auction.

In fact Darlow was not in Monty's Company and he survived the war. His citation reads: 'For great gallantry on 13th October (1914), in volunteering to go forward to a place where extreme danger was to be expected, and helping to bring in Major Christie [D Company] who was dangerously wounded'.[12] The *Daily Mail* article goes on to say that the medal was to be auctioned:

> with a 1945 newspaper cutting headlined: The private who helped to save Monty. The first person article describes how after rescuing their badly wounded commanding officer, a Major Christie, Pte Darlow and a colleague returned under fire to the battlefield to save others. 'Most of the officers were badly wounded and unconscious' he wrote. 'Lieutenant Montgomery was one of them and I recall placing him near the stretcher on which lay my dying commanding officer.'

It is noteworthy that if Darlow was indeed the author of this article he makes no claim to have actually *saved* Monty.

There were several bidders at the auction, but Darlow's DCM was apparently bought by his grandson. The Trustees of the Royal Warwickshire Museum, having been outbid for the medal, subsequently wrote to him to ask if he would consider having it put on display in their museum in Warwick. He did not reply.

One of the soldiers who certainly claimed to have been involved in rescuing Monty and bringing him back to the Battalion Aid Post was Private H W Jackson of the Royal Army Medical Corps (RAMC). He wrote later:

> The unit's [Warwicks] officer was one of the casualties but no one could venture out in daylight to find out if he was still alive . . . After a short talk, Captain Phillips [21 Field Ambulance RAMC] decided to make a quick run through enemy fire to a haystack where an infantry NCO would be waiting. Our troops in the trenches were told to hold their fire. I followed Captain Phillips to the haystack. The infantry NCO indicated where we were to make for to pick up the officer. All three of us crawled behind one another . . . During one of the stops I stretched my right arm out and my fingers touched something which I pulled towards me . . . It was a ladder and as we had no stretcher each time we moved I pulled it along with me. On reaching the ground where the action had taken place, we spread out, keeping sight of each other, to try to find the officer. It was sometime afterwards that I looked towards Captain Phillips and saw him raise his arm . . . Captain Phillips had found the wounded officer, who was still alive but in a serious condition. We placed him on the ladder and started to move back along the ground with our officer and the NCO at the top part and myself at the foot end of the ladder. After some time and covering quite a bit of ground they stopped and whispered down to me to pull the ladder away when the word was given, which I did. I crawled towards them and they had now got the seriously wounded officer lying on the inside of a greatcoat. We raised him from the ground, then quickly made for the stretcher-bearers who were waiting to take him from us . . . Little did I know that the officer we rescued was Field Marshal Lord Montgomery of Alamein, who many years later, by a strange coincidence, confirmed that he was the seriously wounded officer we brought in when he was Lieutenant Montgomery of the Royal Warwickshire Regiment.[13]

It would not be unreasonable to surmise therefore that, after saving Major Christie, Darlow was indeed one of the stretcher-bearers mentioned in Private Jackson's article. As for the brave man who actually died trying to save Monty, it seems unlikely that we shall ever know his name.

From the Regimental Aid Post Monty was evacuated to an RAMC

Advanced Dressing Station. He was not expected to live and 'as the Station was shortly to move, a grave was dug for me'.[14] Fortunately, when the time came for the move he was still alive and after a thirty-mile journey he was admitted to a French military hospital in St Omer.

(Map 1)

Monty spent three days at St Omer before being evacuated by hospital train and ship (the *St David*) to the Royal Herbert Military Hospital in Woolwich near London, which he reached late on 18 October. He remained there until 5 December when, after an amazing recovery, he was granted three months' leave. The knee wound had proved to be superficial, but his right lung was permanently damaged and he suffered from breathlessness for the rest of his life. He was told that his days in a combat infantry battalion were over. But there was some consolation. Monty had been promoted to the rank of captain and on 1 December he learned that he had been awarded the Distinguished Service Order (DSO)[15] for: 'conspicuous gallant leading on 13 October, when he turned the enemy out of the trenches with the bayonet. He was severely wounded'.

Monty's time in direct contact with the enemy may have been over, but his contribution to the war effort was set to continue until victory was achieved. In February 1915 he was declared fit for home service (not to be sent abroad) and appointed Brigade Major (Chief of Staff) of the 91st Infantry Brigade. This high profile job would normally have gone to a graduate of the Staff College, but the desperate shortage of regular officers dictated otherwise.

The 91st Brigade was one of those being formed from the thousands of volunteers who had flocked to the colours in an early enthusiasm to 'teach the Germans a lesson' and at this stage it was only a training Brigade. Monty, despite his very limited combat experience, was delighted to be given virtually a free hand in setting and supervizing the training standards laid down – indeed, he himself set many of those standards since his commander was 'a very nice person, but quite useless, and it would be true to say that I really ran the Brigade and they all knew it'. The 91st was subsequently renumbered the 104th and sent to France in January 1916. Monty was re-graded as medically fit for overseas service and remained in his post of Brigade Major.

By January 1916 the Western Front had solidified and the line of opposing trenches stretched virtually 300 miles from the English Channel to Switzerland – the horrors of trench warfare with its lack of mobility and domination by artillery and machine guns had arrived.

In July Field Marshal Haig launched a major offensive on the Somme. Monty's Brigade was in reserve for the opening phases of the campaign – a campaign in which the British suffered 57,470 casualties (including

19,000 killed or died of wounds) on the first day alone, and which by the time it ended in November, had cost the Allied forces approximately 600,000 casualties for a gain of only some ten kilometres of ground. Monty wrote later: 'The so-called "good fighting generals" of the war appeared to me to be those who had a complete disregard for human life'.[16] The 104th Brigade was inevitably drawn into the bloodbath and by 23 July it had put in three major attacks, the last costing it a third of its strength. Monty was slightly wounded in the hand by shrapnel on the 26th, but remained at duty. The Brigade, exhausted and decimated, was withdrawn from battle on the 31st, but put back in the line again after only four days; it remained there until the end of August when, while the holocaust on the Somme continued for another two months, it left for the quieter Arras front. At the time Monty kept his feelings about the slaughter to himself, but he wrote later:

> The conflict which began in August 1914 in Europe developed into the bloodiest war in history. The only impressive results were the casualties – and these had a profound influence on my military thinking. A large number of those killed had no known grave; in some cases corpses formed part of the trenches, and were devoured by rats.[17]

He was also becoming disillusioned about the leadership in the Army:

> There was little contact between the generals and the soldiers ... I never once saw the British Commander-in-Chief, neither French nor Haig, and only twice did I see an Army Commander.[18]

In January 1917 the 29-year-old Monty was promoted to the rank of major and transferred to the Headquarters of the 33rd Infantry Division where he became the General Staff Officer Operations (GSO 2). Then, in July 1917, after a short course at a Staff School in France, he was appointed GSO 2 Training in the Headquarters of IX Corps. As such he witnessed as a staff officer, but did not directly participate in, another bloodbath – the Third Battle of Ypres, better known as Passchendaele. It lasted from 31 July until 17 November and cost the Allies 310,000 men. In October, just before the conclusion of the campaign, Monty became the GSO 2 Operations of the Corps.

On 21 March 1918 the Germans launched their 'Spring Offensive'. Directed against the British part of the Western front and using new tactics which saw carefully trained stormtroopers infiltrating through selected breaches in the line, it was highly successful. In just two weeks the British suffered 175,000 casualties and were driven back some forty miles to the very outskirts of Amiens. IX Corps was not directly involved in the fighting, but became responsible for a reserve defensive line, known as the GHQ line, fifty miles behind the original front. Fortunately the German offensive ran out of steam before it reached the GHQ line and on 1 April IX Corps was moved north to the valley of the Lys river where its six Divisions, at a cost of 27,000 casualties, carried out a successful defensive operation on the Kemmel Ridge (Map 1A) against a second German offensive.

Following the Battle of the Lys, IX Corps moved to the Soissons area in the French sector to lick its wounds and retrain. It was not to be left in peace for long though for on 27 May, following the greatest artillery barrage of the war, the Germans broke through at the junction between the French and British to a depth of some twelve miles and reached the Marne. Fortunately the enemy salient was successfully sealed off, but the Battle of Chemin-des-Dames decimated IX Corps and by 30 May its strength of over 100,000 men had been reduced to little more than that of a division (15,000 men).

The casualty figures quoted above are perhaps incomprehensible to a generation separated by eight-five years from the events that occasioned them. Not surprisingly they made an indelible impression on those involved – not least on Major Bernard Montgomery.

Monty's superiors must have thought very highly of his abilities as a staff officer, for on 18 July 1918 he was promoted to the rank of 'brevet lieutenant colonel' and given the important appointment of General Staff Officer Grade 1 (Chief of Staff) of the 47th (London) Infantry Division. The 'brevet' rank was much sought after since it was only conferred on those expected to reach high rank; there was however a snag – the recipient did not receive the pay of the rank!

As GSO1 (Chief of Staff) of the 47th Division, Monty played an important role in the BEF's final offensives of August to October 1918. He was meticulous in the instructions he issued on behalf of his very senior and experienced commander, Major General Goringe, and soon earned the latter's liking and respect. Monty makes little mention of these final offensives in his *Memoirs*, other than to say that in order to get accurate information on the course of the fighting, 'we' devised a system of sending officers with wireless sets up to the headquarters of the forward battalions. The system often failed because of the unreliability of the radios, but it nevertheless proved worthwhile and Monty was to use the same system to good effect in WWII.

On 3 September Monty was writing to his mother:

> These are stirring times and everyone is being pushed to the limit of their endurance. We really have got the Bosche on the hop, he is thoroughly disorganized and it looks as if we might get away beyond our old battlegrounds and get into country as yet untouched by shells

etc. The Division has been wonderfully successful and we have never failed yet to do what we set out to do.

The final German collapse came as a surprise to the fighting men. Monty wrote home on 28 October: 'I think that Germany's allies will drop off one by one, but that she will go on to the end, as she is going to get such rotten terms that she will fight it out unless a revolution does them in'. In the event a mutiny in the German fleet and a revolution in Munich did just that and on 10 November the Kaiser abdicated.

By the time the Armistice was signed on 11 November 1918, Brevet Lieutenant Colonel Bernard Montgomery DSO had been awarded the French Croix de Guerre and 'Mentioned in Despatches' eight times. Although a 'Mention' was the lowest of the honours that could be awarded to an officer or a soldier, the fact that he received it so often is remarkable.

Monty was of course by then a hardened soldier with little or no interests outside the Army. He had been appalled by the carnage of four years of war and the lack of professionalism and imagination shown by the top generals:

> The fact that [Field Marshal Haig's] Chief of Staff had no idea of the conditions under which the troops had to live, fight, and die, will be sufficient to explain the uncertainties that were passing through my mind when the war ended'.[19]

Fortunately for those under his command in the Second World War, he did not forget the lessons he had learned in the First, although, as we shall see, being closely involved in four years of carnage inevitably made him more cautious and 'casualty conscious' than others with less experience.

NOTES

1   'Direct fire' is defined as fire from a weapon operated by someone who can physically see the target.
2   *The Antelope* (Royal Warwickshire Regiment magazine), 1938, Vol. 14.
3   Montgomery, *Memoirs*, p. 32.
4   Montgomery, Brian, *A Field Marshal in the Family*, p. 159. This was almost certainly an exaggeration; according to its War Diary the Battalion lost eight officers and fifty-four men on 26 Aug 14.
5   The Battalion War Diary records: 'Party under [Lt] Col Elkington arrived St Quentin where Col Elkington surrendered at the Mayor's request on a German threat to bombard the town. This surrender he later withdrew, and then left the town, alone. The men, under Lt Cooper, found their way to Ham'. Elkington later joined the French Foreign Legion, and saw active service during which he was both wounded and decorated for his bravery.

After the war his rank in the British Army was restored and he was awarded the Distinguished Service Order!

6   Montgomery, op. cit., p. 32.
7   Letter to father dated 27 Sep 14.
8   Ibid.
9   *The Antelope*, 1938, Vol. 14.
10   Montgomery, *Memoirs*, pp. 33–4.
11   According to a letter written by a Mr Norman Cliff to the *Observer* newspaper (published 7 Apr 67), this account, allegedly in Monty's own handwriting, was originally held in the Regimental Headquarters of the Royal Warwickshire Regiment in Warwick. Unfortunately there is no longer any trace of it.
12   Appendix VIII – 1st Battalion Royal Warwickshire Honours/Decorations 1914–1918 – Other Ranks.
13   *The Military Historical Society Bulletin*, Vol. XXX, No. 118, dated Nov 79.
14   Montgomery, op. cit., pp. 33–4.
15   The Military Cross was not instituted until Dec 1915.
16   Montgomery, op. cit., p. 35.
17   Montgomery, *A History of Warfare*.
18   Montgomery, *Memoirs*, p. 35.
19   Ibid, p. 36.

CHAPTER V

Patton – February 1915 to May 1917

(Map 2)

George Patton did not want a second child, but Beatrice was insistent and in February 1915, at the Patton family home in Southern California, she produced another daughter. To his intense relief Georgie, still on his course at Fort Riley, Kansas, missed the birth and, hiding his disappointment that it was not a boy, declared himself 'delighted'. He also wrote to Beatrice: 'have it named out there where you can get more advice. All I know is that I don't like the sound of either Ruth or Ellen'[1] – the names of his mother-in-law and mother. She promptly had the baby christened Ruth Ellen!

In June 1915 Patton graduated second from his Troop (company) commander's course and was granted two and a half months' leave. He spent it with his family in Massachusetts. The most significant event during this leave was a near fatal accident when his car overturned on the way back from a polo match. Patton was accident-prone – he had already suffered numerous injuries at West Point playing football or during various other athletic activities and had suffered bad falls from horses in 1913 and again in the spring of 1915.

During the summer of 1915 Patton learned to his horror that his Regiment, the 15th Cavalry, was destined to relieve the 8th Cavalry on constabulary duties in the Philippines. He had no intention of being relegated to a backwater in the Pacific and immediately travelled to Washington and the War Department to petition for a better posting. Who he saw is unrecorded, but he got his way and soon received orders to report in mid-September to the 8th Cavalry in Fort Bliss, Texas. Georgie was over the moon. Beatrice was not. They returned to Fort Riley, packed up their now quite large household, including his eleven horses, and despatched the whole lot to his father's estate in Southern California.

Fort Bliss was an isolated military reservation on the outskirts of a small Wild West border town called El Paso. It was the Headquarters of the officer responsible for guarding the US–Mexican border from Arizona to an outpost in the Sierra Blanca mountains ninety miles south-east of El Paso – Brigadier General John 'Black Jack' Pershing.[2] He had 5,000 troops under his command. Georgie and Beatrice agreed it was no place for her and they began another period of separation.

The main body of the 8th Cavalry had yet to arrive in Fort Bliss from the Philippines and Patton, who had few duties and was due to take the examination for promotion to lieutenant, settled down once more to his studies. In the event he passed easily but he was again shocked to be told that as soon as a lieutenant's vacancy occurred in the 15th Cavalry he would be transferred to it. This meant he would end up in the Philippines after all.

Patton had, nevertheless, arrived in the Mexican border area at a good time from the point of view of his career. A month after his arrival the United States recognized Venustiano Carranza as the new President of Mexico. Woodrow Wilson's government had provided Carranza with military supplies during his struggle to gain power, but he was in fact a ruthless revolutionary and no better than the man he had overthrown. One of Carranza's supporters was the notorious bandit leader, Pancho Villa; he had expected the Americans to support him rather than Carranza for the Presidency and when they failed to do so he swore revenge against the United States – that revenge took the form of raids across the border, with the aim of terrorising the Americans living in the nearby towns in Texas, New Mexico and Arizona. Carranza supporters were also engaged in similar burning and looting operations. Patton may have been denied a chance to participate in the great European war but at least he had a chance of seeing some action on the Mexican border.

In mid-October two Troops of the 8th Cavalry, including Patton's, were sent to the nearby small town of Sierra Blanca in the mountains of that name on border protection duty. Whilst one Troop remained in reserve to protect the thirty-mile stretch of railroad to El Paso, the other manned the border outposts which were 100 miles and a three-day journey away by horse. The setting in Sierra Blanca itself was that of the classic Hollywood Western – about twenty houses, fifty people, cowboys and renowned gunfighters, a hotel, a saloon, a sheriff and a town marshal. Needless to say, Patton's profanity, generosity in the saloon, and quickly proven ability with a gun made him an instant hit with the locals.

There were two or three alarms concerning raids by Villista or Carranzista bandits in the Sierra Blanca area during Patton's time there, but none resulted in any direct clashes with the cavalry. Nonetheless, Georgie enjoyed the roughness of the posting and was no doubt surprised when Beatrice joined him for the last few weeks of his tour. Amazingly she fitted in well, and by the time they left to return to Fort Bliss in early 1916, they had both become popular with the locals. Perhaps it was her popularity or maybe because of her husband's behaviour, we shall never know, but Beatrice decided to join Georgie on a permanent basis. She returned to Massachusetts to collect the children and Georgie applied for a quarter on post at Fort Bliss.

Since the beginning of the year Pancho Villa and his men had terrorised both Mexicans and Americans in a series of raids south of the border involving kidnapping, murder, rape and pillage; at least seventeen US citizens had died in these raids. And then, on 9 March, Villa with about 400 bandits attacked the small border town of Columbus, New Mexico, in an act of revenge for American support for his rival Carranza. It is also said he was searching for a man called Sam Ravel to whom Villa had given money to buy arms. Ravel never delivered the weapons nor returned Villa's money. Whatever the reason and despite a military garrison of some 600 troops, eight soldiers were killed and ten Americans civilians were wounded in an orgy of killing, looting and burning.[3] Villa is said to have lost about 100 men. News of the Columbus attack reached Fort Bliss a day later and within three days Washington had ordered Pershing to mount a 'Punitive Expedition' against Pancho Villa. On the 12th Patton learned, to his utter disbelief and disappointment, that his Regiment was not to be included in the Expedition – he was to be denied his first chance of real action. In characteristic manner, Georgie determined to do something about this unacceptable situation, and after applying through various intermediaries to join Pershing's staff, he even turned up at the General's quarters and said he was prepared to carry out any task just as long as he could join the force. The fact that Pershing[4] had become friendly with Patton's 29-year-old, unmarried and attractive sister Nita during her visit to Fort Bliss may well have helped his case but, whatever the reason, Patton's persistence won the day and Pershing appointed him an extra Aide-de-Camp (ADC).

In 'Black Jack' Pershing, George Patton found his role model general – an autocrat, intolerant of weaklings, a strict disciplinarian, a perfectionist and a stoic who eschewed the comforts of life. He delighted in being in the presence of a general who slept on the ground and carried only a single blanket and his toilet kit.

Pershing's expedition was mounted not from Fort Bliss but from Columbus. Preparation time was wholly inadequate but the force set off as ordered on 15 March. It was doomed to failure from the start. Modern technology, including six reconnaissance aircraft (all of which crashed in the first month), dirigible balloons, radios and motor vehicles, favoured the 5,000-strong American force, but there was little chance of finding Villa in the desert and Sierra Madre mountains of northern Mexico. It was an area where many of the peasants were sympathetic to Villa's cause, and as well as the many excellent hiding places for men who knew the country like the backs of their hands, the US cavalry columns threw up clouds of dust on the dirt trails in dry weather or wallowed in mud when it rained.

Carranza's men were also searching for Villa and in a clash with them he was hit in the knee and forced to go into hiding in the mountains. He hid for two months keeping only thirty of his men with him.

By June Woodrow Wilson had decided that there was a distinct possibility of an all-out war with Mexico and gave orders that the Pershing force was to withdraw to the small Mexican town of Dublan about 100 miles south of the US border. There it was to set up a major garrison and act as a back up for Carranza's troops. It no longer had the mission of directly capturing or killing Pancho Villa. This withdrawal only served to encourage the latter, however, and on 15 September he attacked the town of Chihuahua with some 2,000 men. Despite a garrison of several thousand Carranza troops, the attack was successful and Villa freed many of his men who were being held prisoner there.

In January 1917 President Wilson decided to call off the Punitive Expedition, and in early February, less than a year after it had set out, Black Jack Pershing led 10,690 men and 9,307 horses[5] back across the border. Pancho Villa was still a free man[6] and the only real success the Expedition could claim was that it had at least kept him and his bandits away from the US border. There had in fact been very little fighting between Pershing's troops and the Villistas.

What part did George Patton play in the Punitive Expedition? His position as an extra aide to Pershing was unauthorized and so for presentational purposes Patton was attached to Pershing's old Regiment, the mainly white officered, but otherwise black 10th Cavalry. This was slightly ironic for someone who considered himself a 'Southern gentleman'. In today's world George Patton would undoubtedly be labelled a 'racist', but 'he was a product of his times and clearly distrusted both blacks and Jews; the former were simply considered inferior, whereas the Jews were distrusted and often despised for their success'.[7] Patton's views about the Mexicans, expressed to Beatrice a month after entering their country, were very forthright:

Now there is nothing left but for us to take the country and exterminate the present inhabitants [;] they are so far behind that they will never catch up [;] they are much lower than the Indians. They have absolutely no morals.[8]

As an ADC to Pershing, Georgie was unlikely to see direct action against the bandits. He often travelled with the General in his entourage of three motorcars but his duties were basically routine and boring. This was particularly so after June when the force withdrew into a supporting role. In July he wrote to his father: 'We are all rapidly going crazy from lack of occupation.'[9] There were, however, several major incidents of interest during his time in Mexico. The first, and certainly the most exciting from Patton's point of view, occurred on 14 May. He had been put in charge of a foraging expedition comprising ten soldiers and two civilian guides with the task of obtaining a fresh supply of maize. The group was mounted in three Dodge motorcars and Patton used the opportunity to carry out a raid on a nearby ranch where he believed the commander of Pancho Villa's personal bodyguard, Julio Cárdenas, might be hiding. What followed was described in a Boston newspaper under a photograph of Patton and the headline, 'MEXICAN BANDIT-KILLER WELL KNOWN IN BOSTON': 'Patton and his men left the camp in their autos and fought the bandits from their autos, that is to say, they sprang directly from their cars into the fight, putting the encounter in a class by itself.' The full details of this incident have never been confirmed, but a vivid account can be read in Carlo d'Este's superb book, *A Genius for War*. From the point of view of this history it is sufficient to record that Patton's quick thinking and leadership certainly resulted in the death of Cárdenas and two other bandits. Whether Patton himself actually killed any of the bandits was never established, but there seems little doubt that he wounded Cárdenas before someone else shot him dead and that his bullets were amongst those that accounted for the other two. And it was certainly not a one-sided affair – although no Americans were killed or wounded, an examination of Cárdenas's cartridge belt revealed that he alone had fired thirty-five rounds before he died. Patton was of course elated by the incident. The same night he wrote to Beatrice: 'I have at last succeeded in getting into a fight . . . I have always expected to be scared but was not nor was I excited.'[10] And three days later he wrote: 'The Gen [General] has been very complimentary telling some officers that I did more in half a day than the 13 Cav [Cavalry] did in a week.'[11]

On 23 May 1916 George Patton was promoted to the rank of first lieutenant. Fortunately the threat of being posted back to his old Regiment, the 15th Cavalry, in the Philippines had been overtaken by his foreign service in Mexico and once the Punitive Expedition was over he and Beatrice could look forward to life together in Fort Bliss.

In August Black Jack Pershing decided to take a short leave in Columbus. He took Georgie with him, and although Beatrice did not join him, his vivacious sister Nita did. A week of partying, dancing and riding followed and it was soon clear that his General was infatuated, if not in love, with Nita. But whilst it was extremely useful to have a potential family connection with an important senior officer, Patton's ambitious nature could not be hidden – he wrote to Beatrice, 'Nita may outrank us yet'.[12]

A more serious happening occurred in early October. A petrol lamp in his tent caught fire causing severe burns to Patton's face and hands. Fortunately his eyes were not damaged and he was not permanently scarred, and after a short period in hospital, he was granted two weeks' sick leave which he spent in Columbus; Beatrice joined him for a short reunion. When he returned to the routine of garrison life in northern Mexico, however, his morale began to suffer and he began to wonder if his father-in-law's prediction that the Army was a dead-end career might after all be correct. Beatrice did not help when, fed up with their long separation, she suggested he should resign. For Patton this was inconceivable.

In February 1917, following the withdrawal from Mexico, Black Jack Pershing was given command of the Southern Department of the US Army based at Fort Sam Houston and promoted to the rank of major general. Patton was reassigned to the 7th Cavalry at Fort Bliss and given command of A Troop. A month later he took and passed the promotion examination to captain.

On 6 April the United States of America finally declared war on Germany and within four weeks Major General John (Black Jack) Pershing had been appointed to create and command an American Expeditionary Force (AEF) to fight in France. At the beginning of that year the United States Army consisted of only 108,399 officers and men and possessed only 285,000 Springfield rifles, 544 three-inch field guns, enough ammunition for only a nine-hour bombardment and fifty-five obsolescent aircraft.[13]

On 18 May George Patton received a telegram to report immediately to Pershing in Washington. At the time he was on thirty days' leave occasioned by the illnesses of both Beatrice's father and mother. On arrival in the capital Georgie learned that he had been promoted captain and was to command the Headquarters Troop (some sixty-five personnel) of Black Jack's Advance Headquarters. The fact that this was an unofficial appointment did not worry him – at least he was off to war. On the 28th George Patton said goodbye to Beatrice and the same day Pershing's Advance Headquarters embarked in HMS *Baltic* for the eleven-day trip to Liverpool, England. By then the General was privately engaged to Georgie's sister Nita, but it had been decided to postpone the wedding until after the war.

NOTES

1   Letter to Beatrice dated 1 Mar 15.
2   Pershing had been an unpopular instructor at West Point but he was a veteran of the Indian wars and an insurrection in the Philippines and had risen to become one of the most highly respected officers in the Army. He was nicknamed Black Jack as a result of commanding the all-black 10th Cavalry Regt.
3   These figures vary depending on which source is consulted. Carlo D'Este claims eighteen Americans died.
4   Pershing had lost his wife and three daughters in a tragic house fire the previous August.
5   D'Este, op. cit., p. 184.
6   He was assassinated by a number of unknown Mexicans on 20 Jul 23.
7   D'Este, op. cit., p. 172.
8   Letter to Beatrice dated 29 Apr 16.
9   Letter to his father dated Jul 16.
10   Letter to Beatrice dated 14 May 16.
11   Letter to Beatrice dated 17 May 16.
12   D'Este, op. cit., p. 180.
13   Ibid, pp. 188–9.

CHAPTER VI

Patton in WWI

(Map 3)

Black Jack Pershing and his AEF Advance Headquarters, including George Patton, arrived in Liverpool, England on 8 June 1917. The Lord Mayor and a Guard of Honour from the Royal Welsh Fusiliers greeted him before he entrained for London where again he was welcomed by the Lord Mayor and the Commander-in-Chief (C-in-C) Home Forces, Field Marshal Viscount John French. Patton was taken to the Tower of London for a reception by the Honourable Artillery Company, England's senior Regiment, and during his first few days in the capital he signed the King's guest book at Buckingham Palace and dined at White's – the oldest Gentlemen's Club in the world. He was in his element. In the meantime his General was received by King George V, Prime Minister David Lloyd George, Admiral Viscount Jellicoe and the British Minister for Munitions, Winston Churchill. Everyone was delighted to have the Americans 'aboard'.

On arrival in Paris Pershing and his party were just as warmly received by the French C-in-C, Marshal Joseph Joffre and the Minister for War. Patton was billeted in the Hotel Continental, not far from the Advanced

Headquarters in Rue Constantine, but after a short time he arranged to move into a three-bedroomed apartment just off the Champs Elysées, which he shared with a French interpreter, and another American. He loved the atmosphere and social whirl of Paris, and despite the mundane nature of his job, running the day-to-day business of the Headquarters, he was at least kept busy. He did not endear himself to his brother officers however, when he purchased, needless to say with Beatrice's money, a twelve-cylinder, five-passenger Packard automobile.

On occasions Georgie stood in as Pershing's ADC and in this capacity he was with his General on 20 July when the latter visited the British C-in-C in France, Field Marshal Sir Douglas Haig. During the visit he was introduced, not only to Haig, but also to General Trenchard, the pioneer of British aviation and to General Gough, the Fifth Army commander.

During the same month the American 1st Division began arriving in France; it was the advance guard of an Expeditionary Force that would total some two and a half million before the end of the war. Patton met some of the Divisional staff in Paris when they stopped off on their way to the American training area in Lorraine, amongst them the Operations officer, Captain George C Marshall of WWII fame.

In early September Pershing moved his Headquarters from Paris to Chaumont in the south-eastern corner of Lorraine. At the same time he gave orders that no American women were to come to France, ending Georgie's hopes that Beatrice might take up residence in Paris and that he might get to see her during his leave periods.

Although Patton hated his job as Commandant of Pershing's Headquarters he was not entirely unhappy in Chaumont. He was comfortably billeted in the General's château and he enjoyed riding in the local countryside. Nevertheless, he was determined to 'get back to the line again'[1] and command cavalry soldiers. But then in mid-October something happened that changed his whole life – he was hospitalised with jaundice. During his time there he was visited by an officer who had been his troop commander at Fort Myer in 1912 and who had tutored him for his promotion examination in 1915 – Lieutenant Colonel Leroy Eltinge. Georgie had great respect for this officer and was fascinated when he suggested that George should become a 'tank' officer. Heavy tanks had been used by the British with mixed success on the Somme in September 1916, whilst the French, with different tactical ideas, had employed lightly armoured and more mobile armoured tracked vehicles in the spring of 1917. Pershing soon became aware of the potential of this new weapon, and after establishing an AEF Tank Board, recommended the creation of a Tank Department to implement a plan to manufacture and field a force of two hundred heavy and two thousand light tanks, modelled on the British Mark IV and French Renault respectively. Eltinge had been appointed by Pershing as temporary head of the 'AEF Tank Corps'.

On 3 October Patton wrote formally to his General and said he wished to be considered for a command in the new tank force, and a month later he wrote to his father:

> The T [tanks] are only used in attacks so all the rest of the time you are comfortable. Of course there is a fifty percent chance they won't work at all but if they do they will work like hell. Here is the golden dream . . . 1. I will run the [tank] school. 2. Then they will organize a battalion and I will command it. 3. Then if I make good and the T [tanks] do and the war lasts I will get the first regiment. 4. With the same 'IF' as before they will make a brigade and I will get a star.[2]

On 10 November, shortly before his 32nd birthday, Captain George S Patton was detailed as the first officer in the new Tank Corps. He was ordered to proceed to Langres, where he was to report to the Commandant of Army Schools for the purpose of establishing the First Army Tank School. He was given one assistant, Lieutenant Elgin Braine, an artillery officer.

Before Patton could even begin to set up a Tank School he naturally had to learn something about tanks and, in the same week that the British launched their massive armoured attack at Cambrai (Map 1) on 20 November 1917, he began a two week familiarization course at the French tank training centre at Chamlieu. He learned to drive the two-man Renault tank, fire its gun and how its engine functioned. He also discussed tank tactics with French officers, and when Elgin Braine joined him on the second week of the course they were able to arrange a visit to the Renault tank factory to learn about tank design and manufacture.

Patton was not slow to learn the basic lessons of the British attack at Cambrai. It had been led by the entire British Tank Corps of 476 armoured vehicles, including 378 heavy tanks on a seven-mile front and, after catching the Germans completely by surprise, a breakthrough and advance of some four to five miles was achieved in a matter of only six hours. Unfortunately many of the tanks broke down, and when the British failed to exploit the breakthrough, the Germans were able to bring up reinforcements, counter-attack and restore the situation. The major lesson Patton gleaned from this was that if tanks were to be successful they needed close infantry support, but in his 12 December fifty-eight page memorandum addressed to the temporary head of the AEF Tank Corps, Lieutenant Colonel Eltinge, he went on to argue that tanks should adopt the role of cavalry and be used to exploit success. Nevertheless, it was the task of the Tank Corps to assist and not replace the infantry.

In mid-December Patton arrived in Langres. It was an old walled town totally unsuitable for a tank school and it was quickly decided to move to the nearby village of Bourg which had a railhead and good access roads.

By mid-January 1918 the first eighteen volunteer officers arrived and a month later two companies of volunteer soldiers joined. There were no tanks but this did not deter Patton who had been promoted to the rank of major on 26 January. He insisted on a strict regime of hard work, discipline, saluting, athletics, games and general behaviour. He personally wrote the training manuals and devised a tank doctrine. Amongst the many subjects taught were the general employment of tanks on the battlefield, weapon training, map reading, gas drills and camouflage; in addition new drills, carried out on foot because of the lack of tanks, were instituted to teach all ranks the various new commands they would receive and the actions they would need to implement once inside their tanks. Patton worked himself harder than his men, organizing the training, visiting the Renault tank works and his French counterparts, lecturing the AEF colonels and generals on the employment of tanks – even though he did not have any – and even having discussions with the British general who had led the Cambrai attack, General Hugh Elles and the Chief of Staff of the British Tank Corps, Lieutenant Colonel J F C Fuller, a leading expert on the employment of tanks. The latter went on to develop radical theories on armoured warfare and the mechanisation of armies in the 1920s and 1930s.

On 23 March the first ten Renault tanks arrived in Bourg. Since no one else had ever driven a tank before, Patton himself drove each one off the railway flats. His men were immediately given crash courses on their new 'mounts' and as early as 16 April Patton ran a series of field exercises to test his men. Georgie had by now been promoted to the rank of lieutenant colonel and he followed these initial exercises with a demonstration to the Commandant and students of the General Staff School at Langres showing how tanks could, and should, support infantry. It was considered a success and five days later he was appointed to command the 1st Light Tank Battalion of the US Tank Corps. Patton's prediction was coming true – in less than a year he had moved from captain to lieutenant colonel. This rapid promotion was due almost entirely to 'Black Jack' Pershing. As Patton put it in letter to Beatrice: 'General P. had a hell of a time getting me promoted as they said I was too young [he was 32] but he finally put it over.' 300 miles away to the north Monty was still a major and heavily involved in the German 'Spring Offensive'.

In May Patton, frustrated by the lack of tanks – the 1st Light Tank Battalion still had only twenty-five overworked Renaults – obtained permission to spend two weeks with a forward French tank unit. His command of the French language was by now excellent and he admired his hosts, 'I like them much better than the British possibly because they do not drink tea'.[3] But this proximity to the fighting only increased his frustration. He was commanding a unit that had no possibility of going into action until it received its full quota of equipment and that seemed as far away as ever. On 13 June he wrote to Beatrice:

> Sometimes I deeply regret that I did not take the infantry last November instead of the tanks. The Regiment I had a chance to join has been at it now for five months . . . I keep dreading lest the war should finish before I can really do any fighting.

Up to this point the Pershing had allowed some of his formations to be used in the forward areas to gain experience, and indeed two of his Divisions, operating under French Corps, had played vital roles in thwarting the German offensive in late May at Château-Thierry, and an American Marine Brigade had fought a famous battle at Belleau Wood. Nevertheless, Pershing and the American government had steadfastly refused Allied requests to permanently subordinate their units to French or British commanders. They were determined that when the time was right their troops would fight as a complete Army under American command. That time came on 10 August when Pershing assumed command of a fully activated US First Army. By then it had a strength of well over a million men. Furthermore, it had been agreed with the French C-in-C, Marshal Ferdinand Foch, that this Army would be employed west of Verdun, in the Meuse–Argonne sector, and that in early September its first action would be to eliminate the German salient at Saint Mihiel.

Patton was both surprised and thrilled when he received orders on 20 August to report to the head of the Tank Corps, Colonel Samuel Rockenbach, 'equipped for field service'. From the latter he learned that his command was to be expanded and officially designated the 1st Tank Brigade.[4] It would comprise the 344th and 345th Tank Battalions with a total of 950 officers and men and was to participate in the forthcoming offensive. Furthermore his Brigade was to be reinforced with twenty-four Schneider medium tanks of the IV Regiment of the French Army and was to be one of three tank Brigades being committed – the others being a heavy American Brigade using British Mk V tanks (it had been training in England) and a French light Tank Brigade. He was to operate in support of the US V Corps in the northern part of the Saint Mihiel salient, an area considered by Rockenbach to be suitable for only very limited tank operations. On the night of 21–22 August Patton accompanied a French patrol into no-man's-land and subsequently reported that unless there was heavy rain immediately before the offensive, his tanks could carry out their designated task. Two days later the promised Renault tanks began arriving at Bourg.

In the middle of the 1st Tank Brigade's preparations for the forthcoming attack, the plan was suddenly changed and Patton was told that instead of supporting V Corps his Brigade would now support the 1st and 42nd

Divisions of IV Corps in the southern sector. Fortunately the offensive was postponed until 12 September, but even then the last of the Brigade's Renaults did not arrive in the forming up position until two hours before H-Hour.

Four days before the attack Patton issued 'Special Instructions' to his two Battalions:

> No tank is to be surrendered or abandoned to the enemy. If you are left alone in the midst of the enemy keep shooting. If your gun is disabled use your pistols and squash the enemy with your tracks . . . remember that you are the first American tanks. You must establish the fact that AMERICAN TANKS DO NOT SURRENDER . . . As long as one tank is able to move it must go forward. Its presence will save the lives of hundreds of infantry and kill many Germans . . . This is our BIG CHANCE.

Patton watched the offensive begin from a hillside overlooking his sector of the battlefield. Over 3,000 guns participated in a four-hour barrage before ten American divisions totalling 230,000 men, supported by 70,000 Frenchmen, began their advance.[5] His direct superior, Colonel Rockenbach, had told Georgie that he was to remain at his Command Post where he could direct his tanks and at the same time be in direct contact with higher headquarters. He went on to make it clear that Patton was not personally to lead his tanks into battle.

When H-Hour came at 0500 hours the rain, which had begun four days earlier, became torrential and the ground, already mainly marshland, turned into a quagmire. Despite this the 344th Tank Battalion outran the infantry of the 1st Division and reached their objective of Nonsard before they ran out of fuel. Surprisingly, only three broke down. On the right flank, the 345th Tank Battalion had great difficulty breaching the main German trench system and, despite his orders to stay off the battlefield, Patton decided to move forward on foot to see for himself what was happening and if necessary to redirect the Battalion. It was obvious that the lack of inter-arms training was causing untold problems, with the infantry having no idea what the tanks were supposed to be doing and the tanks often being unable to see, let alone contact, the men they were meant to be supporting.

Patton first met the commander of the French Schneider tank detachment at Maiserais and then moved on to Essey (today they are one village) where a Brigade of the 42nd Division under Brigadier General Douglas MacArthur was held up. As more than one historian has noted, a German shell landing in the right place at that moment might have seen the end of two of the greatest WWII commanders! Fortunately Essey was soon taken and Patton, with permission from MacArthur, ordered the few remaining tanks of the 345th Battalion on to the next village, Pannes. Despite Rockenbach's orders he rode on one of the tanks and before long the Germans withdrew from the village leaving it to the combined force of infantry and armour. Patton then moved across the battlefield on foot to the 344th Battalion at Nonsard. Finding its tanks out of fuel he decided to return to his CP to arrange a resupply.

By midday on the 13th both Patton's Battalions had been refuelled and were ready to advance again, but by then the Saint Mihiel salient had been to all intents and purposes eliminated. Indeed the Germans, fully aware of its vulnerability ever since they had captured it in April 1915, had always planned to abandon it in the face of a determined enemy attack and withdraw to the 'Hindenburg Line' behind the Woëvre Plain. In fact they learned of the impending offensive three days before it began and by H-Hour on 12 September two of their divisions were already on their way to the rear. It soon became a jibe in French military circles that the Americans had 'relieved the Germans in the salient'! Nevertheless, the Americans had proved to both friend and foe that they were a major force to be reckoned with. 16,000 prisoners and 443 guns had been taken.[6] From George Patton's point of view, however, it was a disappointment. Although he was thrilled that his tanks had kept going in 'conditions [that] could not have been worse', he felt that the lack of determined German resistance meant that the Tank Corps had been neither fully tested nor able to show its true potential. The bare statistics of the battle were that only two tanks had been lost to enemy fire, forty had failed to negotiate the German trenches and thirty had run out of fuel. Five of his men had been killed and nineteen wounded, of whom only four had been wounded whilst actually inside a tank. As far as Patton's personal performance was concerned there is little doubt that his presence on the battlefield and in the most forward areas did much to inspire his men. On the other hand it earned him no medals (MacArthur won his fifth Silver Star at Essey), merely a severe reprimand from Rockenbach for leaving his Command Post in complete defiance of orders.

On 16 September Patton was able to report that he had 131 Renaults ready for action. It was as well – in ten days time the US First Army was to launch a new offensive in the Meuse–Argonne sector, thirty miles to the north-west.

The Meuse–Argonne offensive was launched on 26 September by the First US and Fourth French Armies on a twenty-four-mile front stretching from the Argonne Forest to the Meuse river. In order to deceive the Germans into thinking the next attack would be towards Metz and Alsace, some American units remained in the Saint Mihiel salient until the last minute. These included fifteen tanks of Patton's 345th Battalion which, in the early evening of the 22nd, motored into no-man's-land in front of the Hindenburg Line. Meanwhile the rest of the 1st Tank Brigade withdrew to the railhead at Saint Mihiel and then moved thirty-three miles to Clermont-en-Argonne where they arrived at night and moved quickly into woods two miles to the north.

Patton's task was to support the two National Guard Divisions of I Corps – the 28th and 35th. The 28th was to advance nine miles along the eastern edge of the Argonne Forest with Varennes as its objective, whilst the 35th advanced a similar distance towards Cheppy. The only open ground was a one-mile wide strip running north on the right flank of the 28th Division towards the two objectives and even this had the Aire river running through it forming a tank barrier between the two Divisions. It was obvious to Patton that his tanks could not operate in the forest and he therefore ordered his 344th Battalion to follow the infantry of the 35th Division in the open ground on the right flank.

Patton was determined to do something about the fuel problems experienced at Saint Mihiel and as well as ordering every tank to carry two additional four-gallon containers, he established a 20,000-gallon dump within half a mile of the start line; this was in addition to two large dumps positioned by Rockenbach near the front line.

In a letter to Beatrice dated the day before the attack, Patton wrote:

> Just a word to you before I leave to play a little part in what promises to be the biggest battle of the war or world so far . . . If the Bosch fights he will give us hell but I don't think he intends to fight very hard . . . I will have two battalions and a group of French tanks in the show, in all about 140 tanks. We go up a stinking river valley which will not be at all a comfortable place in a few hours.

This time he attempted to placate Rockenbach by siting his Headquarters alongside that of the 35th Division and telling him that he would always keep six to ten runners with him. This clearly indicated that he would not necessarily remain at his Headquarters! In the event Patton had with him in his forward Headquarters his Reconnaissance and Signals officers, twelve runners, telephones with plenty of cable and a number of carrier pigeons.

At 0230 hours on 26 September nearly 3,000 guns opened fire on the German positions. 'During the three hours preceding H-Hour, the Allies expended more ammunition than both sides managed to fire in the [American] Civil War.'[7] Then, at 0530 hours in dense fog, nine American Divisions, four of which had never been in action before, began their advance. Patton remained at his Headquarters until 0630 hours, but then, true to form, he began to follow in the tracks of the 344th Battalion's Renaults. 'It was terribly foggy and in addition they were shooting lots of smoke shells so we could not see ten feet.'[8] Perhaps not surprisingly, when the fog finally began to lift Patton and his group found themselves under heavy fire and in front of the leading tanks which had become bogged down in the German trench works. He was in fact only some 500 yards short of the 35th Division's objective of Cheppy. Even more serious was the fact that the tanks had once again outpaced the American infantry who were disorganized and in some cases fleeing the battlefield. Patton's group took cover behind a railway embankment. He described what happened next in a letter to Beatrice:

> All at once we were shot at . . . with shells and machine-guns. Twice the infantry started to run but we hollered at them and called them all sorts of names so they stayed. But they were scared and some acted badly . . . none did a damn thing to kill Bosch. There were no officers there but me.[9]

He soon realised that the only hope of getting the attack going again was to get some of his tanks through the trench system so that they could deal with the German machine-guns. However, just at this moment his reserve tank companies started to arrive, along with a number of French Schneider heavy tanks attached to his Brigade, resulting in heavy congestion and producing a prime target for German artillery. Messages carried by one of his officers and his batman to the stalled tanks produced no results and so finally:

> I went back and made some Americans hiding in the trenches dig a passage. I think I killed one man here. He would not work so I hit him over the head with a shovel. It was exciting for they shot at us all the time but I got mad and walked on the parapet . . . At last we got five tanks across and I started them forward and yelled and cussed and waved my stick and said 'come on'. About 150 doughboys [infantrymen] started but when we got to the crest of the hill the fire got fierce right along the ground. We all lay down.[10]

The tanks finally managed to advance, and despite the intense German shell and machine-gun fire, Patton is said to have waved his walking stick above his head and shouted, 'Let's go get them, who's with me?'. About a hundred infantrymen apparently followed him, but after crossing the crest line they came under fire and soon went to ground again. Only Patton and six men, including his batman Private Jo Angelo, continued to move forward beside the lead tanks.

> I hoped the rest would follow but they would not and soon there were only three [of us] but we could see the machine-guns right ahead so we yelled to keep up our courage and went on. Then the third man went down.[11]

Soon after this Patton was struck by a machine-gun bullet in the upper left thigh, 'and [it] came out just at the crack in my bottom about two inches to the left of my rectum. It . . . made a hole about the size of a dollar where it came out'.[12]

Patton's batman managed to drag him into a shell hole and apply bandages to stem the bleeding, but there was no hope of either man getting back to a place of real safety whilst the heavy German fire continued. The time was about 1100 hours and it was to be another two hours or more before they could be rescued. Eventually two Companies of the 344th Tank Battalion managed to outflank the Germans and they were soon joined by men of the 35th Division's 138th Regiment. At about 1330 hours this joint force finally secured Cheppy. In the meantime a medical orderly of the 35th Division had looked after Patton and he was eventually evacuated by stretcher to an ambulance two miles away. Private Angelo insisted on staying with him. He was later awarded a Distinguished Service Cross for saving Patton's life.

By nightfall on the 26th the 1st Tank Brigade had ninety-seven out of 140 tanks still combat ready, but two days later only fifty-three tanks were still in action.

On the 29th Patton and one of his badly wounded company commanders were moved by 'cattle train' from the evacuation hospital where they had been initially cared for, to a base hospital near Dijon. On 2 October he was able to write to Beatrice:

> The hole in my hip is about as big as a tea cup and they have to leave it open. I suffer not at all except when they dress the wounds. I look as if I had just had a baby . . . Still we broke the Prussian guard with the tanks so it is all fine.

Ten days later he wrote again:

> I feel terrible to have missed all the fighting. It seems too bad but I had to go in when I did or the whole line might have broken. Perhaps I was mistaken but anyway I believe I have been sited [sic] for a decoration. Either the Medal of Honor or the Military Cross [he almost certainly meant Distinguished Service Cross]. I hope I get one of them . . . Peace looks possible but I rather hope not for I would like to have a few more fights.

On 17 October Patton heard that he had been promoted to the rank of Colonel. He immediately wrote to Beatrice, addressing the envelope to 'Mrs. Colonel G S Patton, Jr'. At the end of the month he managed to get a transfer to a hospital in Langres where he soon became an outpatient and within days he was able to return to Bourg and reassume command of the Tank School.

And the Meuse–Argonne campaign? The Argonne Forest was finally cleared of enemy on 9 October and the whole campaign ended with the Armistice. The fighting had cost the Americans over 122,000 men and the Germans 100,000. In the case of Patton's 1st Tank Brigade only eighty out of its 834 men were still fit for duty.

Colonel George S Patton's direct participation in WWI had lasted only two days; in fairness though, it has to be said that they could hardly have been more dramatic or eventful. 'The War to end all Wars' ended at the eleventh hour of the eleventh month of 1918 – Patton's 33rd birthday. He wrote in his diary, 'Peace was signed and Langres was very excited. Many flags. Got rid of my bandage. Wrote a poem on peace'.

300 miles away to the north near Tournai in Belgium (Map 1), Brevet Lieutenant Colonel Bernard Montgomery wrote the following entry in the 47th (London) Division War Diary:

> Early in the morning news received from Corps HQ that hostilities were to cease at 1100 ... The Divisional Commander will hold a conference at 10.00 on 12th Nov, for all COs on the duties of Commanding Officers during the Armistice.

350 miles to the east in Bavaria, Corporal Adolf Hitler spent 11 November guarding Russian prisoners.

Having heard about the activities of both our prima donnas in WWI it is time to consider what they had learned from their experiences. In the case of Monty it is clear that the horrendous casualties suffered by the British Army left an indelible impression on him and a determination whenever possible to use materials, rather than men, to achieve his aims. He became convinced that carefully organized set-piece battles, rather than undisciplined mobile operations, were the only way to ensure victory and avoid heavy casualties.

Patton, comparatively shielded from the horror of the mass casualties, had come to the opposite conclusion. The slogging infantry attacks of WWI, following behind massive artillery barrages, appalled him. His attitude is summed up in the following extracts from his 'Field Notebook 1921–22':[13]

> To move swiftly, strike vigorously and secure all the fruits of victory is the secret of successful war.
> War means fighting. Fighting means killing, not digging trenches.
> When the enemy wavers throw caution to the winds ... A violent pursuit will finish the show. Caution leads to a new battle.
> Ride the enemy to the death.

One could say that these differing attitudes stemmed from their military backgrounds – one an infantryman, the other a cavalryman. One thing is certain – these attitudes, nurtured in France in WWI, would come to fruition in WWII.

NOTES

1 Letter to Beatrice dated 19 Sep 17.
2 Letter dated 6 Nov 17.
3 Letter to Beatrice dated 19 May 18.
4 Later re-numbered as the 304th Tank Brigade.
5 *Final Report of Gen. John J. Pershing* – Washington, DC: Government Printing Office, 1919, pp. 38–43.
6 Ibid.
7 D'Este, *A Genius for War*, p. 254.
8 Letter to Beatrice dated 28 Sep 18.
9 Ibid.
10 Ibid.
11 Ibid.
12 Ibid.
13 Box 59, George S Patton Papers, Library of Congress, Washington, DC.

CHAPTER VII

Montgomery between the World Wars

Soon after the Armistice Monty was posted to the Headquarters of the British Army on the Rhine as a Grade 2 staff officer in the Operations Branch (SO 2 Ops). Owing to the rapid reduction in the size of the Army as a whole, he was required to revert to the rank of major. There were of course no 'operations' per se and he had few interesting duties. One perk that did come his way was to escort one of the C-in-C's distinguished visitors[1] round some of the WWI battlefields by car. The tour of over 1,000 miles included Saint Mihiel, Verdun and Chemin-des-Dames; he wrote to his mother: 'he is a rich man and I get all my expenses paid'.

Soon after the signing of the Versailles treaty in the summer of 1919, Monty was told that his job in Cologne was to be axed. He had already decided that the only way to obtain further advancement was to gain a place at the Staff College in Camberley, England, but selection was by nomination, rather than competitive examination, and he had been bitterly disappointed when his name had failed to appear on the list of candidates for that year. His problem was that he had no friends in high places – in fact he had very few friends at all. He was even more distraught when he found his name missing yet again from the list of candidates for the 1920 course. Determined to rectify matters he made a direct approach to his C-in-C, General Sir William Robertson, during a tennis party at the latter's residence in Cologne. It was perhaps fortunate that Robertson was the first Field Marshal in the British Army to have started as an ordinary soldier and he was sympathetic. Monty's name was soon added to the list. Robertson went even further, and to fill the gap before the Camberley course starting the following January, he arranged for Monty to be promoted to the temporary rank of lieutenant colonel and given command of the 17th Battalion of The Royal Fusiliers, stationed nearby. The Battalion was part of the British occupation force, but its soldiers were virtually all conscripts under the age of 20 who wanted to forget matters military as soon as possible and return to civilian life. Monty did his best to keep them busy and, as well as continuing with military training which he was obliged to do, he ensured that his men attended discussion groups and received advice about their impending demobilization. It was a frustrating time for a dedicated professional soldier like Monty who had already decided, 'to dedicate myself to my profession, to master its details, and to put all else aside'.[2]

Monty spent Christmas 1919 with his parents and on 22 January 1920, once again in the rank of major, reported to the Staff College for the one-year course. He did not enjoy his time there. Not surprisingly, having already served as a Brigade Major (Chief of Staff of a Brigade) and Chief of Staff of a Division, and as a Grade 2 Staff Officer in both a Division and a Corps – all under active service conditions – he found the course boring and less than challenging. It certainly did not live up to his hopes and expectations and he appears to have made this obvious to his fellow students, who found him boringly professional, and to some of his instructors. 'I must admit that I was critical and intolerant . . . I believe I got a good report, but do not know as nobody ever told me if I had done well or badly.'[3]

Monty graduated in December 1920 and the following January he was appointed Brigade Major (Chief of Staff) of the 17th Infantry Brigade, based in Cork, southern Ireland. It was to be another year before Prime Minister Lloyd George's Government in London created the Irish Free State and Monty walked straight into another war – this time with the Irish Republican Army (IRA). He wrote later:

> In many ways this war was far worse than the Great War . . . It developed into a murder campaign in which, in the end, the soldiers became very skilful and more than held their own. But such a war is thoroughly bad for officers and men; it tends to lower their standards of decency and chivalry, and I was glad when it was over.[4]

In a letter to his father dated 1 March 1922, he explained what it was like from his perspective:

The situation is really impossible; we have had two officers murdered in the last fortnight; ambulances and lorries are held up almost daily by armed men and the vehicles stolen ... The Provisional Government have no authority of any sort or description here; the south is entirely ruled by the IRA who publicly state ... that they owe no allegiance ... Our policy is that we do not care what anyone does, or what happens, so long as the troops are left alone and are not interfered with; any civilian, or Republican soldier or policeman, who interferes with any officer or soldier *is shot at once* ... Three armed civilians held up one of our closed cars the other day; they thought it was empty except for the chauffeur, and that they would be able to steal it. Unluckily for them there were three British officers inside it; they opened fire at once through the windows with revolvers; two of the civilians were killed, but the third escaped. It was a good lesson for them ... The IRA get no pay ... When they want money they go round the town and forcibly collect 5/- a head from every resident; this happens once a week ... I shall be heartily glad to see the last of the people and of the place.

Furthermore, the fact that his parents' home in Moville had been raided by eight members of the IRA who stole mattresses and blankets from the beds, various daggers, spears, and wooden clubs collected by his father in the Pacific, and a few old muskets and pistols, did little to endear the Republican cause to Montgomery. A year later he set out his thoughts on the problem to a brother officer:

To win a war of that sort you must be ruthless; Oliver Cromwell, or the Germans, would have settled it in a very short time. Nowadays public opinion precludes such methods; the nation would never allow it and the politicians would lose their jobs if they sanctioned it ... The only way therefore was to give them some form of self-government.[5]

At the end of May 1922 Monty, to his great relief, was transferred to the 8th Infantry Brigade in Plymouth, again as Brigade Major (Chief of Staff), but in the summer of 1923 he was posted once more, this time to be a Grade 2 Staff Officer in the Headquarters of a Territorial Army (TA) Division – the 49th – in York. Since there was no Grade 1 Staff officer in a TA division, he was effectively the Chief of Staff. He had survived the 'Geddes Axe', which reduced manning levels in the Army to the minimum thought necessary to garrison India and Egypt and other territories under British control, but not to man another Expeditionary Force like the BEF in 1914. Another major war involving the British Empire was considered almost impossible by the Government of the day.[6] Monty wrote later:

An extensive use of weed killer is needed in the *senior* ranks after a war; this will enable the first class younger officers who have emerged during the war to be moved up . . . Opportunity was taken to get rid of a great deal of inefficient material in the lower ranks, but in the higher ranks much dead wood was left untouched.[7]

Monty spent much of his free time in Plymouth and York coaching young officers for the examinations which had been introduced for entrance to the Staff College. It was an occupation he clearly enjoyed and at which he was good. In the same way he introduced sand-table tactical exercises for the part-time officers and NCOs of the 49th Division, an innovation unheard of in the TA.

Apart from the few months Monty had spent with the Royal Fusiliers in Cologne, he had been away from Regimental Duty (service in an active duty battalion or unit) for eleven years and in early 1925 he was posted back to his original Battalion – the 1st Battalion of The Royal Warwickshire Regiment – in Shorncliffe. It must have seemed like coming home for it was in Shorncliffe that he and the Battalion had been stationed in 1913 on their return from India. Monty took command of a company, but his Commanding Officer, who had spent WWI in New Zealand and therefore lacked experience, was delighted to hand over responsibility for the unit's tactical training to the very experienced and obviously talented new arrival. Monty's professionalism, however, did not endear him initially to his brother officers who were far more interested in sport, hunting and social pleasures. Even so, they soon came to appreciate his talents, especially when they resulted in the Battalion acquitting itself well during the annual manoeuvres on Salisbury Plain. One of Monty's innovations was to take four of the young officers, including his brother who had by now joined the Regiment, on a battlefield tour in France and Belgium. It was carried out on bicycles and covered the retreat from Mons, Le Cateau, St Quentin, Météren, where Monty had been wounded, Ypres and Lille.

It was during his time with the Royal Warwicks that Monty accompanied his Commanding Officer and his wife to Dinard in France for a golfing holiday. He was by now a keen golfer and it was during this vacation that he met and apparently fell madly in love with a 17-year-old called Betty Anderson. Her father was in the Foreign Department of the Government of India and the family was home on leave. Monty was 37. Betty found this intense officer charming but boring and almost inevitably she refused his proposal of marriage. This was hardly surprising if, as is reported by his brother, Monty spent time on the beach drawing 'pictures for her in the sand to illustrate his ideas for the employment of armoured fighting vehicles' and 'how he would position his tanks . . . to be used in conjunction with infantry'.[8]

In January 1926 Monty was again promoted to the rank of brevet lieutenant colonel and posted back to the Staff College in Camberley as an instructor. Before he took up this appointment, however, he decided to take a skiing holiday in Lenk in the Bernese Oberland. He must have known Betty Anderson and her parents were due to be there as well for he was standing in the foyer of the Wildstrubel hotel when she walked in. Whether he thought his new rank and persistence might gain her hand is not clear, but his proposal of marriage was again turned down and Monty had to admit defeat. There was, nevertheless, to be a major consolation which would lead to marriage. On the same holiday Miss Anderson introduced him to a Mrs Betty Carver and her two boys. She was a widow, her husband having been killed at Gallipoli in 1915, and the sister of an officer who was to be one of the great pioneers of armour warfare and who would command the 79th Armoured Division (an experimental formation) in WWII – Sir Percy Hobart. 'I soon made friends with the boys and with their mother, and the holiday passed pleasantly.'[9]

Although Monty had not enjoyed the Staff College as a student, he was thoroughly at home there as an instructor.

> In my case it seemed that here was an opportunity for three years hard study; I knew enough by then to realise that the teacher learns much more than his students. And these three years would be spent working closely with certain other instructors already there, ones who were known to me as some of the best officers in the Army.[10]

Probably the most famous of these, and certainly one of the most influential in Monty's case, was the Director of Studies, Alan Brooke, destined to become the Chief of the Imperial General Staff (CIGS) in WWII. Amongst the most famous students during his time there were Miles Dempsey, later to command the Second British Army in Normandy, and Richard O'Connor, later to be a fellow Divisional commander in Palestine and even later to command VIII Corps in Normandy.

Monty's wide experience and talent as a lecturer ensured his success at Camberley. The students found him dictatorial and very demanding, but they enjoyed his sharp wit and obvious ability.

In January 1927 Monty took a second skiing holiday at Lenk and again met Mrs Carver and her two boys. 'This time I saw a great deal of Betty Carver and by the time the holiday was over I had fallen in love; for the first and only time in my life.'[11] It must be assumed that since he had twice asked another woman to marry him in the previous twelve months, this latter comment, which appears in his official *Memoirs*, was made in deference to his son, stepsons and their mother.

Monty and Betty Carver were married in Chiswick Parish church on 27 July 1927 in front of the two families and a few guests. His brother was his best man and his father conducted the service, following which Monty said 'Goodbye, goodbye, we're going off now, straight to our honey-moon'.[12] With that he opened the car door for Betty, took the wheel himself and set off to Switzerland. To the amazement of family and friends, including the best man, there was no Reception.

For a man who had spent the whole of his adult life as a bachelor, living in officers' messes, marriage to a woman with sons aged 12 and 13, meant a major change in life style. Surprisingly, Monty adapted to it with ease and 'a time of great happiness then began'.[13] An indication of how well Monty got on with his stepsons, for whom he came to have a great affection, can be gauged by the fact that they both later became regular Army officers. The Montgomerys lived in one of the Staff College married quarters – bungalow number 17 in the grounds of the Royal Military College, Sandhurst – and a year later David, Monty's only child, was born. Betty was 40.

In early 1929 Monty left the Staff College and was given the task of rewriting the War Office *Infantry Training Manual*. He was attached to his old Battalion of the Royal Warwicks which had by now moved to Woking, thirty miles outside London, and the family lived in a married quarter in Inkerman Barracks.

> I decided to make the book a comprehensive treatise on war for the infantry officer. All my work had to be approved by a committee in the War Office and some heated arguments took place; I could not accept many of their amendments ... I then recommended that the committee should disband and that I should complete the book in my own time; this was agreed. I produced the final draft, omitting all the amendments the committee had put forward. The book when published was considered excellent, especially by its author.[14]

Monty was appointed second-in-command of the Battalion in July 1930 and at the end of that year he was told that he was to be the next Commanding Officer. On 17 January 1931, at the age of 43, he was promoted to the rank of substantive (permanent) lieutenant colonel. That month the Battalion sailed for Port Said in Egypt whence it was to take the train to Jerusalem. He was also to be 'OC Troops Palestine', with authority over another Battalion in Haifa and Arab cavalry in the Jordan valley. Betty and David were able to join him in June and for just under a year Monty and his 'very good Colonel's Lady' were able to enjoy not only the Holy Places, but also some of the wonders of the ancient world like Petra and Baalbec. However, life was not all smooth for Monty. His insistence on promotion by merit rather than seniority did not go down well in his Battalion and as a renowned 'Staff Officer' (he had after all served for a total of only two years at Regimental duty since the end of WWI), he was viewed with suspicion by some of his officers and many members of his

Warrant Officers' and Sergeants' Mess. He was certainly unpopular with
the Governor and members of the civilian Foreign Service in Jerusalem:

> Among the many guests who used to come to lunch and dinner at
> Government House was the colonel in command of the Warwick-
> shires, the Regiment that was garrisoning the Holy City. We all took
> a great dislike to Colonel Montgomery as he used to lecture us on the
> luxurious lives that we led . . . He had been particularly censorious at
> dinner the previous Thursday, not even sparing Princess Alice
> [Countess of Athlone] from his strictures.[15]

At the end of the year the Royal Warwicks, with their families, moved to
Alexandria, a major 'flesh-pot' in the Middle East at that time and Monty
found himself under the eyes of both a Brigade commander and the C-in-
C Egypt. Fortunately they were tolerant superiors – his lack of interest in
ceremonial drill parades, derogatory remarks about a neighbouring
Battalion of the Brigade of Guards and a Cavalry Regiment that he
considered amateurish, and actions such as abolishing formal and
compulsory Battalion Church Parades on Sundays and setting up a
Regimental brothel, would have landed him in serious trouble with most
superiors at that time. As it was they were both highly impressed with his
professionalism and the training standards achieved by his Battalion and
he received excellent annual reports, albeit with caveats that he should
curb 'a certain high-handedness' and 'cultivate tact, tolerance and discretion'.

During the time Monty was in Egypt his father died; he was 85. Monty
wrote later: 'It was a tremendous loss for me. The three outstanding
human beings in my life have been my father, my wife, and my son.'[16]

On Christmas Eve 1933 the Battalion, complete with the officers' and
senior ranks' families, sailed for India. Its next station was Poona, near
Bombay. Here Monty immediately landed himself in trouble. His
immediate superior was a Guardsman who believed that foot drill was
the basis of all training – indeed that it was the 'be all and end all' of
military training – and that ceremonial parades, including Sunday
Church Parades, were much more important than field manoeuvres. By
coincidence he had written Volume I of the Infantry Training Manual –
Drill, whilst Monty had written Volume II – *Tactics*. Needless to say they
did not get on. A classic example of their relationship and one that gives
another insight into Monty's character is quoted by his brother in his
book *A Field Marshal in the Family*. During a formal inspection of the
Battalion, the Garrison commander halted his horse in front of Monty
and said: 'Colonel Montgomery, you are not positioned properly in front
of your regiment in mass formation. You are six paces too far to your
right. Please take up your correct position now.' Monty apparently

saluted and then gave the order: Royal Warwickshire. Six paces right close. March.'[17]

Fortunately for Monty within three months he was offered, and accepted, the appointment of Senior Instructor at the Indian Army Staff College in Quetta, near the border with Afghanistan, in what is now Pakistan. He moved there in June 1934 with the rank of Colonel. 'We had three very happy years there, except for the earthquake in May 1935.'[18] The Quetta earthquake of 31 May 1935 was one of the worst, if not the worst, ever experienced in the sub-Continent. The entire town was destroyed, 30,000 people killed and many thousands injured and maimed. Fortunately for the Montgomerys the Staff College was four miles from the town and as well as no damage being caused, no one there was hurt. Betty and David had to return to England for eight months and Monty became fully involved in organizing and running a refugee camp.

Unknown to Monty, in the same month as the Quetta earthquake, he had been selected to command the next regular infantry brigade to become available and two years later, in May 1937, after more than six years abroad, he returned home to command the 9th Infantry Brigade in Portsmouth. He was thrilled – not just because it was promotion to the rank of brigadier and a senior command, but because his Brigade was part of the 3rd Infantry Division which would be part of any BEF in the event of war. And by now Monty was convinced that war with Nazi Germany was a certainty.

After two months' leave in northern England, Monty assumed command of his Brigade and took it to a training camp on Salisbury Plain. Betty and 9-year-old David went to a hotel at the seaside for the rest of his school holidays. Then disaster struck. Whilst sitting on the beach Betty was stung on the leg by an insect, septicaemia set in and despite the amputation of her leg, within two months she was dead. Monty was devastated.

> I was utterly defeated. I began to search my mind for anything I had done wrong, that I should have been dealt such a shattering blow. I could not understand it; my soul cried out in anguish against this apparent injustice. I seemed to be surrounded by utter darkness; all the spirit was knocked out of me. I had no one to love except David and he was away at [boarding] school.[19]

Inevitably Monty threw himself back into his work and dedicated himself entirely to the Army. 'I made the 9th Infantry Brigade as good as any in England and none other could compete with us in battle on the training area.'[20] Within a year he was promoted again, to the rank of major general and posted to Palestine, a country for which Britain was responsible under a mandate from the League of Nations. Arriving at the beginning of

November 1938 he took command of a new Division, the 8th, one of two charged with quelling an Arab rebellion against the influx of Jewish immigrants. His Headquarters was in Haifa and he was responsible for the northern half of the country. No sooner had he arrived, however, than he received a message from the War Office informing him that he was to be offered the post of General Officer Commanding the 3rd Infantry Division in England when the present incumbent moved on the following December. It was the best major general's command in the British Army – Monty was elated. In the meantime he set about sorting out the Arab rebellion with a vengeance.

Having come to the conclusion that the campaign was not a nationalist movement such as the one he had faced in Ireland, but rather was one that was 'being waged by gangs of professional bandits', he dealt with it accordingly. He ordered his troops to: 'hunt down and destroy the rebel gangs. They must be hunted relentlessly; when engaged in battle with them we must shoot to kill . . . This is the surest way to end the war'.[21] His edict proved highly effective and by the beginning of 1939 most of the Arab rebels in his sector had been either killed or captured. He was able to write to the Military Secretary in the War Office:

> the rebellion out here as an organized movement is smashed; you can go from one end of Palestine to the other looking for a fight and you can't get one; it is very difficult to find Arabs to kill; they have had the stuffing knocked right out of them. I shall be sorry to leave Palestine in many ways as I have enjoyed the 'war' out here.

Monty's obvious high spirits were soon dashed though, when towards the end of April, he fell seriously ill. On 24 May he was admitted to hospital, paralysed and with a rising fever. He was found to have a patch on his lung and tuberculosis was suspected. Despite, or perhaps because of, his condition, Monty demanded to be sent home by sea and incredibly the sea voyage seemed to do the trick. Monty later recalled:

> I walked off the ship at Tilbury in good health . . . I went direct to Millbank [Army] Hospital in London and asked for a thorough medical overhaul; this took three days and the verdict was that there was nothing wrong with me. I asked about the patch on my lung; it had disappeared.[22]

One result of this illness was that he never smoked again; neither would he allow others to smoke in his presence.

By the time Monty had enjoyed some leave and been declared fit for duty, Britain was in the process of partial mobilization for war with Hitler's Germany. His hopes of taking over the 3rd Division, however, were dashed when he was told that the mobilization crisis had led to all previously announced appointments being cancelled; the current commander of the 3rd Division was therefore to continue in post. Monty was told his name was now in a pool of major generals awaiting employment. Needless to say he was not prepared to let matters rest and he contacted his friend Lieutenant General Sir Alan Brooke, Director of Studies at the Staff College when Monty had been an instructor there, and now GOC Southern Command. The 3rd Division was part of his Command. Brooke made overtures in the right places in the War Office and the existing commander of the 3rd Division, who at this critical time in the United Kingdom's history, had rather surprisingly asked for and been granted two months 'fishing leave' in Ireland, was sent off to Bermuda to be the Governor as originally planned. Bernard Montgomery took command of the 3rd Infantry Division on 28 August 1939, three days before the Germans invaded Poland and just six days before war was declared.

NOTES

1   Sir Peter Fryer.
2   Montgomery, *Memoirs*, p. 37.
3   Montgomery, op. cit., p. 39. The author had the same experience in 1960.
4   Ibid.
5   Letter to Major A E Percival dated 14 Oct 23. The author, who was one of the first soldiers on the streets of Londonderry in August 1969 and who completed three operational tours in Ulster and one as Chief of Staff Operations at HQ Northern Ireland, held similar views to Monty's when he left Ulster in 1971.
6   From a strength of three and a half million in 1918 the Army had been reduced to 370,000 by the end of 1920.
7   Montgomery, op. cit., p. 40.
8   Montgomery, Brian, *A Field Marshal in the Family*, p. 195.
9   Montgomery, op. cit., p. 42.
10 Ibid, p. 41.
11 Ibid, p. 42.
12 Montgomery, Brian, op. cit., p. 207.
13 Montgomery, op. cit., p. 42.
14 Ibid, p. 41.
15 Runciman, *A Traveller's Alphabet*, 1931, Jerusalem.
16 Montgomery, op. cit., p. 19.
17 Montgomery, Brian, op.cit., pp. 224–5.
18 Montgomery, op. cit., p. 43.
19 Ibid, p. 44.
20 Ibid, p. 45.
21 National Archives, London, file WO 216/111.
22 Montgomery, op. cit., p. 48.

CHAPTER VIII

Patton between the World Wars

As we have heard, Patton fully expected to be awarded a DSC or even a Medal of Honor for his exploits in the Meuse–Argonne campaign and he was devastated when he heard, on 17 November, that he was to receive neither. He had in fact been recommended for a DSC by the head of the Tank Corps, Samuel Rockenbach, but the American Expeditionary Force (AEF) Adjutant General disapproved the citation before it could reach the C-in-C, General Pershing. In his usual fashion Georgie would not let matters rest and he soon persuaded Rockenbach to submit a further recommendation – this time with eleven first-hand accounts of Patton's valour – and at Bourg on 17 December, in front of the whole of the 1st Tank Brigade, he received the coveted medal. He already held a French Croix de Guerre, and thanks to a recommendation by the Commandant of the AEF Schools, he was also to be awarded the Distinguished Service Medal.

After Christmas Patton learned that whilst he was to prepare his men for a move back to the United States, he personally was destined, like Monty, for occupation duties in the Rhineland. Again he was devastated and once more he lobbied senior members of the AEF staff to allow him to accompany his men back to the States. No doubt they were aware of his close association with Pershing and Patton got his way; on 1 March he and his men boarded the SS *Patria* in Marseilles for the journey home.

TANK FIGHTERS OF NEW YORK AMONG 2,110 BACK HOME. COLONEL PATTON TELLS HOW BIG MACHINES BY HUNDREDS ATTACKED GERMANS – so read the 18 March 1919 caption of the *New York Herald Tribune* under a photograph of Georgie. He was the darling of the press, not just in New York, but also in Washington and as far afield as Los Angeles. Although he naturally revelled in this adulation it was to be short-lived. Like most 'conquering heroes', Patton and his men were soon to be forgotten.

Following its return to the States the 1st Light Tank Brigade, renumbered as the 304th, was assigned to Fort Meade, Maryland, the new home of the Tank Corps. Within a month, however, Patton was detached on temporary duty to a board of veteran Tank Corps officers tasked with making recommendations as to how a future Corps should be structured, trained and employed in war. During his absence from his Brigade, Patton was temporarily replaced by a Lieutenant Colonel Dwight D Eisenhower, a former infantry officer who had been posted to the Tank Corps and who, during the war, had set up and run the largest tank training centre in the United States. When Patton returned to his Brigade in the late summer, Eisenhower, known always to his friends as 'Ike', took over a Battalion of brand new Mk VIII Liberty tanks; they had been manufactured in the

States, but not in time for the war. Ike was five years younger than Patton and shared his passion for riding, hunting and shooting. A major difference between the two officers, however, was money – Georgie and Beatrice had plenty whereas Ike and his wife Mamie had to survive on army pay. There were few married officers' quarters in Fort Meade and when both wives joined their husbands they had no choice other than to live in parts of a disused wooden barracks. The Pattons and Eisenhowers worked hard to transform their spartan surroundings into reasonable homes and improve their standards of living – the Pattons helped by a housekeeper, governess, an English cook, six Mexican servants, stables for a dozen horses and two cars. The Eisenhowers on the other hand were forced to live very quietly.

Like many other soldiers returning from war, especially one who had found it exhilarating, George Patton found it hard to settle down to the humdrum life of peacetime soldiering. Fortunately he and Ike soon became firm friends – as Eisenhower wrote later, they: 'got along famously. Both of us were students of current military doctrine. Part of our passion was our belief in tanks – a belief derided at the time by others'.[1] This was certainly true; the majority of their contemporaries believed that infantry and artillery were the major combat arms, but as Ike put it:

> George and I and a group of young officers thought that this was wrong. Tanks could have a more valuable and spectacular role. We believed . . . that they should attack by surprise and mass.[2]

Both officers expounded their views in the *Infantry Journal* where they not only fell on deaf ears, but in the case of Eisenhower, led to him being reprimanded by the Chief of Infantry and told that he should keep his ideas, which were 'incompatible with solid infantry doctrine' to himself or 'be hauled before a court-martial'.[3]

By June 1920 the US Army had shrunk from a wartime strength of over three and a half million to under 200,000 and as the people of America increasingly embraced pacifism and isolationism, the boys who had returned from France as heroes found themselves unwanted and even despised. For Patton these views were not just unbelievable, they were unacceptable. He wrote to his sister Nita:

> We are like the people in a boat floating down the beautiful river of fictitious prosperity and thinking that the moaning of the none too distant waterfall – which is going to engulf us – is but the song of the wind in the trees . . . our politicians are blind and mad with self delusion.[4]

While Patton was able to enjoy his recreational pursuits of hunting, polo, steeplechasing and competitive swordmanship, his military career took another knock in June 1920 when he was demoted to the rank of captain. The same thing happened to Ike a month later and even the head of the Tank Corps, Rockenbach, was reduced to the rank of colonel. The fact that Georgie was promoted to major a day after his demotion did little to satisfy a man with his ambitions. His only consolation was that, thanks to Rockenbach, he was allowed to remain in command of the 304th Brigade; when more senior officers arrived in Fort Meade they were either sent to other units or absorbed into the Headquarters. But Patton became more and more disillusioned about his own future and that of the Tank Corps. He had been bitterly disappointed when in 1919 his former idol Pershing had recommended to a Congressional Committee that the Tank Corps should be restricted in size and placed under the Chief of Infantry 'as an adjunct of that arm'. And when it became clear that his stated preferences for future duty – a place at the School of the Line at Fort Leavenworth or a posting to London as Military Attaché – were not going to be met, he decided it was time to return to a more gentlemanly and enjoyable life in the cavalry. He submitted his application for a transfer in the summer and it was approved in mid-September. On 28 September Patton reviewed the 700 men of the 304th Brigade for the last time. He made a typical Georgie speech, including the words:

> When I have cussed out or corrected any of you, men or officers, it has been because according to my lights you were wrong, but I have never remembered it against you. I have never asked any of you to brace more, work more [or] fight more than I have been willing to do myself; with the result that in keeping up with you in France I had to get shot.

In October 1920, as Major Bernard Montgomery approached the end of his year at the British Staff College, Major George Patton was ordered to report to the 3rd Cavalry Regiment at Fort Myer, Virginia. It had been an eventful seven years since he had last served there.

Before continuing with the story of Patton's life before the outbreak of WWII, readers may wish to know what happened to the relationship between his sister Nita and General 'Black Jack' Pershing. Recall that they had become privately engaged in 1917, but had decided not to announce the engagement or get married until after the war. Pershing stayed on in France until September 1919, enjoying the adulation of the rich and famous and it came as something of a bombshell when Nita received a letter telling her that Black Jack's feelings for her had 'gone' and that they should delay their marriage until they 'returned'. To rub salt into the wound he failed to invite her to a victory ball in Paris at which he was the guest of honour – even though she was only a short distance away across the Channel in London at the time. To Patton's delight Nita immediately broke off the engagement. According to Georgie's daughter, Ruth Ellen, he had never considered Pershing good enough for his sister anyway – Black Jack's father had after all been a brakeman on the railroad! Ruth Ellen went on to record that her father was 'relieved at having the taint of favoritism or nepotism removed from whatever his future might hold'.

Patton was given command of the 3rd Squadron of the 3rd Cavalry at Fort Myer and as a major in command he was at last entitled to a decent officer's quarter – a rather grand one in fact. It was brick built and in a wonderful setting overlooking the Potomac and the city of Washington.

The role of the 3rd Cavalry was mainly ceremonial – parades for visiting heads of states, funerals, Presidential inaugurations and the like. Patton found himself once more in the limelight, which suited him well, and he revelled in spectacular riding displays which were part of the regular routine of the Regiment. He also found himself with plenty of time to indulge in his passions of polo – he was a member of the Army team – fox hunting, steeplechasing, tennis, squash and swordsmanship. And on top of all this physical activity, Georgie found time to read and add to his huge personal library, as well as joining Beatrice in a hectic social whirl. On the 'down' side, however, he was graded 'below average' by his commanding officer for tact. This was hardly surprising – during this period he became well known for serious losses of temper and sometimes for outrageous behaviour, such as inviting ladies to view his wound scars. This inevitably meant lowering his trousers! Nevertheless, despite his tantrums and indiscretions, Patton was accepted for the five-month Advanced Officers' Course at the Cavalry School at Fort Riley. He reported there in January 1923, by which time the Army had been reduced to a strength of only 137,000.

Patton did well on his course – well enough to be selected to attend the Command and General Service School at Fort Leavenworth,[5] Kansas – the equivalent of the British Staff College at Camberley. He reported there in the September but Beatrice, who was pregnant again, remained in Massachusetts with their two daughters. She gave birth to a son on Christmas Eve. Georgie was present at the birth and was overjoyed to at last have a son to carry on the family name – the baby was christened George Smith Patton IV. It was only after the birth of his son that Patton began to relax as a father and enjoy his children. For a long time after his return from France he had been extremely strict with his little daughters, seemingly unable to accept the fact that they were not boys. Ruth Ellen, who was too young to know him before the war, described him as 'an ogre', and even Beatrice's entreaties for him to be more tolerant and loving had little effect. Fortunately the birth of young George changed every-thing and during the summer of 1924 she was able to write to Aunt Nannie that her husband: 'seems like his old self again . . . he is just like a kid –

every stern line has gone out of his face and . . . the kids . . . are having a grand time with him'.[6]

Patton enjoyed the Leavenworth course both academically and socially. He and Beatrice, unlike the majority, had the money to indulge themselves and entertain lavishly – on one occasion they gave a dinner at the Fort golf club for 120 guests. Georgie graduated twenty-fifth out of 248 and was graded an 'honor' student. Whether this had anything to do with the fact that the Commandant was an old acquaintance who, as Commandant of the AEF Schools in France, had been instrumental in him being awarded the Distinguished Service Medal is unknown. Certainly he tried to retain Patton as an instructor on his staff, describing him as ' one of our best students' who 'has demonstrated that he understands the theory as well as the practice of war'. Nevertheless, the War Department refused his request and in July 1924, Patton reported for duty as the G-1 (Chief Personnel Officer) at the First Corps Area Headquarters in Boston. It is perhaps noteworthy that Patton passed his carefully prepared Command and General Service School course notebook on to Eisenhower who attended Leavenworth in 1925 and passed out top.

The Pattons were in Boston for only nine months before a new posting took Georgie to Hawaii; nevertheless, it was a particularly happy time, especially for Beatrice who had her family and many friends in the immediate neighbourhood. True to form the Pattons 'lived it up', renting a large house with stables and paddocks near the beach in Beverly and employing an English nanny and a houseful of English servants. Georgie was not stretched professionally during this short assignment at First Corps and seems to have spent most of his time writing military papers for various publications, including the *Cavalry Journal*. When he left for Hawaii in March 1926, to join the staff of the 13,000 strong Hawaiian Division, Beatrice and the children stayed behind for a further nine months; post-natal complications had followed George's birth and the Hawaiian climate, hot and humid, was considered unsuitable for her. By the time she did arrive, complete with governess, she found Patton had organized a suitable home with two Japanese housekeepers and three grooms for his large collection of polo ponies and horses. The only thing to mar their happiness was the loss of many of their personal possessions, including Beatrice's piano and most of Georgie's books, due to a fire in the hold of the ship taking him out there.

The whole Patton family came to love Hawaii but the death of Georgie's father in June 1927 cast a dark cloud over their lives. Patton was inconsolable for a considerable time. Part of the emotional tribute he wrote a month later read:

> Oh darling papa, I never called you that in life as both of us were too self-contained but you were and are my darling . . . God grant that

you see and appreciate my very piteous attempt to show here your lovely life. I never did much for you and you did all for me. Accept this as a slight offering of what I would have done.[7]

A second bitter blow to Patton's morale came later that year when he was relieved of his position as Chief Operations Officer (G-3) and became Chief Intelligence Officer (G-2) – a far less important and prestigious appointment. The circumstances are not completely clear but it appears that he criticized on paper the performance of a brigade commander and some of the regimental commanders and this, coming from a relatively junior major, was too much for the senior officers of the Division. Patton's Commanding General gave as his reasons for sacking his G-3, 'too positive in his thinking and too outspoken'.[8]

In April 1928, just before they left Hawaii, the Pattons bought their first and only house – *Green Meadows*. It was a large colonial mansion located near Beatrice's home in Massachusetts. They were able to spend the late spring setting up their new home, but in the early summer Georgie had to report for his new assignment in the Office of the Chief of Cavalry in Washington. Beatrice stayed behind, intent on restoring her new home to some of its former glory, while Georgie rented a large house near Washington Cathedral – it had once been the summer White House of a former President! But he did not stay there for long; the following year his old riding companion, Henry Stimson, became Secretary of State under President Hoover and bought it. When Beatrice and the children moved down to join him, the family moved into a large rented house in north-west Washington – needless to say, it was ideal for entertaining. Once more the Pattons were able to indulge in their treasured delights of socializing, fox hunting and horse shows, and in the case of Georgie, steeplechasing and polo. They also bought a boat which they kept on the Potomac.

In 1929 Patton turned down a posting to London as Military Attaché. It was not an easy decision but as a very protective father he was determined to make sure his daughters married well:

> We have two marriageable daughters . . . If we go to London it stands to reason that one or both of them will marry an Englishman. Englishmen, well-bred Englishmen, are the most attractive bastards in the world, and they always need all the money they can lay their hands on . . . They are men's men, and they are totally inconsiderate of their wives and daughters.[9]

Georgie and Beatrice always made sure their daughters had suitable escorts and it is hardly surprisingly that in 1929 the eldest, Bee, was introduced to the most outstanding cadet at West Point – a man she married five years later and who became a four-star general.[10]

In September 1931 Patton was sent on a nine-month course at the Army War College[11] – a sure indication that he was being groomed for senior command and/or staff appointments. Each student was required to write a research paper during his time there and Patton's, in which he outlined his ideas on how America might fight its next war, was allegedly graded a 'work of exceptional merit'.[12]

Patton's studies were interrupted by the death of Aunt Nannie. His mother had already passed away in October 1928 and he took the opportunity of Nannie's funeral to write the following tribute:

> I have always prayed to show my love by doing something famous for you, to justify what you called me when I got back from France, 'My hero son' . . . In a few moments we will bury the ashes of Aunt Nannie. All the three who I loved and who loved me so much are now gone . . . I have no other memories of you but love and devotion. It is so sad that we must grow old [he was 46] and separate. When we meet again I hope you will be lenient for my frailties. In most things I have been worthy. Perhaps this is foolish but I think you understand. I loved and love you very much. Your devoted son G S Patton, Jr.[13]

Patton's attempts to lobby for the appointment of Commandant of Cadets at West Point at the end of the War College course came to nothing. Instead, in July 1932, he returned to Fort Myer as Executive Officer of the 3rd Cavalry and walked into one of the more unpleasant episodes of his military career. The following extract from the website of the Library of Congress, Washington DC, explains briefly what happened:

> The Great Depression of the 1930s had spread economic misery, despair, and heartbreak across America and nearly one-third of working Americans were unemployed and desperate for some relief. Many veterans of World War I felt that the federal government owed them a particular debt for their sacrifice and service during the war. They began to organize and demand that Congress approve an early payment of pension funds that was not due until 1945. In the summer of 1932, about 20,000 unemployed veterans and their families travelled to Washington, D.C., from across the United States to lobby Congress. Some of these 'Bonus Marchers' camped out in shacks and tents, which they mockingly called 'Hoovervilles' after President Herbert Hoover. Others occupied abandoned and partially dismantled buildings near the Capitol. Although the marchers were not disorderly or unruly, the Hoover administration and local officials feared this group of around 5,000 might turn into a mob. The tense situation exploded on July 28, 1932, when a marcher was killed during a scuffle with police, and federal troops were called in to

restore order. One of the first federal officers to arrive in Washington, D.C., was Major George S. Patton. His cavalry troops[14] met up with infantry at the Ellipse, near the White House. Patton and the federal troops, equipped with gas masks, bayonets and sabers, marched up Pennsylvania Avenue, firing gas grenades and charging and sub-duing the angry crowd. Later that night, Patton and the federal troops cleared out the marchers' camp in Anacostia, with some tents and shacks catching fire in the process. By the following morning, most marchers had left Washington, but the incident left bitter memories and affected Patton deeply. He called it the 'most distasteful form of service' and later wrote several papers on how federal troops could restore order quickly with the least possible bloodshed.

Although Patton described the incident as a 'distasteful form of service', he wrote in one of the 'several papers' mentioned above:

> Bricks flew, sabers rose and fell with a comforting smack, and the mob ran. We moved on after them, occasionally meeting serious resistance . . . Two of us charged at a gallop and had some nice work at close range.

It is also of interest that General Douglas MacArthur, the Chief of Staff of the Army at the time, personally directed the afternoon's operation, appearing on horseback and in full dress uniform – much to the disgust of Dwight Eisenhower who was one of his Military Assistants. MacArthur is also said to have ignored President Hoover's order, passed through the Secretary of War, that the military were not to pursue the veterans back across the river to 'Hooverville'.

The following morning Patton found himself in another embarrassing situation. The soldier who had saved his life in France, Joe Angelo, was one of the veterans involved and was brought before him on the picket lines around Anacostia. Patton is alleged to have exclaimed: 'I do not know this man. Take him away and under no circumstances permit him to return'. He then apparently explained to officers present:

> That man was my orderly during the war. When I was wounded, he dragged me from a shell hole under fire. I got him a decoration for it. Since the war my mother and I have more than supported him. We have given him money. We have set him up in business several times. Can you imagine the headlines if the papers got wind of our meeting here this morning! Of course, we'll take care of him anyway![15]

Whether Patton spoke the truth on this occasion or was angry and embarrassed to be confronted by Angelo is unclear. The available evidence indicates the latter.[16] Similarly it is unknown whether the Pattons ever did in fact properly 'take care of him'.[17] This author, having already said he found it strange that Montgomery either did not remember, or did not bother to find out, the name of the soldier who saved his life, finds Patton's behaviour in relation to his saviour just as incomprehensible.

The duties of the Executive Officer at Fort Myer were not onerous and Patton was able to indulge in all his favourite pursuits during his three years there. He and Beatrice were co-sponsors of the famous Cobbler Hunt and were inevitably popular with the Washington 'horsey set'. The only highlights of this period appear to have been his promotion to the rank of lieutenant colonel in March 1934 (Monty was three years ahead of him) and the marriage of his eldest daughter in June of the same year. It took place in the same church where Georgie and Beatrice had married twenty-four years earlier.

In the spring of 1935 Patton received orders for a second tour of duty as Chief Intelligence Officer (G-2) to the Commanding General in Hawaii. Beatrice was thrilled to be returning to a place she had come to love but Georgie was bitterly disappointed. He was 50 years old and his career seemed to be going nowhere. The previous year he had purchased a forty-foot schooner and to everyone's amazement he announced he was going to sail it to Hawaii. He duly moved the boat by rail from Washington to the Pacific coast and set off with an amateur crew of six on a voyage of 2,238 miles. Beatrice, who had volunteered to be the cook, spent most of the fifteen days afloat in her bunk asleep or being seasick.

The Pattons' second tour in Hawaii was not a happy one. Four major incidents blighted their time there. First, a serious fall from a polo pony gave Georgie concussion, as a result of which he was never again able to hold his drink. From then on he showed the effects of alcohol after just a couple of drinks. Second, he failed again, in 1936, to gain the appointment of Commandant of Cadets at West Point and third, his marriage nearly came to grief. Despite his highly visible love for Beatrice, he had an affair with her 21-year-old half sister, Jean Gordon, when she came to stay with them, taking her on an unchaperoned horse-buying expedition to another Hawaiian island. Fortunately for Patton Beatrice forgave him. According to their daughter Ruth Ellen, she said:

> Your father needs me ... So, if your husband ever does this to you, you can remember that I didn't leave your father. I stuck with him because I am all that he really has, and I love him and he loves me.[18]

The fourth incident was a public admonishment from his Commanding General. It occurred during a polo match when Patton swore at the opposing team captain. He was called before the general, publicly relieved of his captaincy of the Army team for using foul language in front of ladies and insulting his competitors, and told to leave the field. After a protest by the opposing team captain he was allowed to continue, but the incident did little for his relationship with his superior.

In June 1937, after just two years in Hawaii, Patton was posted to the 9th Cavalry Regiment in Fort Riley, again as Executive Officer. Whilst out riding with Beatrice during his leave before reporting for duty, however, her horse lashed out and its hoof broke Patton's leg. It was a very serious injury leading to thrombosis and he came close to death. Recuperation lasted six months and once again he fell into a deep depression. Unbelievably, when he was able to hobble to the stables he beat Beatrice's horse with a crutch and threatened to kill it. Not surprisingly, the marriage reached another low point.

By February 1938 Patton was fit enough to take up his post at Fort Riley and both his spirits and the state of his marriage began to recover. He enjoyed being back amongst cavalrymen and his morale received a huge boost when, on 1 July that year, he was promoted to the rank of colonel (Monty was by now a major general) and appointed to command the 5th Cavalry Regiment at Fort Clark, Texas.

Fort Clark was a military backwater on the Mexican border, but Patton was in his element. He threw himself into command with a vengeance and his men soon learned that he was serious in his demands for 'spit and polish' and realistic training – something new in their lives and a nasty shock. After only five months, however, his tour was cut short and he was summoned back to Washington to command the 3rd Cavalry at Fort Myer. The social demands on the life of the Commanding Officer at Fort Myer meant that he needed a large private income and Patton was an obvious choice for the post – few officers in the US Army had his sort of money. He was, nevertheless, furious, for although he would once again be in the presence of senior military and political figures, he felt he was being taken away from real soldiering and vented his anger on those around him – particularly Beatrice whom he blamed in that it was *her* money that had brought him to this position!

Patton's behaviour in the year leading up to the outbreak of WWII in Europe became more and more extreme and placed a great burden on his family. He was convinced that his career had stagnated and that he was already too old for high command. His outbursts of temper became more and more frightening and everyone, including his officers, tried to stay out of his way. However, the outbreak of a major war, even if America was not involved, did wonders for his morale and he at once began to write letters to officers in high positions, reminding them of his existence. He need not have bothered. The new Chief of Staff of the Army was General George C Marshall who had known Patton in France in WWI. In a notebook in which Marshall recorded the names of officers he thought promising, Georgie's had already been entered – with a footnote saying:

'George will take a unit through hell and high water. Keep a tight rope round his neck. Give him an armored corps when one becomes available'.[19] It is also of note that one of Beatrice's riding companions at this time, and an occasional lunch guest at the Pattons, was the wife of the President of the United States – Eleanor Roosevelt!

NOTES

1   Eisenhower, *At Ease: Stories I Tell to My Friends*, p. 169.
2   Ibid, p. 170.
3   Ibid, p. 173.
4   Letter dated 19 Oct 19.
5   Since renamed 'The Army Command & General Staff College'.
6   D'Este, *A Genius for War*, p. 333.
7   Ibid, p. 340.
8   Patton Papers, Vol II, pp. 889–90.
9   Patton to his wife – D'Este, op. cit., p. 345.
10 John K Waters.
11 In those days located in Washington, on the site of what is now Fort McNair.
12 D'Este, op. cit., p. 349.
13 Ibid, p. 350.
14 It is not clear why Patton rather than the commanding officer of the 3rd Cavalry was in charge of the 200 troopers.
15 D'Este, op. cit., p. 354.
16 Ibid, p. 351 & p. 874, Note 30.
17 In 1939 Patton, allegedly in reply to a pleading letter on Angelo's behalf from an ex-captain, sent a cheque for $25 and a letter saying, 'My mother and I helped him considerably, but due to changed conditions I am not able to do as much for him now as then.' – Ibid, p. 877, Note 5.
18 Ibid, p. 359.
19 Ibid, pp. 377–8.

CHAPTER IX

Montgomery – September 1939 to August 1942

(Map 4)

Hitler failed to follow up his successful invasion of Poland with an immediate attack in the west and a 'Phoney War' developed with neither side taking offensive action. This lasted until 10 May 1940 when the full fury of the German Blitzkrieg was unleashed on France and the Low Countries. In the intervening period the British Expeditionary Force

(BEF), which had arrived in France the previous September, was located east of Lille, near the frontier with neutral Belgium. It spent its time digging trenches and constructing pill-boxes and anti-tank obstacles in the area. All the senior officers realised, however, that if, as seemed likely, the Germans violated Belgian neutrality, their formations would have to be rushed forward some 100 miles to try to hold the enemy on the line of the Dyle river. The Belgian authorities, understandably in political but not in military terms, refused to offer any facilities to the British until they were actually attacked.

'In September 1939 the British Army was totally unfit to fight a first class war on the continent of Europe'[1] – so wrote Monty in 1958. He went on to point out that the BEF lacked proper communications and an efficient administrative system and that the transport in his 3rd Infantry Division was 'inadequate and completed on mobilization by vehicles requisitioned from civilian firms . . . It consisted of civilian vans and lorries'.[2] In the case of weaponry his anti-tank guns were also totally inadequate and 'I never saw any . . . [British] tanks during the winter or during the active operations in May . . . and we were the nation which had invented the tank and were the first to use it in battle'.[3]

There is no point in a book such as this in describing the military campaign in Belgium and France in May/June 1940, so only the part played by Monty and his 3rd Division will be covered and that only in outline.

Monty's soldiers landed at Cherbourg on 30 September and moved over 300 miles by rail, in cattle trucks like their 1914 predecessors, to the area just south of Lille – their motor transport had been unloaded at Brest where much of it was looted by French dockers. The Division's mission was to defend part of the Franco–Belgian border just to the east of Lille; though in the event of Belgium being invaded it was to move forward nearly 100 miles and occupy a sector behind the Dyle river astride Louvain. Montgomery immediately set to work to prepare his men for these tasks and 'the 3rd Division certainly put the first winter to good use and trained hard'.[4]

> I trained the division for this [latter] task over a similar distance moving westwards, i.e. backwards into France. We became expert at a long night moves and then occupying a defensive position in the dark, and by dawn being fully deployed and in all respects ready to receive attack. This is what I felt we might have to do; and it was.[5]

Monty was less interested in the 'spit and polish' and saluting side of soldiering, but at the insistence of his Corps commander, Alan Brooke (later Lord Alanbrooke), he was •forced to issue a confidential memorandum on these subjects to his commanding officers. It stated:

1. I am not satisfied with the general standard of discipline, turnout, smartness, soldierly bearing, and so on that I notice in the Division.
2. I see men lounging about in the streets with their tunics open, hats on the back of their head, cigarettes behind their ears . . . At night . . . a good deal of drunkenness and a great deal of shouting and singing in the streets. We have got to keep the men in hand . . .

I know there are many difficulties; we have many men who have been soldiers only a few weeks, and we have large numbers of reservists who may tend to pull our standard down unless we are careful. But I will not allow any let-up in this matter, whatever the difficulties, and all officers . . . will give this subject their immediate attention.

He was much more concerned about the dangers of venereal disease and again landed himself in serious trouble with his C-in-C and Corps commander for giving orders that condoms (French letters to the British and *capotes anglaises* to the French) were to be made available in unit shops and 'Early Treatment' rooms in every company. He also wrote that if a soldier needed 'horizontal refreshment' he 'would be well advised to ask a [military] policeman for a suitable address' of properly inspected brothels in Lille. Despite his superiors' outrage he got away with these orders and earned for himself the title 'General of Love'. Not everyone, however, agreed with this epithet. Many officers found his self-assertive manner, relatively casual dress and obvious conceit difficult to cope with; nevertheless, they were well aware that one step out of line or any sign of inefficiency would land them in serious trouble.

With the exception of his own Corps commander, Monty was highly critical of his superiors. The British C-in-C, Lord Gort, he described as 'a most delightful person, a warm hearted friend . . . [but] he was not clever and he did not bother about administration . . . Gort's appointment to command the BEF in September 1939 was a mistake; the job was above his ceiling'.[6] And he described the command and control arrangements of the forces available in France in May 1940, set up by the French Supreme Commander, General Gamelin, as 'a complete dog's breakfast'. There is no doubt that he was right.

The Blitzkrieg (lightning war) that hit the Allies on 10 May took them completely by surprise and was a repeat of what had happened in Poland only nine months earlier. Monty wrote later that his Division 'did everything that was demanded of it' and this is true. By 11 May it had reached its designated Dyle position astride Louvain where, not without some difficulty, it took over from a Belgian division; nonetheless, the collapse of major parts of the French Army, occasioned by the drive by German Panzer divisions – one commanded by Monty's future adversary Erwin Rommel – through the supposedly impenetrable Ardennes, was to ensure a retreat far worse than that of 1914.

The first direct attack against the 3rd Division came on 15 May. This was beaten off, but on the same day German tanks burst across the Meuse at Sedan and the crisis began. By the 20th the Germans had reached the Somme at Abbeville in a vast turning movement and by the 23rd the Division was back more or less where it had started – at Roubaix near Lille. In the intervening period it had successfully occupied a blocking position on the Escaut canal for four days. On 27 May Monty was ordered to disengage his Division and move it that night over twenty-five miles to the north-east to fill a gap left by the Belgians on the Yser Canal – a gap on the direct British withdrawal route to Dunkirk. This very difficult operation, directly across the line of the northern German advance, was completed successfully; but, on arrival on the Yser Monty learned that during the night the King of the Belgians had surrendered his Army to the Germans. A further rapid withdrawal was ordered and during the night of the 29th his exhausted men took up positions on the eastern side of the Dunkirk perimeter. The next morning Monty's Corps commander, Brooke, told him that he had been ordered back to England and that Monty was to take over the Corps. His new command, however, was to last only three days.

Later that day, Monty, along with the commander of I Corps, Lieutenant General Barker, attended Lord Gort's final briefing in France. He was appalled when he heard the C-in-C give orders that Barker's Corps was to make the final stand at Dunkirk, cover the evacuation of the rest of the BEF and then if necessary surrender along with the French forces in the Dunkirk area. He asked for a word in private and told Gort that Barker was 'in an unfit state to be left in final command';[7] he then went on to recommend that his friend Harold Alexander, the commander of the 1st Infantry Division, be given command of Barker's Corps. Amazingly Gort acquiesced. Monty then gave orders for the evacuation of his own II Corps from the beaches the following night. Fortunately for the British, Hitler had ordered his Panzer forces to halt when they were within sight of Dunkirk and the destruction of the BEF be left to Hermann Goering's Luftwaffe. It failed in this task and over 366,000 British, French and Belgian troops were evacuated to England in what became know as 'the Miracle of Dunkirk'[8] Much of the credit for the successful evacuation of the II Corps troops, first from jetties at La Panne and Bray-Dunes and when that became impossible, from Dunkirk itself, must go to Monty. He remained completely calm and gave clear, decisive orders. After remaining at Bray-Dunes until the early hours of 1 June, he joined his Chief of Staff and ADC, who had been wounded by a shell splinter, and walked the ten miles to the great mole at Dunkirk. There they embarked on a Royal Navy destroyer and later that day landed in Dover.

On his return to England Monty did an extraordinary thing – he banned his soldiers from taking leave to see their families and loved ones. This order may seem puzzling and heartless, but to a totally dedicated professional soldier like Montgomery it was a natural thing to do – his country was in great danger and having conducted a successful withdrawal it was necessary to regroup immediately and face the enemy again. Unfortunately for Monty he failed to appreciate that the people of the United Kingdom, encouraged by Churchill, believed Dunkirk was a victory, rather than an ignominious defeat, and that those who had returned home were heroes. According to Monty's Intelligence Officer, Lieutenant Colonel 'Kit' Dawnay, when his commander visited one of his Battalions the soldiers jeered him; that night he rescinded his order and gave everyone forty-eight hours' leave.

Only the men of the BEF returned to England – some 400 tanks, 2,474 artillery pieces, 63,879 vehicles and 650,000 tons of supplies and ammunition had been destroyed or were abandoned during the three-week campaign in Belgium and France.[9] Monty's officers and men, now located in and around Frome in the West Country, were amazed therefore when, within a few days of their return home, the Division received not only reinforcements, but also a complete replacement of weapons and equipment. There was only enough for just one division at that time in the whole country and the 3rd received it all. The reason was simple – it was destined to return to north-west France to continue the fight. France, however, capitulated on 17 June, the expedition was cancelled and the Division was ordered to take up linear defensive positions on the Sussex coast between Brighton and Littlehampton, ready to resist the expected German invasion. Monty described later how his men carried out this order:

> [We] descended like an avalanche on the inhabitants of that area; we dug in the gardens of the seaside villas, we sited machine-gun posts in the best places, and we generally set about our job in the way we were accustomed to do things in an emergency.[10]

One of his Brigade commanders, Brian Horrocks, gave more details:

> Monty used to pay constant visits. 'Who lives in that house?' he would say pointing to some building, which partly masked the fire from one of our machine-gun positions. 'Have them out, Horrocks. Blow up the house. Defence must come first'.[11]

Monty went on:

> Mayors, County Councillors, private owners, came to see me and demanded that we should cease our work; I refused, and explained the urgency of the need and that we were preparing to defend the south coast against the Germans.[12]

Monty was in fact appalled that his Division was being used in a static role and that it had been ordered to defend the whole coastline rather than specific strongpoints. When the Prime Minister, Winston Churchill, came to visit on 2 July, he took his chance and recommended that the 3rd 'Iron' Division, being the best equipped in the Army, should be provided with civilian buses to give it mobility and then given a counter-attack role. He did this without consulting his Corps commander. Needless to say Churchill liked the idea and within twenty-four hours he issued one of his 'Action this Day' minutes. Monty got his buses and the Division moved at once to Gloucestershire in central England to train in its new role. His Corps commander was of course furious.

Churchill had found Monty quite obnoxious and 'common' as a person, but he had been impressed by his energy and enthusiasm and this would stand 'the little man', as Winston dubbed him, in good stead in the years to come. A small anecdote concerning their meeting is worth relating. During dinner that night at the Royal Albion Hotel in Brighton, Monty refused to drink anything other than water and said he did not smoke; he added that he was 100% fit. Winston, with a drink in one hand and a cigar in the other, replied that he was 200% fit!

Monty was no longer with the 3rd Division when it moved to central England. On 22 July he was promoted to the rank of lieutenant general and given command of V Corps in Hampshire and Dorset. He took over from the man who had just finished commanding the ill-fated expedition to Norway, General Sir Claude Auckinleck, who now became C-in-C Southern Command. As such he was Monty's direct superior. Unfortunately he was a man for whom Monty had no time and later came to actively dislike, some say despise.

Monty claimed later that from the time he took over V Corps his 'real influence on the training of the Army then in England' began.[13] He started as he intended to continue – by sacking most of Auckinleck's staff and getting rid of many overweight and over-age officers in the Corps. But he had hardly had time to settle into the job when, in April 1941, he was transferred to XII Corps which covered the likely invasion sector in Kent and Sussex. And then, just seven months after that, in November 1941, he was moved up to be C-in-C South-East Command. He now found himself commanding most of the anti-invasion forces in the country and so, in typical Monty fashion and on his own authority, he changed the name of his command to 'South-Eastern Army' and his own appointment to 'Army Commander'. His new appointment enabled him to boast that 'the ideas and the doctrine of war, and training for war, which began as far west as Dorset, gradually spread along the south of England to the mouth of the Thames'.[14]

One of Monty's major priorities in this training for war was physical and mental fitness and he was ruthless in weeding out those who could not reach his required standards. Officers had to be 'full of binge', by which he meant that they should be looking forward to a good fight and have the 'glint of battle' in their eyes – it could almost have been Patton speaking!

During his short time with XII Corps Monty ran a series of major exercises to train and test all ranks under his command. They were codenamed BINGE, MOREBINGE and SUPERBINGE and his dissatisfaction with some of the results led to numerous senior commanders being sacked and replaced with others better known to Monty. 'A number of heads are being chopped off – the bag to date is three Brigadiers and six COs', he wrote shortly after his arrival in the Corps to his former Intelligence Officer, Kit Dawnay. In many ways he was, of course, in his element, but secretly he felt he was being sidelined from the main events taking place in the Mediterranean – this was particularly so after Hitler attacked the Soviet Union in June 1941 and the direct threat to Great Britain receded.

During his time in England Monty was tireless in his determination to bring all ranks up to the standards he believed essential for success in battle. He made it clear that there were no bad soldiers, only bad officers; he rammed home the need for a constant regrouping of infantry, armour, engineers and artillery to meet differing situations; he emphasised the need to attack on relatively narrow rather than wide fronts, the need for commanders to be well forward so that they could see for themselves and so that their subordinates did not have to come back to them, and the need for close air support to be made available whenever possible to those fighting on the ground – in fact, although he was probably unaware of it, he was quite simply telling his commanders to follow the German example!

Monty's time in southern England was not without its hiccups and difficulties. His most personal tragedy occurred in January 1941 when the warehouse in Portsmouth where all the furniture from his 1938 house with Betty and most of the family belongings were stored, was set on fire by an incendiary bomb and destroyed. (Readers will recall that the Pattons lost most of their personal possessions during the second move to Hawaii.) Monty thus lost all the precious mementoes of his marriage – except his son David. His treatment of the boy, however, was to say the very least, strange, especially when one remembers the unhappy time he had had with his own mother. He had not even bothered to go and see him after returning from Dunkirk and one of his most trusted subordinates, Brigadier Bill Williams, said later that Monty 'treated David terribly – it broke our hearts to see it'.[15] After Betty's death he refused his sister's offer to be a surrogate mother and when the war broke out he gave strict orders that David was never to be allowed to visit his grandmother or any other member of the family. Certainly the poor boy saw little of his father in the ten years following his mother's death. He spent most of his school holidays in a series of 'holiday homes for children' and Monty vetoed a suggestion that he should be sent to Canada as an evacuee.[16] Although David is said to have never complained about his childhood, Monty himself admitted that 'My son had an unsatisfactory life from then [1938] onwards . . . I was never able to make a home for him again until 1948'.[17]

There were other unfortunate incidents during 1940. He clashed a number of times with his superior, General Sir Claude Auckinleck, over training and tactics. To the latter's intense irritation Monty went over his head twice in an attempt to influence the postings of officers and soldiers into and out of his Corps, and on other occasions Monty actually contradicted or countermanded the instructions of his predecessor and the man who was now his boss. Shortly after taking over XII Corps he issued an operation instruction condemning Auckinleck's strategy of trying to defend the whole coastline; he instituted instead a policy of defending only critical points and localities. Such directives, and his well-known statement that there were only two solutions to most military problems – his own and the wrong one – did little for his popularity with his fellow generals. On one occasion he actually countermanded one of Aucklinleck's direct orders. The C-in-C had given specific instructions that in view of the threat of a German invasion, soldiers were never to be parted from their personal weapons. Monty cancelled the order on the grounds that a soldier could hardly be responsible for his rifle if he went for a swim in the sea or was in the back row of a cinema with his girl-friend![18]

Inevitably Montgomery's growing arrogance and apparent determination to seek the limelight also upset many middle rank officers (majors, colonels, etc.) as well as his contemporaries and superiors. He was adamant that all soldiers should see and hear their commanders and he began the habit of addressing his men informally in groups – in cinemas, on sports fields and so on – and this was seen by many as pure showmanship. His new rule of allowing three minutes for coughing and then banning it whilst he spoke soon became legendary. And his order banning wives from potential operational areas near the south coast of England did little for his popularity amongst the middle rank and senior officers it mainly affected – few below the rank of major could afford to have their wives with them. Monty wrote:

> If an officer's wife and family were present with him in or near his unit area, and the attack came, an officer would at once be tempted to see to their safety first and to neglect his operational task . . . The whole future of England . . . was at stake . . . Moreover, since the men could not have their families with them, the officers shouldn't either. The wives must go. And they did.[19]

Actions like the ones mentioned above soon increased his standing and popularity with his soldiers and junior officers. They were not slow to appreciate his informality and obvious determination to drag at least *his* part of the British Army out of the mould in which it had been stuck since WWI – indeed its rigid class system and many of its operational practices had changed little since the Boer War at the turn of the century.

In April 1942 Montgomery, as 'Army Commander', held the largest training exercise ever seen in England. Operation TIGER involved some 100,000 troops and the two Corps in the South-Eastern Army, Monty's old XII Corps and I Canadian Corps. He described it as 'a real rough-house lasting ten days'. One of the observers was Major General Dwight Eisenhower. He reported officially to Washington that Monty was 'a decisive type who appears to be extremely energetic and professionally able'. Privately, according to his driver, Kay Summersby, Eisenhower called him a 'son of a bitch'. Ike was renowned for his temper and this outburst stemmed from Monty admonishing him for lighting a cigarette in his presence!

An event that would haunt Monty for the rest of his life occurred during the last three months of his command of the South-Eastern Army – the Dieppe raid (Map 1). Undertaken for political rather than military reasons, this pre-invasion 'reconnaissance in force' was launched to placate Soviet and American demands for a 'Second Front' in France – demands that Churchill and the British Chiefs of Staff had rejected as impracticable. Many books and articles have been written about this disastrous operation and this author does not intend to go into the details. The basic facts are as follows: originally planned for 21 June, the raid was twice delayed as a result of unsatisfactory, some would say disastrous, rehearsals. The troops eventually embarked on 7 July, but the weather prospects were not good and certainly unsuitable for the employment of airborne troops. The operation was therefore cancelled and the following day the men were dispersed back to their camps. The raid was eventually launched on 19 August, lasted nine hours and resulted in 3,369 Canadian casualties (roughly 2,000 became prisoners), about 900 naval, Royal Marine and Commando casualties and the loss of 106 Allied aircraft and sixty-seven aircrew. If it achieved nothing else, however, it did at least show the Allied Chiefs of Staff that a great deal of very careful planning and coordination would be required for a real 'Second Front'.

The basic plan for the raid originated in Admiral Mountbatten's Combined Operations Headquarters. Subsequently it was opened up to critique by military, naval and air force staffs and commanders. The original idea of a pincer attack from the flanks was soon rejected in favour of a frontal assault on Dieppe, preceded by heavy bombing on the main defences and paratroop attacks to take out coastal batteries on either side of the port. This plan was approved in principle by the Chiefs of Staff on

13 May 1942, but later altered to delete the bombing and substitute commando, rather than airborne, attacks on the German coastal batteries.

Monty has been severely criticized, particularly by the Canadians, for the disaster at Dieppe and Mountbatten later tried to shift some of the blame for what happened from himself to his Army colleague. Let us look therefore at Monty's involvement in the planning of the operation. He certainly did not come into the picture until after 13 May and he was only brought in then because the troops chosen for the main assault, the 2nd Canadian Infantry Division, were part of his command. As a consequence C-in-C Home Forces, General Paget, made him 'responsible for the Army side of the planning'.[20]

From the outset Monty did not favour the use of a Canadian Division:

> I mentioned to him [C-in-C Home Forces] that it was not right to use inexperienced Canadians for the operation . . . Having expressed my fears, I could do no more but acquiesce; to do otherwise would have been to lower the morale of the Canadian troops . . . if they wanted to be used . . . their wish would be agreed. And they did want to be used.[21]

In January 1942 Monty had been warned by the CIGS to 'go easy' on the Canadians. This followed his criticism of their tactical doctrines and training methods and his insistence that they should follow *his* directives. Then, having come to the conclusion that most of their most senior officers were 'useless, quite useless', he went on to lecture the Canadians on the way things should be done. Not surprisingly relationships went from bad to worse. Lieutenant General Crerar resisted Monty's right to give orders to his Corps and refused to address him on paper as 'Army Commander'; instead he wrote to him as 'C-in-C South-Eastern Command'. The crisis came in February 1942 when Crerar insisted that in the event of a German invasion, Canadian troops in reserve could only be used with the consent of the Canadian Government or its authorized representative. Monty called this 'playing politics' and 'bellyaching'. Their relationship never recovered.

With regard to the details of the plan for the raid, Monty wrote in 1958:

> Certain modifications had been introduced in to the revised [19 August] plan. The most important were – first, the elimination of the paratroops and their replacement by commando units; secondly, the elimination of any preliminary bombing of the defences from the air. I should not myself have agreed to either of these changes.[22]

With regard to elimination of the preliminary bombing, this is untrue. The decision to dispense with it was taken at a meeting at Combined

Operations Headquarters on 5 June. Mountbatten was in America at the time and Monty, as the senior Home Forces representative, 'was in the chair at the meeting where the decision was taken; and he is not on record in the minutes as having demurred'.[23]

With regard to the cancellation of the first raid in July and the resurrection of the plan, albeit revised again, in August, Monty had this to say:

> It was reasonable to expect that [after the cancellation of the original raid] it [the objective and details of the raid] was now a common subject of conversation in billets and pubs in the south of England ... Once all this force was 'unsealed' and dispersed, I considered the operation was cancelled and I turned my attention to other matters. But Combined Operations Headquarters thought otherwise; they decided to revive it and got the scheme approved by the British Chiefs of Staff towards the end of July. When I heard this I was very upset; I considered that it would no longer be possible to maintain secrecy. Accordingly I wrote to General Paget, C-in-C Home Forces, telling him of my anxiety, and recommending that the raid on Dieppe should be considered cancelled 'for all time'. If it was considered desirable to raid the Continent, then the objective should not be Dieppe. This advice was disregarded. On 10th August I left England to take command of the Eighth Army in the desert.[24]

It was as well he did – had he still been Commander South-Eastern Army in the aftermath of the costly and abortive raid the repercussions might well have prevented him from going on to become a world-famous and successful commander. It has to be said though, that the Dieppe operation remains a question mark against his military record.

Monty's appointment to command the Eighth Army was accidental. Alan Brooke, the Chief of the Imperial General Staff and a Monty 'fan', had recommended him for that appointment in early August but Churchill had had other ideas. As we shall learn shortly, the latter was far from satisfied with the situation in the Middle East and was determined to make major changes in the command structure in that theatre. Monty of course had no knowledge of the impending changes and he was amazed to receive a telephone call from the War Office on 7 August informing him that he was to take over the First (British) Army and command the 'Northern Task Force' in Operation TORCH, an Anglo–American invasion of French North Africa, planned for November. The overall commander was to be the major general he had recently ticked off for smoking in his presence – Ike! And the American appointed to command the other (Western) Task Force in TORCH was none other than George S Patton! Our two prima donnas were due to meet with Eisenhower in London the following morning, but as events turned out they would have to wait a little longer before their paths crossed. On 8 August Monty received a second call from the War Office. It informed him that an aircraft carrying the commander-designate of the Eighth Army in Egypt had been shot down and that General Gott had been killed. Monty was to fly out and assume command at once. Without seeing, or even telephoning his son David before he left, he arrived in Egypt on 12 August. He had again given strict instructions to the couple looking after the boy[25] that David, now at Winchester, was 'on no account' to visit his grandmother and that they were 'in complete and absolute charge. If any members of my family chip in and want to advise, see them right off'.[26]

NOTES

1 Montgomery, *Memoirs*, p. 49.
2 Ibid.
3 Ibid, p. 50.
4 Ibid, p. 58.
5 Ibid, pp. 58–9.
6 Ibid, p. 52.
7 Ibid. p. 64.
8 Barnett, *Engage the Enemy More Closely*, gives a grand total of 366,162.
9 Smurthwaite, Nicholls & Washington, *Against All Odds: The British Army of 1939–1940*, p. 6.
10 Montgomery, op. cit., p. 68.
11 Horrocks, *A Full Life*, p. 94.
12 Montgomery, op. cit., p. 68.
13 Ibid, p. 70.
14 Ibid.
15 Horne, *The Lonely Leader*, p. 39.
16 Ibid.
17 Montgomery, op. cit., p. 47.
18 Montgomery, Brian, *A Field Marshal in the Family*, p. 259.
19 Montgomery, op. cit., pp. 72–3.
20 Ibid, p. 75.
21 Lord Montgomery Deposit, IWM, Aug 62.
22 Montgomery, op. cit., p. 76.
23 Fergusson, *The Watery Maze*, p. 171.
24 Montgomery, op. cit., p. 76.
25 Maj & Mrs Tom Reynolds – no relation to the author. He had been the headmaster of David's preparatory school in Hindhead.
26 Horne, op. cit., p. 50.

CHAPTER X
Patton – September 1939 to October 1942

Following the outbreak of war in Europe, George Patton's morale improved enormously. Before September 1939 he had felt that, as commanding officer of the 3rd Cavalry Regiment, he was in a military backwater and that he was already too old to gain further advancement. Then three things happened to change the picture completely: the appointment of his old acquaintance, General George Marshall to be the Army Chief of Staff, Marshall's decision to create 'an Armored Force' and a rapid expansion of the United States Army.

As Chief of Staff of the Army, Marshall was allocated the best officer's quarter at Fort Myer and Patton, never one to miss a trick when it came to ingratiating himself with people of influence, immediately offered to put him up in his own house while the quarter was being prepared for its new occupant. He wrote to Beatrice on 27 July 1939: 'Gen George C Marshall is going to live at our house!!! . . . I think that once I can get my natural charm working I won't need any letters from John J P [Pershing] or any one else'. Just to make sure, he went even further – in the September he presented the new Chief of Staff with a set of eight silver stars, ordered from a New York jeweller, in honour of his promotion. Marshall accepted them and wrote: 'I will wear these stars with satisfaction and honor to the Army'. From then on he usually addressed Patton by his first name, or even 'Georgie', a practice he never extended to other subordinates including Eisenhower and Omar Bradley.[1]

Marshall approved the establishment of an autonomous 'Armored Force' in the spring of 1940 and in June that year Patton, convinced that his future was there rather than in the cavalry, wrote to its head, Major General Chaffee, and asked to be placed on a list of potential brigade commanders. He received a reply saying: ' I need just such a man of your experience in command' and the following month Patton was posted to Fort Benning, Georgia, where one of the Brigades of the new 2nd Armored Division was being formed. Fortunately the Division was being commanded by an old cavalry friend, Brigadier General Scott, and from a list of potential commanders sent to him by Chaffee, he selected Georgie to command the 2nd Armored Brigade. Marshall also had a hand in Patton's move. He wrote to Georgie that he thought: 'it would be just the sort of thing you would most like to do at the moment. Also, I felt that no one could do that particular job better'.[2]

On 24 July Patton left Fort Myer in a handover ceremony that left him in tears. A month later, as commander of the understrength and ill equipped 2nd Armored Brigade, he was promoted to the rank of brigadier general. His joy at becoming a general officer was tempered, however, by the state of his marriage which, following his infidelity in Hawaii and outrageous behaviour in Fort Myer, was clearly on the rocks. Beatrice did not accompany him to Fort Benning and Georgie was distraught. After a few weeks though she succumbed to his entreaties and joined him. Letters proclaiming:

> For so long when I have done anything worthwhile you have always been in the gallery. It is hard to have no gallery anymore and I feel quite sorry for myself but more sorry for you because I have shattered all your ideals.[3]

and, 'I love and miss you terribly but can see no future [as] I have hurt you too much',[4] worked the necessary magic.

During the autumn of 1940 Chaffee, ill with cancer, was forced to give up his dual roles as commander of the Armored Force *and* the Armored Corps and handed temporary command of the Corps to Scott, now a major general. This left a vacancy at the 2nd Armored Division and Patton moved up to take it. These appointments were made permanent in the December and in April 1941 Patton was made a major general. He was still one rank behind Monty, who readers will recall had become a lieutenant general in July 1940, but he was certainly on his way. So was the US Army – by the end of the year it had reached a strength of 620,000 and within another six months it would be nearly one and a half million. In the case of the 2nd Armored, by April 1941 it had grown to a strength of 14,000.

By this time George Patton had earned his nickname 'Old Blood and Guts'. No one dared call him that to his face but he clearly knew about it and revelled in it. The nickname was certainly appropriate for as well as drilling his Division, itself nicknamed 'Hell on Wheels', with all the techniques he deemed essential for successful armoured warfare, Patton was as usual a stickler for strict discipline and the highest standards of dress. Like Monty in England he was determined to instil in his men the doctrines and methods demonstrated by the Germans in Poland and France and the need for mixed groupings of tanks, infantry, artillery and engineers to meet specific operational needs.

Patton's behaviour during his time at Fort Benning was often outrageous and embarrassing to many of those who witnessed it. Nevertheless, his exploits as the commander of the 2nd Armored were beginning to bring him fame again (or was it notoriety?) and in the summer of 1941 he appeared on the front cover of *Life* magazine, wearing his 'Green Hornet' uniform in front of a tank. He had designed it himself 'for his tankers' and it comprised green padded jodhpurs, a pea green double-breasted jacket fitted at the waist with brass buttons that ran up over the right shoulder, a pearl-handled pistol slung under his left arm and a helmet with a raised band that looked like a halo!

Patton's temper continued to land him in trouble. On one occasion he allegedly ordered an unfortunate military policeman who had tried to arrest him for speeding within Fort Benning to, 'get your ass out of the 2nd Division area'. On hearing this, the post commander, Major General Fredendall, for whom Georgie had no time, ordered him to apologise. This was not the first time that Patton had had to apologise to a soldier – nor would it be the last. But despite all his indiscretions and posturing, Georgie became more and more popular with his men and it was not long before former and current 'tankers' were applying for transfers to the 2nd Armored. One officer Patton would have liked in his Division was Eisenhower. Even before he assumed command Patton had written to Ike, still only a lieutenant colonel, saying that he would like to have him as either his Chief of Staff or as a Regimental commander, whichever he preferred. Unfortunately for Georgie, in June 1941 Ike was moved to Fort Sam Houston, Texas, as the Third Army Chief of Staff.

During the six months before the Japanese attack on Pearl Harbor in December 1941, Patton's 2nd Armored Division participated in three major manoeuvre exercises – inter-Corps in Tennessee, inter-Army in Louisiana and between the First Army and IV Corps in the Carolinas. The Louisiana exercise was the largest ever carried out in the United States, involving 400,000 men and twenty-seven divisions, and the manoeuvres in the Carolinas included I Armored Corps which comprised the 1st Armored Division and Patton's 'Hell on Wheels'. Each of the exercises had its highlights – good and bad. On the first, the 2nd Armored made a name for itself by deploying at night without lights and under radio silence; during the second, after being trapped and subsequently routed, it went on in a later phase to spearhead the I Armored Corps attack. This involved an advance of some 400 miles and was achieved in typical Patton fashion by slipping out of the designated manoeuvre area and using civilian gas stations to overcome petrol shortages. It is not clear who paid for the petrol but it may well have been Georgie! George Marshall witnessed the final phase in the Carolinas exercise and 'recalled with relish the splendid performance of a certain George S Patton'. He was less pleased with the performance of others:

> Thirty-one of the forty-two army, corps and divisional commanders were either relieved or shunted aside to make way for a new generation of commanders, which included Omar N Bradley, Terry Allen, Leonard T Gerow and Patton's classmate, William H Simpson.[5]

By December 1941 both Patton's future and the future of the Armored Force were assured. On 15 January Georgie was appointed to command I Armored Corps.

Another officer who had also excelled himself during the Louisiana manoeuvres was Ike. As Chief of Staff of the Third Army he was credited with devising the strategy that won the 'war' between it and the Second Army. His meteoric rise to Supreme Commander began immediately afterwards when he was promoted from lieutenant colonel to brigadier general.

Patton's flamboyant arrival at his Corps Headquarters in Fort Benning was typical of the man. Preceded by a dozen outriders in polished helmets and an honour guard from the 2nd Armored Division, he arrived standing in the back of his command car; after then ordering the sergeant of the guard to 'Post the colors', he saluted as the American flag and his two star general's flag were unfurled and then at precisely 11 o'clock he announced: 'I assume command of I Armored Corps. At ease!'.

Patton's time with I Armored Corps at Fort Benning lasted only two months. In March 1942, whilst retaining command of the Corps, he was selected to command a new Desert Training Centre being set up in Arizona and California. After a four-day reconnaissance he selected an 18,000 square-mile area, 200 miles east of Los Angeles. It was completely uninhabited and conditions there equated very much with those to be found in North Africa. But he was not pleased with his new assignment – he felt that once again he was being rusticated. Nonetheless, he set to work with a vengeance to train the men of the Armored Force to cope with desert conditions – within a month of arrival they were required to run a mile in fifteen minutes with rifle and full pack. He was everywhere – leading, teaching, driving, supervizing, cajoling. And needless to say, he was constantly writing to his bosses, Generals Devers (head of the Armored Force) and McNair (commander Army Ground Forces), telling them of his progress – and his achievements!

Despite the fact that Patton felt he was once again in a military backwater, events on the other side of the world were about to bring him to the foreground of history in a very short time. They began, following the fall of Tobruk in June 1942 and the clear Axis threat to the Suez Canal, with Roosevelt offering Churchill military assistance. Churchill asked for Sherman tanks to reinforce the Eighth Army, but at Marshall's suggestion a fully equipped Armored Division was offered instead, and Patton was immediately summoned back to Washington to prepare the necessary plans for its move overseas. It was soon realised, however, that it would take too long to get there and in the event the Americans sent 300 un-manned Shermans and 100 howitzers instead. In the meantime Georgie had landed himself once more in trouble – this time with George Marshall. On studying the requirement to send his beloved 'Hell on Wheels' Division to help the British, he had immediately suggested that two divisions would be better than one – no doubt with himself in command! Marshall was furious; he ordered Patton back to California and sent one of his secretaries (presumably male) to escort him to the plane.

By the middle of 1942 the Americans and British had reached agreement that the war against Germany would take precedence over that against Japan; however, the American demand for a direct cross-Channel attack that year against 'Fortress Europe' had been deemed totally impracticable by the British. In an attempt to reach a compromise Churchill suggested seizing French North Africa later that year and even though this idea was viewed with suspicion in Washington, where it was seen as possibly safeguarding Britain's imperial interests rather than trying to win the war, it was eventually accepted by Roosevelt and his Chiefs of Staff. Three invasion forces, two American and one British, would land simultaneously and neutralize the French in Morocco and Algeria. They would then invade Tunisia and in concert with the British Eighth Army advancing from Egypt, trap the Axis forces in North Africa. The overall commander of this joint enterprise was to be none other than Dwight D Eisenhower! After the Louisiana manoeuvres Marshall had brought Ike back to Washington to head the War Plans Division, after which he had been sent to London in April 1942 to coordinate planning with the British. In June Marshall appointed him to command all US troops in the newly designated European Theater of Operations (ETO) in the rank of lieutenant general. The following month Ike wrote to Patton and warned him that his services would soon be required. Georgie's reaction to his former subordinate's incredible elevation is not recorded, but it must have come as a great, and perhaps unpleasant, shock.

Patton's worry that he had been rusticated did not last long. His success in running the Desert Training Center was obvious to everyone, including Marshall, and at the end of July he was again summoned to Washington and told that he was to command the Western Task Force in Operation TORCH – the invasion of Morocco. He had no time to return to California but immediately sent for some of his most trusted staff to join him. He had hardly settled into his new headquarters, however, when he was ordered to London to help Ike plan the invasion.

Although Georgie was billeted in one of the best hotels in the capital, Claridges, he found London drab and did not enjoy his time there. He wrote in his diary[6] that he was 'not, repeat not, pro-British'. And he was certainly unimpressed with both the joint Anglo-American planning team for TORCH and the US naval planners. But his dissatisfaction did not end there – he did not trust Mark Clark, Ike's deputy, and he even found the Supreme Commander 'not as mentally rugged as I thought; he vacillates'.[7]

Patton returned to Washington in mid-August and before long had fallen out with the man responsible for carrying the invasion force across the Atlantic and landing it, Admiral Hewitt. The situation became so difficult that the Chief of Naval Operations, Admiral King, asked Marshall to sack Patton and get someone more amenable and flexible to command the Western Task Force. With Ike's support Marshall refused and Georgie survived. The relationship between the naval and military staffs was far from good, however, and not helped by insufficient time, only eleven weeks, for planning, training and rehearsals. And Patton and Hewitt had still not resolved all their differences as late as 21 October when they were summoned to the White House to see Roosevelt. Georgie wrote in his diary that he arrived there:

> with the hope that he [Roosevelt] would put some heat on Hewitt about the necessity of [the] landing. As nothing came of it, I said, 'The Admiral and I feel that we must get ashore regardless of cost, as the fate of the war hinges on our success'. Roosevelt replied, 'Certainly you must'.

Patton visited his ailing, 81-year-old hero, Black Jack Pershing, in the Walter Reed Army hospital before leaving for North Africa and received his blessing, and Beatrice said goodbye to him in the naval dockyards at Norfolk, Virginia. On 23 October he wrote in his diary: 'This is my last night in America. It may be for years or it may be forever. God grant that I do my full duty to my men and myself'. That same night, 7,000 miles away in Egypt, the massed guns of Montgomery's Eighth Army fired the opening barrage in the battle of El Alamein! At 0810 hours the following morning Naval Task Force 34 slipped out of Norfolk, bound for Morocco – the prima donnas were moving towards their first meeting.

NOTES

1 Eisenhower, David, *Eisenhower at War 1943–1945*, p. 62.
2 Letter dated 19 July 40.
3 Letter dated 27 Aug 40.
4 Letter dated 3 Sep 40.
5 D'Este, *A Genius for War*, p. 397.
6 Begun in Jul 42 and available with the Patton Papers in the Library of Congress, Washington.
7 D'Este, op. cit., p. 419.

CHAPTER XI

Montgomery in North Africa – August to November 1942

(Map 5)

The story of the British Army in North Africa from 1940 until August 1942 is one of small victories followed by large defeats. It started with the Italians crossing into Egypt from Libya in 1940 and then digging in. The British Western Desert Force, under Major General Richard O'Connor, then attacked and drove them back to El Agheila, halfway to Tripoli. However, the arrival of German troops under Rommel and then Churchill's order to divert troops to Greece soon changed that picture; by March 1941 the British were forced to give up most of the ground they had regained. Two counter-offensives in May and June produced disappointing results, but in November the Eighth Army under a new commander, General Sir Claude Auckinleck, mounted a highly successful offensive that not only relieved the besieged port of Tobruk, but went on to reach El Agheila once again. This success was in turn short lived; Rommel counter-attacked and routed the Eighth Army. Tobruk fell and the Germans were eventually halted in July 1942, as much by exhaustion and lack of supplies as by military action, between the Qattara Depression and a small village on the coast called El Alamein.

Auckinleck, who was by then C-in-C Middle East Command as well as the commander of the Eighth Army, reported that he would be unable to launch a counter-offensive before mid-September and on 3 August Churchill decided to fly to Egypt and sort matters out himself. He acted in a typical Churchillian manner. His first action was to split the Middle East Command into two – Egypt, Palestine and Syria, to be called the Near East Command, and Persia and Iraq to be a new Middle East Command. He then invited Alan Brooke, the CIGS, who had accompanied him, to take over in Egypt. When Brooke declined the offer Churchill told the War Cabinet in London that he was appointing Harold Alexander and that Montgomery was to be given the First Army in his place. Auckinleck was to be moved to the new Persia/Iraq Command and Lieutenant General 'Strafer' Gott, the XIII Corps commander, was to take over the Eighth Army. Readers will recall that it was only when the latter was killed on 7 August that Churchill was forced to accept Brooke's original recommendation of Monty for the Eighth Army.

Arrival

Monty was of course delighted to learn that his old friend Alexander was to be his C-in-C. But there was a problem; when he arrived in Cairo on 12 August he found that Aucklinleck had decided to stay on until the 15th and that, although the latter had appointed someone to stand in during his absence in Cairo,[1] the Auk was still in fact the official commander of the Eighth Army.

> I arrived there soon after 10 a.m. and was taken straight to see Auckinleck. He asked me if I knew he was to go. I said that I did. He then explained to me his plan of operations; this was based on the fact that at all costs the Eighth Army was to be preserved 'in being' and must not be destroyed in battle . . . If Cairo and the Delta could not be held, the army would retreat southwards up the Nile. I listened in amazement to this exposition of his plans . . . he then said I was to go down to the desert the next day and spend two days at Eighth Army HQ, getting in the picture and learning the game . . . I was not to take over till the 15th of August, the day on which he would himself hand over to Alexander.[2]

Monty knew that it was a waste of time discussing any changes of policy with either Aucklinleck or his Chief of Staff, both of whom were being sacked, so he called in the Deputy Chief of Staff, Major General John Harding. Alexander was present at the meeting. Harding had been a student of Monty's at the Staff College and he had a high regard for his abilities. With Alexander's agreement, he told Harding that he wanted to create a reserve armoured corps similar to Rommel's and that the 300 Sherman tanks due to arrive in Suez from America on 3 September would provide the necessary equipment for the armoured divisions of that corps. He asked if this was a realistic plan. Harding asked for the afternoon to consider it and when Alexander and Monty returned to his office at 1800 hours they were told that it *would* be possible – 'This was splendid and we told him to go ahead'.[3]

Monty's first day in Egypt was not restricted to high-level meetings. During the afternoon he bought himself 'clothes suitable for the desert in August' and he also interviewed and accepted a second ADC – Captain John Poston. He had been Gott's ADC and knew the desert. He was to stay with Monty until the last week of the war when he was killed in Germany.

After spending the night at the British Embassy, Monty set off for Eighth Army Headquarters at 0500 hours on 13 August. He picked up Brigadier Freddie de Guingand, the Brigadier General Staff of the Eighth Army and an old friend, on the way and by the time they reached the desert HQ Monty had already decided that he would appoint him as his

Chief of Staff with full powers over all branches of the Headquarters – this was something unheard of in the British Army at that time.

Monty was singularly unimpressed with Auchlinleck's Eighth Army Headquarters. 'The whole atmosphere . . . was dismal and dreary . . . No one could have a high morale . . . if we stuck ourselves down in a dismal place like this and lived in such discomfort.'[4] Although he was not due to take command for another two days he decided to take action at once. He told the acting Army commander, Ramsden, to return to his Corps (XXX) and then wrote a telegram to Auckinleck's Headquarters in Cairo saying that he had assumed command of the Eighth Army from 1400 hours.

> This was disobedience, but there was no comeback. I then cancelled all previous orders about withdrawal. I issued orders that in the event of enemy attack there would be *no* withdrawal; we would fight on the ground we now held and if we couldn't stay there alive we would stay there dead.[5]

Monty's subsequent actions left his staff flabbergasted. He immediately left the Headquarters 'in case any repercussion came from GHQ about my sudden seizure of command' and went to visit the commanders of the New Zealand and Australian Divisions in XIII Corps; there he explained his future plans. Then, on arrival back at *his* Headquarters he addressed the entire staff. He again explained his policy of no withdrawal and told them that two new Divisions currently defending areas in the Nile delta were to be brought forward to the Alamein position; furthermore, all ammunition, water and rations were to be stored in the forward areas and all motor transport was to be sent back to the rear areas. He then gave orders that the Headquarters was to move as soon as possible to a site on the sea-shore near the Desert Air Force Headquarters, where they would jointly make plans for an offensive that 'would hit Rommel for six right out of Africa . . . But I had no intention of launching *our* attack until we were ready'. Then to everyone's amazement he cancelled a previous order forbidding tents and ordered that the senior officers' mess, a 'meat safe' wire cage designed to keep the flies out, was to be torn down to, 'let the poor flies out'.[6] 'Let us all be as comfortable as possible', he decreed. Finally, he publicly appointed Freddie de Guingand to be Chief of Staff of the Eighth Army and told the entire staff that 'every order given by him [was to] be regarded as coming from me and would be obeyed instantly'.[7]

Monty continued as he had begun – as a new broom sweeping clean. He claimed later that he believed that at this time the men of the Eighth Army:

> were worthy of greater things . . . they had lost confidence in their higher leadership, they lacked a sound battle technique, and they

were deficient of equipment and weapons comparable to those of the Germans ... The morale and determination of our troops was undermined by plans for further withdrawals. The 'atmosphere' was wrong.[8]

He agreed with Churchill's description of an Army 'brave but baffled'. Certainly British morale as a whole was at a low ebb in August 1942 and Monty knew that Churchill, and indeed the British people, desperately needed a victory. He was therefore determined to give them one. But it was to the senior commanders and staff that he first directed his attention. All who heard him, from that first evening in the desert, were left in no doubt that he meant business, that inefficiency and 'bellyaching' would not be tolerated and that orders, 'no longer formed the base for discussion, but for action'.[9] And it was only *after* he had taken a 'grip' on his Corps, Divisional and Brigade commanders that he turned his attention to his men. His basic daily routine involved being woken in his caravan before 0700 hours, spending the whole morning and early afternoon visiting units, inspecting, quizzing officers on their duties and responsibilities and then addressing the men, and then, after discussing policy matters with de Guingand and listening to reports from his liaison officers, he would have an early supper and retire to bed at 2100 hours.

> The Eighth Army consisted in the main of civilians in uniform, not of professional soldiers ... It seemed to me that to command such men demanded not only a guiding mind but also a point of focus ... not only a master but a mascot. And I deliberately set about fulfilling this second requirement. It helped, I felt sure, for them to recognize as a person – as an individual – the man who was putting them into battle. To obey an impersonal figure was not enough. They must know who I was ... But I readily admit that the occasion to become the necessary focus of their attention was also personally enjoyable ... I started ... by wearing an Australian hat – first of all because it was an exceedingly good hat for the desert, but soon because I came to be recognized by it ... Later ... I took a black beret, again for utilitarian reasons in the first place.[10]

And there is no doubt that the 'short, wiry fellow with a bee in his bonnet about PT' soon made a very firm, and for the most part good, impression on officers and men alike. Many of them felt that at last they had a commander who could deal with Rommel – known by now as 'the Desert Fox'.

Churchill visited the re-sited Eighth Army Headquarters near Burg-el-Arab on 20 August on his way back from Moscow. He wrote in Monty's autograph book:

May the anniversary of Blenheim [the Duke of Malborough's great victory on 13 August 1704] which marks the opening of the new command bring to the Commander of the Eighth Army and his troops the fame and fortune they will surely deserve.[11]

Within eleven weeks of taking command Monty and his Eighth Army had given Churchill and the British people not one victory, but two. The first was the seven-day defensive battle of Alam Halfa beginning on 31 August, and the second was the famous attack at El Alamein which began on 23 October and lasted until 4 November. The details of these battles are well known and will not be repeated. From the point of view of this book, Alam Halfa and Alamein, and indeed the subsequent operations carried out by the Eighth Army in North Africa, are important only for what they tell us about Montgomery as a man and as a general.

Alam Halfa

A number of post-war historians have criticized Monty for his performance in the battle of Alam Halfa, claiming that he merely implemented an existing plan devised by Auckinleck and his Chief of Staff, Dorman-Smith, and that he failed to capitalize on his success. Whilst one of his future Corps commanders, Oliver Leese, described Alam Halfa as 'Monty's finest battle', a respected and distinguished historian, Correlli Barnett, has stated that following Alam Halfa, 'Montgomery set out for the top . . . in a second-hand suit of glory'.[12] Whatever view one takes (those interested should read Barnett's book, *The Desert Generals*), one thing is certain – Monty delivered a victory that was desperately needed. Being essentially a realist, he had come to two basic conclusions: one, that 'the standard of training of the Eighth Army formations was such that I was not prepared to loose them headlong into the enemy'; and two, that he needed 'a resounding victory . . . so that confidence of officers and men in the high command would be restored'. It followed that since he was not prepared to go on the offensive until he was fully ready, it made sense to allow Rommel to 'beat up against . . . 400 tanks in position, dug in, and deployed behind a screen of 6-pounder anti-tank guns . . . and to suffer heavy casualties'. This is precisely what happened at Alam Halfa and Monty had his first victory. His answers to those who criticized him for not following up Rommel's withdrawal were that: 'I was not too happy about the standard of training of the Army'; 'the equipment situation was unsatisfactory'; and:

I was not anxious to force Rommel to pull out and withdraw 'in being' back to the Agheila position . . . It was essential to get Rommel to stand and fight and then defeat him decisively . . . Thus the Battle of Alam Halfa ended in the way we wanted.[13]

Rommel was certainly in no doubt about the way Monty had performed:

> There is no doubt that the British commander's handling of this action had been absolutely right and well suited to the occasion, for it enabled him to inflict very heavy damage on us in relation to his own losses, and to retain the striking power of his own force.[14]

Monty wrote to his son David on 8 September: 'The battle I have been fighting with Rommel is over. I have defeated him and that is very good. I expect you will see a good deal about it in the papers. I have enjoyed it all enormously'.

El Alamein

By the time Monty went on the offensive at El Alamein he had replaced a Corps commander,[15] one of his Divisional commanders[16] and his senior artillery officer, and had surrounded himself with a staff mainly of his own choosing.

> Having checked over the leadership problem and made the necessary changes, I was satisfied that I had a team which would collectively handle the task that lay ahead without difficulty. Some of them remained on my staff for the rest of the war.[17]

Monty's decision not to launch the Alamein attack until 23 October met with fierce resistance from Churchill. He demanded that it should take place in September to synchronise with a Soviet offensive and to divert attention away from the landings on the North African coast – Operation TORCH. With Alexander's support, Monty refused – on the grounds that an earlier attack, launched before his men had received additional training and the necessary equipment was in place, would fail:

> if we waited until October, I guaranteed complete success . . . I had told Alexander . . . that, in view of my promise to my soldiers, I refused to attack before October; if a September attack was ordered by Whitehall, they would have to get someone else to do it. My stock was rather high after Alam Halfa! We heard no more about a September attack.[18]

Despite Monty's insistence that his men should be retrained before any offensive, he knew it was impossible to bring them up to the standards he would have liked in the time available:

> By the end of September there were serious doubts in my mind

whether the troops would be able to do what was being demanded
... If I was not careful, divisions and units would be given tasks
which might end in failure because of the inadequate standard of
training. The Eighth Army had suffered some 80,000 casualties since
it was formed, and little time had been spent in training replace-
ments.[19]

In the event he had no choice other than to amend his initial plan and
tailor it to the capabilities of his troops.

On 23 October Monty, despite his misgivings, sent a personal message
to every man under his command:

1. When I assumed command of the Eighth Army I said that the
   mandate was to destroy Rommel and his Army, and that it would
   be done as soon as we were ready.
2. We are ready now. The battle which is now about to begin will be
   one of the decisive battles of history. It will be the turning point of
   the war. The eyes of the world will be on us . . .
3. We have first-class equipment; good tanks; good anti-tank guns;
   plenty of artillery and plenty of ammunition; and we are backed
   up by the finest air striking force in the world. All that is necessary
   is that each one of us, every officer and man, should enter this
   battle with the determination to see it through – to fight and to kill
   – and finally, to win . . .

AND LET NO MAN SURRENDER SO LONG AS HE IS
UNWOUNDED AND HE CAN FIGHT.[20]

After briefing the press on the morning of the 23rd, Monty moved to his
forward Tactical Headquarters, where:

In the evening I read a book and went to bed early. At 9.40 pm the
barrage of over one thousand guns opened, and the Eighth Army
which included some 1,200 tanks went into the attack. At that
moment I was asleep in my caravan; there was nothing I could do and
I knew I would be needed later.[21]

Readers will recall that as Monty fell asleep, George Patton was about to
sail from Norfolk, Virginia for Morocco.

No battle goes exactly according to plan and Alamein was no exception.
The various crises are well chronicled and need not be repeated. Monty
claimed afterwards, arrogantly but accurately, that, 'If I had not stood firm
and insisted that my plan would be carried through, we would not have
won at Alamein'.[22] This is undoubtedly true. Despite some over-
optimistic objectives and several serious mistakes made during its

implementation, the battle of El Alamein was still a decisive, if not total, victory, and the credit for this must go to the man who devised the original plan, amended it as necessary as the battle developed and brought it to a successful conclusion in the time frame envisaged – Bernard Montgomery. Many others would have lost their nerve – indeed, some of the senior commanders did, but fortunately for the troops who did the fighting, not the Army commander.

Needless to say, in the post-war years numerous armchair critics criticized Monty for his handling of the Alamein battle. A number of them undoubtedly raised some very valid points, but this author prefers to let the basic statistics of the battle itself speak for themselves: Monty lost 13,560 men killed, wounded and missing and some 500 tanks, of which all but 150 were repairable; Rommel lost some 57,000 casualties, the vast majority of them becoming prisoners of war, 450 tanks and over 1,000 anti-tank guns and artillery pieces. By any standards these figures indicate that Alamein was a clear and decisive victory for the Eighth Army. Monty described it in typically 'Monty' terms to Allied war correspondents on 5 November; dressed in a grey pullover and wearing a black Royal Tank Regiment beret he said:

> It has been a fine battle. There is no doubt of the result. Two nights ago I drove two armoured wedges into the enemy and I passed three armoured Divisions through those places. They are now operating in the enemy's rear. Those portions of the enemy's armour which can get away are in full retreat. Those portions which are still facing our troops down in the south will be put 'in the bag'. It is complete finish. I did not hope for such a complete victory; or rather I hoped for it but I did not expect it. After twelve days of very hard fighting, the Eighth Army and the Allied air forces have gained a complete victory . . . But we must not think that the party is over. We have no intention of letting the enemy recover. We must keep up the pressure. We intend to hit this chap for six out of North Africa.

Monty then went on to describe the capture of the commander of the Afrika Corps,[23] General von Thoma, and a discussion he had had with him over dinner in his Headquarters the previous evening (von Thoma also spent the night in Monty's Headquarters as his guest). He said that when he had asked von Thoma if the Germans had a character sketch of the Eighth Army commander, von Thoma had said that indeed they did; they saw him as a hard, ruthless man who had brought a new form of tactics to the desert.

As Monty was speaking his troops were beginning their controversial pursuit of Rommel's forces – but more of that in a later chapter.

Three days after the Eighth Army began its advance westwards, George

Patton's Western Task Force, part of Operation TORCH, landed near Casablanca. The TORCH plan foresaw the neutralisation of French North Africa, and then a rapid thrust into Tunisia. With the Eighth Army advancing towards Tunisia from the east and the TORCH forces driving in from the west, the Axis forces in North Africa would surely be trapped and eliminated.

As we shall hear in the next chapter the TORCH landings were successful and on 11 November George Patton received the unconditional surrender of the French forces in Morocco. On the same day Monty was promoted to the rank of general and became 'Sir' Bernard Montgomery.

NOTES

1 Lt Gen. W H Ramsden.
2 Montgomery, *Memoirs*, p. 94.
3 Ibid, p. 96.
4 Ibid, p. 99.
5 Ibid, p. 100.
6 De Guingand, *Operation Victory*, p. 139.
7 Montgomery, op. cit., p. 102.
8 Montgomery, *El Alamein to the River Sangro*, p. 9.
9 Montgomery, *Memoirs*, p. 107.
10 Ibid, p. 111.
11 Ibid, p. 106.
12 Barnett, *The Desert Generals*, p. 266.
13 Montgomery, op. cit., p. 110.
14 Liddell Hart, *The Rommel Papers*, p. 279.
15 Ramsden (XXX Corps).
16 Renton (7 Armoured [Armd] Div).
17 Montgomery, op. cit., p. 114.
18 Ibid, p. 117.
19 Ibid, p. 119.
20 Ibid, pp. 127–8.
21 Ibid.
22 Ibid, p. 139.
23 Von Thoma's Afrika Corps was part of Rommel's 'German–Italian Panzer Army Afrika'.

CHAPTER XII

Patton in North Africa – November 1942 to April 1943

(Map 6)

Operation TORCH

Although TORCH was the first major Anglo/American operation of WWII it has never been given the prominence of the Normandy invasion or even the raid on Dieppe. It may be useful therefore to provide readers with some background information. Commanded by General Eisenhower from a Headquarters in Gibraltar, Operation TORCH was designed to gain control of Morocco and Algeria from the 100,000 Vichy French troops stationed there, and then to attack the Axis forces in Tunisia, crushing them against the British Eighth Army advancing from the Western Desert. The final phase of TORCH would see bases established for air and sea operations against the continent of Europe. As it turned out the destruction of the Axis forces in North Africa took much longer than expected and the bases eventually established were used, controversially, for land invasions of the 'soft underbelly' of Hitler's Europe.

Phase I of TORCH involved three Task Forces: the Eastern Task Force, comprising 33,000 British and American troops, was aimed at Algiers; the Center Task Force, with 22,000 Americans carried mainly in British ships flying the American flag, was to take Oran; and the 32,000 strong American Western Task Force, commanded by George Patton, was to land, as we have already heard, in Morocco and capture Casablanca. D-Day for this extremely complicated operation, which was launched directly from ports in the United States and Great Britain, was 8 November.

The fiercest resistance to Operation TORCH was encountered by the Center Task Force in Oran. The men of the 1st US Infantry Division, attempting to encircle the city from the flanks, were engaged in heavy fighting on the 8th and 9th, but on the 10th a thrust by armour of the 1st US Armored Division finally entered the city from the south and at noon the French surrendered. The Americans suffered some 600 killed, wounded and missing.

The Eastern Task Force had a rather easier time of it. British and American troops landing to the west and east of Algiers respectively[1] met no little or no opposition; but when some 700 Americans landed from two British destroyers[2] in an attempt to secure the main harbour, they were surrounded and after suffering seventy-nine casualties they surrendered. Fortunately, and by chance, Admiral Darlan, the Deputy to Vichy France's head of Government, Marshal Pétain, was visiting his sick son in a hospital in the city when the Allies landed. He soon realised that the situation was hopeless and after conferring with Pétain by radio, he agreed a ceasefire with Major General Mark Clark, Eisenhower's deputy, early on 10 November. The ceasefire though applied only to Algiers. Incidentally, Clark had been landed from a British submarine on the 9th.

How did Patton's Western Task Force fare in Operation TORCH? Strangely, he makes little mention of it in his book *War As I Knew It*. Nevertheless, the operation is well recorded. Carried across the Atlantic in 102 ships, the Task Force was organized into three Task Units: the Northern Unit, under Major General Lucien Truscott, with 9,000 men of the 9th Infantry and 2nd US Armored Divisions, was to land at Mehdia and was tasked with capturing the airport at Port Lyautey (today Kenitra); the Southern Unit, under Major General Ernie Harmon, with 6,000 men and 100 tanks, was to land at Safi, some 150 miles south-west of Casablanca. Its mission was to protect the Task Force from a counter-attack from the direction of Marrakech. The Center Unit, under Major General Jonathan Anderson, with 16,500 men, mainly from his own 3rd Infantry Division, and eighty tanks, had the main mission of taking Casablanca. It was to land at Fedala (now renamed Mohemmadia), a small fishing port roughly fifteen miles north-east of the city. Patton and his Headquarters, carried in the Task Force flagship, the *Augusta*, were also to land at Fedala.

Morocco

Georgie found the two-week voyage across the Atlantic extremely boring. For something to do he read the Koran which he described as 'a good book and interesting'. The officers' mess in the *Augusta* was 'the best I have ever seen' and fearing that he would get fat, he exercised vigorously, including 'running in place 480 steps in my cabin'.[3] On 8 November he got up at 0200 hours and went on deck to see the lights of Fedala and Casablanca shining across a calm sea. But things did not go quite according to plan. At 0650 hours the invasion fleet began exchanging fire with French shore batteries and an uncompleted battleship, the *Jean Bart*, in Casablanca harbour, and at 0715 six French destroyers came out of the harbour in an attempt to interfere with the landings. They withdrew under heavy fire from the US ships, but were followed by a light cruiser and two destroyers. This happened at about 0800 hours just as Patton was about to go ashore. The first salvo fired by the *Augusta* 'blew our landing boat [which was still on the davits] to hell, and we lost everything except my pistols'.[4] Far more important than the loss of Georgie's personal kit, however, was the loss of his Headquarters' radios. He had no way therefore of communicating with Eisenhower in Gibraltar or his Northern and Southern Task Units. The naval engagement went on for another three hours and was well remembered by Patton who later wrote: 'I was on the main deck when a shell hit so close it splashed water all over me, and later on the bridge, one hit even closer, but I was too high to get wet'.[5]

Patton eventually got ashore at 1320 hours, 'getting very wet in the surf. There was still quite a fight going on, but I had no bullets'.[6] By this time, unbeknown to Georgie, Harmon's Southern Task Unit had landed successfully at Safi against light opposition; but in the north at Mehdia, Truscott's men, after suffering a chaotic landing, were facing a tricky situation with French shelling interrupting reinforcements. It was to be another two days before they would capture the airport and by then they would have suffered seventy-nine dead and many wounded.

The situation at Fedala, where Patton had landed, was no better. The wide, sandy beaches were cluttered with men and supplies landed in the wrong place and groups of curious Arabs getting in the way! The men of Anderson's 3rd Division had secured the waterfront by the evening, but French naval gunfire and armed resistance still interrupted the flow of reinforcements. The overall situation was not helped by the fact that Patton, who spent the night in a blacked-out hotel in Fedala, had no direct communications with his C-in-C in Gibraltar, his own North and South Units or even the *Augusta*.

The following morning found a very angry Patton down on the chaotic beach amongst landing craft that were taking half an hour to unload and back off. Needless to say, in a typical Georgie manner, he was soon directing affairs and even recovering the body of a drowned soldier himself. His short temper was soon evident; when he found a sobbing GI on the beach he:

> kicked him in the fanny and he jumped right up and went to work . . .
> As a whole the men were poor and the officers worse. I saw one
> Lieutenant let his men hesitate to jump into the water. I gave him hell.
> I hit another man who was too lazy to push a boat.[7]

That afternoon he returned to the *Augusta* exhausted and the following day he received a message from Eisenhower: 'The only tough nut [Casablanca] left is in your hands. Crack it open quickly'.

On 11 November:

> I decided to attack Casablanca this day with the 3rd Division and one
> tank battalion. It took some nerve as both Truscott and Harmon
> seemed in a bad way, but I felt I should maintain the initiative. Then
> Admiral Hall [the naval Chief of Staff] came ashore to arrange for
> naval gunfire and air support and brought fine news. Truscott has

taken the airfield at Port Lyautey and there are forty-two P-40s on it. Harmon is marching on Casablanca.[8]

Unknown to Patton, the fascist French Resident General in Morocco, August Noguès, had decided during the night of the 10th that further resistance was pointless and he sent word at 0430 hours on the 11th that he was prepared to negotiate a surrender. Patton's reply was typical – he told Noguès to cease hostilities at once or he would launch an all-out attack.

> At 6:40 [on Georgie's 57th birthday] the enemy quit. It was a near thing, for the bombers were over their targets and the battleships were in position to fire. I ordered Anderson to move into the town and if anyone stopped him, to attack. No one stopped him, but the hours from 7:30 to 11 were the longest in my life so far. At 2 o'clock, Admiral Michelier and General Noguès came to treat for terms. I opened the conference by congratulating the French [he spoke good French of course] and closed it with champagne and toasts. I also gave them a guard of honor – no use kicking a man when he's down.[9]

Patton's Western Task Force, including naval personnel, suffered 337 killed, 637 wounded and 122 missing during Operation TORCH.[10]

With the fighting over, Patton's main task was to ensure that the French and Moroccan leaders cooperated with the Allies and saw the Nazis as their common enemy. To this end he began an intense diplomatic campaign, a campaign for which he was strangely well suited. He had already written to the Sultan of Morocco on 10 November assuring him that he and his men had come not as conquerors but as friends (a precursor of similar assurances given to Iraqis sixty-one years later!) and he now began a round of high-level visits to ingratiate himself with everyone who mattered in the country. On 16 November he made what also amounted to a 'state' visit to the French Resident General, Noguès, and the Sultan of Morocco in Rabat, and on the 22nd, the fifteenth anniversary of the Sultan's Accession, he paid a second visit; on this occasion he began his speech:

> Your Majesty, as a representative of the great President of the United States, as the commander of a huge military force in Morocco, I wish to present the compliments of the United States on this occasion, the fifteenth anniversary of your ascension to the throne of your ancestors, and I wish to assure you that so long as Your Majesty's country, in cooperation with the French Government, cooperates with us and facilitates our efforts, we are sure, with the help of God, to achieve certain victory against our common enemy, the Nazis.[11]

The full meaning of his words was not lost on his audience.

Further diplomatic gestures, such as attending a Requiem Mass for French as well as American dead on the 23rd and a luncheon with Noguès on 8 December at which he met the French Governor of Dakar, followed. And one of the highlights of this period was a spectacular parade by Franco–American troops in Rabat where he was allegedly cheered by 100,000 Arabs shouting 'Vive l'Amérique!'.[12] Patton was of course in his element – his picture was on the front page of all the American papers and an NBC report described him as, 'a combination of Buck Rogers, the Green Hornet, and the man from Mars ... the rootin', tootin' hip-shootin' commander of American Forces in Morocco.'[13] And even his marriage seemed to be coming together again. Beatrice had written to him on 8 November: 'Darling Georgie, I realise that there are months and perhaps years of waiting and anxiety ... but there can be no separation between us except by amputation'.

Despite all the pageantry and adulation, Patton was in fact very concerned that the war was once more leaving him behind. He was acutely aware that his troops were gradually being whittled away to provide reinforcements to Tunisia and he saw no future for himself on the western periphery of the Mediterranean war zone. His morale had already suffered a major blow when his rival, Mark Clark, was promoted to the rank of lieutenant general in early December and given command of a newly formed Fifth Army. This elevation followed his successful surrender negotiations with French Admiral Darlan. The fact that both Eisenhower and Clark had been his juniors and both lacked his combat experience, merely rubbed salt into the now open wound.

On 17 November Patton flew to Gibraltar to meet Eisenhower, but his C-in-C had made no decision on the future employment of his force and he came away even more depressed. He found the attitude of the British officers on Ike's staff quite objectionable and he felt his boss was falling too much under the influence of the British: 'We wasted a lot of time at lunch with the Governor of the Rock, an old fart in shorts with skinny legs. I truly fear that London has conquered Abilene'.[14]

By early December it was clear that the Allied invasion of Tunisia was getting nowhere. Immediately following the TORCH landings Hitler, fearing that the Tunisian ports would be used for an invasion of southern Europe, ordered a massive reinforcement of the country; by the end of November there were 20,000 Axis troops there and this figure grew to 100,000 during December, including the 10th Panzer Division. And as if this was not bad enough, a 500-mile supply line between Algeria and Tunisia, appalling weather and muddled Allied leadership ensured a winter stalemate.

On 9 December Eisenhower summoned Patton to meet him in Algiers. Georgie's plane was nearly shot down by Allied anti-aircraft guns, but he arrived safely and was ordered to visit the Tunisian front and find out why Allied tank losses were so high. He drove at once to British Lieutenant General Anderson's First Army Headquarters where, following various briefings and visits to the V Corps[15] and 78th Division Headquarters, he formed the firm impression that poor leadership was the basic problem. He later reported that he was astonished and disgusted to find the general commanding the 78th Division did not even get up until after 0800 hours! It is said that Patton's subsequent Anglophobia had its roots in this visit. Certainly from this time on he had a very poor opinion of British officers.

Patton's report to Ike on tank losses, not surprisingly, blamed the inadequacy of the 37mm gun on the Grant tank. Its only hope was to immobilize the German Mk IV with a lucky hit on the tracks or possibly the optics. All the Allied tanks at this stage of the war were hopelessly under-gunned.

Patton's next major task was the security of the Casablanca Conference in January 1943, when Roosevelt and Churchill and their Chiefs of Staff met in the mansion-like Hotel Anfa to sort out a future strategy for the war. The details of the conference need not concern us, only the result – to the consternation of General Marshall and many other Americans, it was agreed that Operation OVERLORD, the cross-Channel invasion of France, was to be delayed, North Africa would be cleared of enemy and then Sicily, followed by Italy, would be invaded in the summer.

Georgie and Mark Clark, who was the official host, not surprisingly failed to get on, but Patton managed to gain the limelight when he was officially appointed to greet his President; in typical Patton fashion, he arranged to line the route from the airport with most of the 40,000 troops under his command. He followed this by entertaining lavishly each evening in the luxurious villa he had taken over as his quarters. He included amongst his guests Roosevelt, Churchill, Marshall, and the Chief of the Imperial General Staff, General Sir Alan Brooke. The latter wrote later, but with the benefit of hindsight of course:

> I had already heard of him [Patton], but must confess that his swashbuckling personality exceeded my expectation. I did not form any high opinion of him ... A dashing, courageous, wild and unbalanced leader, good for operations requiring thrust and push but at a loss in any operation requiring skill and judgement.[16]

It was during the Casablanca Conference that Eisenhower decorated Georgie with a second Distinguished Service Medal and mentioned that he was considering appointing him 'Deputy Commander for Ground Forces'. In the event, Churchill persuaded Roosevelt that once Monty's Eighth Army came under Ike's command, Alexander should become his

Deputy. Georgie was not in fact disappointed: 'I think I was fortunate in not being made Deputy C-in-C to Ike. I guess destiny is still on the job. God, I wish I could really command and lead as well as just fight'.[17] He was, however, angered when he heard that II US Corps was to be placed under British command: 'We have sold our birthright ... I am shocked and distressed'.[18]

In February 1943 Patton met General Sir Bernard Montgomery for the first time. He had accepted an invitation by Monty to attend a study period in Tripoli (Map 5) for senior officers from England and those serving in the Middle East, to go through the lessons learned in the fighting so far. It was not really Georgie's scene and he is said to have only attended to relieve his boredom in Morocco. As it turned out, he was the only American officer there and was described by Monty as: 'the commander of an armoured Corps; an old man of about sixty'.[19] His alleged remark that: 'I may be old, and I be stooped, but it just don' mean a thing to me!' is probably apocryphal, but his views on Monty are given in an entry in his diary dated 14 February: 'small, very alert, wonderfully conceited, and the best soldier – or so it seems – I have met in this war. My friend General Briggs says he is the best soldier and the most disagreeable man he knows'.

On 19 February Patton's morale received a major boost when he heard that he was to command the American element in the forthcoming Anglo/American invasion of Sicily; he was elated, but then on 4 March, he suddenly received a message from Ike's Chief of Staff, calling him to meet Eisenhower at Maison Blanche airport near Algiers and warning him that he would probably be taking over II US Corps from Lloyd Fredendall in Tunisia. Readers may recall that Fredendall had been the post commander at Fort Benning in 1941 and Patton had formed a very low opinion of him at that time. Ike confirmed the appointment during their half hour meeting on the 5th, without saying why he was sacking Fredendall, and then went on to warn Patton that he must cooperate with the British to the fullest extent possible and on no account was he to criticize them. Patton then flew on to Constantine to meet Alexander who, it will be recalled, had been appointed Land C-in-C the previous month. The latter, 'was very friendly and complimentary in his remarks, stating that he wanted the best Corps commander he could get and had been informed that I was that man'.[20]

Tunisia

(Map 7)

Following the successful landings in Algeria, the Allied operation in Tunisia had not gone according to plan. First Army, under British

Lieutenant General Kenneth Anderson, the senior Allied commander in Tunisia, had been activated on 9 November and tasked with advancing overland from Algiers to seize Tunis and the ports of Bizerte, Sousse, Sfax and Gabes. 'Army' in this case, however, is a complete misnomer – when it began its advance on 11 November, First Army comprised only one weak Division of two Brigades and a small armoured force, totalling about 12,300 men.[21] During the rest of November a third British Brigade[22] reinforced the Division and CCB of the 1st US Armored Division also operated under its command, but even this force was still inadequate to deal with the Germans defending the major objectives of Tunis and Bizerte. There had been no Axis troops garrisoning Tunisia when the Allies landed on 8 November, but German troops arrived by air at El Ariana airfield near Tunis within twenty-four hours and this advance guard was rapidly reinforced from Sicily and southern Italy. A week later 5,000 Axis troops, with armour, had seized all the key points in Tunis and Bizerte, the ports of Sousse, Sfax and Gabes and the inland town of Kairouan. By the end of the month, while American troops guarded the rear areas and the southern flank, British troops had advanced to within fifteen miles of Tunis over some of the most inhospitable terrain in the world, in ever worsening weather and under constant air attack by the Luftwaffe; but by then there were over 20,000 Axis troops in Tunisia and they were still being reinforced with German armour and German and Italian infantry to form eventually what became known as the 100,000 strong Fifth Panzer Army under General von Arnim. During December First Army was also reinforced by the addition of a British Armoured Division[23] and more American troops, bringing it up a strength of some 67,000, but any chance of an early victory had now gone. On Christmas Eve, at a conference between Eisenhower and Anderson, it was decided to abandon any further attempts to take Tunis and Bizerte until the rainy season had ended. By this time, however, it was clear that despite their common language, the British and US Armies were operating with completely different procedures and practices, often with disastrous results. Joint actions to date had made it clear that 'differences of terminology and organization . . . would have to be ironed out at brigade and battalion level.'[24] It was also clear that Eisenhower as C-in-C, based 400 miles away in Algiers and completely lacking in combat experience, could not possibly be expected to run the whole ground campaign in Tunisia. On 24 January 1943 he therefore delegated the entire Tunisian front to Anderson and placed Fredendall's II US Corps of some 32,000 men under his command. Sadly, Fredendall, an arrogant, foul-mouthed Anglophobe, was one of the least capable American generals in WWII.

In mid-February the Germans saw their chance to split the Allied front in Tunisia by attacking II US Corps; on the 14th two of von Arnim's Panzer Divisions attacked at Sidi-Bou-Zid and five days later Rommel struck at the Kasserine Pass. Fredendall's men, badly deployed and equipped, were overwhelmed in both cases, losing ninety-eight tanks, suffering over 6,000 battle casualties, and another 3,000 lost as prisoners of war. One of Ike's aides wrote in his diary on 23 February: 'proud and cocky Americans today stand humiliated by one of the greatest defeats in our history'.[25] Eisenhower, realising that Fredendall had lost control, sent for Ernie Harmon, who was training his 2nd Armored Division in Morocco for the invasion of Sicily. He appointed him Deputy commander of II Corps and told him that his first job: 'is to do the best you can to help Fredendall restore the situation. Then you will report to me whether you should relieve Ward [the Divisional commander at Kasserine] or Fredendall'.[26] Amazingly, the latter willingly turned his command over to Harmon 'whose firm leadership was a key factor in stabilizing the US front during the critical days after Rommel's breakthrough'.[27] The British took a different view as to why Rommel decided to pull back and regroup. Montgomery claimed that in response to a 'very real cry for help on the 20th of February' from Alexander, in which he was asked 'to relieve the pressure on the Americans', he 'speeded up events and by 26th February it was clear that our pressure had caused Rommel to break off his attack against the Americans'.[28] Certainly the threat posed by the Eighth Army's presence in his rear, coupled with stronger American resistance on their front, was enough to make Rommel rethink his strategy.[29] On 6 March he launched a major attack with three Panzer divisions against Monty's leading Corps at Medenine, fifty miles south-east of Gabes.

The most serious consequence of the Sidi-Bou-Zid and Kasserine debacles was the damage done to the reputation of the US Army in North Africa. Alexander, by then Deputy C-in-C Mediterranean and commander of the Anglo/American 18th Army Group[30], wrote to the CIGS on 3 April: 'If this handful of Divisions here[31] are their best, the value of the remainder must be imagined';[32] and even more forcibly later:

> They simply do not know their job as soldiers and this is the case from the highest to the lowest, from general to the private soldier. Perhaps the weakest link of all is the junior leader, who just does not lead, with the result that their men don't really fight.[33]

Monty was more generous:

> It was the old story; lack of proper training allied to no experience of war, and linked with too high a standard of living. They were going through their early days, just as we had had to go through ours. We had been at war a long time and our mistakes lay mostly behind us.[34]

After reading Harmon's damning after-action report[35] and hearing similar criticisms from Alexander, Eisenhower decided to sack Fredendall and offer II Corps to Harmon. However, he refused on the grounds that having recommended that Fredendall should be sacked, it was morally impossible for him to take over. As we have heard, Ike immediately decided to bring in George Patton to do the job.

Patton arrived at II Corps Headquarters at 1000 hours on 6 March – the day Rommel attacked Monty's men at Medenine. Our prima donnas were in the same theatre of operations, little more than 100 miles away from each other and engaged against the same enemy.

Georgie was appalled by what he found: 'No salutes. Any sort of clothes and general hell.'[36] It was obvious that morale was low after the Kasserine Pass disaster and he knew he had little time to put things right before his Corps would have to attack in support of a major offensive by Monty to break through the German defences on the Mareth Line. Since re-training the Corps in the time available, ten days, was out of the question, he decided the only thing he could do was to tighten up on discipline and try to inspire some leadership qualities in his officers.

Patton was surprised to find Major General Omar Bradley already in II Corps Headquarters as Eisenhower's 'personal observer'. Fredendall had not taken to his arrival kindly and Georgie was no less pleased to find he had a 'spy' in his camp. He quickly arranged with Ike's Chief of Staff for Bradley to become his subordinate as Deputy Corps commander.

Patton's 'blitz' on II Corps took the usual forms – strict uniform regulations, including the wearing of ties and no rolled up shirt sleeves, the proper wearing of steel helmets, correct saluting, etc. – all these measures enforced by heavy fines. But Georgie went much further. As well as haranguing his officers and soldiers, he closed the Corps mess at 0600 hours in the morning, told all officers to wear their rank on the front of their helmets, even though it made them a more conspicuous target, and generally made life less comfortable for everyone. 'These Patton reforms promptly stamped his personality upon the Corps. And while they did little to increase his popularity, they left no doubt in anyone's mind that Patton was to be the boss.'[37]

Patton had not been in a good mood when he arrived at II Corps. He had been expecting to command the American Western Task Force in the forthcoming invasion of Sicily and now he found himself a Corps commander again and under *British* command; in addition, he was desperately worried about his son-in-law, Lieutenant Colonel John Waters, who had been reported as missing in action after the fighting at Sidi-Bou-Zid. It would be several weeks before he was listed as a prisoner of war (PW). These factors may explain to some extent his occasional outrageous behaviour at this time. Certainly it shocked Bradley, who wrote after the war:

Whenever he addressed men he lapsed into violent, obscene language. He always talked down to his troops . . . His language was studded with profanity and obscenity. I was shocked . . . Yet when Patton was hosting at the dinner table, his conversation was erudite and he was well-read, intellectual and cultured. Patton was two persons: a Jekyll and Hyde.[38]

Other examples of Patton's extraordinary behaviour at this time included driving around in a heavily escorted command car with sirens screaming and his general's two-star and the II Corps flags flying and having a half-track with a 50-calibre machine gun standing guard outside his sleeping quarters.

On 12 March Georgie learned that he had been promoted to the rank of lieutenant general. To his surprise and delight his ADC, Dick Jenson, produced two sets of three silver stars and a three-star flag he had been carrying in anticipation of just such an event. That night Patton wrote in his diary: 'Now I want, and will get, four stars'.

II Corps resumed operations under its new commander on 17 March. Five weeks later, with the situation in Tunisia much improved, Patton handed over command to Omar Bradley and returned to Morocco to train the American component for the invasion of Sicily. His short period with II Corps is significant for his defiance of orders, confrontations with Allies and very questionable behaviour with some of his officers. This latter point was later emphasised by Omar Bradley who claimed that Patton's style of command was often demeaning and controversially, that he was unpopular with his subordinates. But let us take each of these allegations in turn – first, his defiance of orders.

It had been made very clear to Patton that II Corps' role in the offensive against the Fifth Panzer Army was both secondary and diversionary. With three infantry and a single armoured Division,[39] two British reconnaissance squadrons (companies)[40] and a total strength of just over 88,000 men, its mission was to attack von Arnim's flank and divert his attention and reserves away from Montgomery's Eighth Army push along the coastal plain through the Mareth Line towards Gabes. To this end Patton was initially under strict instructions not to advance beyond the range of mountains known as the Tunisian Eastern Dorsal; this ran from Fondouk, through Faid and Maknassy, to El Guettar.[41] In spite of this directive, Patton resolved to launch an offensive of his own. He would pay lip service to Alexander's Directive by feinting towards Fondouk and Faid with two infantry Divisions,[42] while his main thrust would be made to the south-east by his 1st Armored Division with an additional infantry Regiment. It would, in accordance with Alexander's Directive, recapture the area south of the Kasserine Pass, secure forward airfields for the RAF and then take Gafsa which was to become a forward logistic base for the

Eighth Army; his remaining infantry Division[43] would then move on through El Guettar to Gabes on the coast – thus cutting off the Axis forces opposing Montgomery's advance.

In the event, and despite torrential rain and appalling ground conditions, the first part of II Corps' advance went well. Gafsa was found to be 'free of defenders',[44] El Guettar was occupied on the 18th and the 1st Armored Division reached Maknassy on the 22nd. The most serious fighting came the following day when a sizeable proportion of the German 10th Panzer Division[45] launched two heavy counter-attacks along the Gabes–Gafsa road to the east of El Guettar. Despite some initial German successes which caused heavy American casualties, the re-inforced 1st Infantry Division eventually beat off these attacks. This did wonders for American morale: 'By WWII standards the Battle of El Guettar was a minor engagement, but for the US Army it was a significant victory',[46] and in fact this 'minor engagement' was a great help to the British advance. As Monty put it later, the American action: 'assisted our [Eighth Army] operations above all by containing 10 Panzer Division'.[47] Be that as it may, Patton's attempt, begun on 30 March, to push on to Gabes and cut the link between Rommel's German–Italian Panzer Army and von Arnim's Fifth Panzer Army, although eventually authorized and indeed ordered by Alexander, failed. The 1st Armored Division Task Force, sent forward by Patton and commanded by one of his WWI compatriots, was simply not strong enough. After three days' fighting it had made little progress and it was clear that II Corps had been brought to a halt on the line of the Eastern Dorsal. Subsequent pleas by Alexander for it to advance again to cut off von Arnim's troops retreating as a result of Monty's victory at Wadi Akarit on 6 April, were apparently rejected. Whether this was due to a failure of communications or because of the very infantry casualties already sustained is unclear. Whatever the reason it resulted in Roosevelt expressing his disappointment to Eisenhower that Georgie's II Corps had not only failed to break out from the Eastern Dorsal, but that it had not even reached a position where it could shell the retreating Axis forces. General Marshall went on to complain that American newspaper reporters were voicing open criticism of American failure in Tunisia. Faulty censorship had:

> allowed stories to go out that attributed specifically and apparently almost exclusively to American units the blame for not securing a more decisive victory over Rommel in the south and cutting him off during his retreat. This has had a most disheartening effect at home and apparently morale is suffering badly.[48]

Patton's first confrontation with the British in Tunisia came on 1 April when he sent a situation report claiming that his forward troops had been continuously bombed all morning and that a total lack of air cover had allowed the German air force to operate almost at will. It could well be that the report was written in anger – Patton's beloved ADC, Captain Dick Jenson, had been killed that morning by a 500-pound bomb dropped by a German bomber and he had unashamedly wept over the body.

Needless to say Patton's report infuriated the Allied Tactical Air Commander, New Zealander Air Vice Marshal Arthur Coningham, who retaliated with a message suggesting that II Corps was not battle-worthy! After an intervention by Air Chief Marshal Sir Arthur Tedder, the commander of Allied Air Forces in the Mediterranean, US Lieutenant General Carl Spaatz and Coningham's American Deputy, Brigadier General Kuter, Coningham visited Patton the following day. The latter received him wearing a polished helmet and his pearl-handled pistols. A shouting match quickly developed with both men banging Patton's desk. Georgie refused to accept an oral apology and Coningham responded by saying that he was proud of his air force and would not have it criticized. In the end Coningham climbed down and agreed to send a message to all the original recipients of the report retracting his remark. Georgie had won – although he soon received a letter from Ike admonishing him for his unwise distribution of his original message.

Patton's second confrontation was with British General Sir Harold Alexander who, at a meeting on 11 April, made it clear that II Corps was to be given a secondary role in the forthcoming Allied offensive to take Tunis and Bizerte. He also mentioned that one of his British Corps commanders had reported that the US 34th Infantry Division had been 'no good' when it had been placed temporarily under his command for a specific operation (more details of this will be given in the next chapter). Patton responded with two strong letters: one demanding that his Corps should be given an equal role with the British in the future offensive, and a second demanding that the 34th Division should in future remain under II Corps command in order to prove its worth. Alexander reluctantly agreed. A corollary to this incident is that both Patton and Bradley blamed Eisenhower for failing to restrain the British and for allowing one of their generals to publicly criticize an American Division. Patton wrote in his diary on 11 April: 'God damn all British . . . I will bet that Ike does nothing about it. I would rather be commanded by an Arab. I think less than nothing of Arabs'. And he followed this up a day later with: 'Ike is more British than the British and is putty in their hands. Oh, God, for John J Pershing'.

The last allegation concerns Patton's extraordinary behaviour with his subordinate commanders. Three examples will suffice. The worst was probably his treatment of an old friend, Terry Allen, the commander of the 1st Division. During the fighting at El Guettar Patton appeared at Allen's Headquarters early one morning and to everyone's amazement demanded to know why there were slit trenches surrounding it. When told they were for protection against air attack, he then asked Allen which one was his. When Allen pointed it out Patton went over and urinated in it.

The second example again occurred during the El Guettar battle. Patton arrived unexpectedly at one of the 9th Division's Regimental Head-quarters and found the Divisional commander, Major General Manton Eddy, conferring there with the Regimental commander. He immediately tongue-lashed Eddy for not being forward with his troops. Eddy later recalled that in the whole of his career he had never been talked to as Patton talked to him that morning. The third example was similar. During the attempt to break through at Maknassy, Omar Bradley recalled that Patton told the commander of the 1st Armored Division, Major General Orlando Ward, to: 'Get off your ass; get a pistol in your hand, and lead that attack yourself'. Georgie recorded in his diary: 'Now my conscience hurts me for I fear I have ordered him to his death, but I feel it is my duty'.[49] In the event the attack failed, Patton decorated Ward with a Silver Star and then, twelve days later, he sacked him.[50] In fairness to Patton, however, it has to be pointed out that Ward was the only divisional commander he sacked in the whole of WWII.

Before Patton left Tunisia he laid flowers on the grave of his ADC, Dick Jenson, in the military cemetery at Gafsa. He had just received a letter from his widow in which she said: 'You gave him the happiest years of his life'.[51] Patton had been in Tunisia for forty-three days. His command of II Corps had not been as glorious as he might have hoped, but one way or another he had left an indelible impression on his men. His diary entry for 17 April records that he had: 'fought several successful battles, com-manded 95,800 men [an exaggeration], lost about ten pounds, gained a third star and a hell of a lot of poise and confidence'. Three weeks after Patton left Tunisia the war in North Africa ended.

NOTES

1   11 British Infantry (Inf) Brigade (Bde), part of 78 Inf Division (Div) & combat teams from 34 US Inf Div.
2   3rd Battalion (Bn) of the 135th Inf Regiment (Regt) landing from HMS *Broke* and *Malcolm*.
3   Patton, *War As I Knew It*, p. 5.
4   Ibid, p. 6.
5   Ibid.
6   Ibid, p. 7.
7   Patton's personal Diary, 9 Nov 42.
8   Patton, op. cit., p. 7.
9   Ibid, pp. 7–10.
10   D'Este, *A Genius for War*, p. 439.
11   Patton, op. cit., pp. 15–16.

12 D'Este, op. cit., p. 443.
13 Ibid, p. 454.
14 Diary, 17 Nov 42.
15 At this time V Corps comprised only one Div (the 78th Inf), but in Dec it was reinforced with the 6th Armd Div.
16 Alanbrooke Diary, Liddell Hart Centre, King's College, London.
17 Diary, 28 Jan 43.
18 Ibid.
19 Letter to Brooke dated 15 Feb 43.
20 Diary, 5 Mar 43.
21 78 Inf Div with 11 & 36 Bdes & Blade Force comprising a tank bn, a motorized inf company (coy), an artillery battery (bty), some armoured cars & 1st Parachute (Para) Bn.
22 1 Guards Bde.
23 6 Armd Div.
24 Ray, *Algiers to Austria*, p. 30.
25 D'Este, op. cit., p. 458.
26 D'Este, *Eisenhower Allied Supreme Commander*, p. 396.
27 Ibid.
28 Montgomery, *Memoirs*, p. 158.
29 Rommel was appointed C-in-C Army Group Afrika on 23 Feb 43. As such he took von Arnim's Fifth Panzer Army under command.
30 18th Army Group comprised First British Army (Anderson), Eighth British Army (Montgomery) & Fifth US Army (Clark).
31 1st Armd & 1st, 9th & 34th Inf Divs.
32 Alanbrooke Papers, Liddell Hart Centre, King's College, London.
33 Nicolson, *Alex*, p. 211.
34 Montgomery, op. cit., p. 158.
35 According to Patton's diary dated 2 Mar 43, Ernie Harmon described Fredendall as a moral and physical coward.
36 Letter to Beatrice dated 13 Mar 43.
37 Bradley, *A Soldier's Story*, pp. 44–5.
38 Ibid.
39 1 Armd, 1, 9 & 34 Inf Divs.
40 Derbyshire Yeomanry – II Corps AAR dated 10 Apr 43.
41 First Army Letter of Instruction dated 2 Mar 43.
42 9 & 34 Inf Divs.
43 1st Inf Div.
44 Howe, *Northwest Africa: Seizing the Initiative in the West*, p. 548.
45 Two Pz (Panzer) & two Pz-Gren (Grenadier) Bns with support from motorcycle & arty Bns.
46 D'Este, op. cit., p. 475.
47 Montgomery, *El Alamein to the River Sangro*, p. 58.
48 Diary of Harry C Butcher, Naval Aide to Eisenhower, dated 16 Apr 43.
49 Diary, 24 Mar 43.
50 He was replaced by Harmon.
51 Letter dated 16 Apr 43. Jenson had been his ADC since early 1941.

CHAPTER XIII
Montgomery – El Alamein to Tunis

(Map 5)

The victory at El Alamein made Monty a national hero and he followed it with an extraordinary advance of some 1,850 miles that culminated in the total destruction of the Axis forces in North Africa. Egypt was freed in a week, Libya in three months and Tunisia, admittedly with vital help from Anderson's First Army, in six months – a remarkable achievement by any standards. Yet still, soon after the end of WWII, critics took up their pens and with the benefit of hindsight, pointed out what they considered to be the errors and omissions in Monty's plans and in the way he exercised command. They accused him of excess caution, sluggishness, failing to exploit his advantages, failing to listen to his subordinates, isolating himself from his staff, and of becoming increasingly dictatorial and conceited. Their task was of course a relatively easy one, carried out as it was in the comfort of their homes and with access to the full records of the fighting – not for them the stresses and dangers or the confusion of battle experienced by the subject of their criticisms. Some of the points raised by Monty's critics are of course completely valid and to some extent he brought many of them upon himself by his arrogance and conceit; nevertheless, it should never be forgotten that Montgomery and the men of the Eighth Army delivered the British Empire's first great land victory in WWII.

From the purposes of this book it is unnecessary to go into the particulars of the seven major battles fought between El Alamein and Tunis – El Agheila, Buerat, Medenine, Mareth, El Hamma, Wadi Akarit and Enfidaville – a plethora of excellent books are available for readers interested in the details.[1] Instead, this author will attempt to paint a picture of Monty, as a man as well as a general, during this campaign.

The Pursuit

Montgomery's experiences in WWI made him cautious by nature and it follows that throughout his later career he favoured a step-by-step approach to any problem and a series of carefully prepared set-piece battles, fought after a careful logistical build-up, rather than the 'Blitzkrieg' type operations so favoured by the Germans – and indeed George Patton! It has to be remembered that he had no direct experience in the handling of armour and no experience of 'the pursuit'; quite the opposite in fact, and so it is hardly surprising that his first aim was not the immediate and complete destruction of Rommel's forces, but rather the capture of the El Agheila position over 800 miles from Alamein, where he calculated he would face his first serious opposition. Monty knew that Rommel's forces had been severely weakened, but he was determined to avoid the mistakes of his predecessors, and he was certainly not going to allow himself to be caught off-balance, being counter-attacked by Rommel and being forced back to where he had started. He wrote later:

> As we approached El Agheila I sensed a feeling of depression, particularly among some of those officers who had participated in our previous offensives and withdrawals; I did not feel depressed at the prospect myself.[2]

Monty admitted later that he: 'kept a firm hand on the battle [pursuit to Agheila] in order to ensure the master plan was not "mucked about" by subordinate commanders having ideas inconsistent with it'. He went on to claim that 'Rommel's forces were saved from disaster' on 6 and 7 November because three Divisions were 'bogged in the desert, unable to move, and it was not possible even to get petrol to them', and again on the 15th, 16th and 17th because of very heavy rain.[3] But the causes of the relatively slow follow-up after Alamein were more complicated: the lack of thrust and professionalism shown by some of his most senior commanders and a general inexperience in the 'pursuit', 'advance to contact' and 'encounter battle' phases of war, led to a chaotic situation, compounded by logistical failures and an almost total lack of traffic control.

From Alamein onwards Monty commanded from a 'Tactical Headquarters' (Tac HQ), leaving his Chief of Staff, Freddie de Guingand, to run his 'Main Headquarters' where the bulk of his operational staff were located, and a 'Rear Headquarters' where his logistical staff were to be found. This system was new to the British Army and may well have led to some of his initial problems. Tac HQ consisted of some thirty to forty vehicles including a close protection troop (platoon) of cavalry, three caravans, and an armoured command vehicle manned by three operational staff officers and a signals officer. By this time Monty had two ADCs with him – John Poston and a new officer, Johnny Henderson, who had joined him just after the breakout from Alamein. Of the three caravans, Monty used one as his sleeping quarters, another as his map room and the third for guests. From the armoured command vehicle he could communicate, in theory at least, with de Guingand at Main Headquarters, at least one of his Corps Headquarters, and sometimes Air Marshal Coningham, the Desert Air Force commander. There is no doubt that by locating himself basically at Tac HQ, Monty intended to disentangle himself from the detailed running of his Army and get physically closer to his senior commanders. This commendable desire to be well forward, as exemplified by Rommel of course, led almost at once to two surprising and potentially dangerous situations:

> A reconnaissance party was sent forward to select a site for my head-quarters in the Mersa Matruh area ... The party took a road leading down to a place on the shore called Smugglers Cove ... [and] was captured.[4] I myself with a small escort was moving well forward in rear of the leading echelons of the Army ... [when] I ran into a sharp engagement which was going on a few hundred yards in front; we had bumped into an enemy rearguard which was trying to hold us off while they cleared Mersa Matruh ... If I had gone down the road to Smugglers Cove, it is possible I would have run into the enemy; if so, I'm pretty clear that I wouldn't be writing this book today.[5]

Later on that same day, 7 November, his Tac HQ actually set up *ahead* of the leading Corps and Divisional Headquarters[6] and: 'was now the leading HQ in Eighth Army'.[7]

Monty put on a great show of being pleased with the way the advance from Alamein to the western Egyptian border had progressed. On 12 November he issued a message to his Army which included the words:

> In three weeks we have completely smashed the German and Italian Army, and pushed the fleeing remnants out of Egypt, having advanced ourselves nearly 300 miles up to and beyond the frontier ... There is some good hunting to be had farther to the West, in Libya; and our leading troops are now in Libya ready to begin.[8]

But the reality was very different. He knew that Rommel still had a large force to be reckoned with and he was far from pleased with the way the initial advance had gone; so much so that he sacked the commanders of X Corps (Lumsden) and the 10th Armoured Division (Gatehouse).

A major and immediate requirement at this time was to seize the airfields south of Derna; these were needed, not just to give air cover for a further advance, but to provide protection for a convoy due to sail on 16 November from Alexandria to Malta. The island fortress was in dire straits from food and fuel shortages. Fortunately Rommel's rapid withdrawal saw this requirement met on 15 November. Then, while a small element of the Eighth Army crossed the desert towards El Agheila to act as a threat and hasten the enemy out of Benghazi, the bulk of the Army followed the coast road, taking Benghazi on the 20th, Agedabia on the 23rd and reaching El Agheila a day later. Over 800 miles had been covered in just over a month – and this in spite of major administrative difficulties such as refuelling and the forward repair of heavily used equipment. The German retreat has been described as: 'the longest and most precipitate retreat in German military history'.[9] Axis casualties between 23 October and 23 November were calculated as 61,000 men killed, wounded, missing or captured, 536 tanks, 720 anti-tank guns and 430 artillery pieces.[10] And yet Monty was still criticized for not sending a much stronger armoured force across the desert with the aim of cutting off Rommel's main force in the Benghazi sector. These critics ignore two basic facts: one, immediately following the two-week battle of El Alamein, the Eighth Army was disorganized and suffering from battle-fatigue; and two, Monty, despite his message to his troops on 12 November, was still worried that Rommel might suddenly strike back:

> As we approached the Agheila position I sensed a feeling of anxiety in the ranks of the Eighth Army. Many had been there twice already; and twice Rommel had debouched when he was ready and had driven them back.[11]

After reaching El Agheila Monty therefore halted his Army; firstly, to make sure that it was capable of resisting any German attack, and secondly, in order to build up supplies of petrol, food and ammunition for his own forthcoming attack. The daily air force fuel requirement alone was quite staggering – 1,400 tons – and with the port of Benghazi not yet operational, all supplies still had to be delivered along a single road.

Monty's advance from Agheila to Tripoli has been described as 'pedantic'; despite that, perfectly reasonable explanations for his decisions and actions appear in his book *Memoirs*, written in 1958. After stating that his ultimate objective at this time was Tripoli,[12] he goes on to point out that by 18 November, following the success of the TORCH landings, it was clear to him that whereas his Army had: 'The long sea route via the Cape to Egypt, a small railway terminating at Tobruk, the indifferent port of Benghazi, and the 760 miles of road from Benghazi to Tripoli', Eisenhower's forces in Tunisia had: 'a short sea route to the ports of N. Africa; and . . . a good railway and road system which stretches nearly to the Tripolitanian border'. Therefore 'from the communication point of view alone', and in view of the fact that Eisenhower was facing, in Monty's view, only minimal opposition, it was obvious that: 'the capture of Tripoli should be undertaken from the *West*' (author's emphasis).[13] Hence his decision not to rush his advance and incur unnecessary casualties.

El Agheila

Ironically, neither Monty nor Rommel wanted a serious battle at El Agheila at the end of November. Rommel had flown back to see Hitler and recommended a total evacuation of North Africa, but after this plea failed he was at least able to persuade Field Marshal Kesselring, C-in-C South, that a phased withdrawal to Buerat, 200 miles east of Tripoli, was the best plan. Monty on the other hand, with his supply lines stretching more than 800 miles all the way back to Alexandria and insufficient combat troops in the forward area, knew that he could not begin the operations against the Agheila position until the beginning of December at the earliest. He decided therefore: 'to attempt bluff and manoeuvre, and to bustle Rommel to such an extent that he might think he would lose his whole force[14] if he stood to fight'.[15]

Monty carried out a detailed reconnaissance of the Agheila area with Lieutenant General Oliver Leese, the commander of XXX Corps, and then after giving him the necessary orders, flew back to Cairo to discuss the future operations of his Army and the problems of its logistical support with his own C-in-C, Harold Alexander. At least one critic has implied that by doing so and by not attacking the Agheila position at once, Monty allowed Rommel to first reorganize and then withdraw his battered forces successfully. Such criticisms ignore the realities of the situation.

Monty 'spent a very pleasant weekend in Cairo . . . staying at the British Embassy'.[16] He wrote to his son's guardians: 'I must say it is rather pleasant to live in a nice house again. And also to have a good bath and proper haircut by a good barber', and he later recalled that his 'appearance at St George's Cathedral for the Sunday evening service, where I read the lessons, created quite a stir. It is a strange experience to find oneself famous and it would be ridiculous to deny that it was rather fun'.[17] In fact it must have been a very busy weekend for as well as meeting Alexander, Monty visited his Chief of Staff, Freddie de Guingand, who had been evacuated to hospital suffering from a gallstone, and had even persuaded the doctors to agree to a three-week convalescence instead of their preferred three months, and then to follow Alexander's example and have his portrait painted by the South African Official War Artist, Neville Lewis. During the two-hour sitting, Lewis showed Monty a photograph of himself painting Field Marshal Smuts; this caused Monty to send an immediate signal to his Headquarters demanding the attendance of the commander of his Army Film and Photographic Unit, Captain Geoffrey Keating. The following day Keating duly photographed Monty having his portrait painted and, according to Lewis, a copy was sent to the United States by wireless with a caption saying: 'Desert Rat takes time off from chasing Desert Fox to sit for his portrait'. By now Monty was becoming very aware of the value of PR (Public Relations) and he was using it quite ruthlessly to gain publicity for both himself and the Eighth Army – much to the irritation of more conservative senior officers in Cairo and at home. But Monty had no worries about that; he gave express orders that Keating and the editor of the two Eighth Army newspapers,[18] Captain Warwick Carlton, both of whom were the major agents for this publicity, were not to be moved from their present positions without his express authority. And the soldiers of the Eighth Army? At last they had found themselves members of a victorious Army, famous at home and even in America, and they revelled in the glory.

On his return to his Headquarters just east of Benghazi, Monty learned that the 'bluff' part of his plan had worked. Rommel, unnecessarily nervous in view of Monty's relative weakness, was already splitting his force by ferrying his immobile Italian troops back to a better defensive position at Buerat. Monty therefore immediately brought forward the start of a long outflanking move by two days to 11 December and his main frontal attack to the 14th. Again the details of the battle of Agheila need not concern us. Suffice it to say that by the night of the 16th it was all over. As already mentioned, Rommel had no intention of fighting an all-out battle at Agheila and when he found himself being outflanked by armour[19] and General Freyberg's New Zealand Division, he ordered the bulk of his forces to pull back. Long afterwards the commander of XXX Corps, Oliver Leese, wrote:

> It was sad to see Rommel get away, but in my opinion it was firstly too big a risk to forfeit our firm base at Agedabia by sending *all* our tanks on with the New Zealanders and secondly I don't think we could have brought up sufficient ammunition and petrol to supply a large force of tanks by the time Rommel started to withdraw. Finally I am very doubtful whether even a larger force of tanks at General Freyberg's disposal could have stopped the Panzer Corps breaking out by night on the open desert ground.[20]

Certainly Monty was not disappointed with the results. He wrote two letters on 18 December; the first to Brooke: 'We turned the enemy out of a very strong position by aggressive tactics ... he got a very severe mauling'.[21] And the second to Freddie de Guingand in hospital in Cairo: 'I have had a look at the famous Agheila position. It is immensely strong and we have been saved considerable casualties by not having to attack it seriously; it was a complete mass of mines'. With that he moved his Tac HQ forward to be near his leading Corps Headquarters, where he was: 'well placed to direct the reconnaissance of the Buerat position and to draw up the plan for the advance to Tripoli'.[22]

Tripoli

By mid-December Monty had decided that:

> the Eighth Army needed a halt during which it could pull itself together and get ready for the final 'jump' to Tripoli ... I ordered that

... no offensive operations would take place until after Christmas ... and we would spend that day in the happiest way that conditions in the desert allowed. It was very cold. Turkeys, plum puddings, beer, were all ordered up from Egypt ... I decided to attack [to break through to Tripoli] on the 15th of January.[23]

But the problem was not so much that the Army needed to 'pull itself together'; it was much more one of logistics.

The problem is petrol. I require 1,200 tons of petrol delivered daily by sea into Benghazi. At present this is not being done and I am having to move 800 tons daily by road from Tobruk [800 miles].[24]

The logistic problem was severely aggravated on 4 January when very heavy gales created havoc and destruction in Benghazi. By the 12th its capacity had fallen from 3,000 tons per day to 400 tons. Monty had no option other than to 'ground' the three Divisions of his X Corps and use its transport to bring forward the shortfall in petrol and supplies from Tobruk (800 miles away) and Benghazi (300 miles away). On 28 December he wrote to the CIGS:

I am getting on with my preparations and am making forward dumps of petrol, supplies and so on. I shall have completed these by 14 January ... I am building up my tank strength and will have over 400 for the party [advance to Tripoli] ... Once I get to Tripoli I will not be able to operate west of that place and towards Tunisia until the port of Tripoli is working well ... I cannot operate west of Tripoli with my base 800 miles away at Benghazi and only one road!

As an aside and on a more personal note, Monty took advantage of this lull in the campaign to fly Neville Lewis forward to his Headquarters for more portrait sessions. A second official war picture on behalf of the South African Government was painted showing him in a plain jersey, with no badges of rank but wearing his Australian hat with its many badges, and then Lewis painted a second one, commissioned for Monty's son David, showing him wearing his Royal Tank Regiment beret. The artist offered it to him for nothing but Monty insisted on giving him a cheque for £100. The painting was eventually taken back to England by Winston Churchill after his visit to the Eighth Army the following February. Amazingly, Monty wrote to his son's guardians instructing them very firmly that only David was to have the portrait – they must never let any other member of the family, including his mother, have it.

Various critics, at the time and in later years, have described Montgomery's plans for the advance to Tripoli as ponderous. They belittle

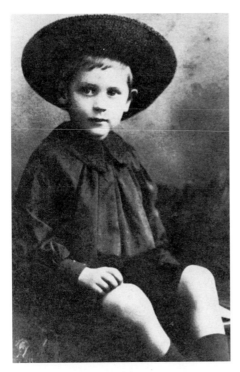

1. Montgomery, aged four.

2. Patton, aged five.

3. Montgomery, aged 18.

4. Patton aged 18 at the Virginia Military Institute.

5. Montgomery, aged 27, with DSO medal ribbon.

6. Patton, aged 32, with Renault tank in France, 1918.

7. Montgomery's wife, Betty, and son, David, in 1936.

8. Beatrice, 'Little Bee' and Patton in 1915.

9. Lieutenant General Montgomery, commanding XII Corps, with Churchill in 1941.

10. Major General Patton, commanding the 2nd Armored Division, in Louisiana in 1941.

11. Ike promotes Patton to be a 3-star general in Tunisia, March 1943.

12. Montgomery before the battle for Tripoli, 15 January 1943.

13. Patton at Gela, Sicily, 12 July 1943.

14. Montgomery and Patton meet in Sicily, 25 August 1943.

15. Patton, Eisenhower and Montgomery at the latter's HQ in Sicily, 29 August 1943.

16. Patton apologising to the 1st Infantry Division, 27 August 1943.

17. Montgomery on leave in the UK with his son David and Major and Mrs Reynolds, David's guardians.

18. Montgomery with men of the SAS Brigade, April 1944.

19. Patton with American troops in the UK before D-Day.

20. Montgomery, with 'Hitler' and 'Rommel'.

21. Patton with 'Willie'.

22. Allied Supreme Command for D-Day. Seated left to right: Tedder, Eisenhower, Montgomery. Standing left to right: Bradley, Ramsay, Leigh-Mallory and Bedell-Smith.

23. Montgomery's first press conference in Normandy, 11 June 1944.

24. Montgomery decorates Major General Maxwell Taylor, commander 101st Airborne Division, 12 June 1944.

25. Patton at a press conference in Normandy, August 1944.

26. Patton on the move in the Ardennes.

27. Bradley, Eisenhower and Patton in Bastogne, February 1945.

28. Montgomery, 'Lightning Joe' Collins (left) and Matt Ridgway in the Ardennes, January 1945.

29. Montgomery at Schloss Ostenfelde, Germany, June 1945.

30. Patton rides 'Favory Africa', the Lipizzaner stallion Hitler had chosen as a gift for Emperor Hirohito of Japan.

31. Patton and Jimmy Doolittle at a press conference in Los Angeles, June 1945.

32. Patton in grim mood with his sister Nita (centre) in Los Angeles in the summer of 1945.

33. Patton hands over command of Third Army to Lucian K Truscott, 7 October 1945.

34. Last known photograph of Patton and Ike, 15 October 1945.

35. Montgomery with Stalin, 10 January 1947.

36. Monty greeting Ike, the first Supreme Commander of NATO, in Paris on 7 January 1951.

37. Montgomery with his daughter-in-law, May 1953.

38. Montgomery enjoying the evening of his life at Isington Mill.

his supply problems and ignore the fact that in less than ten days his tactics rattled Rommel into abandoning, almost without a fight, his heavily mined defences at Buerat, and prevented him from preparing a proper defence on the very defensible Tarhuna–Homs line, 200 miles farther to the west and only fifty miles from Tripoli. The fact that Monty did this with only one Corps (XXX), rather then the two he had planned for (XXX and X), is also often ignored by these critics. In fairness however, it has to be pointed out that Rommel's heart was no longer in the fight – by the end of 1942 he was convinced that Tripoli was of little further value and that the Axis forces in Tunisia and Tripolitania should be united under one command.

At 0400 hours on 23 January, after an advance of 1,200 miles and three months to the day since Alamein, the 'Desert Rats' entered Tripoli. Once again the details of this final advance to Tripoli need not concern us – except to mention that in order to ensure that his breakthrough at Buerat was followed up with a proper pursuit, Monty decided to command the centre and right wings of the attack himself, whilst Oliver Leese commanded those on the outflanking left wing. He did this most effectively from his Tac HQ; as Rommel put it: 'The British commander was now conducting his operation far more energetically than he had done in the past'.

From his pre-war experiences in the Middle East, Monty knew the potential dangers of a city like Tripoli and he determined that his Army would 'retain its toughness and efficiency'. With this in mind he therefore forbade:

> the use of houses, buildings, etc., for headquarters and troops; all would live in the fields and in the desert . . . Having given these orders . . . I drove into the city with Leese and we sat in the sun on the sea front and ate our sandwich lunch . . . Our ADCs and police escort sat not far away, also having lunch. I asked Leese what he thought they were talking about after many months of monastic life in the desert; he reckoned they were speculating on whether there were any suitable ladies in the city . . . I decided to get the Army away from Tripoli as early as possible.[25]

Eleven days after Tripoli fell to the Eighth Army the first re-supply ship entered the harbour and Winston Churchill and the CIGS flew in to stay with Monty. The following day he put on a triumphal Victory Parade for the Prime Minister, complete with flanking tanks and anti-tank guns, a march-past by the Highland Division, a review of the New Zealand Division, visits to XXX Corps artillery and engineer units, an inspection of the Desert Air Force at the local airfield and a tour of the harbour.

I showed him soldiers that I do not believe you would see in any other Army in the world; magnificent fighting men from all over the world; the parade and march past in the main square of Tripoli was a wonderful sight; the PM was deeply moved . . . The morale is right up on the top line and the sick rate is 1 man per 1,000 per day; you cannot want anything better than this.[26]

Medenine

(Map 7)

Readers will recall that in mid-February, as part of the Casablanca agreement, Monty's Eighth Army was placed under the overall command of the C-in-C North Africa – Dwight D Eisenhower. Along with Anderson's First Army and Mark Clark's Fifth, it became part of British General Sir Harold Alexander's 18th Army Group. They will also recall that following his success against the Americans at Sidi-Bou-Zid and the Kasserine Pass, Rommel pulled back and regrouped for an attack against the Eighth Army. This was launched with three Panzer Divisions on 6 March at Medenine, twenty miles south-east of Mareth.

'After Rommel had pulled out from the First Army front I thought it likely it would be my turn to be attacked next: and it was' – so wrote Monty in his *Memoirs*.[27] He 'was not very strong on the ground at the time', still having only XXX Corps available, but he had been building up his strength for an assault on the Mareth Line, timed for 19 March.

Described as 'perhaps the best executed brief defensive battle of WWII',[28] Monty: 'fought the battle the same way as I had at Alam Halfa . . . I refused to move to counter any of his thrusts. I refused to follow up when Rommel withdrew'.[29] The Germans lost fifty-two tanks out of 160; the British lost none and suffered only 130 casualties. Three days later, Rommel, already a sick man, left Tunisia, never to return.

Mareth

On 20 March Monty issued another message to his soldiers telling them that:

In the battle that is now to start, the Eighth Army:
(a) Will destroy the enemy now facing us in the Mareth position.
(b) Will burst through the Gabes Gap.
(c) Will then drive northwards on Sfax, Sousse and finally Tunis.[30]

The Mareth Line fortifications, originally built by the French to protect Tunisia from an invasion by Mussolini's troops, were very strong and well protected by minefields. Monty's tactics for breaching it involved a frontal attack on the eastern or coastal flank, designed to break through, or if that failed to at least draw the enemy reserves to that part of the defensive line; at the same time he would launch a force of 200 tanks and 27,000 men round the western or desert flank, a distance of some 250 miles, with the aim of breaking in behind the Axis defences at Mareth. Monty was convinced that his enemy would be forced to give way on one front or the other. It is interesting that his strategy for the campaign in Normandy in June 1944 followed exactly the same pattern.

Liddell Hart wrote later: 'In many respects, Mareth was his [Monty's] finest battle performance of the war'. Others have described it as misconceived or claimed that he miscalculated. Certainly it is true that by the 23rd, the main frontal assault by Leese's XXX Corps, launched on far too narrow a front and with insufficient forces, had failed with heavy casualties and, as Monty put it himself in his *Memoirs*: 'We lost all our gains. We were back where we had started two days before'. This was the first time since Monty had taken command that elements of the Eighth Army had been forced to retreat and some members of his staff began to worry. But, in his *Memoirs*, Monty went on to point out that:

> By 9 a.m. on 28th March we were in full possession of the famous Mareth Line, after a battle lasting only one week. Having received a setback on our right, we recovered quickly and knocked the enemy out with a 'left hook'.[31]

This was true. Having been woken up in his Tac HQ by a 'very upset' Leese at 0200 hours on 23 March, Monty decided to close down the XXX attack and ordered Horrocks, with his X Corps Headquarters and his 1st Armoured Division, to take command of the already strong New Zealand 'left hook'.

> The enemy was made to commit his reserves in desperation and piecemeal, as at Alamein; we committed ours in one concentrated blow on a narrow front. The outstanding feature of the battle was the blitz attack [at El Hamma] on the left flank, in daylight, on the afternoon of 26th March ... The enemy was making ready for our usual night attack; instead he was assaulted in the afternoon with great ferocity ... This blitz attack was the most complete example of the close integration of land and air power up to that time.[32]

Needless to say though, Monty sacked the Divisional and Brigade commanders responsible for the failed frontal attack on the Mareth Line![33]

Wadi Akarit

Although the 'blitz attack' against El Hamma was successful and Gabes was reached on 29 March, a further attempt to advance north towards Sfax was soon halted on what many strategists have called 'the best natural defensive position in North Africa' – the Wadi Akarit. As described in the last chapter, the attempt by George Patton's II US Corps to cut off the Axis forces by breaking through to the coast at Gabes had also come to naught, and Monty was now faced with another major battle. This time, however, he made sure that his frontal assault was strong enough. On 3 April he signalled to Alexander: 'I am attacking with three infantry Divisions . . . and will pass NZ [New Zealand] Div and 1st Armoured Div through the hole thus made. I will keep the 7th Armoured Div in reserve'. The attack, not surprisingly, was successful. Launched at 0415 hours on 6 April, it took only twenty-four hours for the Wadi Akarit position to fall. Oliver Leese recalled later:

> Large numbers [7,000] of prisoners were taken with their boots off. So complete was our surprise that the 21st and 10th Panzer Divisions, which were operating against the Americans [Patton's II Corps] in the Guettar area, were not able to return in time to intervene.[34]

The Eighth Army's 200-mile advance from the Wadi Akarit to Sousse was completed in six days – Leese's XXX Corps took Sfax on 10 April and Sousse two days later, whilst Horrock's X Corps, moving on the open inland route, reached Kairouan on the 11th. Prior to this the British IX Corps, part of First Army, with the US 34th Infantry Division under command, had been ordered to strike into the rear of the retreating Axis forces from Fondouk; but, according to the British Corps commander, Lieutenant General John Crocker, the US Division failed to take the heights covering the Fondouk Pass and this delayed the advance of the British 6th Armoured Division, so allowing large numbers of Axis forces to get away to the north. This accusation by Crocker about the performance of the US 34th Infantry Division led to the confrontation, mentioned in the last chapter, between Patton and Alexander.

This failure allowed the remaining Axis forces in front of Monty's men to reach the relative security of the hills around Enfidaville (today Enfida), fifty miles south of Tunis. But before we describe the final phases of the war in North Africa, there is an interesting incident which shows a strange side to Monty's character and one that did little to endear him to his American allies. Two months previously, Ike's Chief of Staff, Bedell Smith, had visited Monty in Tripoli and they had discussed how soon the Eighth and First Armies could join up north of Gabes. Monty had claimed that he would be in Sfax by 15 April and Bedell Smith had said that if he could achieve that Eisenhower would give him anything he asked for; whereupon Monty had asked for a B-17 Flying Fortress, complete with crew (to remain on the US payroll); it was to be his personal property until the war ended. Bedell Smith, presumably thinking this was a joke, agreed, but on 10 April Monty claimed his prize and six days later he got it! There is apparently no evidence that this extraordinary act caused Ike any *personal* distress, but it certainly led to consternation in his Headquarters, damaged Anglo/American relations in general and led to Monty being 'properly ticked off by Brooke, the CIGS'.[35] Not that he cared: 'It made me a thoroughly mobile general' he later recalled.

Living as he did at his Tac HQ, Montgomery was surrounded by much younger men, many of whom 'respected him, admired him and perhaps even loved him',[36] and this, coupled with his successes on the battlefield, clearly added to his egotism. Even his Chief of Staff, de Guingand, said later:

> Many of us noticed he became more dictatorial and more un-compromising as time went on; and we felt that this was not only due to the strain of war, but also because he did not live with officers of his own age.[37]

Monty revelled of course in the adulation of his young officers and soldiers. A Private Glaister had written to him on 23 December:

> You have made us proud to belong to the 8th Army . . . on behalf of thousands of us here in Libya – on behalf of this great brotherhood, thank you sincerely . . . God bless you, Sir, and guide you at all times.[38]

Reflecting on this idea of a 'great brotherhood', Monty wrote later:

> We were a 'brotherhood in arms'. We did what we liked. We dressed as we liked. What mattered was success, and to win our battles with a minimum of casualties. I was the head of the brotherhood. I was pretty tough about mistakes and especially mistakes which cost lives; I would allow no departure from the fundamentals of the master plan.[39]

And there were other manifestations of this growing egotism. A film, *Desert Victory* (the story of the battle of Egypt), had been made by the Eighth Army Film Unit, and was being shown, not only in British cinemas, but also in South Africa, Australia, New Zealand, and America – even Stalin had been sent a copy. Little wonder then that this now world-famous soldier could write to his son's guardian: 'You ought to have got more than £6 odd for my Tripoli message, in South Africa it would certainly have fetched £50 . . . They will become very historic in years to come'.[40] Certainly Ike, who had visited Monty just before the Wadi Akarit battle, found him 'unquestionably able, but very conceited.[41] Monty in turn wrote in his diary:

> Eisenhower stayed the night with me. He knows practically nothing about how to make war, and definitely nothing about how to fight battles. He is probably quite good at the political stuff.

It has to said though, that having won four major battles in a single month and advanced another 500 miles, Monty and his Eighth Army had much of which to be proud.

Tunis

Anyone who visits the Tunis area today can see that the open plain immediately to the west of the city was, as Rommel put it later, 'an ideal place for motorized forces to assemble for an attack . . . and consequently represented an "Achilles Heel" for our [Axis] front.' It is hardly surprising then that Monty says in his *Memoirs* that he wrote to Alexander on 10 April and:

> recommended that the First Army should [make the final assault in Tunisia]; the plain west of Tunis was suitable for armour whereas my Army was likely to be faced with difficult and mountainous country at Enfidaville.[42]

However, it is noteworthy that a day later he signalled Alexander to say that he was going to try to 'gate-crash' the enemy position at Enfidaville, and that on the 15th he approved orders for a major attack to go in on the 19th or 20th designed to break through to the north along the narrow coastal plain between the sea and the beginning of the Atlas mountains to the west. In fact Monty believed that a joint offensive by the First and Eighth Armies would result in the enemy being forced to withdraw into the Cape Bon peninsula where his Eighth Army, having broken through from the south, would be well placed to inflict the final blow.

On 16 April Alexander issued a directive that was fully in accordance with Monty's wishes. It ordered First Army to make the final assault on Tunis, with II US Corps taking Bizerte.

Monty, in accordance with this directive, agreed that he would:

> face up now to the Enfidaville position and will make things very unpleasant there for the Bosche about 21 April; that will get him looking my way before First Army goes in on 22 April.[43]

The Eighth Army attack at Enfidaville went in in fact on 19 April and certainly attracted German attention. Von Arnim had to reinforce his Italian troops with three German divisions. Unfortunately the First Army attack on Tunis from the west failed and when Monty returned from a three-day visit to Cairo on the 26th, he found what he described as a 'dog's breakfast'. He had been in Cairo to look at the plans for the invasion of Sicily, Operation HUSKY, which was due to take place in just over two months' time. Unlike George Patton, who was to command the American element in that invasion and who had handed over II US Corps to Bradley so that he could devote himself entirely to the training of the American troops involved, Monty was expected to continue commanding the Eighth Army in Tunisia *and* be responsible for the British part of HUSKY. His plea, made only two days before, that he, his Headquarters and the Eighth Army divisions due to take part in HUSKY should be withdrawn from the Tunisian campaign, had been rejected. The reasons for this highly unsatisfactory state of affairs will be explained in the next chapter.

Monty decided initially that the best way to sort out the 'dog's breakfast' was for his men to attack again at Enfidaville in an attempt to break through towards the Cape Bon peninsula, but when this failed he pleaded with Alexander to come and discuss the crisis with him; at the time he was in bed at his Headquarters at Sousse with tonsillitis and influenza. The latter did so on the 30th and Monty, have given up hope of inflicting the final blow in Tunisia, agreed to transfer an Armoured Division, an Infantry Division, and an Armoured Brigade[44] to First Army. He also sent his Armoured Corps commander, Brian Horrocks, to take over IX Corps from Crocker who had been wounded during the fighting west of Tunis.

At 0300 hours on 6 May the reinforced First Army renewed its attack. Horrocks wrote in his memoirs, *A Full Life*: 'The two infantry divisions punched the initial breach, and at 7.30 a.m. I was able to order the two armoured divisions forward'.[45] In less than thirty-six hours Tunis and Bizerte had been captured and Monty was able to remember with pride:

> The first troops to enter Tunis were those of our own 7th Armoured Division. They had earned this satisfaction. Organized enemy resistance ended on the 12th May, some 248,000 [including about 100,000 Germans] being taken prisoner.[46]

An Allied Victory Parade with 30,000 troops, 14,000 of whom were from Great Britain and its Empire, but with only 'a token number of American GIs of Bradley's II Corps',[47] took place in Tunis on 20 May. Eisenhower, Harold Macmillan (as Churchill's personal representative), Alexander and Anderson headed the reviewing party; Monty had returned to England four days earlier after telling Brooke that: 'I must get home [before HUSKY] for a short rest'.[48] George Patton and Omar Bradley were relegated to a minor stand occupied mainly by French civilians and junior officers. Georgie, in a fury, described the parade as 'a god-damned waste of time', but Bradley was more forceful, feeling that it seemed:

> to give the British overwhelming credit for the victory in Tunisia. For Patton and me the affair merely served to reinforce our belief that Ike was now so pro-British that he was blind to the slight he had paid us and, by extension, the American troops who fought and died in Tunisia'.[49]

American casualties in North Africa were 18,221, including 2,715 killed and 6,528 lost as PWs;[50] British and British Empire casualties from 23 October 1942 to 12 May 1943 totalled 38,090, including 6,230 killed and 10,600 captured,[51] but some 60% of this total were in Anderson's First Army.

NOTES

1 Nigel Hamilton's *Monty: Master of the Battlefield 1942–1944* is strongly recommended.
2 Montgomery, *El Alamein to the River Sangro*, p. 46.
3 Montgomery, *Memoirs*, p. 142.
4 Monty's stepson, Colonel Dick Carver, was a member of the reconnaissance party in question, but he managed to escape and return to British lines a month later.
5 Montgomery, op. cit., p. 142.
6 Lumsden's X Corps & Gatehouse's 10 Armd Div.
7 Monty's diary 7 Nov 42.
8 Montgomery, op. cit., pp. 143–4.
9 Ibid, p. 63.
10 Ibid.
11 Montgomery, op. cit., p. 146.
12 Ibid, p. 140.
13 Letter to Brooke dated 18 Nov 42.
14 Rommel had some 50,000 Axis troops and about thirty-five tanks in the El Agheila position.
15 Montgomery, op. cit., p. 146.
16 Ibid, p. 146.
17 Ibid, p. 147.
18 The daily *Eighth Army News* & weekly *Crusader*.
19 The 4th Light Armd Bde.
20 Hamilton, op. cit., pp. 90–1.
21 The Germans are said to have lost twenty tanks, thirty guns, many vehicles & 500 POWs.
22 Montgomery, op. cit., p. 147.
23 Ibid, p. 148.
24 Monty's diary 25 Dec 42.
25 Montgomery, op. cit., p. 155.

26 Letter to Deputy Director Military Operations, War Office, London, dated 6 Feb 43.
27 Page 158.
28 Hamilton, op. cit., p. 157.
29 Montgomery, op. cit., p. 159.
30 Ibid, p. 161.
31 Ibid, p. 162.
32 Ibid, pp. 162–3. Twenty-two squadrons of ground attack aircraft took part.
33 Maj Gen J Nichols (50 Inf Div) & Brig Beak VC (1st Inf Bde).
34 Hamilton, op. cit., p. 218.
35 Montgomery, op. cit., p. 164.
36 Chalfont, *Montgomery of Alamein*, p. 198.
37 Ibid.
38 Montgomery, op. cit., p. 152.
39 Ibid, pp. 172–3.
40 Letter to Phyllis Reynolds dated 20 Mar 43.
41 Hamilton, op. cit., p. 210.
42 Montgomery, op. cit., p. 164.
43 Letter to Alexander dated 12 Apr 43.
44 7th Armd Div, 4th Indian Inf Div & 201st Guards Armd Bde.
45 4th British (First Army) & 4th Indian (previously Eighth Army) Inf Divs & 6th (First Army) & 7th (previously Eighth Army) Armd Divs.
46 Montgomery, op. cit., p. 165.
47 D'Este, *Eisenhower Allied Supreme Commander*, p. 425.
48 Letter to CIGS dated 13 May 43.
49 Bradley, *A Soldier's Story*, p. 109.
50 D'Este, *A Genius for War*, p. 487.
51 Ellis, *WWII Data Book*.

CHAPTER XIV

Countdown to Sicily

(Maps 6 & 8)

Montgomery

On 16 February 1943 General Alexander told Montgomery that he was to command the British (Eastern) Task Force in the forthcoming invasion of Sicily – Operation HUSKY. On seeing the outline plan Monty signalled back:

> In my opinion the operation planned in London breaks every common sense rule of practical battle fighting and is completely theoretical. It has no hope of success and should be completely recast.[1]

The plan he was complaining about envisaged half a dozen or so dispersed landings by individual brigade groups on the north-western, south-western, southern and south-eastern coasts of Sicily. For a man who was convinced that battles could only be won by a concentration of force at a critical point, this was a recipe for disaster. Four days later Monty repeated his views to the CIGS, adding:

> I have given my views to Alex as to how it ought to be recast . . . I am very sorry for Alex, for there is no doubt he found a real 'dog's breakfast' over the First Army and has had a dreadful time.[2]

This was true. Instead of having the time to supervize the planning of HUSKY, Alexander was spending his whole time trying to sort out the 'dog's breakfast' Anderson's First Army was making of the Tunisian campaign. It therefore fell to Monty, whose Eighth Army was having to provide the formations and units for the British Task Force, to take on the task of turning a thoroughly bad plan into one that had some chance of success. In doing so he made himself highly unpopular and enabled his critics, then and since WWII, to accuse him of seeking to enhance his own interests and those of the Eighth Army at the expense of George Patton and the US Army. The following simple chronology of the events leading up to the invasion of Sicily should allow the reader to make up his own mind about this accusation.

3 April – although Monty had by now been promised an extra Division for his part of HUSKY, the plan still involved dispersed landings. He therefore wrote to Alexander: 'have no intention of doing some of the things they [the planners] suggest'.[3]

5 April – Alexander agreed that the landing craft needed for Monty's extra Division would use those assigned for the American landings on the north-west coasts and that the US landings in the Palermo sector would be postponed until D+5 at the earliest.

9 April – Monty reluctantly accepted the amended plan.

10 April – Ike issued the amended plan for HUSKY.

17 April – Monty wrote to Alexander: 'Crux of the matter is that unless Eighth Army is freed from present battle operations [in Tunisia] and sent back to get down to HUSKY the success of that operation will be in grave danger'.[4]

19 April – Monty met Eisenhower and Alexander in Algiers and put forward the following proposal: The Eighth Army would stay in Tunisia and assist Anderson's First Army, but de Guingand and part of Monty's staff would go back to Cairo to take over the planning of the British part of HUSKY, and he himself would commute between Tunisia and Cairo to supervize the planning. This suggestion was agreed and Monty went

away convinced that he, not Headquarters 18th Army Group, was in charge of the British part of HUSKY.

23 April – Monty flew to Cairo and after seeing the existing plan, wrote to the CIGS:

> They want me to operate in little Brigade Groups all over the place. I refuse . . . We cannot go on in this way. Unless we can get a good and firm plan at once, on which we can all work, *there will be no HUSKY in July*. I hope this is realised at your end.[5]

24 April – Monty sent a cable to Alexander saying that he could now say: 'quite definitely that we require two more divisions, assault loaded and to be landed on D-Day in the Gulf of Gela (on the southern coast of the island) if the invasion of Sicily is to be a success'.

29 April – Alexander convened a conference in Algiers to sort out the problems, but Monty fell ill with influenza and tonsillitis and could not attend; the other attendees decided that they could not approve any amendments to the previously agreed plan unless Monty presented any new proposals himself.

30 April – Alexander flew to see Monty and after agreeing a final strategy for the Tunisian campaign (see previous chapter), he also agreed to an abandonment of the American (George Patton's!) Western Task Force's landings in the west of Sicily in favour of a single concentrated landing in the east. The same day Monty wrote to the CIGS: ' The proper answer is to bring two USA Divisions in to land . . . on the south coast [Gela], and get the aerodromes. And chuck the Palermo landings for the present'. He then went on to suggest a full-scale conference in Algiers on 2 May.

2 May – Monty arrived in Algiers to find that the aircraft bringing Alexander to the conference had been delayed by low cloud and that Ike's Naval and Air Deputies, Cunningham and Tedder, both British, refused to sit down without him. Monty remembered later:

> I went to look for Bedell Smith, Chief of Staff to Eisenhower. He was not in his office and I eventually ran him to ground in the lavatory. So we discussed the problem there and then. He was very upset; he said that for political reasons it was essential to reach a final decision and get on with the job. I said it was far more important to do so for military reasons, and that I could give him the answer to the problem at once; he asked me to do so. I said the American landings up near Palermo should be cancelled and the whole American effort put in on the south coast, astride Gela . . . with the object of securing the air fields that were considered so essential by our air forces. The Eighth Army and the Seventh US Army[6] would then land side by side, giving cohesion to the whole invasion.[7]

Bedell Smith conceded that Monty's idea was the best solution to their problems and immediately convened a staff planning conference – with Monty present! Needless to say Monty's views, forcefully but coherently expressed, won the day and he returned to his Headquarters in Tunisia confident that when the new plan was put to Alexander, as C-in-C 18th Army Group, and then to Ike, as C-in-C North Africa, it would be approved. Later that evening he added a rider: 'Consider proper answer would be to put US Corps under me and let my Army HQ handle the whole operation of the land battle'!

3 May – Alexander signalled Monty: 'Your plan has been approved by C-in-C'. He did not, however, address the proposal that Monty should be the overall commander of the joint invasion force.

5 May – Monty again pressed Alexander: 'Only one commander can run the battle . . . It seems clear that Eighth Army HQ should command and control the whole operation, with 2 US Corps included in Eighth Army'.

6 May – Monty wrote in his diary:

> The proper answer is to let Alexander finish off the Tunisian war, and to cut him right out of HUSKY. With the new plan it is a nice tidy command for one Army HQ, and Eighth Army should run the whole thing . . . I have done my part in the Tunisian war coming 2,000 miles from Egypt. I should now pull out and should run HUSKY.

Ever the realist though, he wrote to Brooke the same day: 'For political reasons I don't think they will agree to 2 US Corps being in my Army; they will insist on a separate American task force. So we will have to make the best of that'.[8]

7 May – At another conference in Algiers, Bedell Smith, on behalf of Ike, ruled that the American contribution to HUSKY was indeed to be a separate expedition. This meant that Alexander would be the overall commander of the invasion force with Monty and Patton commanding their respective Task Forces. Monty wrote in his diary: 'It was something to get that clear, as the organization for command and control can now be worked out'. And a few weeks later he wrote: 'Fighting the Germans is easy; the tiring thing is the way one has to keep one's own show from going off the rails'.

As mentioned in the last chapter, Monty returned to England 'for a short rest' before the opening of Operation HUSKY. He arrived in England on 17 May, having flown home in 'his' Flying Fortress which had 'been fitted up as a very comfortable little study for me, with two armchairs and a table for writing etc'.[9]

In a letter dated 7 May he had made it quite clear that he had no wish to see any of his family except his son David: 'I find the various members of my family are apt to be very trying, and particularly my mother – who is now on the 80 mark ... It will be my one desire to see *none* of them'.[10]

The day after his arrival Monty had tea at Buckingham Palace with the King and Queen and the Princesses Elizabeth and Margaret. That evening he went to the theatre where he was 'completely mobbed by the crowd'[11] and the following day:

> A Thanksgiving Service for the end of the war in Africa was held in St Paul's cathedral on 19 May; I was in London but was not asked to attend. It was explained to me *after the service* that it was desired to keep my presence in England a secret. Yet to my delighted surprise, wherever I went I was followed by crowds. The incident made me realise that if I were pretty popular with a lot of people, I was not too popular in some circles.[12]

On his way back to his Headquarters on 2 June Monty met the CIGS and Churchill in Algiers. From the former he received a few 'home truths'. Recalling the dressing-down he administered, Brooke wrote in his diary:

> He requires a lot of educating to make him see the situation and the war as a whole outside the Eighth Army orbit. A difficult mixture to handle, brilliant commander in action and trainer of men, but liable to commit untold errors, due to lack of tact, lack of appreciation of other people's outlook. It is most distressing that the Americans do not like him, and it will always be a difficult matter to have him fighting in close proximity to them.

And he followed this up with a letter to Monty dated 22 June, in which he wrote:

> If I told you a few home truths I feel confident that you bear no ill will ... I have had to fight several pretty tough battles for your benefit. That is the reason why I am so *very* anxious that you should not do things that lay you open to criticism and seriously detract from your value as a higher commander ... That is why I felt it desirable to bring home to you the importance of your relations with allies and other Services.

Following his 'dressing-down' by the CIGS, Monty met Churchill. His diary entry records that the Prime Minister: 'cross-examined me a good deal about the plan for Sicily. I expressed confidence in our plan ... this was only natural, since it was my plan!'.

On the eve of the invasion of Sicily he wrote in his diary:

> My Army is in tremendous form, the soldiers are very enthusiastic,

and are soberly confident of the issue. So am I myself. But I am under no illusions as to the stern fight that lies ahead.

Patton

Readers will recall that on 17 April, just as Monty was demanding to be relieved of responsibility for the Tunisian campaign, George Patton handed over II US Corps to Omar Bradley and returned to Morocco. His I Armored Corps, now located in Rabat and re-designated the Western Task Force, was the American element of Operation HUSKY. Georgie's experiences in Tunisia had disillusioned him, and what particularly rankled was the fact that all the senior commanders in the upcoming invasion of Sicily, other than Eisenhower, were British – the Allied Naval Forces were commanded by Admiral Sir Andrew Cunningham, the Air Forces by Air Chief Marshal Sir Arthur Tedder and the Land Forces by Harold Alexander. Ike had no authority to replace any of them and the only person he could sack was the commander of the US element of the invasion force – Georgie Patton!

Patton had not been invited to participate in the overall planning of HUSKY and when he saw the final plan on 3 May he was both disappointed and angry. He found that his Task Force, which was similar in size to Monty's,[13] was to play second fiddle to the British. The Americans 'would act as the shield in [Alexander's] left hand while the Eighth Army served as the sword in his right'. It seemed to the Americans that 'Alexander was simply not prepared to entrust the Seventh Army with anything more than a secondary role in the campaign'.[14] Nevertheless Patton controlled his anger in public and when asked by Alexander if he was satisfied with the plan, he allegedly replied: 'General, I don't plan – I only obey orders'.[15] In fact he was devastated. He wrote in his diary:

> The US is getting gypped. Only an act of God or an accident can give us a run for our money. On a study of 'form', especially in the higher command, we are licked. Churchill runs this war . . . I have greater ability than these other people and it comes from . . . a belief – an unshakable belief – in my destiny. The US must win – not as an ally, but as a conqueror.[16]

Back with his own staff, Patton was apparently much more forthright; he allegedly told them: 'This is what you get when your Commander-in-Chief ceases to be an American and becomes an Ally'.[17] If this report is true, it was an extraordinary display of disloyalty to his C-in-C.

Patton met with his own staff and the artillery commander of the 82nd Airborne Division, Brigadier General Maxwell Taylor, on 5 May to plan the American part of HUSKY. In just one hour he set out his concept of operations and then, like Monty, he left his staff to work out the details. It was also during May that Patton appointed a new ADC – Lieutenant Colonel Charles Codman, a distinguished aviator from WWI, a cultured Bostonian and a fluent French speaker. He was to remain with Georgie for the rest of the war.

In the middle of May Patton was thrilled to learn that General Marshall had decided that the American contribution to HUSKY was to be given equal status with the British by upgrading it to 'Army' status. On landing in Sicily the Western Task Force was to be known as the Seventh US Army. Georgie's ambition of commanding a Field Army was to be fulfilled.

The full Western Task Force plan was presented, along with those of the Eastern Task Force and the Naval and Air Forces, to Eisenhower and all the senior Allied commanders on 21 June in Algiers. Patton spoke for only six minutes but was convinced that 'we stole the show'.[18] Monty was not present, being involved first with King George VI's visit to the Eighth Army and then spending his time visiting every unit in his XIII Corps in the Cairo area, and subsequently flying to Tunisia and Malta to see the 78th and 51st Highland Divisions of his XXX Corps and his 1st Airborne Division units. At the end of this round of visits he had therefore 'seen every unit taking part in HUSKY', had 'been seen by all the men, and [had] addressed all the officers'.[19]

Needless to say, George Patton was also busy visiting his units in the run-up to HUSKY. Preceded by motorcycle escorts and usually arriving in a command or staff car with sirens screaming, he too ensured that every man under his command saw him and in most cases heard him.

Patton exuded confidence in front of his staff and soldiers, but behind this facade lurked his life-long obsession with fate and death. Five days before HUSKY he wrote to Beatrice:

> I doubt I will be killed or wounded, but one can never tell. It is all a question of destiny . . . When you get this you will either be a widow or a radio fan, I trust the latter. In any case I love you.

And to his brother-in-law, Frederick Ayer, he wrote on the same day:

> It is not a goodbye [but] if we should not meet again until we get to the other side, I am assured on credible authority that the heavenly foxes are fast, the heavenly hounds keen, the fogbank fences high and soft, and the landings firm.

Monty seems to have had no such misgivings.

Also on 5 July Patton wrote in his diary:

> At no time did Ike wish us luck or say he was back of us – fool . . . I

131

am leading 90,000 men in a desperate attack and eventually it will be over 250,000. If I win I can't be stopped! If I lose I shall be dead.

NOTES

1 Signal dated 13 Mar 43.
2 Letter to Brooke dated 17 Mar 43.
3 Alexander Papers, National Archives, London.
4 Ibid.
5 Letter dated 23 Apr 43.
6 The US 'Western Task Force' was re-designated 'Seventh US Army' on the day of the Sicily landings – 10 Jul 43.
7 Montgomery, *Memoirs*, pp. 177–8.
8 Letter dated 6 May 43.
9 Letter to the Reynolds dated 7 May 43.
10 Ibid.
11 Letter to Phyllis Reynolds dated 18 May 43.
12 Montgomery, op.cit., p. 183.
13 Patton's Task Force comprised three inf divs and one armd div; Monty's had four inf divs, an independent (indep) inf bde & one armd bde.
14 D'Este, *A Genius for War*, p. 513.
15 Ibid, p. 494.
16 Diary dated 22 May 43.
17 D'Este, op. cit., p. 495.
18 Ibid, p. 499.
19 Diary dated 9 Jul 43.

CHAPTER XV

Sicily

(Map 8)

HUSKY was the only operation in WWII in which Monty and Patton participated as equals – they were both Army commanders. It is also noteworthy that the initial assault force, more than eight divisions, was in fact larger than that used in the invasion of Normandy, making HUSKY numerically, in terms of men landed on the beaches and frontage, the largest amphibious operation of WWII.

The basic plan saw Monty's Eastern Task Force of some 115,000 men with four infantry Divisions (including one Canadian Division), an independent Infantry Brigade and a Canadian Armoured Brigade[1] making the main effort, with a landing on a forty-mile front in south-east Sicily from the Pachino Peninsula to Syracuse. Patton's Western Task Force of some 66,000 men with one Armoured and three infantry

Divisions[2] was to land in the Gulf of Gela between Licata and Scoglitti and then move rapidly inland to seize the airfields just north of Gela. Monty and Patton had never met to discuss the overall plan, but they were both clear that the Western Task Force's mission was to protect the Eighth Army's left flank as it made the main thrust towards Messina. The opposition facing the Allied Task Forces totalled ten Italian infantry divisions, of which six were immobile coastal formations, the Hermann Goering Panzer Division and two similarly re-formed Panzer-Grenadier Divisions.[3] Plentiful reinforcements were, however, available from mainland Italy. It is also important to understand the topography of the island – as Monty put it:

> Sicily is very mountainous and [vehicle] movement off the roads and tracks is seldom possible. In the beach areas there was a narrow coastal plain, but behind this the mountains rose steeply . . . It was apparent that the campaign in Sicily was going to depend largely on the domination of main road and track centres.[4]

To fully understand the difficulties facing Monty and Patton one has to go to Sicily, see the ground for yourself and understand the extent to which Mount Etna dominates the north-east third of the island. And even then one has to remember that none of today's highways with their wide surfaces, tunnels and super viaducts existed in 1944. Of the four narrow roads that led north from the landing beaches, only two went all the way to Messina – one running along the eastern coast from Catania and the other turning east after reaching the northern coast. Monty planned from the outset to make his main thrust up the east coast and, as we shall soon learn, it did not take long for Georgie to realise that if he was to reach Messina before Monty he had no choice other than to strike north and then east along the northern coast road, Highway 113.

The 2,760 ships and landing craft carrying the two Task Forces came from as far afield as Scotland, the USA, Algeria, Tunisia, Libya, Egypt and Beirut. They rendezvoused off Malta (Map 5), where Ike, Monty and Admiral Sir Andrew Cunningham had located themselves, and with the help of bad weather, which led the defenders to believe no landings were possible, the American and British troops stormed ashore against virtually no opposition some two hours before dawn on 10 July. Inevitably, many things failed to go exactly according to plan, particularly the airborne operations which had preceded the landings. The US 82nd and British 1st Airborne Divisions suffered very heavy losses due to badly trained pilots, high winds and heavy anti-aircraft fire, both enemy and friendly. Nearly 400 aircraft and 137 gliders were involved. Thirty-six of the gliders landed in the sea, drowning 252 men of the British 1st Air Landing Brigade and only twelve gliders reached their objectives. Some 3,400 US paratroopers, who should have been dropped north-east of Gela, landed over a thousand-square-mile area of south-eastern Sicily; their commander, Brigadier-General Jim Gavin, came down over thenty-five miles from his intended landing site. Nevertheless, Monty's insistence on an over-whelming concentration of ground forces ensured overall success.

Monty was so elated with the success of the landings that at 1030 hours on D-Day he went in person to see Admiral Cunningham to express his 'great appreciation of the work of the Navy' and he followed this up with a letter to Air Chief Marshal Sir Arthur Tedder congratulating him on the fact that 'the Allied Air Forces had definitely won the air battle'. These were generous gestures since both men detested Monty and had vigorously opposed his plan for the invasion – Tedder on the grounds that air cover could not be guaranteed before the capture of the Gela and Comiso airfields, and Cunningham saying that he would not commit the navy without guaranteed air cover. Both had finally given way.

Monty's enthusiasm was translated into firm directives that evening when he signalled both his Corps commanders, Leese of XXX Corps and Dempsey of XIII Corps, to 'operate with great energy' towards Noto and Avola in the first case and Syracuse in the second. He then embarked in the destroyer HMS *Antwerp* and landed on the Pachino Peninsula at 0700 hours the following day. His morale received another boost when he learned that the whole peninsula was secure and that the port of Syracuse had been captured intact. With an arrogance that would have caused problems with anyone other than Alexander, he signalled:

> Everything going well here . . . No need for you to come here unless you wish. Am very busy myself and am developing operations intensively . . . Have no, repeat no, news of American progress . . . if they can . . . hold firm against enemy action from the west I could then swing hard with my right with an easier mind. If they draw enemy attacks on them my swing north will cut off enemy com-pletely.[5]

It was clear that Monty was telling his C-in-C how subsequent operations should be developed and this did not bode well for future relationships between the Seventh and Eighth Armies.

George Patton had embarked in the American Naval Task Force commander's flagship *Monrovia* four days before the landings. He wrote in his diary on 9 July: 'I have the usual shortness of breath I always have before a polo game. I would not change places with anyone I know right now'.

Following the successful American landings Gela was captured by midday. Patton remained aboard the *Monrovia* throughout D-Day, but when the enemy launched a major counter-attack in the Gela sector on the morning of the 11th he could restrain himself no longer and at 0930 hours he disembarked, wading ashore:

> resplendent in an immaculate uniform complete with necktie neatly tucked into his pressed gabardine shirt, knee-length polished black leather boots and his ever-present ivory-handled pistols strapped to his waist.[6]

He arrived at the Ranger Headquarters in Gela just in time to witness a second enemy counter-attack being beaten off. He then went on to see the commander of the 1st Infantry Division, Major General Terry Allen. Needless to say he could not resist interfering and issued orders that the Division was to push inland, ignoring a strong German pocket of resistance to its rear. This was in direct contradiction of the Corps commander's orders. The latter, Omar Bradley, wrote later: 'He countermanded my Corps order to the Div without consulting me in any way. When I spoke to him about it George apologized and said he should not have done that. But George didn't like it'.

Thanks to a British newspaper correspondent who never even went ashore in the first two days of the invasion,[7] the *New York Herald Tribune* and *Los Angeles Evening Herald-Express* carried wildly exaggerated reports of Georgie's first actions in Sicily. 'Patton leaped ashore to head troops at Gela' trumpeted the former, whilst the latter had the headline: 'Patton led Yanks against Nazi tanks in Sicily' and its account read that he: 'leaped into the surf from a landing boat and personally taking command, turned the tide in the fiercest fighting of the invasion of Gela'. Nothing could have been further from the truth. The Rangers, the men of the 1st Infantry Division and the tanks of CCB of the 2nd Armored Division beat off the counter-attacks without any help from Patton. At 1900 hours he was back on the *Monrovia*; that evening he noted in his diary: 'This is the first day in this campaign that I think I earned my pay'.[8]

Patton was not alone in bypassing the normal chain of command and giving orders directly to divisional commanders. Monty went even further. The commander of the 50th Infantry Division recalled that on 12 July:

> I got a message, return at once to your Headquarters, Army commander wants to see you ... Monty explained to me that he was going to drop parachutists ... and that I'd got to get forward as fast as possible to relieve them ... Monty gave these instructions to me, not Dempsey [his Corps commander] ... Usually in an army, the Army commander would give orders to the Corps commander and he would summon the divisional commander. Monty was

determined to impress his personality on the chap who was doing the job. That's the answer![9]

And the commander of the 51st Highland Division later remembered that during the same day Monty had gone even further and given orders directly to one of his Brigade commanders.[10]

12 July was a pivotal day in the relationship between Monty and Patton. At 2200 hours the Eighth Army commander signalled Alexander:

> My battle situation very good . . . Intend now to operate on two axes. XIII Corps on Catania and northwards. XXX Corps on Caltagirone–Enna–Leonforte. Suggest American Div at Comiso might now move westwards to Niscemi and Gela. The maintenance and transport and road situation will not allow two Armies both carrying out extensive offensive operations. Suggest my Army operates offensively northwards to cut the island in two and that the American Army holds defensively . . . facing west.[11]

It is quite clear from the above that Monty, having received no directions of any sort from Alexander as to how future operations should be developed, had decided to take matters into his own hands and do the C-in-C's job for him. In doing so he uncharacteristically split his Army and departed from his normal principle of concentration of force.

A look at the map shows that in fact Monty's proposals made sound military sense – as well as thrusting directly towards Messina, he would, by cutting inland towards Enna, be outflanking the Axis forces facing the Americans north of the Gulf of Gela. But Alexander did nothing and the US 45th Infantry Division continued moving up the Vizzini–Enna road (Highway 124). Monty wrote later in his diary:

> The battle in Sicily required to be gripped firmly from above. I was fighting my own battle and the Seventh American Army was fighting *its* battle; there was no co-ordination by 15th Army Group.[12]

Frustrated by the lack of response from Alexander, Monty again took matters into his own hands and ordered the 51st Highland Division, 23rd Armoured Brigade and the 1st Canadian Infantry Division to move up Highway 124 – right across the path of the advancing 45th US Division!

On 14 July Alexander finally responded to Monty's request and moved the inter-Army boundary – a boundary that had been agreed long before the landings. This resulted in the 45th Division being completely wasted; it was forced to pull back all the way to Gela and then move west to the left flank of the 1st Division!

Omar Bradley, commanding II US Corps, was understandably furious. He recalled later:

> We had a boundary for II Corps which went through Ragusa to the north to Vizzini ... Just before we got there, we got [an] order changing the boundary – switching us off to the north-west and giving that road as boundary to the British including the road ... I was peeved ... They [the new orders] were so obviously wrong and impractical. We should have been able to use that road, even if we would have shifted to the left – used it to move to the left.[13]

In the event Monty's attempt to drive north-west and outflank the enemy in front of the Americans came to nothing – by the time the British, lacking mobility, reached Highway 124 and the sector south of Vizzini, the Germans had brought in armour and were able to hold on. Oliver Leese, the XXX Corps commander, said later that he thought the decision to move the boundary and pull the 45th Division back was a mistake:

> I often think now that it was an unfortunate decision not to hand it [the Caltagirone–Enna road] to the Americans ... They were making much quicker progress than ourselves, largely owing, I believe, to the fact that their vehicles all had four-wheel drive ... We were still inclined to remember the slow American progress in the early stages in Tunisia, and I for one certainly did not realise the immense development in experience and technique which they had made ... I have a feeling that if they could ... [have been allowed to drive] straight up this road [Highway 124], we might have had a chance to end this frustrating campaign sooner.[14]

Monty's thrust towards Catania was also frustrated when the Germans suddenly and dramatically reinforced their defences with a strong parachute force.

But what was the reaction of the commander of the Seventh US Army to these dramatic events? On 12 July Eisenhower had visited Patton who was still on board the *Monrovia*. Ike was in a bad mood and had already sent a signal blaming Patton's command for a tragedy the previous evening when Allied naval forces had shot to pieces an aerial convoy bringing in a Regimental Combat team of the 82nd Airborne Division. Sixty pilots and eighty-one paratroopers had died. Ike demanded an investigation and ordered that action be taken against those responsible. Not content with that, he proceeded to castigate Patton for the inadequacy of his progress reports and, as if that was not bad enough, he left without saying anything positive about the successful landings in the Gulf of Gela.

The following day Patton wrote in his diary: 'Perhaps Ike is looking for an excuse to relieve me . . . If they want a goat, I am it'.

There is no doubt that the confrontation with Ike affected Georgie deeply and it may well have made him reluctant to challenge Alexander's decision to change the inter-Army boundary. Maybe he would have done so if Alexander had come clean with him during a visit on the 13th. By then the latter knew of Monty's suggestion that the boundary should be changed, but he made no mention of it and, unforgivably, Patton was left in the dark for several more hours. He did, however, obtain the C-in-C's agreement to expand his operations to the north-west and take Agrigento, but only provided he continued to protect the Eighth Army's left flank and did not get involved in a major engagement. Patton and the commander of the 3rd Division, Lucian Truscott, agreed that a 'reconnaissance in force' would meet Alexander's requirement.

When Patton learned of the inter-Army boundary change on 14 July he determined that it was time to stop playing second fiddle to the British. This resolution was strengthened even further when on 16 July, he received a message from 15th Army Group instructing him to occupy a defensive line running northwards from Caltanissetta with the aim of protecting Monty's XXX Corps as it swung east towards Leonforte. Patton knew that the Eighth Army's several thrusts were in trouble after encountering strong German resistance and with only relatively weak Italian forces on his front he saw his chance. 'Monty is trying to steal the show and with the assistance of Divine Destiny [Eisenhower] he may do so', he wrote in his diary that evening. The following day he arrived without warning at Alexander's Headquarters in Tunisia and suggested that his Army should advance on two fronts – Bradley's II Corps driving north to Termini, while a Provisional Corps made up of the 2nd Armored, 3rd Infantry and 82nd Airborne Divisions under his Deputy, Major General Geoffrey Keyes, cleared the western part of the island. In fact Georgie's eyes were not set on Termini, but rather on the capital of Sicily – Palermo. Alexander was clearly caught off guard and instead of taking control of his two strong-willed subordinates and ordering Monty to concentrate on holding the Germans in place and Patton to forget western Sicily and instead drive north and then east to Messina to cut off the Axis forces in the north-east of the island, he agreed – and the campaign dragged on for another month.

Although Brigadier General Maxwell Taylor, the artillery commander of the 82nd Airborne Division, described the Provisional Corps' advance into north-western Sicily as: 'a pleasure march, shaking hands with Italians asking, "How's my brother Joe in Brooklyn?" Nicest war I've ever been in!',[15] it was in fact extremely unpleasant for many of the GIs who had to march over 100 miles through very rugged country in stifling heat and swirling dust. Nevertheless, Palermo fell to Truscott's 3rd Infantry

Division on 21 July and his men were greeted by thousands of flag-waving Sicilians.

When Patton himself arrived in Palermo – after modestly allowing Keyes, the Provisional Corps commander, to enter first, he was greeted with cheers of 'Long Live America' and 'Down with Mussolini!'.

He quickly established his Headquarters in the Royal Palace and 'had it cleaned by prisoners for the first time since the Greek occupation [241 BC]', and it was there that he was visited by the Cardinal of Palermo's representative, ate 'K-rations on china marked with the cross of Saxony' and 'got quite a kick about using a toilet previously made melodious by constipated royalty'.[16]

On 23 July Bradley's II Corps reached the northern coast at Termini and Patton lost no time in ordering it to turn east – he was determined to beat Monty to Messina. As he gave these orders he was probably remembering a passage in a letter he had written to his wife only three days earlier: 'If I succeed, Attila will have to take a back seat'.

But the week between 17 and 23 July was not an entirely happy one for George Patton. In two separate incidents a captain and a sergeant of the 45th Division killed seventy-three Italian prisoners in cold blood and at their court-martial the defence attorneys argued that they had only been following orders given in a speech delivered by Patton to the 45th Division on 27 June. In it he had warned members of the Division to watch out for enemy soldiers raising their arms in apparent surrender but then shooting or throwing grenades. They should watch out for this type of treachery and 'kill the s.o.b's' unless they were certain of their real intention to surrender.[17] This defence was rejected, but Patton was later the subject of an official Inspector General's investigation in England in 1944, and although the latter concluded that there was no culpability on his part, some of 'the mud stuck' and a later investigation by an American historian concluded that Patton's actions had verged on a war crime.[18]

What did Monty make of the Seventh Army's advances to Palermo and Termini? By the time Bradley's II Corps reached the latter on 23 July, Monty realised that his own dispersed thrusts, aimed at bypassing Mount Etna via Adrano on the west side and Fiumefreddo on the eastern coast road, were getting nowhere. The ground was the most difficult in the whole of Sicily and the Germans were inevitably making good use of it. After the war he blamed a lack of coordination of the land, sea and air efforts for the delay in gaining:

> control of the island more quickly, and with fewer casualties . . . the Supreme Commander was in Algiers, Alexander . . . was in Sicily; Cunningham, the Naval C-in-C, was in Malta; whereas Tedder, the Air C-in-C had his Headquarters in Tunis. When things went wrong, all they could do was to send telegrams to each other.[19]

In fact there were two basic reasons for this delay – one, Alexander's failure to coordinate the Seventh and Eighth Armies; and two, Monty's failure to understand early enough the topographical difficulties involved in trying to advance past the east and west sides of Mount Etna. On 19 July Monty had signalled Alexander outlining his axes of advance round either side of Mount Etna and suggesting that:

> when the Americans have cut the coast road north of Petralia, one American division should develop a strong thrust eastwards towards Messina so as to stretch the enemy who are all Germans and possibly repeat the Bizerte manoeuvre' [i.e., cut them off].

This made complete military sense but, as we have already heard, by the 17th Patton had persuaded Alexander to allow him to drive towards the north-western part of the island and when the C-in-C tried to restrain Georgie by sending him a new directive on the evening of the 19th it was too late. The directive, in accordance with Monty's suggestion, ordered Patton to first cut the coastal road north of Petralia and only then to move on Palermo. However, the Seventh Army Chief of Staff, Brigadier General 'Hap' Gay, kept the first part of the message from Patton, ensured the remainder took a long time to be decoded and then asked for it to be repeated on the grounds that it had been garbled! By the time this problem had been resolved the advance guard of Keyes' Provisional Corps was already in Palermo and Monty's idea of an American division helping him, at least in the short term, to unhinge the opposition in front of his Army had been frustrated.

By 23 July Monty realised he had been over-ambitious and that the cost of trying to break through the German defences astride Mount Etna, known as the Etna Line, was going to be too great. Two days earlier he had closed down XIII Corp's drive up the east coast and he now sent a message to Patton inviting him to come and discuss the capture of Messina and offering: 'Many congratulations to you and your gallant soldiers on securing Palermo and clearing up the western half of Sicily'. Privately of course he believed Georgie's Palermo escapade had been a completely wasted effort.

Patton met Monty at Syracuse airfield on the 25th. Expecting the worst and mistrusting his comrade's intentions, he was astounded when Monty suggested that the Seventh Army should use both the major roads north of Mount Etna (Highways 113 and 120) in a drive to capture Messina. In fact Monty went even further and suggested that his right-hand, or southern, thrust might even cross the inter-Army boundary and strike for Taormina, thereby cutting off the two German divisions facing the Eighth Army; the latter would 'take a back seat'. The same evening Georgie wrote in his diary:

I felt something was wrong, but have not found it yet. After all this had been settled, Alex [Alexander] came. He looked a little mad and, for him, was quite brusque. He told Monty to explain his plan. Monty said he and I had already decided what we were going to do, so Alex got madder and told Monty to show him the plan. He did and then Alex asked for mine. The meeting then broke up. No one was offered any lunch and I thought that Monty was ill bred both to Alexander and me. Monty gave me a 5-cent lighter. Someone must have sent him a box of them.

Monty described the 'plan' in his own diary:

the Seventh American Army should develop two strong thrusts with (a) two divisions on [Highway 120] (b) two divisions on [Highway 113] towards Messina. This was all agreed.

How can we explain Monty's surprising generosity in offering the 'prize' of Messina to Patton? A major factor was certainly his wish to avoid further British and Canadian casualties[20] in an attempt to breach the Etna Line. Another was his wish that his Army, not Patton's, should mount the main invasion of the Italian mainland. As early as the 23rd he had signalled Alexander:

Consider that the whole operation of war on to mainland must now be handled by Eighth Army as once Sicily is cleared of enemy a great deal of my resources can be put on to the mainland. I will carry the war into Italy on a front of two Corps.

By giving Patton the main role in finishing off the enemy in Sicily, Monty planned to rest the two Corps just mentioned in preparation for the forthcoming invasion. They would then assault the 'toe' of Italy in conjunction with a landing in the Gulf of Gioja by the X British Corps sailing direct from North Africa.

On 28 July Monty flew to Palermo in his B-17 Flying Fortress for further discussions with Patton. Unfortunately the landing strip was too short, but 'the pilot did the most amazing job . . . He put all the brakes on one side and revved one engine and swung the whole thing round – which wrote it off. That was the end of it'.[21] Monty emerged from the wreck seemingly unperturbed, to be met, not by Patton but, by an ADC. It was Georgie's way of getting back at him for his rudeness in Syracuse. Nevertheless, he then put on a typical Patton reception with motorcycles and scout cars to escort Monty to the palace in Palermo where a band and guard of honour were waiting to greet him. After a formal lunch the two men reviewed their future plans and Monty again emphasized the importance of the Seventh Army's thrust to Messina. He wrote in his diary:

> We had a great reception. The Americans are very easy to work with. I discussed plans for future operations with General Patton. Their troops are quite first class and I have a very great admiration for the way they fight.

But Patton was still very wary of Monty's intentions and sent a note to the commander of the 45th Division: 'This is a horse race in which the prestige of the US Army is at stake. We must take Messina before the British. Please use your best efforts to facilitate the success of our race'.[22]

George Patton's behaviour during the last three weeks of the campaign in Sicily can only be described as extraordinary. He castigated Omar Bradley for the tactics being employed by his II Corps, telling him:

> I want you to get into Messina just as fast as you can. I don't want you to waste time on these manoeuvres [outflanking enemy resistance], even if you've got to spend men to do it. I want you to beat Monty into Messina.[23]

And on another occasion[24] he allegedly accused the commander of the 3rd Infantry Division, Lucian Truscott, of being 'afraid to fight'.[25] Bradley stated later that:

> Patton was developing as an unpopular guy. He steamed about with great convoys of cars and great squads of cameramen . . . To George, tactics was simply a process of bulling ahead. Never seemed to think out a campaign. Seldom made a careful estimate of the situation. I thought him a shallow commander . . . I disliked the way he worked, upset tactical plans, interfered in my orders. His stubbornness on amphibious operations, parade plans into Messina sickened me and soured me on Patton. We learned how not to behave from Patton's Seventh Army.[26]

The reference to amphibious operations was in relation to three landings made on the north coast of Sicily during the advance to Messina, known to the Americans as 'end runs'. Patton did not in fact interfere in the first successful landing, but he ordered the second to take place earlier than Bradley and Truscott wished, ending in a minor disaster, and he ordered the third to take place despite the fact that the 3rd Division had already advanced beyond the landing site!

Georgie's 'parade plans into Messina' again reflected badly on him as an Army commander. Although a patrol of the 3rd US Infantry Division had entered the city on the evening of 16 August, Patton gave orders that no formed units were to enter 'until he could make triumphal entry'. Bradley recalled that he 'had to hold our troops in the hills instead of pursuing the fleeing Germans in an effort to get as many as we could. [The] British nearly beat him into Messina because of that'.[27]

At 1000 hours on 17 August George Patton led an American column into Messina. Ike's liaison officer with Patton, Major General John Porter Lucas, who was in the following vehicle, recorded in his diary: 'We entered the town about ten-thirty amid the wild applause of the people . . . The city was completely and terribly demolished'. German long-range artillery fire landed near the third vehicle, wounding its occupants, but this did not deter Patton who proceeded on to the central piazza where he met British troops who had landed south of the city near Scaletta on the 15th.[28] The commander of the British force, Brigadier J C Currie, saluted Patton 'dazzling in his smart gabardines', and is reported to have said, 'General, it was a jolly good race. I congratulate you'. The film *Patton* gives a completely false version of this event. Monty himself is depicted leading a British column into Messina, only to be greeted by Patton with a smirk on his face having beaten his archrival into the city. As Monty's Chief of Staff, Freddie de Guingand, put it later:

> Absolute cock, in the film: Monty marching at the head of the Highlanders – all balls! . . . It was all balls that, about who was going to get to Messina first. We were *delighted* when we heard that Patton had got to Messina first.[29]

But Patton's triumph was to be short lived. Two weeks previously, on the very day that he had learned that Eisenhower was to award him the DSC for 'extraordinary heroism' at Gela on 11 July (an award 'I rather feel I did not deserve . . . but won't say so'[30]), he had called in at the 15th Evacuation Hospital where he encountered a Private Charles H Kuhl of the 26th Infantry Regiment of the 1st Division. Seeing no visible wounds Patton asked him why he was in the hospital. On being told that he was not wounded but 'I guess I can't take it', Patton called him a coward, ordered him out of the tent and when the terrified soldier remained motionless, 'slapped his face with a glove, raised him to his feet by the collar of his shirt and pushed him out of the tent with a final kick in the rear'.[31] That night Patton wrote in his diary: 'Companies should deal with such men, and if they shirk their duty, they should be tried for cowardice and shot'.

A week later, in the 93rd Evacuation Hospital, Patton's behaviour was even more outrageous. He encountered a regular Army artilleryman, Private Paul G Bennett, shivering on his bed. On being told by Bennett that 'I can't stand the shelling any more', Patton lost his temper, called him 'a goddamned coward', ordered the receiving officer not to admit this 'yellow bastard' and then shouted at Bennett, 'You ought to be lined up against a wall and shot. In fact, I ought to shoot you myself right now, God damn you!'. Patton then pulled out his pistol and waved it in the terrified soldier's face, after which he ordered the hospital commander to 'get that man out of here right away'. He then slapped Bennett across the face. Not content with this, when Patton saw Bennett break down in tears he returned to his bed and hit him a second time. By then a number of doctors and nurses had arrived on the scene and were witnessing the confrontation; it was only brought to an end when the hospital commander interposed himself between Bennett and Patton.[32]

Patton went from the 93rd Evacuation Hospital directly to the II Corps Headquarters where incredibly, he bragged to Bradley about the incident with Bennett. But Bradley, although he was shocked and disgusted by Patton's behaviour, was not prepared to go over his head and report him to Eisenhower, and the following day when he received a written report of the incident from the surgeon of the hospital, he ordered his Chief of Staff to put it away in a sealed envelope in a safe. There was, however, clearly no way such an offence could be kept quiet for long. One of the 93rd Hospital nurses told her boyfriend, a captain in Public Affairs, and he passed the story on to American press and radio correspondents attached to the Seventh Army. On 19 August a written summary of the incident was presented to Ike's Chief of Staff in Algiers, confirming a similar report sent three days earlier to Eisenhower's Chief Surgeon, Brigadier General Frederick Blessé, by the II Corps Chief Surgeon.

Following Blessé's report, Eisenhower wrote an extremely strong letter of censure to Patton on the 17th – the day Messina was captured! In it he stated that there could be no excuse for 'the abuse of the sick, nor exhibition of uncontrollable temper in front of subordinates'. It went on: 'I must so seriously question your good judgement and your self-discipline, as to raise doubts in my mind as to your future usefulness', and after concluding: 'that [such] conduct . . . will *not* be tolerated in this theater no matter who the offender may be', Ike ordered him to 'make in the form of apology or otherwise such personal amends to the individuals concerned as may be within your power'.[33]

Three days later Patton was ordered to meet Major General Lucas at Palermo airfield; he was told that Lucas was carrying a personal message from Ike. That message, according to Lucas's diary entry for 20–21 August, was to the effect that Georgie was to apologise, not only to the individual soldiers concerned, but to every Division in the Seventh Army!

On 21 August Patton shook hands with Bennett and apologised, but that night he wrote in his diary: 'It is rather a commentary on justice when an Army commander has to soft-soap a skulker to placate the timidity of those above'. The following day he addressed the doctors, nurses and enlisted men who had witnessed the two incidents, expressing his belief that cases of shell-shock were most tragic, admitting that he had over-stepped himself, but then going on to say that such men might well be helped from their own self concern by being made to direct their anger at someone else. His audience was apparently unimpressed and considered his words fell well short of an apology. He also apologised to Private Kuhl, telling him that 'if you will shake my hand in forgiveness, I'll be much obliged to you'.

Patton's apologies to his Divisions were sometimes charged with emotion and had widely differing results. In most cases he talked of regret 'for occasions when I may have harshly criticized individuals' and he usually mentioned 'certain incidents that had better be forgotten'. He apparently used 'earthy language' and the general reaction of the troops is said to have been one of quiet indifference.[34] In the case of his old 2nd Armored Division there was general disbelief about the incidents and he was received enthusiastically, whilst in that of the 1st Infantry he was heard in stony silence and there were even said to have been a few boos. The reaction in the 9th Infantry varied – in the case of one Regiment he was cheered after his opening word and he left in tears without saying another, whilst in another Regiment the men released blown-up condoms that floated over his head, again causing him to leave with a different type of embarrassment. Truscott's 3rd Infantry cheered him with shouts of 'No! General, No! No! No!'. For many of his men he clearly remained the hero of the hour but, according to correspondent Quentin Reynolds of *Collier's* magazine, there were 'at least 50,000 American soldiers on Sicily who would shoot Patton if they had the chance'.[35]

Despite Patton's indiscretions Eisenhower was determined to save him 'for service in the great battles still facing us in Europe'[36] and he hid the full details of the slapping incidents from General Marshall in Washington. In a letter to his superior dated 24 August, he attributed the success of the Sicily campaign to Patton's 'energy, determination and unflagging aggressiveness', and then went on to say that Georgie:

> continues to exhibit some of those unfortunate personal traits of which you and I have always known and which during this campaign have caused me some most uncomfortable days. His habit of impulsive bawling out of subordinates, extending even to the personal abuse of individuals, was noted in at least two specific cases. I have had to take the most drastic steps; and if he is not cured now, there is no hope for him. Personally, I believe that he is cured ... because fundamentally he is so avid for recognition as a great military commander that he will ruthlessly suppress any habit of his own that will tend to jeopardize it.

Ike explained his need to keep the services of his brilliant if unorthodox subordinate to the media reporters who had sent the report of the slapping incidents to his Chief of Staff on 19 August and asked for their cooperation. Surprisingly, an unofficial gentleman's agreement was reached and for the time being at least Patton was safe from media and Congressional attention.

Patton's pride in taking Messina was soon dashed when in early September, Marshall announced that his subordinate, Omar Bradley, had been selected to command the First US Army – the US Army earmarked for the cross-Channel invasion of Europe. When Mark Clark's Fifth and Monty's Eighth Army landed in Italy a few days later, Patton realised that his Seventh Army was probably destined for disbandment or at best used to provide reinforcements to Mark Clark's and that he personally had been side-lined. When Bradley paid his final courtesy call on Georgie on 7 September, he found him isolated in his palace in Palermo and 'in a near-suicidal mental state . . . This great proud warrior, my former boss, had been brought to his knees'.[37]

What of Monty in the final days of the Sicily campaign? Having handed over the baton for Patton to 'win the race' for Messina, he had turned his attention to the forthcoming invasion of Italy. The impression given in a letter to his son's guardians at this time is one of quiet satisfaction and calm:

> All goes well here. I am extremely fit . . . I keep my HQ always high up, above the plain country; it is cooler here, and there are less mosquitoes. The present view from my caravan is quite wonderful . . . with Mount Etna towering above and dominating everything. I have begun to collect birds, of which I have always been very fond. I now have some canaries.[38]

The reality was very different. His short visit to London the previous May had convinced him that the planning for the forthcoming cross-Channel invasion of France was in the same chaotic state as he had experienced before the invasion of Sicily, and this led him to urge the CIGS to move Alexander back to England to 'take hold' of the situation. In a letter to Earl Mountbatten, the Chief of Combined Operations, dated 25 July, he indicated his great concern over this situation and said that in his view the only way to sort it out was to move Alexander and himself back to London to take charge. The letter also made clear his overall ambitions:

> I also feel Alex and myself cannot *both* leave here if it is the intention to carry on against Italy and knock her out of the war. Someone will be required to command the field armies for Eisenhower i.e. 15th Army Group; we shall probably have three Armies, two American [Patton's Seventh and Clark's Fifth] and one British [the Eighth] . . . If

Alex and I *both* go home there is *no one* out here who could command three armies and knock Italy out. So if Alex goes home, as I think he must, then I must stay here and take on his job – and knock Italy out. I could come home early next year, in the spring, to help Alex.

But the suggestion was ignored; Alexander stayed in the Mediterranean and Monty's hopes of commanding the 15th Army Group were dashed. On the same day that he wrote home about collecting canaries, he had no other option but to write to Mountbatten: 'I think as things go at present it is probably right to leave the 1st XI out here'.

Two days later Monty received, to his delight, a signal from Alexander's Headquarters placing X British Corps under his command for the invasion of Italy. Little did he know that on that very same day Eisenhower had charged Mark Clark's Fifth Army with the main assault on the mainland and told him that the X British Corps would be under *his* command. It was to be another three weeks (on 16 August) before Alexander confirmed to Monty that Clark's Fifth Army would carry out the main assault (Operation AVALANCHE), landing south of Naples at Salerno on about 10 September with the British X Corps under command. Monty was disappointed, but being a realist he realised that the Salerno landing made the Gulf of Gioja operation by X Corps redundant. Nevertheless, he was disgusted at the duplicity of the planning staffs and also bitterly disappointed that due to a lack of landing craft his own landing on the 'toe' of Italy could only be carried out by one rather than the two Corps he had envisaged.

The end of the Sicily campaign brought little satisfaction to our prima donnas. Within a few days Patton realised he was in deep trouble over the slapping incidents and Monty was aware that just as the Seventh Army had been sidelined into a subsidiary and supporting role in HUSKY, so his Eighth Army would be in AVALANCHE. His only consolation was that at least his Army would be the first to land on the continent of Europe. But he was also depressed about the outcome of the Sicily campaign. Due to the bungling and lack of direction and coordination by both Eisenhower's and Alexander's Headquarters, 40,000 Germans, 60,000 Italians and some 10,000 vehicles, including forty-seven tanks, had escaped in a skilfully executed withdrawal across the Straits of Messina. Admittedly the Axis forces had suffered 160,000 casualties, of which 140,000 were prisoners, but the cost to the Allies had been heavy – 12,843 British Commonwealth casualties and 8,781 Americans; these figures can be doubled if one takes into account those who were evacuated with malaria. Monty blamed the higher command for the failure to stop or at least heavily interfere with the Axis withdrawal. As early as 7 August, having seen the latest RAF reconnaissance reports and aware that the Etna Line had finally been broken by his XXX Corps, he noted:

There has been heavy traffic all day across the Straits of Messina and the enemy is without doubt starting to get his stuff away. I have tried hard to find out what the combined Navy – Air plan is in order to stop him getting away; I have been unable to find out. I fear the truth is that there is NO plan . . . The trouble is there is no high-up grip on this campaign . . . It beats me how anyone thinks you can run a campaign . . . with the three Commanders of the three Services about 600 miles from each other.

Surprisingly, Monty did not include Ike in his criticism – it was after all the latter's responsibility to coordinate the activities of his Service commanders. Eisenhower finally did so on 9 August, but even after that there was still no coherent interdiction plan and Monty could do nothing other than to watch his enemy escape and his rival claim the limelight.

But if Monty's morale had been lowered by the failure of the higher command to end the Sicily campaign satisfactorily and the muddle and deceit in the planning of the forthcoming Italian operation, he at least had the consolation of being idolised by the majority of his men. Unlike Patton who, as already mentioned, was thoroughly disliked and even hated by many of his officers and soldiers, Monty's popularity had never been higher and much of the affection he earned was due to his informality and the fact that a day never went by throughout the whole campaign without him visiting one of his units. Not for him the outriders, flags, shiny stars and smart uniform; instead, an old shirt or jumper, baggy trousers and a rather over-sized, dusty beret. As one Canadian colonel wrote later: 'He had us break ranks and gather round his vehicle. He then gave us permission to smoke and extolled the fighting virtues of Canadian troops and flattered us'.[39] Thus the Canadians, who had resented his heavy-handed training methods when under his command in the South-Eastern Army in England in 1942, had come to admire him in same way as his British soldiers.

On 17 August Montgomery wrote in his diary:

Operation BAYTOWN is an invasion of the mainland of Italy, so as to secure the 'toe' and open up the Straits of Messina for the Navy. I said [to Alexander] I would do the operation on night 30/31 August. It will not be easy to do it in the time, as the demolitions on the roads [in Sicily] are very extensive. But it will be done somehow.

On the day George Patton 'apologised' to the doctors and nurses of the 15th and 93rd Evacuation Hospitals, he wrote in his diary: 'I seem to have made Divine Destiny [Eisenhower] a little mad, but that will pass'. That same day Monty added another section to his diary entitled 'Some Reflections on the Campaign in Sicily – July/August 1943'. Among his more stringent comments were the following:

Eisenhower is a very 'big' man who takes the large view and keeps clear of all detail; Bedell Smith [Ike's Chief of Staff] implements all the big decisions and keeps the whole show on the rails.

The whole set-up at 15 Army Group [Alexander's Headquarters] has been bad; the planning for operations, the grip on the battle and the conduct of the war generally, has been a complete failure.

Alexander has great personal charm and a sterling character; so much so that he likes to reach agreement whatever may happen, quite regardless of whether that agreement will win the battle . . I have not got those fine qualities that he possesses, and because I fight for the things that matter I make certain enemies. But I win the battle . . . So we are a good team and I believe each of us is necessary to the other.

NOTES

1   5, 50, 51 British Inf Divs, 1 Canadian Inf Div, 231 Indep UK Inf Bde & 23 UK Armd Bde, & 1st Canadian Armd Bde. No 3 Commando & Nos 40 & 41 Royal Marine Commandos were also in support.
2   2 Armd Div, 1, 3 & 45 Inf Divs & two Ranger Bns under Lt Col William Darby.
3   The Hermann Goering Pz Div & the 15th & 29th Pz-Gren Divs had all been virtually destroyed in the Tunisian campaign.
4   Montgomery, *El Alamein to the River Sangro*, p. 86.
5   Alexander Papers, PRO London.
6   D'Este, *A Genius for War*, p. 506.
7   Ibid, p. 897, Note 13.
8   Patton, *War As I Knew It*, p. 56.
9   Hamilton, *Monty, Master of the Battlefield 1942–1944*, pp. 302–3.
10   Ibid, p. 302.
11   Montgomery Papers.
12   18th Army Group was renumbered before Op HUSKY – it was the sum of the two Army numbers, 7 & 8.
13   Bradley Commentaries WWII, Chester B Hansen Collection, Military History Institute, Carlisle, Pennsylvania.
14   D'Este, op.cit., p. 514, Note 32.
15   Hamilton, op. cit., p. 319.
16   Letter to Beatrice dated 27 Jul 43.
17   Attributed to Brig Gen Wedemeyer – D'Este, op. cit., p. 509.
18   Ibid, p. 510.
19   Montgomery, *Memoirs*, p. 188.
20   By 27 Jul 43 the Eighth Army had suffered some 5,800 casualties.
21   Monty's ADC in an interview with Nigel Hamilton, 13 Aug 81 – Hamilton, op.cit., p. 330.
22   Patton to Troy Middleton, 28 Jul 43.
23   Bradley Commentaries.
24   The planned amphibious landing at Brolo.
25   D'Este, op. cit., p. 527.
26   Bradley Commentaries.

27 Ibid.
28 Lt Col J Churchill with men of 2 Commando & a battlegroup from Brig Currie's 4 Armd Bde including arty and engineers (engrs).
29 Hamilton, op. cit., p. 335.
30 Letter to Beatrice dated 18 Aug 43.
31 Report of the Hospital Commanding Officer – D'Este. op. cit., p. 533.
32 D'Este, op. cit. p. 534.
33 The Eisenhower Papers, Vol 2, pp. 1340–1.
34 D'Este, op.cit., p. 541.
35 Ibid, p. 536.
36 Eisenhower, *Crusade in Europe*, p. 199.
37 Bradley & Blair, *A General's Life*, p. 208.
38 Letter to Phyllis Reynolds dated 3 Aug 43.
39 Col Strome Galloway, *The General Who Never Was*.

CHAPTER XVI

Montgomery in Italy

(Map 9)

It will be remembered that Monty had said he would do everything possible to launch Operation BAYTOWN (the assault across the Straits of Messina) during the night of 30/31 August. On 19 August, however, he sent a signal to Alexander saying that he had been given no objective for the operation and in the absence of any other directive he assumed it was to secure the Straits for the Navy and to act as a diversion for the main Fifth Army landings at Salerno (AVALANCHE). He went on to say that: 'the landing craft and naval personnel given me make an invasion of Europe with *any* object *in the face of opposition* quite impossible'[1] and that current delays had already made it impossible to launch BAYTOWN as early as 30 August. He conceded, however, that AVALANCHE, 'must have priority'.[2]

Monty's demand for a proper directive from Alexander was met on 20 August when he received a half sheet of notepaper(!) from Alexander, written in his own handwriting(!), confirming Monty's assumption and adding that:

> in the event of the enemy withdrawing from the 'toe', you will follow him up with such force as you can make available, bearing in mind that the greater the extent to which you can engage enemy forces in the southern tip ... the more assistance will you be giving to AVALANCHE.[3]

Monty could not believe the naivety of the overall plan – as early as 10

August his Chief of Staff, de Guingand, had expressed his views at an Eighth Army planning conference:

> If AVALANCHE is a success, then we should reinforce *that* [author's emphasis] front for there is little point in laboriously fighting our way up southern Italy. It is better to leave the enemy to decay there or let him have the trouble of moving himself up from the 'foot' to where we are concentrated.

But Monty's hope that BAYTOWN would be cancelled was not to be. Eisenhower called a conference to discuss the invasion on 23 August. All the senior commanders attended and were told of the negotiations going on with the Italians to secure an armistice and the hope that the moment the Allies landed on the mainland the Italians would change sides and fight the Germans. Monty argued that they would never 'fight the Germans properly' and mentioned that at least four German divisions could, and almost certainly would, be concentrated against Clark's Fifth Army, but 'everyone was so pleased about the Italians fighting on our side that it was considered the situation would be good. I was unable to agree'.[4] That night he recorded in his diary: 'Clarke [sic] expounded his plan . . . and it seemed to me to be open to criticism'.

Eisenhower was infuriated by the delay in launching BAYTOWN; in an interview with the American Official Historian in February 1949 he said that he had 'told Alexander I believed we could do it in a rowboat. We sat there in Messina from 17 August until 3 September'.[5] What he had failed to realise, however, was that if the Eighth Army was required to fight its way from the 'toe' of Italy to Salerno, as Alexander had now indicated, a large, balanced force would have to be landed and that would require more than a few 'rowboats'. Ike should have realised that Monty's concern about unnecessary casualties, refusal to take risks and generally cautious nature, would inevitably result in a carefully planned operation involving strong artillery, naval and air support and that this would take time to organize. There was simply no way Monty would risk harming his reputation or that of the Eighth Army by putting an inadequate force onto the mainland of Italy in a rushed and disorganized manner. Nevertheless, he did consider a much simpler, alternative operation. On 27 August five small landing parties were put ashore on the 'foot' of Italy to assess the general situation; if their reports were favourable, Monty hoped to be able to cancel BAYTOWN and simply 'ferry 5 Div across from Catania' (Map 8), but 'having had no news from the parties [by the 29th], I decided that the planned [full] operation of invading the mainland of Italy would go ahead without any change'.[6]

Monty's original plan of putting two Corps ashore had been dashed due to the shortage of landing craft and bridging equipment. Instead, XIII

Corps alone, with just two Divisions, would be responsible for the Eighth Army's campaign on the mainland. The 1st Canadian Infantry Division would advance up the east coast and the British 5th Infantry Division up the west, supported if necessary by two Commandos and the 231st Independent Infantry Brigade in a series of 'left hooks'.

On 29 August Monty invited Eisenhower, Patton, Bradley, Patton's Chief of Staff (Gay), Provisional Corps commander (Keyes) and 3rd Divisional commander (Truscott) to lunch at his headquarters in Taormina (Map 8). Using the owner's silver, china and table linen, he was the perfect host – 'trying to make up for not feeding me last time' recorded Patton. Despite the fact that Georgie was quieter than usual – perhaps because he was carrying his letter of apology to Ike for the slapping incidents[7] – he still managed to entertain Monty and his guests with his 'earthy' wit. In a conversation about soldiers being allowed to talk to local civilians, he allegedly said: 'I say fornication ain't fraternization! That is, if you keep your hat on and your weight on the elbows!'. Monty apparently roared with laughter. After the lunch Ike pinned the Legion of Merit[8] on Monty's chest and they then drove up to Messina where they could see the Italian mainland only two miles away. Their conversation is not recorded but Ike must have been fully aware of Monty's plans and intentions.

BAYTOWN was eventually launched during the night of 2–3 September. It began with a barrage fired by 192 guns – seventy-two British 25-pounders, eighty American medium and forty-eight American heavy guns[9] – the latter all courtesy of George Patton! Then at 0430 hours on 3 September, the fourth British anniversary of the outbreak of the war, the men of the 1st Canadian and 5th British Divisions set foot on the mainland. 'Opposition was slight' and 3,000 prisoners were taken. Monty wrote to the CIGS that night:

> At 1030 hrs I stepped ashore myself on the mainland of Europe just north of Reggio. It was a great thrill once more to set foot on the Continent from which we were pushed off three years ago, at Dunkirk . . . I have enjoyed it all greatly. The Germans evacuated Reggio before we got into the town . . . There is no doubt that some of my chaps are getting tired . . . Continuous and hard fighting is a great strain. The only person who does not get tired is myself. I have the feeling you think I am idle and ought not to go to bed after dinner and read a novel, or do some quiet thinking in bed. But I can assure you, that if I did not do this I could not possibly go on with the business at the present tempo and pace.

Just under seven hours after Monty landed, General Castellano signed the Italian armistice authorized by Marshal Badoglio in a secret meeting with

Eisenhower's Chief of Staff, Bedell Smith. Monty's views on this were expressed to his son's guardian, Phyllis Reynolds, on 9 September:

> If you analyse the matter [getting rid of Mussolini and agreeing an armistice] in cold blood there is no doubt that the Italians have carried out a really good double-cross; they changed sides on one day!! I wouldn't trust them a yard, and in any case they are quite useless when it comes to fighting.

On a more personal note he added:

> I have made the Navy give me a fast Motor Launch; it does 20 knots and is well armed, and has a crew of two officers and fifteen ratings. I use it to cross over to Messina, or to nip round the coast . . . So now I have: one aeroplane [a C-47 Dakota], one Motor Launch, five motor cars . . . I forgot to mention . . . one DUKW. This is a large lorry which can go on the road or on the sea.

Two days later, as the British advance began to suffer delays caused by demolitions and the German rearguards, Monty learned from Alexander that news of the Italian surrender would be broadcast on 8 September, following which American airborne troops would land near Rome, the Eternal City would be seized by Italian troops stationed nearby and other Italian troops would take Taranto, Brindisi, Bari and Naples. Early the following morning a major element of Clark's Fifth Army would land at Salerno and the V British Corps at Taranto. The latter was to come under Monty's command 'when I get within supporting distance of it'.

Monty could hardly believe his ears. He wrote in his diary:

> I told him [Alexander] . . . that when the Germans found out what was going on, they would stamp on the Italians . . . I said he should impress on all senior commanders that we must make our plans so that it would make no difference if the Italians failed us . . . They were carrying out a colossal double-cross, and we must not trust them too much, or tell them our plans just at present . . . The Germans were strong about Rome and Naples, and could concentrate against AVALANCHE quicker than we could build up; if there was any danger of a disaster to AVALANCHE we should cancel it, and put that effort into Taranto and so get a firm grip on southern Italy.

Alexander passed on Monty's views to Eisenhower but it was too late, the die was cast – the AVALANCHE convoys were already at sea. Nevertheless, the Eighth Army commander continued to express his worst fears. On 7 September, two days before the Salerno landings, he pointed out to

Alexander the fact that the Germans had twenty divisions in Italy, including five armoured divisions, whereas the Allies had only two Divisions in the 'toe' and even after landing three more at Salerno, would still total only five.[10] He went on to say that the shortage of shipping was making his build-up very slow and he could not get over to the mainland the units he needed to speed his advance and for port development. Again his warnings and pleas fell on deaf ears.

Monty's worst fears were soon confirmed – the Italians did not react as expected, the American airborne operation near Rome had to be cancelled, the Germans occupied the city the following day and AVALANCHE immediately ran into trouble. Six German divisions were concentrated against it by 12 September and a day later the situation was so serious that plans were actually made to abandon the landing and evacuate the troops; Patton even foresaw the possibility of 'a second Gallipoli'.[11]

By 9 September, the day of the Salerno landings, Monty's troops had advanced a distance of some 100 miles, albeit it against little more than strong German rearguards.

> They were strung out and the infantry were definitely tired. I decided they must be rested . . . I gave orders that they are to halt . . . and to 'wind up' their tails; they will then rest for two days . . . I have XXX Corps, with three divisions, in Sicily, but cannot bring them over to Italy as I have no craft or shipping for the purpose.[12]

A day later Monty gave orders that the two Divisions of Dempsey's XIII Corps were to move north in three or four days' time and secure the neck of the Calabrian peninsula. This delay was in spite of a signal from Alexander telling him that it was, 'of the utmost importance that you maintain pressure upon the Germans so that they cannot move forces from your front and concentrate them against AVALANCHE'. This was Monty at his most cautious and obstinate. He noted in his diary that: 'We are about to become involved in large scale operations on the mainland of Europe and there was no firm plan known to me as to how those operations were to be developed'. The Eighth Army therefore 'would not move beyond the Castrovillari neck until the situation was clearer'. Even on the 13th, when he knew that Clark was in deep trouble at Salerno, he did not move and it was only on the 14th that he gave orders for offensive action. Patrols pushed forward and two days later the advance guard of the Eighth Army made contact with Clark's Fifth Army some forty miles south-east of Salerno – led by a group of journalists in two jeeps, 'impatient at the deliberate character of Eighth Army's advance'.[13] By then the Fifth Army had satisfactorily resolved its own crisis; even so, Monty still felt able to claim that he had 'saved their [Fifth Army's] bacon'. His 20 September diary entry goes even further:

The original idea was that my Army was not to operate beyond the Catanzaro neck. But in actual fact I had to operate some 200 miles beyond that neck, and go very quickly too, and if I had failed to do so the whole of Fifth American Army would have been pushed into the sea.

And ten days later he was still complaining that: 'Some of the things I was asked to do, and the way the whole party was stage-managed, is past all belief'.[14] In fact Monty had refused to take any risks and had gone out of his way to ensure that his Army was always 'balanced' and ready for the unexpected. In his later years Monty was more gracious; he wrote:

I have never thought we had much real influence on the Salerno problem; I reckon General Clark had got it well in hand before we arrived. But we did what we could. We marched and fought 300 miles in seventeen days, in good delaying country against an enemy whose use of demolitions caused us bridging problems of the first magnitude. The hairpin bends on the roads were such that any distance measured on the map as say 10 miles, was 20 miles on the ground and in some cases 25. But, in my view, Fifth Army did their own trick without our help – willing as we were.[15]

How can Monty's obstinacy and apparent sluggishness be explained? Perhaps by the fact that he was annoyed that his role in the invasion of the Italian mainland was merely supportive and diversionary? Or by the fact that he believed the AVALANCHE plan was flawed and that if it failed the Germans would then concentrate their efforts against his relatively weak Army? Or maybe, as has been suggested by his biographer, Nigel Hamilton, he had deliberately decided to make Alexander pay for his mistakes in not formulating and issuing a positive and coherent overall plan before the invasion? Almost certainly it was a combination of all these factors, but whatever the truth, Montgomery's role in the first phase of the Italian campaign is less than exemplary and one can only wonder, as did Eisenhower, what might have happened if George Patton had been in command in the 'toe' rather than Monty. Ike 'felt certain Patton would have burned shoeleather as he did in Sicily'.[16]

Montgomery came in for a great deal of criticism both at the time and after the war for the slowness of his advance from Reggio. One eminent historian described it as 'Ambling leisurely northwards, Monty's men found it like a holiday picnic after Sicily and Africa'.[17] In order to keep things in proportion, however, it is interesting to compare the Eighth Army's advance with that of the Americans in the Gulf War of 2003. Monty's two infantry Divisions covered some 300 miles through extremely difficult and mountainous terrain, with numerous rivers, in seventeen days; the American 3rd (fully) *Mechanized* Infantry Division (author's emphasis) took exactly the same number of days (20 March to 5 April) to cover virtually the same distance (Kuwait to Baghdad) across a flat desert with only one river to cross!

Monty's last three months in Italy were frustrated by weather, a lack of resources and the failure of his masters to set out a clear strategy. We need not go into the details of his campaign. Suffice it to say that on 17 September Field Marshal Kesselring ordered the Germans to conduct a fighting withdrawal back to the Gustav Line – a natural defensive position centred on Cassino. This they did with typical Teutonic skill and thoroughness. On the Allied side, following the link up of the Eighth and Fifth Armies, Monty's was transferred to the Adriatic side of the Apennine mountains and after taking Foggia with its complex of vital airfields on 27 September, it fought its way up to and across the Trigno (7 November), Sangro (30 November) and Moro (10 December) rivers. In the same period Mark Clark's Fifth Army occupied Naples on 1 October, crossed the Volturno and by 15 January had closed up to the Gustav Line.

Let us look now at some of the reasons for Monty's frustration during this period. First of all he was fully aware that by the end of October the Germans had twenty-four divisions in Italy to an Allied total of fourteen and, coupled with this disparity in strength, he was still angry at the lack of direction from the top. The reasons for Eisenhower's failure to interfere are complex and need not concern us. Those interested should read Carlo D'Este's *Eisenhower Allied Supreme Commander* and Nigel Hamilton's *Monty Master of the Battlefield 1942–1944*. As far as Monty was concerned 'the basic trouble was that we became involved in a major campaign lacking a predetermined master plan'.[18]

In his personal diary he was even more forthright: 'the indecision and lack of grip at 15th Army Group is bad – it is more than that, it is a scandal ... Alexander is the nicest chap I have ever known, but he does not understand the conduct of war'.[19] Monty himself was in no doubt as to how and why the Italian campaign should be conducted:

> It is a mistake to drive the German armies from Italy. I would keep them there, with a hostile population, and difficult communications which we bomb daily. But we must have as much of Italy as ... to enable our air forces to be able to reach the southern German cities and the Roumanian oil fields. I would like to establish ourselves in the valley of the Po ... We would ... constitute a very serious threat to Germany in several directions: eastwards into Austria, northwards into south Germany and westwards into southern France. We could play on this and keep the Germans guessing – and thus help OVERLORD [the cross-Channel invasion of France].[20]

These views reflected those of Winston Churchill.

Another factor was his worry over supplies and repairs. On 29 September, after taking the Foggia airfields, he signalled Alexander that he was being forced to halt for at least ten to fourteen days because, 'I have no reserve stocks and the whole admin business in rear is in a bad way and must be tidied up'.[21] And by 4 October he claimed he was facing:

> a major administrative breakdown ... We had over five hundred vehicles off the road wanting new engines; instead of having base workshops in Italy with a pool of spare engines, the vehicles had to be sent back to Egypt for repair and returned later. A serious medical scandal was narrowly averted; we could not clear our sick and wounded from our hospitals and Casualty Clearing Stations.[22]

And then, as already mentioned, the weather broke at the end of October and by 9 November:

> the whole country was completely waterlogged, the mud was frightful and no vehicles could move off the road, which was covered in 'chocolate sauce'. The wet season was on us, and ... we now began to pay dearly for the loss of time in Sicily.[23]

But despite all these problems and in the absence of any orders to the contrary, Monty continued to battle his way up the east coast of Italy. In fact, along with Mark Clark, he had now set his eyes on Rome. By early October he had developed a plan for taking the city but, as he told Eisenhower on the 11th, he could not implement it with only four Divisions; he needed to be reinforced with X British Corps, currently operating under the Fifth Army. When Mark Clark, quite understandably, refused to give it up the plan had to be abandoned. By 18 November, however, Monty had developed a new plan to attack across the Sangro with three Divisions, 400 tanks and a 'very powerful air effort', aimed at reaching the Rome–Pescara lateral road and then swinging west to outflank the Germans facing the Fifth Army. In a letter to the CIGS dated 18 November, he wrote that this should allow Rome to 'fall to Mark Clark's Army'. Nevertheless, he hoped to 'accompany the N.Z. [New Zealand] Division into Rome! ... When we have captured Rome I shall want some leave. I shall probably write a book entitled "Alamein to Rome" – I don't think'.[24] But it was not to be; by 10 December the rain had brought operations to a complete standstill and although the Eighth Army had reached Ortona, it was clear that Rome would not be captured in 1943. 'I understand Caesar used to go into winter quarters about this time, when he commanded an army in these parts!!! And very wise too!!', Monty wrote to Mountbatten. And as he waited for the rains to stop and his doubts increased about ever reaching Rome before Christmas, Monty's thoughts turned to the cross-Channel invasion of France. He wrote to Major General Simpson, the Director of Military Operations in the War Office: 'Eventually I believe you must cross the Channel . . . [and] I consider you must *at once* begin to prepare the instrument or weapon, and get the plan properly shaped. That means you must transfer from here some good chaps who really understand the business'.[25] A few days later, on the 27th, he underlined these sentiments with another letter to Simpson:

> We must get the Army in England in good shape, and tee-up the cross-Channel venture . . . I am not certain from what I hear that the Army in England *is* in good shape. Some fresh air seems to be needed. A good deal of dead wood needs to be cut out, and the whole show made younger, and more virile.

Monty then went on to suggest that the Italian front should be closed down for the rest of the winter, followed by a spring offensive to draw German troops away from the Channel coast. It was already clear that Monty saw himself as the 'fresh air' needed to make the army in England 'more virile' and as one of the 'good chaps' needed to command an Army – or even an Army Group! On 4 December he wrote again, 'The "great ones" . . . will now presumably re-group the generals . . . if they make mistakes, and get the generals in the wrong places, we will have endless trouble'. Fortunately 'the great ones' did not get it wrong; early on 24 December Monty learned from Brooke that Alexander was to stay in Italy and that he was to command the 21st (Allied) Army Group in the forthcoming invasion of Normandy under Eisenhower as Supreme Commander. Both Churchill and Eisenhower would have preferred Alexander for the 21st Army Group, but the CIGS, aided by a recommendation by Marshall, eventually persuaded Winston that Monty was the better choice. He of course was elated: 'It was a relief and an excitement . . . I was not sorry to leave the Italian theatre'.[26] In typical Montgomery fashion he immediately signalled the War Office with a demand that he be allowed to bring back to the UK his Chief of Staff, his Chiefs of Intelligence and Administration, his senior armoured adviser and his Head Chaplain. When he was told his Chief Administrative Officer was to stay in Italy he decided to take him anyway and 'chance the anger in London'.

On 27 December Monty flew to Algiers (Map 6) to see Eisenhower who told him he: 'had only a sketchy idea of the [OVERLORD] plan and that it did not look too good'.[27] Furthermore, Ike wanted him: 'to take complete charge of the initial land battle, and that he would place the American armies in England under my command for the landing [in France] and subsequent operations'.[28] Monty was to:

act as his representative in London until he himself could get there. I was to analyse and revise the plan [OVERLORD] and have it ready for him on his arrival in England about the middle of January ... I replied that I thought his Chief of Staff, Bedell Smith, should be in London with me ... I also asked that he should give Bedell a statement in writing that I was to act for him.[29]

Monty's farewell meeting with the officers and men of his Headquarters was charged with emotion. He started by telling them that 'this is not going to be easy, but I shall do my best. If I happen to find difficulty in speaking on occasions, I hope you will understand'. He finished it by reading out his farewell message to the Eighth Army in which he expressed his 'great regret' at leaving. Freddie de Guingand described the final moments in his book *Operation Victory*:

> We cheered him and then he walked slowly out to his car; I followed feeling very uncomfortable, for I had tears on my cheeks ... As my Chief talked to this trusted few, I could not help thinking of Napoleon and his Marshals, for here surely there was to be found the same relationship, born and tempered by mutual esteem and success in battle.

On 31 December Monty flew to Marrakech (Map 6) to spend the night and New Year's Day with Churchill, who was recovering from pneumonia, and his wife. He found the Prime Minister studying a copy of the OVERLORD plan and was surprised to be given it and asked for his opinion. Monty complained that he was not his military advisor and had not had a chance to discuss it with any responsible naval or air authority. Churchill still wanted his 'first impressions', so Monty did not 'see in the New Year' with his hosts, but went to bed early and studied the plan – he did not like what he saw and said so in a short paper which he and Churchill discussed the following day on the way to a picnic lunch in the Moroccan countryside.

> I got to know the Prime Minister and Mrs. Churchill well during that short visit to Marrakech, and it was the beginning of a friendship which developed into my becoming a close friend of them both ... Eisenhower had refused to allow me to ... [fly home] in my Dakota two-engined aircraft ... so I transferred to an American four-engine C-54 aircraft. I filled my own plane with oranges and told the pilot to make his way to England ... I reached London on 2 January [and] he followed the next night. [30]

NOTES

1   In fact the overall shortage of landing craft meant that it was impossible to launch AVALANCHE and BAYTOWN simultaneously. Once the latter was completed, Monty's landing craft were required for AVALANCHE.
2   Montgomery, *Memoirs*, p. 191.
3   Ibid, p. 192.
4   Ibid, p. 193.
5   D'Este, *Eisenhower Allied Supreme Commander*, p. 449.
6   Diary entries.
7   In it he wrote: 'I am at a loss to find words with which to express my chagrin and grief at having given you, a man to whom I owe everything and for whom I would gladly lay down my life, cause to be displeased with me' – Eisenhower, *Crusade in Europe*, p. 201.
8   When awarded to a foreigner, this was the equivalent of the US Distinguished Service Medal.
9   Montgomery, *El Alamein to the River Sangro*, p. 111.
10 Fifth Army in fact comprised two Corps – X British with two inf & one armd divs, & VI US with four inf divs; however, only three inf divs could be landed in the first wave.
11 Diary dated 15 Sep 43.
12 Diary dated 9 Sep 43.
13 Chalfont, *Montgomery of Alamein*, p. 216 and 'Whicker's War', British TV, Channel 4, Aug 2004.
14 Letter to Brig Frank Simpson, Director of Military Operations in the War Office, dated 30 Sep 43.
15 Montgomery, *Memoirs*, p. 196.
16 Diary of Harry C Butcher (Ike's Naval Aide) dated 16 Sep 43.
17 Horne, *The Lonely Leader*, p. 65.
18 Montgomery, op. cit., p. 199.
19 Diary dated 27 Oct 43.
20 Letter to CIGS dated 14 Oct 43.
21 Copy in personal diary.
22 Montgomery, op. cit., p. 200.
23 Ibid, pp. 196–7.
24 Letter to Simpson dated 10 Nov 43.
25 Letter dated 23 Dec 43.
26 Montgomery, op. cit., p. 204.
27 Ibid, p. 210.
28 Ibid, p. 205.
29 Ibid, p. 210.
30 Ibid, p. 213.

CHAPTER XVII

Patton in Exile

George Patton had been devastated by the selection of Omar Bradley, his recent subordinate, to command the First US Army in the forthcoming invasion of Normandy, and his morale continued to suffer during September 1943 as he watched his Seventh Army dwindle in strength as it was used to provide manpower and equipment for both Clark's Fifth Army and the US Army in England. Eisenhower had appointed him as the reserve commander of the Fifth Army in case anything happened to Clark, but this was small compensation. Georgie failed to appreciate two things: one, that simply saying sorry for the slapping incidents was not enough and two, that but for Eisenhower he would have been sent home in disgrace. As a result he continued to privately criticize his saviour in a most vicious way, blaming his 'punishment' as he saw it for, 'doing my plain duty to a couple of cowards.[1] And his anger was restricted not just to his immediate superior – another diary entry, dated 10 September, reads: 'Sometimes I think there is a deliberate campaign to hurt me; certainly it is hard to be victimized for winning a campaign . . . Hap [his Chief of Staff] thinks the cousins [the British] are back of it because I made a fool of Monty'. And despite the fact the Monty had openly spoken of his admiration for the Seventh Army's performance in Sicily and had chastised the editor of the Eighth Army newspaper for publishing a report that Patton was being investigated for some sort of offence, Georgie continued to criticize his rival and made it clear to his associates that he believed the British were promoting Monty as a war hero at his personal expense. 'That is why they [the British] are not too fond of me . . . I know I can outfight the little fart any time'.[2] He was also deeply incensed to learn from an author friend of his ADC who visited him in Palermo, that at home the American newspapers had given the impression that Sicily had been a cakewalk for his Seventh Army while Monty's Eighth had done most of the fighting.

By 11 November 1943, Patton's 58th birthday, his morale had hit rock bottom. He wrote in his diary: 'One year ago today we took Casa [Casablanca]. Now I command little more than my self-respect'. Indeed, his Army numbered less than 5,000 and six days later, as he sat in his palace in Palermo, he wrote: 'Pretty soon I will hit bottom and will then bounce'. The 'bottom' came a few days later when the story of the slapping incidents reached a columnist, Drew Pearson. He used it on his syndicated weekly radio programme and soon Patton's name was in every newspaper and on everyone's lips. A number of Congressmen and Senators demanded his immediate dismissal, but Secretary of War Henry Stimson wrote a letter to the Senate defending Eisenhower's decision to retain him for the forthcoming battle in France and amazingly the furore soon died down. Equally amazingly, he received messages of support from the parents of some of his men and according to his ADC, Charles Codman, 89% of Georgie's personal mail was supportive. A notable exception was General 'Black Jack' Pershing who, to Patton's great disappointment, became one of his sternest critics. He never replied to any of Georgie's letters after he became aware of the slapping incidents.

How did Patton spend his five months in exile? He first of all visited the ground over which his men and the British had fought, wrote *Sidelights on the Sicilian Campaign*[3] (which tells you absolutely nothing about the Sicilian campaign), and spent quite a lot of time visiting Greek, Carthaginian, and Roman archaeological sites. In Syracuse he: 'could almost see the Greek triremes, the Roman galleys, the Vandals, the Arabs, the Crusaders, the French . . . who, to mention only a few, have successively stormed, or attempted to storm, that harbor'.[4] He had tea and dined with some of the more important citizens of Palermo including 'a very fat Bourbon princess with a black beard which she shaves' and her girlfriend 'who should be a wrestler but is actually a famous pianist'.[5]

On the military side Patton, as reserve commander, visited the Fifth Army in Italy, but after finding the campaign almost stalemated and morale low, he decided he had no wish to take over. He was also sent to Corsica where he openly inspected French troops, the harbour and Napoleon's birthplace – all part of a cover plan to make the Germans think the Allies were planning a further amphibious operation.

On 8 December Roosevelt, with his personal adviser, Harry Hopkins, landed in Palermo on his way home from the Teheran Conference with Churchill and Stalin. Eisenhower and Patton greeted him. Hopkins comforted Georgie by saying: 'Don't let anything that s.o.b. Pearson [the columnist] said bother you', and his morale was also raised when Ike said he felt sure, 'I would soon get orders to go to the UK and command an Army'.[6]

On 12 December Patton began a 'grand tour' of the Mediterranean, designed again to make the Germans think that some further major operation in that theatre was a possibility. He flew first to Benghazi, then on to Tobruk and El Alamein, noting 'very few wrecked vehicles, guns and practically no wire', then past the Pyramids and finally to Cairo where he stayed in the residence of British General Sir Henry Maitland-Wilson who happened to be away at the time. The following day he toured Cairo, 'a really disgusting place . . . The Egyptian peasant, who abounds in large numbers, is distinctly lower than the Sicilian, who I had previously considered at the bottom of the human curve'; in the afternoon he visited the British Tank School which he found interesting, 'but not anywhere as well arranged as our schools at Knox and Benning' and then 'the famous Shepheard's Hotel' where the cocktails were good but 'cost a dollar and a half apiece'.[7]

On the 14th Patton flew to Jerusalem where, as well as visiting the Holy Places, he 'followed the Way of the Cross, which is a dirty street'. He was also surprised to be followed into the Holy Sepulchre by four secret service bodyguards, noting that, 'People must have very little confidence to fear assassination in such a place'. The following day he found the Pyramids in Egypt 'quite disappointing . . . not as big nor as impressive as those around Mexico City'. That evening he gave a talk on 'landing operations' to some 500 British officers, one of whom wrote later that, 'in all his previous military career he had not learned as much as in my thirty-minute lecture.'[8]

On 16 December Patton visited the British Combined Operations Training Centre on the shores of the small Bitter Lake, where he was asked to repeat his previous evening's lecture. That night he had dinner with Sir Henry Maitland-Wilson who was 'very much interested in my reaction to General Montgomery, but I was very careful in what I said and refused to be drawn out', and on the 17th he visited Polish General Anders and his II Corps. 'His troops are the best-looking, including British and American, that I have ever seen.'[9]

Before returning to Palermo on 20 December, Georgie flew up the Nile and was able to visit the Valley of the Kings, Thebes and the Temples of Luxor and Karnak.

On New Year's Day Patton's morale suffered another blow – he was officially relieved of command of the Seventh Army; Mark Clark took over as a 'caretaker' commander.

> I feel very badly for myself but particularly for the staff and headquarters soldiers who have stood by me all the time in good weather and bad. I suppose that I am going to England to command another army but if I am sent there to simply train troops which I am not to command, I shall resign . . . A Hell of a 'Happy New Year'.[10]

Georgie remained in his palace in Palermo – he had no orders to go anywhere else and nobody in Sicily could order him out.

On 4 January Patton, accompanied as ever by his ADC Charles Codman, flew to Malta for a two-day visit as the guest of British Field Marshal Lord Gort. On the way they were able to see the II US Corps' Tunisian battlefields at the Kasserine Pass, El Guettar and Gafsa, and it gave him:

> a definite idea of the greatness of the American soldier . . . I am glad that when I fought this battle I did not know how hard the country was . . . Had I known how difficult it was, I might have been less bold.[11]

On 5 January Patton toured Malta finding 'the clean-up job which the British have done since the Blitz is worthy of the greatest praise', and the RAF in Malta the 'best dressed and best-disciplined Air Force that I have ever seen, whether it be American or British'.[12]

Four days later Patton again visited the Fifth Army in Italy where he found Mark Clark nervous and worried about the situation at Cassino. The latter and his Chief of Staff 'were most condescending and treated me like an undertaker treats the family of the deceased. It was rather hard to take'.

On 18 January Patton's pride took another severe knock. He was told that in a radio broadcast Eisenhower had announced that Bradley would command all American ground troops in OVERLORD; he realised at once that Bradley would therefore command the US Army Group that would inevitably be established following a successful landing. He also realised that if he did get command of an Army in England, he would be under Bradley's command. He wrote in his diary: 'Well I have been under worse people and I will surely win'.

On 22 January Patton received a signal from Algiers ordering him to the United Kingdom, but giving him no indication of why he was going. Three days later he left Algiers and on the afternoon of the 26th he arrived at an airfield near London to be met by a West Point classmate, a man he detested, Lieutenant General Lee, the Deputy commander of US Forces in England. There was no guard of honour.

NOTES

1   Diary entry dated 21 Sep 43.
2   Diary entry dated 29 Sep 43.
3   To be found in his book *War As I Knew It*.
4   Patton, op. cit., p. 66.
5   D'Este, *A Genius for War*, p. 556.
6   Diary entry dated 8 Dec 43.
7   Patton, op. cit., pp. 71–4.
8   Ibid, p. 76.
9   Ibid, p. 77.
10 Diary entry dated 1 Jan 44.
11 Patton, op. cit., p. 80.
12 Ibid, p. 81.

CHAPTER XVIII

In England before D-Day

On arrival in London in January 1944, Monty, with no home of his own, had to find temporary accommodation – so he moved into Claridges' Hotel. However, this luxury lasted only a short time whilst a flat was prepared for him in Latymer Court, West Kensington, situated just across the road from his old school, St Paul's. Latymer Court also housed his Headquarters Mess whilst the school accommodated his 21st Army Group Headquarters. His office was located in the Headmaster's study, a room he had never been allowed to enter, even when he was a school prefect and captain of both the 1st XV rugby football team and the 1st XI cricket team. He wrote later:

> I had to become a Commander-in-Chief to do so. Many of the people living in that part of London wrote letters asking me to go away. There was a certain amount of enemy bombing going on and we actually suffered some casualties in the headquarters. The inhabitants considered that our presence there was the cause of the bombing, but there was no evidence to justify that deduction ... I asked Admiral Ramsay, the Naval C-in-C for OVERLORD, to live in the mess ... we were a most cheerful party and at dinner each evening the conversation ranged over a wide field.[1]

As mentioned in chapter XVI, Monty believed the outline OVERLORD plan he had been shown by Churchill in Marrakech to be deeply flawed and he immediately set about getting it changed. Accordingly, by 6 January there was a new outline plan that roughly doubled the size of the assault force and the landing zone. A day later Monty explained its basics to his OVERLORD Army commanders. Then on the 13th he summoned all the general officers of the Armies in England to a conference at St Paul's School in which he gave his views on battle fighting and explained his methods of working. 'In short, I gave them the "atmosphere" in which, from then onwards, we would all work, and later would fight'.[2] He then set off on a five-day tour of units of Bradley's First US Army. Some of the Yanks are said to have found his accent affected and irritating, but most of them were apparently amazed that such a senior commander should have taken the trouble to come and see them. In the case of the three Regiments of the 29th Infantry Division, one of which was to suffer grievously on OMAHA Beach, and all of which would take terrible casualties in the months ahead, 'The GIs liked his informality and ... were delighted to be commanded by a general who had thrashed Rommel in North Africa'.

On 21 January Eisenhower called his first Supreme Commander's Conference at Norfolk House. The original OVERLORD plan was presented, only to be demolished by Monty who then explained his own plan. 'The Supreme Commander agreed with General Montgomery ... [and] proposed that General Montgomery should be left in sole charge of the ground battle'.[3] Monty had won the day and the planning staffs went to work on the details: 'I left the details to de Guingand and his staff' – in fact to the combined British and American planning staffs.

George Patton, arriving in London three weeks after Monty on 26 January, was taken straight to SHAEF (Supreme Headquarters Allied Expeditionary Force) Headquarters at Norfolk House in St James's Square, where Eisenhower told him he was to command the Third Army; it was, however, still in the United States! He learned also that until it landed in Normandy, which would not be until a large enough bridgehead had been established by Bradley's First Army, his Army would remain directly under Ike's command. Having recently been Bradley's superior officer, this saved, at least temporarily, any possible embarrassment; it also had the advantage that, unless something very unforeseen happened, Georgie would never be under Monty's command in the 21st Army Group.

Following his meeting with Ike, Patton was given a 'sixty-four-dollar tour' of the severely bomb-damaged capital by Kay Summersby, Ike's Irish born driver, who found him, 'the most glamorous, dramatic general I'd ever met'. She also noted that his image was somewhat marred by 'the world's most unfortunate voice, a high-pitched womanish squeak'.[4]

The following day George Patton who, against his doctors' strong advice, was now smoking twelve cigars a day, welcomed the advance party of the Third US Army at Greenock in Scotland with: 'I am your new commander. I'm glad to see you. I hope it's mutual'; they then moved off to Knutsford (twenty miles south of Manchester) and Peover, five miles farther on (pronounced by the English 'pea-ver' but inevitably called 'piss-over' by the Americans), where the new Headquarters was to be established. Like Monty, Georgie had arranged for his key Seventh Army staff officers to be transferred from Sicily to his new Headquarters, although Eisenhower and Bedell Smith later persuaded him to drop his old Chief of Staff, Gay, in favour of Major General Hugh Gaffey, who had commanded the 2nd Armored Division in Sicily. Gay became Deputy Chief of Staff.

On 3 February Patton returned temporarily to London and moved into an apartment in Mount Street, Mayfair, which he described as an 'Anglican bordello' due to a white bear rug on the bedroom floor, curtains made of pink brocade and a low-lying bed with a silk embroidered cover.[5] He was much more at home when he was able to move into his new quarters in Peover Hall, an eleventh century manor house, which he described to his wife Beatrice as having been last repaired 'in 1627 or thereabouts'. A few days later, in freezing cold weather, Patton addressed his new staff for the first time. He was dressed in a perfectly tailored uniform, bristling with a total of fifteen stars on his cap, collar and shoulders, highly polished cavalry boots and spurs, and carried a riding crop. Beside him was his newly acquired English bull terrier (surely one of the ugliest dogs ever bred?), *Willie*. Amongst the many things he is reported to have said were:

I am here because of the confidence of two men – the President of the United States and the Theater Commander [Ike]. They have confidence in me because they don't believe a lot of goddamned lies that have been printed about me and also because they know I mean business when I fight . . . It is inevitable for men to be killed and wounded in battle. But there is no reason why such losses should be increased because of the incompetence and carelessness of some stupid son-of-a-bitch. I don't tolerate such men on my staff . . . we are fighting to defeat and wipe out the Nazis who started all this goddamned son-of-a-bitchery . . . If you don't like to fight I don't want you around. You'd better get out before I kick you out.[6]

He is also reported to have talked of 'hitting the goddamned Germans with a sock full of shit and when we wipe them out we will go over and get the purple-pissing Japs'.[7]

Monty was determined to see and be seen by as many of those under his command as possible before D-Day and his visits to his troops soon became legendary. He:

inspected two, and often three, parades a day, each of 10,000 men or more. They were drawn up in a hollow square and I first spoke individually to the unit commanders. I then ordered the ranks to be turned inwards and walked slowly between them, in order that every man could see me; the men 'stood easy' throughout so that they could lean and twist, and look at me all the time if they wished to – and most did . . . I explained how necessary it was that we should know each other, what lay ahead and how, together, we would handle the job. I told them what the German soldier was like in battle and how he could be defeated . . . As a result of the meeting between us, I had absolute confidence in them, and I hoped they could feel the same about me.[8]

Typical of Monty's addresses was his final 'Personal Message' to his troops before the invasion:

The time has come to deal the enemy a terrific blow in Western Europe. That blow will be struck by . . . one great Allied team, under the supreme command of General Eisenhower . . . To us is given the honour of striking a blow for freedom which will live in history; and in the better days that lie ahead men will speak with pride of our doings. Let us pray that 'The Lord Mighty in Battle' will go forth with out armies, and that His special providence will aid us in the struggle . . . As we enter battle, let us recall the words of a famous soldier spoken many years ago:- 'He either fears his fate too much, or his deserts are small, who dare not put it to the touch to win or lose it all'. Good luck to each one of you. And good hunting on the mainland.

By the middle of May Monty 'had visited every formation in the United Kingdom [including the Americans, Canadians, Poles, Belgians, Free French, Dutch and Norwegians] ... I must have inspected, and been inspected, by well over one million men'.[9] This remarkable achievement was made possible by the use a special train he had been given called *Rapier*; it comprised four coaches converted into a Headquarters, messes with kitchens and sleeping accommodation with bathrooms. It even had a flatcar attached so that Monty's Rolls Royce could accompany him wherever he went. And by using the train Monty was also seen by thousands of men and women working in factories and on other war work. On 22 February he addressed a representative group of 500 railwaymen at Euston station and on 3 March some 16,000 dockers and stevedores in the London Docks; amazingly he won the support of even their strongly left-wing Trade Union officials. Inevitably these visits became front-page news in the British press and led to a naïve suspicion in some quarters that he had political ambitions.

Monty's son David accompanied his father on some of the visits made during his April 1944 school holidays:

> This trip the train went to Glasgow, where we visited factories and I remember we went to see an international [United Kingdom] football match at Hampden Park. On all occasions, of course, my father was treated as a great hero. Coming out of factories he was virtually mobbed by people and indeed when we went to Hampden Park there was a roar from the crowd for him as he entered the Royal Box. He was treated everywhere with great respect and great affection . . . [he gave the women working in the munitions factories] the feeling that they were part of a team, and that he was going to look after their husbands, etc., and so generate morale at all levels.[10]

In fact Monty saw very little of his son in the months before D-Day and nothing of his mother, or sisters who on two occasions he snubbed 'with a cavalier brutality that shocked his staff'.[11] He did give a lecture at David's school, Winchester, but was forced to write to him: 'I am sorry I have not been able to see more of you these holidays . . . I have very little spare time – if any'.[12] This was of course true.

Naturally Monty revelled in the adulation he received, and he soon became obsessed 'with photographs and portraits of himself'.[13] Following the success of his 'Desert' portraits, he commissioned Augustus John, for a fee of £500, to do another, but he and John failed to get on and he rejected it. Monty later described John as 'dirty, he drinks – and there are women in the background!'. Such criticism, even if he had known about it, would not have worried the artist who was able to sell the portrait, which showed Monty with 'a long, narrow face and made him look like a greyhound'[14] for a much larger sum on the open market.

On 7 April, long before he completed his visits to his troops, Monty was able to call another major conference at St Paul's School. It was attended by just about every general, admiral and air marshal involved in OVERLORD, including of course George Patton, Field Marshal Alan Brooke (the CIGS), Eisenhower and, before its end, by Churchill. Monty opened the conference himself with a ninety-minute address and by the end of the full presentation no one was in any doubt about what was planned and required. Basically, the British were to capture Caen and the high ground to its south-east and then form a shield to protect the American First Army as it cut off the Cherbourg Peninsula and captured the vital port of Cherbourg; then, when there was room enough, Patton's Third Army was to clear Brittany, whilst Bradley's First broke out south-east towards the Seine and Paris. The British Second and First Canadian Armies would be on its left and Patton's Third on its right. The greater part of the German forces would thus be encircled and destroyed. As Bradley put it later:

> The British and Canadian armies were to decoy the enemy reserves and draw them to their front on the extreme eastern edge of the Allied beachhead. Thus while Monty taunted the enemy at Caen, we were to make our break on the long roundabout road to Paris. When reckoned in terms of national pride, this British decoy mission became a sacrificial one, for while we tramped around the outside flank, the British were to sit in place and pin down Germans. Yet strategically it fitted into a logical division of labors, for it was toward Caen that the enemy reserves would race once the alarm was sounded.[15]

In the run-up to D-Day Patton also set about ensuring that the men of the Third Army saw his 'war face' and heard his words of encouragement and exhortation. Travelling in a black Mercedes, escorted by Military Police and wearing a buff and dark green uniform, helmet and his normal high polished cavalry boots, he revelled in being centre-stage. His words were immortalized by George C Scott in the film *Patton* and need not be repeated in any detail. Nevertheless, some of his more memorable statements give a further insight into his character:

> Men, this stuff we hear about America wanting to stay out of the war – not wanting to fight – is a lot of bullshit. Americans love to fight – traditionally! ... Americans love a winner and will not tolerate a

loser. Americans play to win all the time . . . All through your army career you men have bitched about what you call 'this chicken-shit drilling'. That is all for a purpose – to ensure instant obedience to orders and to create alertness . . . Each man must think not only of himself, but think of his buddy fighting alongside him. We don't want yellow cowards in the Army. They should be killed off like flies. If not, they will go back home after the war, goddam cowards, and breed more cowards . . . We want this thing over with. But you can't win a war lying down. The quickest way to get it over with is to get the bastards. The quicker they are whipped, the quicker we go home. The shortest way home is through Berlin . . . Foxholes only slow up the offensive. Keep moving! . . . There is one great thing you men will be able to say when you go home. You may thank God for it. Thank God that, at least, thirty years from now, when you are sitting round the fireside with your grandson on your knee and he asks you what you did in the great World War II, you won't have to say, 'I shovelled shit in Louisiana'.[16]

All seemed to be going well for Georgie and although he was disappointed that his Army was not to be in the first assault on the 'West Wall', his morale was high. Then, just six weeks before D-Day, he found himself in deep trouble again. It began quite innocently when he was invited to speak to an audience of mainly British female volunteers at the opening of the 'Welcome Club for GIs' in Knutsford. In his brief speech he is reported to have said:

The only welcoming I have done for some time has been welcoming Germans and Italians into Hell – I have done quite a lot in that direction and have got about 177,000 there. I feel that such clubs as this are of real value, because I believe with Mr. Bernard Shaw . . . that the British and Americans are two peoples separated by a common language, and since it is the evident destiny of the British and Americans, and, of course, the Russians, to rule the world, the better we know each other, the better job we will do . . . As soon as our soldiers meet and know the English ladies and write home and tell our ladies how truly lovely you are, the sooner the American ladies will get jealous and force this war to a quick conclusion, and I will get a chance to go and kill Japanese.[17]

Unfortunately for Patton, who claimed later that he believed anything he had said was 'off the record', a local newspaper reporter was present at the meeting and the next day an account of his speech appeared in a British paper; this was soon followed by other reports, some of which, even more unfortunately for Georgie, left out his mention of the Russians and changed his word 'ladies' to 'dames'. Within twenty-four hours the American press, eager for another opportunity to pillory Patton, had headlines proclaiming that he had predicted an Anglo-American domination of the post-war world and articles claiming that he had insulted English women. As the *Washington Post* put it: 'General Patton has progressed from simple assaults on individuals to collective assault on entire nationalities'.[18]

Whilst Patton's references to 'Hell' and if true, which seems quite likely, to English and American 'dames' in his speech were undoubtedly a little tactless, the reaction in Washington and indeed at SHAEF Headquarters was seemingly out of all proportion to the seriousness of the incident and, in view of the fact that there is little doubt that Patton *did* include the Russians, grossly unfair. Churchill, who Eisenhower consulted over the matter, dismissed it as 'a storm in a teacup', but not so the Americans. On the 27th Bedell Smith called Patton and told him that he was not to speak again in public without submitting his proposed speech to Eisenhower for personal approval. Georgie was of course shocked and furious; he wrote in his diary: 'Every effort is made to show lack of confidence in my judgement'. Then on the 29th he received a formal letter of censure from Ike that ended:

> I am thoroughly weary of your failure to control your tongue and have begun to doubt your all-round judgement . . . My decision in the present case will not become final until I have heard from the War Department . . . I want to tell you officially and definitely that if you are again guilty of any indiscretion in speech or action . . . I will relieve you instantly from command.[19]

Patton met Eisenhower in London on 1 May and was told that a decision had still not been made as to whether he was to be sacked, reduced in rank and/or sent home. Georgie wrote in his diary: 'I feel like death, but I am not out yet', and to his wife: 'If I survive the next couple of days it will be OK . . . But still I get in a cold sweat when the phone rings'.[20]

Eisenhower was of course consulting Marshall in Washington and was greatly relieved when he received a signal from him on 2 May saying:

> The decision is exclusively yours. My view, and it is merely that, is that you should not weaken your hand for OVERLORD. If you think that Patton's removal does weaken your prospect, you should retain him in command.[21]

This allowed Ike to retain Patton with a clear conscience and on 3 May he sent him a signal telling him to 'Go ahead and train your Army'. The following day he followed it up with a 'For Your Eyes only' message saying that he was retaining him in command, 'solely because of my faith in you as a battle leader'.[22]

Patton had survived, but his reputation was again severely damaged. Henry Stimson, the Secretary of War, wrote to him on the 5th:

> The only way you can hereafter justify yourself and your commander [Ike] is to keep your mouth absolutely shut until you have reached the beachhead and then by successful drive and successful fighting, win back your reputation as a soldier who can contain himself as well as conquer the enemy.[23]

On 5 May Monty set off for Scotland on a series of visits to the Royal Navy. The previous four months had been extremely tiring and he was persuaded to take a few days off, walking and fishing in the Highlands. He failed to catch any salmon, but it was during this short holiday that Monty's 'double', Lieutenant M E Clifton James, joined him and was able to spend hours 'watching his every movement and trying to catch his fleeting expression'.[24] James was of course the 'look alike' officer selected to impersonate Monty in the deception plan designed to make the Germans think the main Allied landings would take place in the South of France. As such James appeared openly in Gibraltar and North Africa whilst Monty himself went about, 'without flying a flag on my car, and I do not wear my black beret'. Nevertheless, he liked James and to the intense annoyance of some in the War Office insisted that he was paid as a four-star general for each day he actually wore a general's uniform.

Like Monty, George Patton was also involved in a major deception plan. His appointment as commander of the Third Army had deliberately been kept secret and instead it was announced that he was the commander of the 1st US Army Group based in south-east England. This bogus Army Group in fact comprised two real Armies, Patton's own Third and the First Canadian, but they were both destined to be follow-on formations in the invasion of Normandy. However, by the use of dummy landing craft, tanks, vehicles, barracks, ammunition dumps, etc. and false signals traffic, the impression was created that Patton's Army Group was the main invasion force and that it would land in the Pas de Calais sector. This deception plan was amazingly successful in that the Germans came to believe that there was indeed a large military build-up in East Anglia and that the main landing would be on the Pas de Calais coast. As most readers will be aware, for a considerable period after the Normandy landings Hitler and many of his senior commanders still believed it was a feint and that larger landings would follow in the Pas de Calais. For his part Patton did his best to ensure that his visits to his Third Army units remained secret and he usually concluded his speeches with the following phrases:

Don't forget, you don't know I'm here at all. No word of that fact is to be mentioned in any letter. The world is not supposed to know what the hell they did with me . . . Let the first bastards to find out be the goddam Germans. Some day I want them to raise up on their hind legs and howl: 'Jesus Christ, it's that goddam Third Army and that son-of-a-bitch Patton again'.[25]

Needless to say the troops loved it.

Although Monty had moved his Headquarters to Southwick House near Portsmouth on 28 April, he still used St Paul's School for the 'Final Presentation of Plans' before D-Day. It was held on 15 May and attended by the King, Churchill, Eisenhower and all the senior commanders. The conference began badly:

Promptly at 9:00 a.m. Montgomery ordered the doors shut; thereafter no one was to be permitted to enter . . . As the conference was about to begin, there was an enormous hammering at the door, which caused Montgomery to look around angrily. The hammering continued, so he finally ordered the doors opened. They were flung wide and in marched George Patton.[26]

Monty ignored the pointed insult and despite the bad start the rest of the conference was a resounding success. Eisenhower, who began the proceedings, 'was quite excellent; he spoke very little but what he said was on a high level and extremely good'.[27] Monty himself gave what was generally described as a quiet, decisive and brilliant presentation. His confidence was clearly evident when he began by saying: 'General Eisenhower has charged me with the preparation and conduct of the land battle'. George Patton, despite his boisterous entrance, said nothing during the conference and little at the lunch afterwards. Bradley recalled, 'This day was clearly not his, and he knew it'.[28]

Monty's Tac HQ for the forthcoming battle in France was set up within the grounds of Southwick House. Capable of being operational in less than an hour after a move, it was organized by a senior Administrative Officer, Major Paul Odgers, and initially consisted of twenty officers and 200 other ranks, including an infantry defence platoon. At the HQ's 'heart' were communications vehicles capable of receiving ULTRA and PHANTOM messages,[29] and three caravans for use exclusively by Monty.[30] One was to be used as his office, one for sleeping ('I would turn out of this caravan for only two people – the King and Winston Churchill'[31]) and one as a map room where he was to be briefed every evening by the team of young liaison officers who were to provide his 'eyes and ears' in the forthcoming campaign. They were headed by his former Eighth Army ADC, John

Poston and two other Desert veterans, Carol Mather and Dick Harden. Monty called them his 'gallant band of knights' and said they were:

> young officers of character and courage; they had seen much fighting and were able to report accurately on battle situations. I selected each personally, and my standard was high . . . some were wounded and some killed.[32]

Also in the Tac HQ were of course his ADCs – two British, Henderson and Chavasse, an American, Ray BonDurrant and a Canadian, Trumbell Warren, of whom Monty had written in 1942: 'I should like you to know I am very fond of you. If anything should happen to me, against Rommel, I would like you to know that I often wish you were my own son'.[33] There were in fact two American ADCs; another, Bill Culver, was located at the 21st Army Group Main Headquarters. Monty had been asked by Bedell Smith to choose between BonDurrant and Culver, but he refused, saying he would take both! Heading this team at Tac HQ was his Military Assistant, Lieutenant Colonel Kit Dawnay, the officer responsible for liasing with Freddie de Guingand at Main Headquarters and in charge of Monty's personal diary.

Readers are already aware of Monty's bet with Bedell Smith in North Africa that resulted in him being loaned a Flying Fortress on a full-time basis, but it will perhaps surprise many that he was in fact quite a keen gambler. As early as 4 March 1943 he had taken bets with de Guingand over the date the German Army would cease fighting as a co-ordinated body, and in the October of that year he accepted a £5 wager from Eisenhower that the war would be over by Christmas 1944. It came as no surprise to his closest associates therefore when Monty opened a betting book in his 'A' Mess at Broomfield House, a modest country house near Southwick. This Mess was restricted to an inner circle of de Guingand and his ADCs who soon noted, however, that Monty 'never *laid* a bet himself, but . . . was always prepared to accept one'.[34]

On 19 May Churchill visited Monty at Southwick House and three days later King George VI had lunch with him and wished him luck. The Churchill visit was charged with tension. The Prime Minister, having reflected on the presentation at St Paul's School on 15 May, had come to the conclusion that the ratio of men with rifles and bayonets to vehicles in the invasion force was wrong and had announced that he wished to discuss the matter with the 21st Army Group staff. Monty would have none of this and in the privacy of his office told Winston bluntly that: 'You can argue with me but not with my staff. In any case it is too late to change anything. I consider that what we have done is right; that will be proved on D-Day'. When the Prime Minister finally did meet the staff he allegedly said, with a twinkle in his eye, 'I wasn't allowed to have any discussion with you gentlemen'.[35] Monty claims they had 'a most amusing dinner', after which Churchill wrote in his autograph book:

> On the verge of the greatest Adventure with which these pages have dealt, I record my confidence that all will be well and that the organization and equipment of the Army will be worthy of the valour of the soldiers and the genius of their chief.[36]

On 21 May Monty attended evening chapel at Winchester College and said goodbye to his son and on the 23rd he began a final tour.

> I was determined to address all officers down to the lieutenant colonel level . . . I visited every corps and divisional area, and spoke to audiences of from 500 to 600 officers at a time. On each occasion it was essential that I should go 'all out'; if one does this properly, energy goes out of you and leaves you tired at the end. It took eight days in all and was an exhausting tour.[37]

On 1 June Monty invited Bradley, Dempsey (Second British Army), Crerar (First Canadian Army) and Patton to another 'final conference' to go over the plans once more, but without the presence of any staff officers. Afterwards they stayed on to dinner during which Monty toasted his Army commanders and Patton, as the oldest Army commander present, returned the toast. Later in the evening he made two major bets with Monty:

> General Patton bets General Montgomery a level £100 that the armed forces of Great Britain will be involved in another war in Europe within ten years of the cessation of the present hostilities [and] General Patton bets General Montgomery that the first Grand National run after the present war will be won by an American-owned horse – an even £10.[38]

In the event Patton lost both bets, but did not live long enough to pay up.

On 2 June Monty addressed all the officers in his Headquarters and that evening Eisenhower dined quietly with him in his Headquarters Mess at nearby Broomfield House. Monty wrote in his diary that night:

> Eisenhower is just the man for the job; he is really a 'big' man and is in every way an allied commander – holding the balance between the allied contingents. I like him immensely; he has a generous and lovable character and I would trust him to the last gasp.

After dinner the two officers went to Southwick for a conference with the weather experts. The forecast was not as good as hoped for, but it was decided to go ahead with OVERLORD on 5 June. Subsequent meetings led to a postponement until the 6th and despite storms in the Channel, the final go-ahead for that day was given by Ike at an early morning meeting on the 5th. Monty was the only 'improperly dressed' officer there, wearing a high-necked fawn-coloured pullover and light corduroy trousers – the others wore conventional uniform. That evening he drove to Hindhead to see Major and Mrs Reynolds, his son's guardians:

> to make final arrangements with them about David . . . Mrs. Reynolds told me afterwards that she knew it was the eve of D-Day – not from anything I said or from the way I behaved, but because I had taken my plain [civilian] clothes and had put them away in a wardrobe.[39]

On his return to Broomfield House Monty, in accordance with his usual practice, went to bed early.

NOTES

1   Montgomery, *Memoirs*, p. 213.
2   Ibid, p. 217.
3   Minutes of Supreme Commander's Conference dated 21 Jan 44.
4   D'Este, *A Genius for War*, pp. 567–8.
5   Ibid, p. 569.
6   Ibid, p. 573.
7   Ibid, p. 574.
8   Montgomery, op. cit., p. 223.
9   Ibid, p. 224.
10   Horne, *The Lonely Leader*, pp. 82–3.
11   Ibid, p. 85.
12   Ibid.
13   Ibid, p. 75.
14   Ibid.
15   Bradley, *A Soldier's Story*.
16   D'Este, op. cit., pp. 602–5.
17   Ibid, p. 586.
18   Ibid.
19   Ibid, p. 588.
20   Letter dated 2 May 44.
21   D'Este, op. cit., p. 590.
22   Ibid.
23   Ibid, p. 591.
24   James, *I was Monty's Double*.
25   D'Este, op. cit., p. 604.
26   Ibid, p. 595.
27   Montgomery, op. cit., p. 236.
28   Bradley, *A General's Life*, p. 241.
29   ULTRA was the codename for the secret decrypts of German

communications traffic, and the PHANTOM service listened to Allied radio
nets enabling Monty to know what was going on the Allied side.

30   They can be seen today in the IWM's military exhibition at Duxford airfield
     in Cambridgeshire.
31   Horne, op. cit., p. 99.
32   Ibid, p. 100.
33   Ibid, p. 101.
34   De Guingand, *Operation Victory*, p. 369.
35   Montgomery, op. cit., p. 238.
36   Ibid, p. 250.
37   Ibid, pp. 238–9.
38   Ibid, p. 215.
39   Ibid, p. 249.

CHAPTER XIX

Return to France

(Map 10)

Montgomery

According to Freddie de Guingand, the Chief of Staff of the 21st Army
Group, Monty 'kept to his office most of D-Day, waiting to see when he
should move to Normandy'. But in his own *Memoirs* Monty claims he
spent the day in the garden at Broomfield House, making a recording for
the BBC of his final message to the troops and receiving reports. 'As the
morning wore on, it was clear we were ashore and that all was going well
as far as we knew. I decided my place was in Normandy; I could do no
good just outside Portsmouth'.[1] In fact the initial reports reaching Monty
were far from precise. It was known that the British airborne landings had
gone well and that five British and Canadian brigades were ashore, but it
was not until 1530 hours that the American beaches were reported clear of
enemy.

By the evening of D-Day Monty's Tac HQ was on its way across the
Channel and shortly afterwards he set sail himself in HMS *Faulknor*. He
wrote in his pocket diary: 'Invaded Normandy; left Portsmouth 10.30'.
With that he went to bed, leaving orders that he was to be woken at 0600
hours and given a report on the battle.[2] In the event the only way he could
really find out what had happened on D-Day and be briefed on the current
situation was to see his Army commanders personally. This he did by
going aboard the USS *Augusta* to meet Bradley, and then having Miles
Dempsey come aboard the *Faulknor*.

The wind and sea had now dropped, the sun was shining, and the 'round the Fleet' trips in the destroyer were delightful; there was plenty to look at, ships everywhere, and block ships and artificial harbours starting to arrive. There was no enemy air action and few signs of battle on sea or land. It was difficult to imagine that on shore a battle was being fought which was deciding the fate of Europe. We anchored off the British beaches at about 8.30 p.m.[3]

Monty went to bed an hour later having asked to be put ashore at 0700 hours the following morning (8 June).

The precise details of what happened to the British and Americans on D-Day and during the first days of the invasion have been described in many books – some good, some bad. For our purposes they need not be repeated, except to say that within four days of the landings the various beachheads had been joined up into one firm base some sixty miles long and three to twelve miles deep, and as Monty himself put it: 'all anxiety had passed'.[4] For those who wish to be reminded of the details, however, or those unfamiliar with them, it is recommended that they read the books listed in this Bibliography.

Monty's arrival and first few hours in France did not go as planned:

We got under way at 6.30 a.m. and began to move in towards the beach . . . The next thing that happened was that a slight shudder went through the ship . . . When he [the first lieutenant] told me we were aground I am reported to have said: 'Splendid. Then the captain has got as close in as he possibly can. Now what about a boat to put me ashore?' I was eventually taken off in a landing craft by some of my staff [from Tac HQ] who were already on shore.[5]

Worse was to follow. The site for his Tac HQ had been selected off a map; it proved to be too near the front line and hence within easy range of enemy artillery. Monty took one look and ordered it moved to a new location. This was done during the afternoon. Fortunately his Canadian ADC, Trumbell Warren, had found the Château de Creullet at Creully,[6] eight miles east of Bayeux, the garden of which was ideal for Monty's caravans. Even so, according to one of his ADCs Monty was, 'tired and rather on edge; nothing was right – yet when Howard Marshall, the BBC rep, called to see him, he showed no sign of tiredness, only confidence'.[7] In fact Monty was delighted with the new site, particularly when the owner's wife, Madame de Druval, produced the only thing he still needed for his personal use – a pot-de-chambre which he kept for the rest of his life! The owner himself, a 75-year-old Marquis, was a supporter of Marshal Pétain and, according to Paul Odgers, 'a dubious ex-cavalry aristocrat'. It appears that he was unaware of the identity of the important guest in his garden until after Monty had left two weeks later.

Monty's decision to move to Normandy on D+2 had caught everyone except his closest confidants by surprise; not least his Chief Medical Officer who, realising that he could not guarantee intimate personal medical services to Monty in the early stages of the campaign, was forced to attach a doctor, Major Bob Hunter, to Tac HQ. The posting was meant to be temporary but Hunter ended up staying with Monty for the rest of the war and even beyond that. His patient was never ill except for the occasional cold, but in the early days of the Normandy campaign Hunter was forced to fly to London twice to fetch new sets of false teeth after Monty broke his dentures on army biscuits – an unlikely 'delicacy' the C-in-C much enjoyed.

Shortly after his arrival in Normandy Monty received a postcard from his mother; addressed to 'HQ 21st Division, Normandy, France', it read:

> I believe you landed at the same spot from which William the Conqueror sailed in 1066. Our ancestor Roger Montgomery was his 2nd in Command – like you. The old Montgomery castle was near Lisieux. Please send photographs.[8]

It is not known whether Monty replied to his mother, but certainly on D+6 he wrote to his son and to the Reynolds expressing his delight at being in Normandy; to David he said:

> All very well here in France and the battle is going according to plan. I have my Tac HQ over here now, with all my caravans, and am comfortably installed and living the open air life. It really pays.

And to Phyllis Reynolds he wrote: 'The French civilians in Normandy do not look in the least depressed; there is plenty of food, plenty of vegetables, cows, milk, cheeses and very good crops'.

The forward location of Tac HQ was surprising in that it was well within enemy artillery range and it was in fact both shelled and bombed during its time at Creully. However, Monty was determined to be on French soil and there were virtually no other options. Less confident C-in-Cs would almost certainly have remained at Southwick House in England where Freddie de Guingand was located with the 21st Army Group Main Headquarters. Indeed, this would have had the advantage of allowing Monty easy and personal access to Eisenhower and his fellow Naval and Air C-in-Cs – but that was not Monty's way. Instead, as soon as a nearby airfield was activated, his Chief Intelligence and Operations officers had to fly over from England in a Dakota each day in order to brief him on SHAEF matters and take back to Main Headquarters his orders and future intentions. The latter could then be passed back up the line to Ike. This somewhat cumbersome system had obvious advantages and disadvantages. Whilst it kept Monty free from the detailed staff work involved in running a successful campaign and placed him much closer to his Army, Corps and Divisional commanders, it isolated and insulated him from his superiors and officers of his own age and seniority. This in turn often led to criticism of his conduct by British and American senior officers at SHAEF and in Bradley's Headquarters – criticism of which Monty was unfortunately unaware.

Monty's life during the first two weeks of the Normandy campaign was, in his view at least, plagued by visitors. Churchill, Brooke and South Africa's General Smuts arrived on the 12th, causing Monty to postpone an important conference with Bradley – much to their joint annoyance. During the visit a German deserter was discovered within fifty yards of Tac HQ causing considerable consternation and a decision to reinforce the infantry defence platoon with commandos and some armoured vehicles. Recalling his visit, Churchill wrote later:

> We lunched in a tent looking towards the enemy. The General [Monty] was in the highest spirits. I asked him how far away was the actual front. He said about three miles. I asked him if he had a continuous line. He said, 'No'. 'What is there then to prevent an incursion of German armour breaking up our luncheon?' He said he did not think they would come.[9]

It is not surprising Monty was in 'the highest spirits' that morning – the Americans had just advanced and captured Caumont, a strategic village on their left flank, half way between Villers-Bocage and St Lô. This allowed Dempsey to launch the British 7th Armoured Division (The Desert Rats) in a wide enveloping movement to outflank the Panzer Lehr Division and advance on Caen – the main British D-Day objective which had yet to be taken. That night Monty signalled de Guingand that this move could be a 'turning point in the battle', and he followed it up with a letter written in almost Pattonistic terms: 'I am enjoying life greatly and it is great fun fighting battles again after five months in England'.

Unfortunately Monty spoke too soon; the British advance through Villers-Bocage was a disaster and Monty was aware of this when his next unwanted visitor arrived on the 14th – Charles de Gaulle! His visit was also a disaster. After deliberately landing on a Canadian rather than a British beach, he arrived at Creully for lunch. Monty wrote in his diary:

> I gave him every facility to go where he liked, but asked him to leave the lodgement area before dark – which he did. His general reception in Bayeux and other places was lukewarm; his staff had to keep shouting, 'General de Gaulle', and pointing to him.

In fact when Monty heard that de Gaulle's speech-making in Bayeux had caused a military traffic jam, he was furious and gave orders that the General was to be sent back to England. Relations between the French 'prima donna' and Monty never recovered. The latter was not the only officer to be angered by de Gaulle. When Eisenhower heard that the Frenchman had claimed in his Bayeux speech that the Free French were liberating France with 'the aid of the Allies', he too was furious.

Shortly after de Gaulle's visit Monty heard that Churchill wanted the King to come over to Normandy. He agreed that this would happen on the 16th, with the proviso that no other VIP should come at the same time; he wrote to the Director of Military Operations in the War Office, 'warn Eisenhower off if he proposes to come the same day, I cannot deal with more than one VIP – and have told the PM [Churchill] today he must not come again just yet'.

The King's visit went reasonably well, although Monty's ADC, Johnny Henderson, who had been supervizing the unloading of Monty's *two* Rolls-Royces earlier that day, recalled in his diary: 'He wasn't allowed to go anywhere else [other than Creully] as there were still snipers about. It is a pity he is not more forthcoming with the troops – never waves to them or shows much sign of interest'.[10] Monty wrote to Phyllis Reynolds afterwards:

> I told the King that I did not think the people of Normandy had any wish to be liberated. When you read in the paper that another town has been 'liberated' it really means that very heavy fighting has taken place around it and that it has been destroyed – that not one house is left standing – and that a good many of the inhabitants have been killed. Such is the price the French are now paying. When they chucked their hand in in 1940 they thought they could avoid all this – but they cannot.

An unfortunate consequence of the King's visit was a BBC report that he had visited Monty in the 'grounds of a château' and a *Daily Mail* article that, according to Johnny Henderson, had 'practically given the route, therefore leaving little doubt in the enemy's mind as to where we were'.[11] Whatever the truth, the Château de Creully, where the BBC outpost was located, was bombed on the 18th and, as Monty put it in a letter to his successor in the Eighth Army, 'heavy gunfire was opened on my HQ two days after that, and I had one killed and two wounded. I then decided to move my HQ, and am having no more visitors!!!'. He had already written to his son on the day of the bombing saying: 'A great deal of bombing and shooting goes on by night, so I have now got my bed put in a hole in the ground and I sleep quite safely below ground level'. On the 23rd Monty's Tac HQ moved to Blay, six miles the other side of Bayeux, just inside the American sector and 'more in the middle'.

Despite Monty's jingoistic statement that it was 'great fun fighting battles again', the battle was not in fact going exactly in accordance with his master plan. The Americans had still not captured Cherbourg and after becoming entangled in what became known as the 'Battle of the Hedgerows'[12] south of OMAHA beach, they were a long way from securing the hinge of their planned breakout – St Lô. British and Canadian attempts to capture or envelop Caen, variously called the bastion, anvil and pivot of the Normandy campaign, had all failed. Monty's demands that 'armoured columns must penetrate deep inland, and quickly, on D-Day'[13] had come to nothing and his overall plan of getting 'control of the main enemy lateral Granville–Vire–Argentan–Falaise–Caen' and having 'the area within it firmly in our possession' seemed as far away as ever.[14] In the corridors of power in London and Washington, the lack of progress and the knowledge that the Allies had already suffered over 30,000 casualties began to cause alarm; the fear that the campaign might bog down into a costly war of attrition returned to haunt the planners. And then to complicate matters further, in the early hours of the 19th a violent three-day storm developed in the Channel. The interruption this caused to the landing of men and supplies[15] inevitably forced the Allies – Americans, British and Canadians alike – to postpone all offensive operations.

On 25 June the British re-opened their attack in the east with an assault by three Corps – Operation EPSOM. Its aim was to cross the Odon and Orne rivers and capture the high ground astride the Caen–Falaise road, thus isolating, and then capturing, Caen. The scale of EPSOM was obvious to all the senior Allied commanders, and although there can be no doubt that it was an essential part of Monty's strategy to draw as much German armour as possible on to the British sector and away from the planned American breakout on the western flank, there is also no doubt that EPSOM was seen by everyone as a major attempt to break through the German defences in the east. Before the attack was launched Monty had written to Eisenhower: 'I shall put VIII Corps through in a blitz attack supported by great air power as at El Hamma'. In fact, EPSOM ended in a sea of mud, cost over 4,000 casualties and sixty-two tanks, and turned out to be the very antithesis of Blitzkrieg. It did, however, ensure that the very powerful II SS Panzer Corps, comprising the 9th and 10th SS Panzer Divisions, recently arrived from the Eastern front, was committed against Dempsey's Second British Army and stayed on that front rather than being freed for use against the planned breakout by Bradley's First US Army. Nevertheless, uninformed critics in the USA and the UK continued to demand the capture of Caen – it seemed to them that since the shortest way to the Seine, Paris and indeed the Rhine was from the eastern flank of the Allied lodgement area, the logical place for a breakout was on that flank. They had no idea of Monty's overall strategy and that it was in fact working – by the end of June there were 725 German tanks on Dempsey's front and only 140 on Bradley's.

The only relatively good news during EPSOM came on the 26th when the Americans finally took Cherbourg; even so, this did little to cheer Monty who was depressed by the weather and worried, firstly by the ULTRA intercept that had told him of the arrival of II SS Panzer Corps, and secondly by the lack of progress in EPSOM. His ADC wrote in his diary:

> The Chief has been in wonderful form for the last fortnight – now again he gets worried and it is advisable to keep well away – let others get the rockets. He gets irritable, doesn't concentrate, fusses over little things.[16]

Monty expressed his concern about the arrival of more Panzer Divisions on the British Second Army front in a letter to the VCIGS, Lieutenant General Sir Archibald Nye, written just before EPSOM. In it he was clearly worried about a, 'great, extravagant armoured battle in the Caen area, with the enemy driving towards Bayeux'.[17] As EPSOM developed, however, he was able to note in his diary that his strategy was working, 'a total of eight PZ divisions all involved in trying to stem my advance west and south-west of Caen; this is excellent'.[18]

The extent of the stalemate in Normandy in June and early July can be gauged by the fact that Monty's Tac HQ remained at Blay for six weeks. And it was in another attempt to break that stalemate that a further attack on the west side of Caen was launched by the Canadians on 4 and 5 July (Operation WINDSOR); but that too failed and this led Dempsey to believe that it would be impossible to take the city without unacceptable casualties unless the attack was assisted by RAF bomber command. Accordingly, and despite the fact that there were no actual German combat units in the city, Caen was devastated on 7 July and by last light on the 9th British and Canadian troops were in possession of all the ground north of the Orne river (Operation CHARNWOOD). Despite this the major mission of securing the high ground between Caen and Falaise had still not been fulfilled and Monty remained under great pressure and criticism. Understandably there is no sign of this in his letters home. On 2 July he sent David some eggs from Normandy, with some chocolate and boiled sweets and a note saying that he now had two dogs; and on the 7th he wrote to Phyllis Reynolds saying:

> All goes well here – except the weather which is completely foul . . . I have been collecting livestock. I now have six canaries, one love bird, two dogs. The dogs are puppies, about ten weeks old. One is a fox terrier, given me by the BBC men in France. I have named him Hitler. The other is a gold cocker spaniel . . . I have named him Rommel . . . Hitler and Rommel both get beaten when necessary . . . both 'coming to heel well'.[19]

Patton

But what of George Patton during this period? He had not been privy to the final discussions as to exactly when OVERLORD would be launched, and he learned about it at Peover through a BBC broadcast at 0700 hours on 6 June. That day he wrote to his son George: 'I wish I was there now as it is a lovely sunny day for a battle, and I am fed up with just sitting'. But that is exactly what Georgie had to do for a month – just sit and lend credence to the deception that when his Army was deployed it would land in the Pas de Calais (Map 4) rather than Normandy. It would appear, however, that Georgie was probably not 'just sitting'. In early July Jean Gordon arrived in England as a Red Cross volunteer, or 'doughnut dolly' as they were often known. Readers may recall that she was Patton's half-sister-in-law and that his wife Beatrice certainly believed that he had had an affair with Jean in Honolulu in 1936. There has been much discussion about their relationship immediately before D-Day. Patton's daughter and Jean's best friend, Ruth Ellen, claimed that it was more like that of a father and daughter; on the other hand his grandson, and his close friend from West Point days, Everett Hughes, both believed he resumed the affair. Needless to say, when Beatrice wrote to Georgie in late July that she had been aware of Jean's presence in England, he wrote back: 'The first I knew about Jean's being here was in your letter. We are in the middle of a battle so don't meet people, so don't worry'.[20]

Patton touched down on a temporary landing strip behind OMAHA beach on 6 July, exactly a year to the day since he had set off from Algiers heading for Sicily. The day before he had written in his diary: 'Why the American army has to go with Monty I do not see, except to save the face of the little monkey'. He remembered later:

> After we landed and drove along the beach, the sight of the destruction of vessels was appalling. Some of this had been done by enemy action, but a great deal of it was due to the storm which raged for several days just after the initial landing.[21]

Although Patton's presence in Normandy was meant to be a closely guarded secret, it was not long before the men on the ground knew about it. Wearing a single pistol he is said to have exclaimed soon after landing:

> I'm proud to be here to fight beside you. Now let's cut the guts out of those Krauts and get the hell on to Berlin. And when we get to Berlin, I am going to personally shoot that paper-hanging goddamned son-of-a-bitch, just like I would a snake.[22]

Patton spent the night of 6 July at Bradley's First Army Headquarters just south of Isigny, 'in the midst of the most infernal artillery preparation I have ever heard',[23] and the next day he drove to his own Third Army Forward Headquarters, codenamed 'Lucky Forward', which had been established in an apple orchard in the grounds of the Château Bricquebec at Néhou, five miles south-east of Bricquebec. Later that morning he and Bradley lunched with Monty at Blay and that evening he wrote in his diary: 'Montgomery went to great lengths explaining why the British have done nothing. Caen is still their D-Day objective and they have not taken it yet'. He did *not* write in his diary that a major attack was to be launched against that city the following day or that progress in the American sector had been equally unsatisfactory.

On 30 June Monty ordered the First US Army to launch a major offensive commencing on 3 July. It was designed to gain the line Coutances–Marigny–St Lô and then:

> to strike straight through, without pause, to the line Caumont–Vire–Mortain–Fougères. Subsequently operations would continue with minimum delays, to successive objectives in the areas Laval–Mayenne and Le Mans–Alençon. A subsidiary thrust was to be launched into the Brittany peninsula.[24]

The offensive did not go well – VIII Corps took twelve days to gain seven miles and VII Corps lost 4,800 men in taking six square miles of ground.[25] By the middle of July the attack was halted and Bradley declared the new primary goal to be St Lô and the road leading west from it towards Périers – a line that Monty and Bradley had originally hoped to reach by 11 *June*! It was to cost the three infantry divisions of XIX Corps 10,077 casualties to achieve this.[26] Nevertheless, by 18 July the 'Battle of the Hedgerows' had finally been won and there was at last enough space for Patton's Third Army. The planned breakout, Operation COBRA, with the objectives specified by Monty on 30 June, could go ahead at last.

Although located in Bradley's operational area, Patton was still under Eisenhower's direct command and was expected to remain so until about 1 August at least. Bradley, not surprisingly, was a little nervous at the prospect of having his old boss serving under him:

> He had not been my first choice for Army commander and I was still wary of the grace with which he would accept our reversal in roles . . . I feared that much of my time would probably be spent in curbing his impetuous habits. But at the same time I knew that with Patton there would be no need for my whipping Third Army to keep it on the move. We had only to keep him pointed in the direction we wanted to go.[27]

NOTES

1 Montgomery, *Memoirs*, p. 249.
2 Horne, *The Lonely Leader*, p. 119.
3 Montgomery, op. cit., p. 252.
4 Ibid.
5 Ibid.
6 Not to be confused with the Château de Creully, half a mile away which was later occupied by the BBC.
7 Henderson diary dated 8 Jun 44 – Horne, op. cit., p. 123.
8 Horne, op. cit., p. 126.
9 Churchill, *The Second World War*, Vol VI, p. 11.
10 Horne, op.cit., p. 140.
11 Ibid, pp. 154–5.
12 It eventually took four US Corps, totalling twelve divisions, to fight their way through the 'bocage' in their sector of Normandy. The 'bocage' consisted of numerous small fields, surrounded by steep banks carrying hedges and trees. Sunken lanes further restricted movement.
13 On 15 May at St Paul's School in London.
14 Ibid.
15 The scale of this interruption can be judged by the following figures: in the period 15–18 Jun, before the storm, the British landed 15,774 soldiers, 2,965 vehicles and 10,666 tons of stores; in the period of the storm, 19–22 June, the figures dropped to 3,982 men, 1,375 vehicles and only 4,286 tons of stores: Ellis, *Victory in the West, Vol I, The Battle of Normandy*, p. 274.
16 Henderson diary dated 27 Jun 44.
17 Horne, op. cit., p. 157.
18 Diary dated 27 Jun 44.
19 Horne, op. cit., p. 163.
20 Letter dated 3 Aug 44.
21 Patton, *War As I Knew It*, p. 90.
22 D'Este, *A Genius for War*, p. 613.
23 Patton, op. cit., p. 90.
24 Montgomery, *Normandy to the Baltic*, pp. 233–4.
25 Center of Military History, US Army, Publication 100–13, *St Lô*, p. 91.
26 Ibid, p. 126.
27 Bradley, *A Soldier's Story*, p. 355.

CHAPTER XX

The Normandy Campaign

(Map 10)

Author's Note

It is impossible to describe the lives of Monty and Patton between July 1944 and May 1945 without going into some of the details of the military operations in Western Europe during that period. Since all the sources consulted by the author do the same, this part of the book will contain fewer personal details than have been provided in previous chapters and of necessity, will concentrate more on the military aspects of their lives.

GOODWOOD

By mid-July the Americans had landed 770,000 troops in Normandy, of which 10% had become casualties, and the British and Canadians 591,000, of which just over 8% had become casualties.[1] Montgomery was facing criticisms from all quarters. The vital port of Cherbourg was still not operational; the Americans had failed to achieve their planned breakout or sufficient space to bring in their troops waiting in England and the United States; German occupation of Caen south of the Orne river was blocking a British and Canadian advance to the Falaise Plain, and insufficient ground had been captured in the British sector for the construction of urgently needed airfields out of German artillery range. It was clear that something had to be done, and done quickly, to break the stalemate. The arrival at this time of four new German infantry divisions complicated matters. Monty knew that their task was to take over from the Panzer divisions on the British front so that the latter could be used in their classic counter-attack role and in particular for operations against the Americans. He knew therefore that he would have to create a sufficient threat on the Caen flank to hold that German armour. Consequently, and having already failed to achieve a breakthrough to the west of Caen, he decided to launch a strong armoured thrust, Operation GOODWOOD, from the bridgehead on the east side of the Orne. As he put it in a letter to Field Marshal Sir Alan Brooke on 14 July:

> The Second Army is now very strong . . . and can get no stronger . . . So I have decided that the time has come for a real 'showdown' on the eastern flank, and to loose a corps of three armoured divisions into the open country about the Caen–Falaise road.

On 15 July Montgomery issued a personal memorandum to the commander of the British VIII Corps, Lieutenant General Sir Richard O'Connor, in which he made his intentions clear:

> To engage the German armour in battle and write it down to such an extent that it is of no further value to the Germans as a basis of the battle. To gain a good bridgehead over the Orne through Caen and thus improve our positions on the eastern flank. Generally to destroy German equipment and personnel, as a preliminary to a possible wide exploitation of success . . . and to fight and destroy the enemy.[2]

Sadly for Monty GOODWOOD was to cause endless controversy and permanently damage his reputation. After the war he claimed that he had:

> never at any time [had] any intention of making the breakout from the bridgehead on the eastern flank. Misunderstandings about this simple and basic conception were responsible for much trouble between British and American personalities.

He then went on to quote an extract from Eisenhower's report on the campaign, dated 13 July 1945, in which Ike had said:

> In the east we had been unable to break out towards the Seine [Map 11], and the enemy's concentration of his main power in the Caen sector had prevented us from securing the ground in that area we so badly needed. Our plans were sufficiently flexible that we could take advantage of this enemy reaction by directing that the American forces smash out of the lodgement area in the west.

Monty construed this as a total misunderstanding of his declared strategy:

> The impression is left that the British and Canadians had failed in the east (in the Caen sector) and that, therefore, the Americans had to take on the job of breaking out in the west. This reflection on Dempsey and the Second Army is a clear indication that Eisenhower failed to comprehend the basic plan to which he had himself cheerfully agreed [at St Paul's School].[3]

In fact Ike had not misunderstood the basic plan. On 6 July he had written to Monty:

> I am familiar with your plan for generally holding firmly with your left, attracting thereto all of the enemy armor, while your right pushes down the peninsula and threatens the rear and flank of the forces facing the Second British Army.[4]

And Monty had replied:

> I am myself, quite happy with the situation. I have been working throughout on a very definite plan, and I now begin to see daylight ... The great thing is to get the First and Third US Armies up to a good strength, and to get them cracking on the southward thrust on the western flank, and then turn Patton westwards into the Brittany peninsula [Map 11]. To sum up, I think the battle is going very well.[5]

In order to guarantee the success of the new British attack, Operation GOODWOOD was opened on 18 July with a devastating aerial bombardment of Caen south of the Orne and the villages lying directly in the path of the attack. The details of what happened between 18 and 21 July need not concern us; it is sufficient to know that only one of the four objectives specified by the Army commander was captured, only 20% of the German armour in the attack area was destroyed and the operation cost over 5,000 British and Canadian casualties and over 250 tanks. On the plus side, however, Monty's main aim of holding the bulk of the German strength on the eastern flank *was* achieved. By the time the Americans launched their major offensive four days later, Dempsey's fourteen divisions were pinning down fourteen German divisions and 625 tanks in the Second Army sector, whereas Bradley's fifteen divisions, plus three of Patton's in reserve, were facing 'a hotchpotch' of formations and battlegroups, amounting to only nine divisions and some 110 tanks.

Be that as it may, one thing is certain; virtually all the senior officers at SHAEF Headquarters, including Eisenhower, considered GOODWOOD a failure. They had expected, and in fairness had been led to believe, that there would be at least a limited breakout. Ike made his famous remark that the Allies could hardly expect to advance through France at a rate of a thousand tons of bombs per mile! Tedder, Leigh-Mallory and all the senior air commanders were equally angry and wanted Montgomery sacked and Eisenhower himself to take command of all land forces; even Churchill began to have doubts about Monty's ability. There can be no doubt therefore that GOODWOOD not only tarnished Monty's reputation forever but also, sadly for him, ended his chance of remaining overall land force commander for the rest of the campaign in Europe. In many ways this loss of reputation was his own fault. As he later admitted: 'I was too exultant at the Press conference I gave during GOODWOOD'. This was true; at that conference he not only gave the impression that a decisive moment in the Normandy campaign had arrived, but even mentioned the words breakout and breakthrough.

COBRA

By 18 July the planning for the American offensive, Operation COBRA, had been completed and Monty had 'approved the scheme'.[6] The attack should have been launched on 20 July, two days after the beginning of GOODWOOD, but in the event it had to be postponed until the 25th because bad weather prevented the heavy aerial bombardment which, as in the case of GOODWOOD, was considered an essential prerequisite.

The period between the opening of GOODWOOD on the 18th and COBRA on the 25th was an extremely uncomfortable time for Monty. On the 19th the CIGS, knowing that most of the senior officers at SHAEF wanted

Monty sacked, flew over to warn him and make him aware that Churchill was furious with him for telling Eisenhower to keep all visitors, including the Prime Minister, away from his Tac HQ during GOODWOOD. Brooke made him write a letter to Winston saying that:

> this is the first I have heard of your visit. I hope that you will come over here whenever you like; I have recently been trying to keep visitors away as we have much on hand. But you are quite different.[7]

It is not clear whether or not Brooke had a hand in it, but that night Monty also invited Eisenhower to visit him, alone, the following day. He did so and to the amazement of his Naval ADC, Harry Butcher, the Supreme Commander, who had spent the whole of the 19th in bed with high blood pressure, listlessness and tinnitus, emerged from the meeting a changed man:

> he went fishing, piloted a liaison plane, threw away the 'slow-down potion' given him for his high blood pressure and told Butcher to telephone Bedell Smith and 'caution him against even hinting at the subject we have been discussing [the sacking of Monty].[8]

It seems clear from this encounter that any misunderstandings between Monty and the Supreme Commander were because they had had far too little eye-to-eye contact. This was mainly due to the fact that Monty, for good tactical reasons, insisted on operating from a forward Tac HQ, far removed from Ike in England, and that the latter visited him only nine times between D-Day and the end of August.

Churchill arrived at Blay the day after Ike's visit. Monty's ADC, Henderson, wrote in his diary:

> It was common knowledge at Tac that Churchill had come to sack Monty ... However, Monty showed not the least nervousness. He shook hands, took him into the Operations caravan – and when they came out Churchill was beaming.

The exact details of what transpired are unknown, but Monty must have turned on the charm; all that is known for certain is that after belittling reports of a 'temporary setback', he went on to brief the Prime Minister on COBRA. The fact that Monty and his Chief of Intelligence were able to share in the contents of Churchill's despatch boxes must have helped to divert attention away from the failing GOODWOOD operation anyway – they contained the first details of the 20 July bomb plot to kill Hitler! Monty sent Winston off with a bottle of cognac and wrote in his diary,

'Everything was made clear. I told him that whenever he got angry in future he was to send me a telegram and find out the truth. He promised to do so'.[9] Actually it had been 'a close-run thing' and there seems little doubt that if COBRA had ended the same way as GOODWOOD, Monty's career would have been over.

Bradley had learned much from his failed offensive in early July when he had attacked in extremely difficult country on a very wide front. For COBRA he accepted Monty's suggestion that he should concentrate his forces on a narrow front just to the west of St Lô and then, after breaching the German defences with a devastating air bombardment and infantry assault, drive for the coast south of Coutances with armoured columns. Nevertheless, COBRA did not begin well; two tragic 'Blue on Blue' bombing incidents caused 757 casualties and initial progress was slow. Bradley reported later that on the first evening of the attack he had, 'little reason to believe we stood at the brink of a breakthrough. Rather, the attack looked as though it might have failed'.[10] Progress came finally on 26 July when VII Corps, under Major General 'Lightning Joe' Collins, crossed the Coutances–St Lô road and made an advance of six miles. The next day the German front, reduced to a thin crust, collapsed and the First Army Divisions swept south and west, taking Marigny and Périers. On the 28th the 4th Armored Division liberated Coutances. By then half a dozen German infantry divisions had been cut to pieces and their parent Corps had disintegrated. As US columns poured down the roads between Coutances and the Vire river, even the Americans were astonished by their success. Bradley wrote in his official report, 'The ensuing period, which the plan had conceived would be a holding and mopping up period, became a vigorous attack period'.[11] He realised that it might now even be possible to implement the plan outlined by Monty on 30 June when the latter had said that once the offensive had started, 'there must be no pause' until it had driven south beyond Avranches and Mortain (Map 11) and had, 'swung up on to the line Caumont–Fougères' (Map 11). Then it was to make a: 'wide sweep south of the bocage country . . . to Le Mans–Alençon' (Map 11). For such exploitation Bradley knew he needed to unleash George Patton! Accordingly he placed Troy Middleton's VIII Corps, which although formally part of Third Army was already fighting under the First Army, under Patton's tactical direction on the 28th. It was a very powerful formation with two armoured and two infantry Divisions. The only other available Third Army Corps, Wade Haislip's XV with three infantry Divisions, was to come under Georgie's command when his Third Army became officially operational at 1200 hours on 1 August.[12]

Patton wasted no time; he went at once to Troy Middleton and arranged to take the Corps under command. The next day he visited its 6th Armored Division which he found:

sitting on a road, while its HQ . . . was engrossed in a study of maps. I asked why they had not crossed the Sienne [a small river running about twenty miles south of St Lô and Coutances]. They told me they were making a study of it at the moment, but could not find a place where it could be forded . . . I then told them I had just waded across it, that it was not over two feet deep and that the only defenses I knew about was one machine-gun which had fired very inaccurately at me . . . They learned the lesson.[13]

On the same day he found a Division of XV Corps digging slit trenches and told them to stop as it was 'stupid to be afraid of a beaten enemy'.[14]

On 30 July Patton's 6th Armored Division took Bréhal and drove past Granville without stopping, whilst the same evening his 4th Armored, still spearheading the advance, entered Avranches without opposition and the next day reached the Sélune at Pontaubault. As Patton described it after the war:

I drove to the CP of VIII Corps at Bréhal. Middleton was very glad to see us as he had reached his objective which was the Sélune and did not know what to do next. [He had been unable to contact Bradley for further orders.] I told him that throughout history wars had been lost by not crossing rivers and that he should get over at once . . . I told Middleton to head for Brest and Rennes [Map 11] . . . and also to create a task force . . . to go along the north coast of the [Brittany] peninsula.[15]

That night Patton addressed his Third Army staff. Included in his harangue were instructions that flanks were, 'something for the enemy to worry about, not us', and that he did not want any messages saying that, 'We are holding our position. We're not holding anything! Let the Hun do that'. He went on:

We are advancing constantly and we're not interested in holding on to anything except the enemy. We're going to hold him by the nose and we're going to kick him in the ass; we're going to kick the hell out of him all the time and we're going to go through him like crap through a goose . . . We have one motto, L'audace, l'audace, toujours l'audace! Remember that gentlemen.[16]

On the day that Patton's Third Army became officially operational, Omar Bradley handed over command of the First Army to Lieutenant General Courtney Hodges and became the commander of the 12th US Army Group, comprising the First and Third US Armies. Nine days earlier the First Canadian Army had been activated under Lieutenant General Crerar and together with the Second British Army it now formed the 21st Army Group. Monty therefore still commanded two Armies. Furthermore, since Eisenhower had yet to move even the command element of SHAEF Headquarters (a Tac HQ) over to Normandy, Monty, as the Land Forces commander, continued to exercise operational control over the 12th US Army Group. As early as 7 July he had written to Brooke: 'He [Ike] has now decided to form the US Army Group, with Bradley in command, and put it under me'. This was confirmed later by Bradley:

> Monty was in operational control of both army groups until September 1st, even though I took over [US] Army Group on August 1st. Ike had not yet moved [his] headquarters over to France. Until SHAEF did come in I was to be under [the] operational control of Monty. Ike did not want to handle [the] campaign from so great a distance.[17]

Patton was of course far from happy with this command arrangement. He did not like *any* US troops being under the control of the 'little fart' as he called Monty.

Brittany

(Map 11)

The Americans were now at the gateway to the Brittany peninsula. In less than a week, they had made a breakthrough of nearly fifty miles and had taken some 18,000 prisoners. The stalemate had come to an end and the war of attrition had suddenly and dramatically been replaced by a war of movement.

At 1030 hours on 1 August Monty gave orders to Bradley that when Patton's Third Army: 'takes up the reins at midday' it was 'to pass one Corps through Avranches straight into the Brittany Peninsula. Its other two Corps will be directed on Laval and Angers [on the Loire]'.[18] This was an extraordinary order in that it was a clear interference in Bradley's sphere of command and one that was not likely to further Anglo/ American relations. Nevertheless, on the same day Bradley gave *his* first orders as an Army Group commander, telling Hodges (First Army) to seize the Vire–Mortain area, and Patton to secure the line St Hilaire(-du-Harcouet)–Fougères–Rennes and then to turn westwards into Brittany. As we have heard, according to Patton he had already issued orders to Middleton to 'head for Brest and Rennes . . . and also to create a task force . . . to go along the north coast of the [Brittany] peninsula' two days earlier. Whether that is true or not makes no difference – on the evening of the 31st, when the 4th Armoured Division captured the bridge at Pontaubault

(Map 10) intact, he certainly told Middleton to send his four Divisions down the single road through Avranches and Pontaubault, and then direct one armoured and one infantry division down the centre of the Brittany peninsula to Brest and a similar force through Rennes to Vannes and Lorient. Meanwhile, XV Corps was to secure the Fougères–Rennes sector.

Georgie was now in his element. The story of how he personally took over in the centre of Avranches and directed traffic for over one and a half hours, has been told many times and depicted on film. He wrote later that it was one of those things 'which cannot be done, but was'.[19] It was certainly an incredible achievement – in seventy-two hours the Third Army moved seven Divisions through the Avranches–Pontaubault 'sheep-race' and across a single bridge.

By the evening of 3 August the 4th Armored Division had advanced forty miles and captured Rennes, and in the days that followed, it and the 6th Armored, 'moved so rapidly that they outran their communications ... VIII Corps and Third Army actually lost track of their locations on several occasions'.[20]

Patton was constantly on the move himself. On 2 August he had 'joined a column of the 90th Infantry Division marching east from Avranches and walked in ranks with them for some hours'. He was worried about the performance of the Division which was under its third commander since arriving in Normandy, and for two miles he spent his time encouraging the men to do better. On the way back from Avranches he came across a soldier who had 'fallen off a bulldozer and been run over ... he was practically split in two. He was still alive and I stayed with him and gave him morphine until an ambulance came'.[21]

By 4 August Brittany had been sealed off and the 4th Armored Division had reached the south coast of the peninsula at Vannes. Middleton had, however, to the fury of Patton, halted his 6th Armored Division half way to Brest in order to take out an enemy force at Dinan. Georgie told the Divisional commander, Robert Grow, to ignore his Corps commander's order, 'Don't take any notice of this order, or any other order telling you to halt, unless it comes from me. Get going and keep going till you get to Brest'. Grow did as he was told, but twenty-four valuable hours had been lost and when he finally reached Brest on the 7th the Germans had withdrawn the coastal garrisons inside the defences of the port and his assault failed.

Meanwhile Hodges' First Army had continued its attacks to the east and south-east. Mortain was captured by Collins' VII Corps on the 2nd and the following day, Bradley ordered Patton to leave minimum forces in Brittany and turn his main forces east. Third Army records do not support suggestions that Patton decided to turn east on his own initiative and seek Bradley's approval afterwards. On the afternoon of the 2nd

Bradley personally stopped the Third Army's 79th Division which was moving west on Patton's order, and directed it south-east to Fougères.[22]

On 4 August Monty, from his new Tac HQ location in the Forêt de Cerisy[23] (Map 10), issued another Directive (M 516); it read:

> Once a gap appears in the enemy front, we must press into it and through it and beyond it into the enemy's rear areas. Everyone must go all out all day and every day. The broad strategy of the Allied Armies is to swing the right flank round towards Paris, and to force the enemy back against the Seine.

He followed this up with another 'General Operational Situation Directive' (M 517) on the 6th. After noting that Third Army troops had reached Vannes on the south coast of Brittany and were rapidly occupying the whole peninsula, it stated that 'No more troops will be used in this task than are necessary, as the main business lies to the east'. It went on to give the order to 'pivot on our left ... swing hard with our right along the southern flank and in towards Paris ... drive the enemy up against the Seine'.[24]

Monty was very happy with his new Tac HQ location. On 5 August he wrote to his son David:

> I now have my caravan headquarters in a large forest, well away from main roads and dust. The dogs [Rommel, Hitler and Keitel] love it. And so do our rabbits; we have six of these and they run about in the Mess and play with the dogs and are very tame ... All goes very well here and we are gaining large tracts of France every day; and collecting in large numbers of prisoners. We took 6,000 yesterday.[25]

It should be noted, however, that he failed to point out that the 'we' above were the Americans and not the British or Canadians.

An interesting insight into the workings of the Tac HQ is provided by the author and playwright, A P Herbert, who as a former friend of Monty's wife Betty, was able to visit the new location:

> One is inclined to imagine the HQ of a great general as a scene of feverish activity and even noise; staff officers bustling about, telephones ringing everywhere, despatch riders roaring in ... there may be such goings on elsewhere, but they are not to be found at Monty's Tac HQ; he considers that the job of the supreme leader in the field is to *think*, and he insists on having time and conditions for thinking.[26]

SPRING and BLUECOAT

(Map 10)

What of the British and Canadians during COBRA? Knowing that he could ill afford to let the German formations in front of Dempsey's Second Army slip away and be used against the Americans, Monty ordered the Canadians to launch an attack (Operation SPRING) to coincide with COBRA. Its aim was to secure the high ground to the south-east of Caen, and to help in this task the Canadian Corps was allocated two British armoured Divisions, giving it a total of four divisions plus an armoured brigade. The successful conclusion of this operation was to be followed by a British XII Corps attack west of the Orne on the 28th and finally the British VIII Corps was to attack through the Canadians down the Falaise road. If and when all this had been achieved, Monty intended to launch several armoured divisions towards Falaise in a re-run of GOODWOOD.

Unfortunately the Canadians were bloodily repulsed and SPRING ended prematurely. Monty realised that he would be unable to launch another attack towards Falaise for several days, but knowing that he had to do something to support COBRA, he decided to mount a second, entirely British operation (BLUECOAT) west of the Orne. Its aim was to provide support for the left flank of COBRA by advancing with two Corps from the Caumont area towards the town of Vire. In doing so Monty hoped to not only help the Americans, but also to get in behind the new front the Germans were trying to form along the Vire river.

Originally scheduled for 2 August, the success of COBRA forced Monty to bring BLUECOAT forward to 28 July. Despite the problems of having to transfer many of the attacking units from the east side of the Orne to the west and of coping with the thick bocage country through which it was fought, BLUECOAT was successful in that it again achieved Monty's aim of holding the bulk of the German armour on the Second Army front – the Germans were forced to commit three Panzer Divisions and three battalions of Tiger tanks against the British advance. Even so the performance of some of the formations in BLUECOAT gave rise to considerable criticism and Monty decided it was time for some senior heads to roll. He had already sacked the commander of the famous 51st Highland Division, Major General Bullen-Smith, on 26 July and he followed this on 2 and 3 August by removing the commander of XXX Corps, Lieutenant General Bucknall, the commander of the equally famous 'Desert Rats' 7th Armoured Division, Major General Bobby Erskine, together with his Chief of Staff and senior artillery officer, as well as Brigadier 'Looney' Hinde, the renowned commander of the 22nd Armoured Brigade. All these officers had been with him in the Western Desert. The performance of some of the senior commanders in SPRING had also been found wanting and it was probably only due to the fact that they were Canadians that they survived.

Mortain

On the morning of 6 August Monty, with Eisenhower's approval, 'issued orders for the advance to the Seine'.[27] On the eastern flank the First Canadian Army, with the 1st Polish Armoured Division and a British infantry Division and tank Brigade under command, was to break out towards Falaise during the night of the 7th–8th (Operation TOTALIZE). At the same time the British Second Army was to continue to advance through the bocage towards the Vire–Vassy road and then turn south-east towards Flers, whilst the American First and Third Armies would thrust across the open southern flank and trap the Germans (Army Group B) in a double envelopment along the Seine – the 'long envelopment'. These plans were made, however, without the knowledge that Hitler had also issued a Directive on 4 August. It ordered von Kluge to launch a counter-offensive from the Vire–Mortain area, aimed first at Avranches, with the aim of cutting off all American forces to the south of that line, and then north-east to the Channel coast to drive the Allies back into the sea. It was a highly imaginative plan, but although it involved the use of eight of the nine Panzer divisions in Normandy and the entire reserves of the Luftwaffe, von Kluge knew it would be impossible to assemble these forces before the collapse of the entire front to the west of the Orne – he also knew that there was no point in arguing! Hitler was also insisting that the attack should not be made until, 'every tank, gun and plane was assembled'. Every detail was specified including the exact roads and villages through which the assaulting troops were to advance. General Blumentritt, Chief of Staff to von Kluge, complained after the war to Milton Shulman, 'All this planning had been done in Berlin with large-scale maps and the advice of the generals in France was not asked for, nor was it encouraged'. The operation was code-named LÜTTICH. Suggestions that the Allies were forewarned of Hitler's intentions through ULTRA intercepts have been effectively dismissed in Ralph Bennett's authoritative book *Ultra in the West*.

(Map 11)

As Patton's tanks approached Le Mans on 6 August, von Kluge began to panic. It was clear that the German southern flank was wide open, but he was reassured by Berlin that afternoon that he 'should not worry about the extension of the American penetration, for the delay [in launching the counter-offensive] would mean cutting off so much more'. Von Kluge knew, however, that the Führer Order was sounding the death knell of the German

Army in Normandy and that any delay in launching the counter-attack would only exacerbate matters. He therefore resolved to attack during the night of the 6th–7th, long before all the necessary forces could be assembled. Although this new plan fell far short of Hitler's vision of a campaign-winning counter-stroke, he surprisingly acquiesced and LÜTTICH, or the Mortain counter-attack as the American called it, went ahead.

LÜTTICH was perfectly summarized by Chester Wilmot in his brilliant book, *The Struggle for Europe*:

> The forty-eight hours, which began on the afternoon of August 6th, settled the fate of the German armies in Normandy. When they should have been withdrawing eastwards to the Seine, Hitler drove them westwards to destruction. While their southern flank was being rolled up, their northern flank gave way, and the sides of the salient from which von Kluge was striving to reach the coast, became a trap ... There were neither natural obstacles, nor prepared defences, nor organized forces to staunch the flow of [the Third Army] armoured and motorized troops who poured through the breach at Avranches and flooded the plain beyond.[28]

Falaise

By 7 August Patton's columns were approaching Le Mans and Bradley suddenly realised that if he could get them to swing north to Argentan and Alençon in a short left hook, he might be able to trap the Germans between Haislip's XV Corps and the Canadian First Army advancing south-east towards Falaise. He described it as: 'an opportunity that comes to a commander not more than once in a century ... We're about to destroy an entire hostile army'.[29] He put this idea to Eisenhower who, not surprisingly, agreed. But what about Monty? After the war he claimed that the 'shorter envelopment' was *his* idea.

> My [overall] plan was to make a wide enveloping movement from the southern American flank up to the Seine about Paris, and at the same time to drive the centre and northern sectors of the allied line straight for the river. In view of the Mortain counter stroke, I decided to attempt *concurrently* a shorter envelopment with the object of bottling up the bulk of the German forces deployed between Falaise and Mortain. It was obvious that if we could bring off both these movements we would virtually annihilate the enemy in Normandy.[30]

Whatever the truth, the necessary orders were issued and on the 8th Patton told Haislip: 'Pay no attention to Monty's goddamned boundaries. Be prepared to push even beyond Falaise if necessary'. By last light on the

12th XV Corps had reached Alençon and Sées, but unfortunately the Canadians, much to Monty's disappointment and eventual irritation, were still struggling to reach Falaise and when Patton asked Bradley for permission to move north from Argentan he refused, fearing 'Blue on Blue' incidents with the Canadians and Poles.

> In halting Patton at Argentan, however, I did not consult Montgomery. The decision to stop Patton was mine alone . . . I much preferred a solid shoulder at Argentan to the possibility of a broken neck at Falaise.[31]

Patton wrote later: 'This halt was a great mistake, as I was certain that we could have entered Falaise and I was not certain that the British would'.[32] He also allegedly asked Bradley if he should: 'continue and drive the British into the sea for another Dunkirk?'![33]

Monty wrote to Phyllis Reynolds on the 14th:

> I have the bulk of the German army in NW Europe nearly surrounded . . . if he escapes me here he can only be driven back on to the Seine – over which river there are now no bridges below Paris, as we have destroyed them all. We will see what happens.

In the event the Canadians did not take Falaise until the 16th and it was another three days before Polish and American troops met up at Chambois (Map 10). Even then the noose was not finally pulled tight until the 21st and in the intervening period thousands of Germans escaped.[34] The carnage in the Falaise Pocket has been described in many books. A member of Monty's Tac HQ, which moved to a position near Chambois shortly afterwards, remembered how flies: 'invaded our camp, bringing infection from the massed corpses in the sweltering Falaise Pocket', and Monty himself, despite his experiences in WWI, wrote in his diary on the 25th, 'I have never seen anything like it before'.

The Seine and Paris

On 14 August Patton claimed that his Army, 'had advanced farther and faster than any army in history',[35] but not content with that he asked Bradley to free two of Haislip's four Divisions for a dash to the Seine. He wrote in his diary that night that he was 'happy and elated'. It was true that the whole of his VIII Corps was still heavily involved in Brittany and that two Divisions of XV Corps were investing the southern side of the Falaise Pocket, but at least the rest of the Third Army, XII and XX Corps, had been freed for what he, like Monty, believed was a far more important task – the creation of blocking forces on the Seine, or 'the long envelopment' as it was called. For once Patton and Monty were in agreement; they realised that following the disaster of the Falaise Pocket, the Germans in northern France were facing another crisis – how to prevent the encirclement and probable destruction of more than 150,000 of their troops west of the Seine. Monty wrote later: 'There was no change in my orders or intentions. I was watching carefully for the mounting of the "wide" envelopment around to the Seine'.[36]

In spite of the fact that the following day SHAEF announced to the world's press that the Third Army, under Lieutenant General George S Patton Jnr, was fully operational on the continent, Georgie's enthusiasm was dampened when Bradley appeared at his forward Headquarters, code-named 'Lucky Forward', and told him that he should not advance beyond Dreux and Chartres. Bradley wanted the Third Army's extended northern flank to be covered by units of Hodges' First Army before any further advance was made. Patton wrote in his diary that he thought Bradley had lost his nerve.[37] His Anglophobia was also in evidence at this time; when he heard that Monty was considering a plan to drop a British airborne division in the Paris–Orléans gap to cut off the German retreat, he is reported to have exclaimed: 'If I find any Limeys in the way, I shall shoot them down'.[38]

In the same way that Monty usually operated from caravans in a Tac HQ, so Patton liked to live and work in two truck trailers at 'Lucky Forward'. He had an ordnance trailer converted to provide him with a parlour complete with desk and a radio for listening to broadcasts, a fully fitted bedroom with washstand, and a bath. The office trailer was a long, removal van type vehicle, fitted with a desk, map boards, normal telephone connected to a radio telephone and a scrambler-type phone with a direct connection to Eisenhower and Bradley. Patton complained that the latter scrambled his words before he uttered them.

Patton's offensive began in earnest at 2030 hours on 15 August and by last light on the 16th his XII Corps on the right had captured Orléans, XX Corps in the centre was fighting in Chartres and the two Divisions of XV Corps had taken Dreux after an unopposed drive of sixty miles. The advance had been ably supported by the fighters and fighter-bombers of Brigadier General Otto Weyland's XIX Tactical Air Command which had been attached to the Third Army since its activation. That evening Monty, perhaps remembering Sicily and Messina, wrote to Brooke: 'The general picture . . . is that Patton is heading straight for Paris and is determined to get there and will probably do so'. A day later, however, he does not seem to have been worried; he wrote to Phyllis Reynolds:

> I now have troops in Orléans, Chartres and Dreux. And I have some 100,000 Germans almost surrounded in the Pocket. The whole purpose of what lies ahead is fascinating.

Readers will not have missed the clear use of the first person singular!

Some commentators have suggested that Patton's Divisions could have gone straight on to the Seine on the 16th, but it was in fact the 18th before the Third Army drive was renewed. It is most likely that Patton was, for once, simply obeying Bradley's order to halt or it may well be that another reason for the pause was the problem of resupply. Certainly on the 17th Monty, after meeting Bradley at Fougères in Brittany, signalled Brooke telling him that the role of Patton's Army:

> has been to stop the enemy escaping through the Paris–Orléans gap and the intention now is to wheel the northern flank of this army up to the Seine about Vernon. But the Corps at Dreux and the one at Chartres are in a very difficult administrative situation and it is doubtful at the moment whether they can move very far until the situation improves.

But not for the first time in their relationship Monty had underestimated Patton. On the 19th a Third Army patrol, having advanced thirty miles in a day, found an intact footbridge over a dam on the Seine at Mantes, thirty-five miles west of Paris and close to Vernon; Patton arrived shortly afterwards, but uncharacteristically failed to order a crossing until he had flown back to consult Bradley who had just had another meeting with Monty. Fortunately permission was given, not only for that crossing, but also for his 7th Armored Division to secure a bridgehead at Melun, thirty-five miles south-east of Paris, and for his XII Corps to cross the Yonne river at Sens (Map 12). By the evening of the 20th the Americans had their first bridgehead over the Seine. Even so the Third Army's rapid advance had not been without considerable losses; in its first three weeks of action it suffered 1,713 killed, 7,928 wounded and 1,703 men missing.[39]

On 20 August Monty moved his Tac HQ to a small village (Proussy), fifteen miles west of Falaise. Paul Odgers wrote later:

> The news was exhilarating, we were out of the bocage; the country stretched for miles before us. It became clear that a faster advance than had ever been planned for would now begin and the HQ was scaled down for active movement.

On 25 August French and American troops of the US First Army entered Paris. The BBC, however, announced that Patton's Third Army had taken the capital. This mistake arose because some of the men in the 2nd French Armoured Division, which *had* been part of the Third Army until as recently as the 17th, were unaware of the change and they told everyone they belonged to the Third. Georgie called it 'poetic justice'!

(Map 12)

On 26 August, the day Patton sent a cable to Eisenhower saying: 'Today I spat in the Seine',[40] Bradley gave orders that the Third Army was to be prepared to advance rapidly to seize crossings over the Rhine between Coblenz and Mannheim and Monty wrote in his diary: 'The Battle of Normandy is over . . . Today, 26 Aug., is D+81; we are well ahead of our forecast'. He was of course referring back to his April briefing in St Paul's School which had predicted that the Seine would be reached on D+90. He did not mention that determined German resistance against the Americans (First Army) and Canadians in the Louviers–Elbeuf (Map 11) sector on the 23rd and 24th had enabled the majority of their 150,000 soldiers east of Falaise to escape across the lower Seine (Map 11). And, unfortunately, he claimed after the war that: 'The outstanding point about the Battle of Normandy is that it was fought *exactly* [author's emphasis] as planned before the invasion'.[41] Although it was true that it had been fought in accordance with the overall strategy and general principles laid down by Monty before, and repeated during, the campaign, he was inevitably forced to make changes to his plan as the situation developed. This was particularly true in relation to the capture of Caen and the vital high ground to its south-east which became an unforeseen battle of attrition.

Monty superseded

It was during his meeting with Bradley at Fougères on 17 August that Monty, still commander of all land forces, first explained his future strategy. His own 21st Army Group would continue on the left, clearing the Channel coast and ultimately securing Antwerp, whilst Bradley's 12th Army Group on the right would move towards Aachen and Cologne, and then the Ruhr, the industrial heartland of Germany. He went on to say that he had not yet spoken to Ike about this strategy, but when he did he would suggest that the US Seventh Army, moving up from the south after its successful landing in the south of France, should be directed on Metz, Nancy and the Saarland. He claimed later that Bradley had 'entirely agreed' this strategy. What Monty did not know at this time was that on the same day Eisenhower had received a letter from Marshall saying that:

> The Secretary [Stimson] and I and apparently all Americans are strongly of the opinion that the time has come for you to assume direct exercise of command of the American contingent.[42]

In accordance with this instruction Eisenhower called a meeting on 20 August at his new Headquarters in Normandy to draw up plans for a change of command and to decide future strategy. Incredibly, Monty did not go himself, but sent de Guingand; he brought back a record of the decisions reached and reported that they were to be sent to the Combined (British and American) Chiefs of Staff. Monty noted that:

> Eisenhower proposes to change the command system on 1st September, to separate the two Army Groups and to command them himself, and to send a portion of the land forces eastwards to the Saar. I cannot agree with these proposals.

His behaviour at this time can only be described as extraordinary – he had not only failed to attend the crucial 20 August meeting, but now, rather than go and see Ike and put his point of view personally, he sent de Guingand back with 'some notes on the problem'.[43] The notes suggested that:

> the quickest way to win this war is for the great mass of the Allied Armies to advance northwards ... [and] to change the system of command now, after having won a great victory, would be to prolong the war.[44]

Not surprisingly de Guingand's two-hour meeting with the Supreme Commander 'was negative' and so Monty asked Ike to come and lunch with him at Tac HQ on the 23rd – the 'Mountain' was required to come to 'Mohammed'. But then from Monty's point of view, it was *he* who was fighting the battle and it would therefore have been quite improper for him to leave his place of duty!

On the 23rd, before Eisenhower arrived at Tac HQ, Monty flew to Laval (Map 11) for another meeting with Bradley and was appalled to discover that the latter was now, 'a whole-hearted advocate of the main effort of his Army Group being directed eastwards on Metz and the Saar ... clearly Ike had been persuading him – or Bedell Smith'.[45]

Eisenhower brought Bedell Smith and his Chief of Administration to the meeting at Tac HQ, but Monty insisted on a private discussion which lasted an hour. During this time he:

> described to him [Ike] my own suggested plan, which had originally been agreed by Bradley. I said that if he adopted a broad front strategy, with the whole line advancing and everyone fighting all the time, the advance would inevitably peter out, the Germans would be given time to recover, and the war would go on all through the winter and well into 1945. I also said that he, as Supreme commander, should not descend into the land battle and become a ground C-in-C ... I said this point was so important that, if public opinion in America

was involved, he should let Bradley control the battle and I would gladly serve under him.[46]

Eisenhower would have none of this, but he did agree that the 21st Army Group was not strong enough to carry out the northern thrust on its own. When, however, Monty went as far as to suggest that he wanted an American Army of twelve divisions to advance on his right flank and that in order to provide this, 'he must stop the man with the ball: Patton and his Third Army'. In this he went too far. Looking at the problem solely through military eyes, he totally failed to appreciate that leaving Bradley with only one Army would infuriate not only Roosevelt and Marshall but also the American public.

> My arguments were of no avail. The 'broad front' strategy was to be adopted and 12 Army Group . . . was to direct its main effort towards Metz and the Saar . . . I was to have 'operational co-ordination' between 21 Army Group and the left wing of 12 Army Group; the term 'operational direction' was cut out of the directive . . . And so we all got ready to cross the Seine and go our different ways.[47]

Monty did in fact obtain agreement that Dempsey's Second Army would be given priority of resupply, but he was furious that he had been refused operational *direction* of the left wing of Bradley's Army Group. When he received Eisenhower's formal directive he wrote in his diary:

> I disagree definitely with Eisenhower's new organization . . . and I disagree definitely with his orders for command (or non-command!) on the left wing. I will, of course, do all I can to make it work; but I shall tell Eisenhower when I next see him that I disagree with it definitely.

Patton did in fact see great merit in Monty's preference for a strong northern thrust and made appropriate plans which he put to Bradley's Chief of Staff – his Third Army would swivel northwards and cut off the enemy fleeing before Dempsey and Hodges at Beauvais. But when Bradley put the plan to Ike, it was ruled out and at 1200 hours on the 24th Georgie was ordered to move east to the Saar. To his anger and disappointment the 12th Army Group was to be split.

The following day Patton met Bradley in Chartres (Map 11). He recalled later:

> Monty had won again and the weight of the operation was to be turned north rather than east. The First Army with nine divisions was to cross the Seine at Melun and Mantes, both of which places had

been captured and bridged by the Third Army ... [after which it] would move on Lille. The Third Army with seven divisions ... was to advance alone in the direction of the line Metz–Strasbourg. So far things were not too bad, as we still had seven good divisions going in the direction in which Bradley and I always wanted to go.[48]

On 30 August British troops reached the Somme at Amiens, men of the First US Army crossed the Aisne at Soissons, and Monty, after a well-publicized crossing of the Seine at Vernon (Map 11), set up his Tac HQ in the Château de Dangu, fifty miles north-west of Paris. For once Monty installed himself *in* the house – but only because he was being painted again! On the 31st he, 'stayed in all day and gave sittings to Mr. [James] Gunn', the new court painter. The latter also started sketching Monty's ADC, Johnny Henderson, but was seen off by Monty declaring, 'You're only here to paint me!'.[49]

Shortly before midnight on 31 August, Monty received a message telling him that the King, at Churchill's instigation, had promoted him to the rank of Field Marshal. He was therefore one rank senior to Ike, but that did little to lessen his disappointment that he was being demoted as commander of the Allied land forces. The following day, 1 September, Eisenhower took command.

Third Army to the Meuse

By 28 August, when Bradley came to visit George Patton at Lucky Forward, the Third Army had suffered a total of 17,908 battle casualties, 6,912 non-battle casualties and had lost 317 tanks.[50] It had, however, captured Château Thierry and Châlons and was approaching Reims. Georgie recalled:

I had considerable difficulty in persuading him to let me continue the attack to the Meuse. He finally assented. The 29th of August was, in my opinion, one of the critical days in this war. It was evident at this time that there was no real threat against us as long as we did not allow ourselves to be stopped by imaginary enemies ... Suddenly it was reported to me that the 140,000 gallons of gas we were to get that day had not arrived. At first I thought it was a back-handed way of slowing up the Third Army. I later found out that ... the delay was due to a change of plan by the High Command, implemented, in my opinion, by General Montgomery. I saw Bradley [and Eisenhower's Chief Operations officer] at Chartres on the 30th. I presented my case for a rapid advance to the east for the purpose of cutting the Siegfried Line before it could be manned. Bradley was very sympathetic, but [the SHAEF staff] did not concur ... We not only failed to get the back gas due to us, but got practically no more ... After receiving the heart-breaking news, I went to our new Command Post at la Chaume, near Sens. There I found that Eddy [the commander of XII Corps] had obtained permission ... to halt at St Dizier [due to lack of fuel]. I immediately called him and told him to continue until the tanks stopped, and then to get out and walk ... In the last war I drained three-quarters of my tanks in order to advance the other quarter and I felt Eddy could do the same.[51]

On 31 August Patton, accompanied by Bradley, flew back to Brittany to see Troy Middleton. Amazingly, and in spite of the fact that the Third Army and VIII Corps Headquarters were 275 miles apart, the latter was still under Georgie's command. Middleton had of course been left to get on with clearing up the Brittany peninsula more or less on his own, but it was an untidy arrangement that suited neither commander and Middleton in particular was incensed that the 12th Army Group administrative organization, known as the 'Communications Zone', had failed to meet his ammunition needs. Brest, Lorient and St Nazaire (Map 11) were still in German hands and Patton was in no doubt about what needed to be done: 'I told Bradley I could not fight on four fronts indefinitely and would like the VIII Corps turned over to someone else'.[52] Bradley agreed – but it was another ten days before VIII Corps was transferred to William Simpson's Ninth Army[53] and eighteen days before Brest fell to the Americans.

At the other end of the Allied front, Patton's troops had reached the high ground east of the Meuse river near St Mihiel (where Georgie had been wounded in WWI) by 1 September. Furthermore, after taking Verdun, they had established a second bridgehead in the northern part of that front, and advanced another six miles to the town of Eix. A day later, as British troops reached the Belgian border near Lille and American patrols of Hodges' First Army were nearing Mons, Eisenhower met Bradley, Hodges and Patton to give them his overall plan. Patton deliberately exaggerated the extent of his Army's advance by claiming that his reconnaissance patrols had already entered Metz and were on the Moselle near Nancy; but the ruse seems to have worked since:

> We finally persuaded General Eisenhower to let ... the First Army and the Third Army go on and attack the Siegfried Line as soon as the Calais area was stabilized [by Monty's 21st Army Group]. Until that time we would be able to get very little gas or ammunition ... It finally ended up with permission to secure crossings over the Moselle and prepare to attack the Siegfried Line whenever I could get the fuel to move.[54]

NOTES

1   Horne, *The Lonely Leader*, p. 225.
2   Stacey, *The Official History of the Canadian Army in the Second World War, Vol III, The Victory Campaign*, p. 168.
3   Montgomery, *Memoirs*, pp. 255–6.
4   Horne, op.cit., p. 201.
5   Ibid, pp. 201–2.
6   Montgomery, op. cit., p. 257.
7   Horne, op. cit., p. 221.
8   Hamilton, *Monty Master of the Battlefield 1942–1944*, p. 739.
9   Horne, op. cit., pp. 222–3.
10   Bradley, *A Soldier's Story*, p. 349.
11   First US Army Report of Operations, 20 Nov 43–1 Aug 44, p. 107.
12   XX Corps had started arriving in Normandy on 24 July but was still not complete by 1 Aug; XII Corps was not complete until 7 Aug.
13   Patton, *War As I Knew It*, p. 94.
14   Ibid.
15   Ibid.
16   D'Este, *A Genius for War*, p. 623.
17   Bradley Commentaries.
18   Hamilton, op. cit., p. 773.
19   Patton, op. cit., p. 96.
20   D'Este, op, cit., p. 628.
21   Patton, op. cit., p. 97.
22   Wilmot, *The Struggle for Europe*, p. 400.
23   He had moved it there to be nearer to Main HQ which had just arrived from England and was located at Le Tronquay, less than five miles away.
24   Horne, op. cit., p. 231.
25   Ibid, p. 240.
26   Ibid, p. 241.
27   Montgomery, *Normandy to the Baltic*, p. 262.
28   Page 406.
29   Bradley, op. cit., p. 424.
30   Montgomery, op. cit., p. 267.
31   Ibid, p. 377.
32   Patton, op. cit., pp. 103–4.
33   D'Este, op. cit., p. 641.
34   The Germans left 10,000 dead in the 'Falaise Pocket' and lost some 50,000 men as prisoners. The 21st Army Group's 2nd Operational Research Section carried out an intensive investigation of the area marked by the towns and villages of Pierrefitte–Argentan–Chambois–Vimoutiers–Trun–Pierrefitte, and called 'The Shambles' in its official report. It found 3,043 German vehicles – 187 tanks and SP guns, 252 artillery pieces, 157 light armoured vehicles, 1,778 trucks and 669 'cars'. According to Horne, *The Lonely Leader*, pp. 250–1, total German losses between D-Day and 22 Aug 44 were estimated at 450,000 including 210,000 PWs, and Allied casualties numbered 209,672 including 36,976 dead – roughly in the ratio of two British and Canadian to three American.
35   Patton, op. cit., p. 104.
36   Montgomery, op. cit., p. 269.
37   Diary dated 16 Aug 44.
38   Horne, op. cit., p. 247.

39 Patton, op. cit., pp. 109–10.
40 D'Este, *Eisenhower: Allied Supreme Commander*, p. 571.
41 Montgomery, op. cit., p. 281.
42 Horne, op. cit., p. 260.
43 Montgomery, *Memoirs*, p. 267.
44 Ibid, pp. 267–8.
45 Horne, op. cit., pp. 262–3.
46 Montgomery, op. cit., pp. 268–9.
47 Ibid, p. 269.
48 Patton, op. cit., p. 113.
49 Horne, op. cit., Note on p. 269.
50 Patton, op. cit., pp. 121–2.
51 Ibid, pp. 115–16.
52 Ibid, p. 117.
53 The Ninth Army did not become operational until 5 Sep 44.
54 Patton, op. cit., p. 117.

CHAPTER XXI

Separate Ways

(Map 12)

The Argument over Strategy

When Eisenhower took over from Monty as land force commander on 1 September, his Headquarters was at Granville on the west side of the Cherbourg peninsula (Map 11) – over 400 miles behind the Allied front line. As Monty put it:

> This was possibly a suitable place for a Supreme Commander; but it was useless for a land force commander who had to keep his finger on the pulse of his armies and give quick decisions in rapidly changing situations . . . Furthermore he was laid up with a bad knee. There were no telephone lines, and not even a radio-telephone, between his Headquarters and Bradley and myself. In the early days of September he was, in fact, completely out of touch with the land battle.[1]

On 4 September, the day the British Second Army captured Antwerp after an advance of 250 miles in only four days, Monty tried once more to persuade Ike to adopt his strategy of 'one really powerful and full-blooded thrust towards Berlin'. He pointed out that there were only sufficient maintenance resources to support one thrust, and of the two available possibilities – north of the Ruhr or via Metz and the Saar – he firmly, and inevitably since he would command it, recommended the one north of the Ruhr. 'In point of fact,' as Monty wrote later, 'it was now almost too late',[2] because on the same day Eisenhower had issued a directive ordering Montgomery's Army Group and two Corps of the First US Army to reach the sector of the Rhine covering the Ruhr and then to seize the Ruhr, and Patton's Third US Army and one Corps of Hodges' First US Army to occupy the sector of the Siegfried Line covering the Saar and then to seize Frankfurt.

As already mentioned, communications between Ike's Forward HQ and Monty's Tac HQ were so poor that Monty did not receive a reply to his 4 September proposal until the 7th and even then it was incomplete, with the second part not arriving until the 9th. Monty was far from satisfied with what he read:

> My intention is initially to occupy the Saar and the Ruhr, and by the time we have done this, Le Havre [Map 10] and Antwerp should be available to maintain one or both of the thrusts you mention. In this connection I have always given and still give priority to the Ruhr . . . and the northern route of advance, as indicated in my directive of yesterday . . . Locomotives and rolling stock are today being allocated on the basis of this priority to maintain the momentum of the advance of your forces, and those of Bradley north-west of the Ardennes.[3]

As Eisenhower saw it, this linking up of the whole front – the First Canadian, Second British, First, Third and Seventh US Armies and French Army B (the latter two advancing up from the South of France) – was mandatory to prevent the costliness of establishing long, defensive flanks along which our troops could have nothing but negative, static missions'.[4] What irritated Monty of course was that Ike's strategy ignored the fact that the Germans, particularly on his front, were incapable of launching any offensive operations that might threaten 'long, defensive flanks'. The SHAEF Intelligence Summary for the week ending 4 September described the German Army in front of Second British Army as, 'no longer a cohesive force but a number of fugitive battlegroups, disorganized and even demoralised, short of equipment and arms'.

Monty was therefore not ready to concede the argument. When the two men met in Ike's aircraft[5] in Brussels on 10 September, the day before Patton's Third and Patch's Seventh US Armies linked up, their conversation was acrimonious. It is said that when Monty *demanded* that priority should be given to *his* advance, Ike put his hand on Monty's knee and said: 'Steady, Monty, you can't talk to me like that. I'm your boss'.[6] But when Ike went on to insist that he *was* giving priority to the northern thrust, Monty would have none of it and replied quite simply that this, 'was *not* being done'. Ike then said that, 'by priority he did not mean *absolute* priority and he could not in any way scale down the Saar thrust'. Monty, frustrated, ended by pointing out that since crossing the Seine he had moved his Headquarters northwards and Bradley had moved his eastwards and that the 'land battle was becoming jerky and disjointed'.

> It was obvious that he [Ike] disagreed with my analysis. He repeated that we must first close to the Rhine and cross it on a wide front; then, and only then, could we concentrate on one thrust. We parted without any clear decision, except that . ., the 'broad front' strategy was to remain in operation. But Eisenhower agreed that 21 Army Group should strike northwards toward Arnhem [Map 13] as early as possible, and he admitted that successful operations in that direction would open up wide possibilities for future action.[7]

This gave Monty his chance and he virtually blackmailed Eisenhower on 11 September by warning him that due to the poor maintenance situation[8] he would not be able to launch his planned offensive to and beyond Arnhem before the 23rd at the earliest and possibly as late as the 26th.

> This message produced results which were almost electric. Bedell Smith came to see me next day to say Eisenhower had decided to act as I recommended. The Saar thrust was to be stopped. Three American divisions were to be grounded and their transport used to supply extra maintenance to 21 Army Group. The bulk of the support of 12 Army Group was to be given to the First American Army on my right and I was to be allowed to deal direct with General Hodges. As a result of these promises I reviewed my plans . . . and then fixed D-Day for the Arnhem operation (MARKET GARDEN) for Sunday, 17th September.[9]

Perhaps not surprisingly, after the confrontation on Brussels airfield and Monty's follow-up, Eisenhower's next letter to Monty, dated 15 September, began: 'Dear Montgomery'![10]

(Map 13)

On 14 September Monty ordered Dempsey's Second British Army, with major elements of the First Allied Airborne Army[11] under command, to secure crossings over the Maas and lower Rhine rivers in the general area Grave–Nijmegen–Arnhem (Map 13). Strong forces were then to be established on the line Arnhem–Deventer–Zwolle, facing east, following which the Second Army would outflank the Siegfried Line by advancing along the northern side of the Ruhr.

In the meantime George Patton, with Bradley's support, was determined to avoid being relegated, as in Sicily, to a minor role. He is said to have, 'frequently reminded his staff that they now had two enemies to fight: the Germans and SHAEF, whose boss was the best general the British had'.[12] He was, however, hamstrung by a severe shortage of essential supplies. It is claimed that when he found a convoy delivering rations, he raged to Bradley: 'I'll shoot the next man who brings me food. Give us gasoline; we can eat our belts'. And to war correspondent Cornelius Ryan, he said: 'Now, if Ike stops holding Monty's hand and gives me the supplies, I'll go through the Siegfried Line like shit through a goose'.[13]

As Patton saw it there was only one way round his difficulties and that was to resort to subterfuge. He had already failed to report captured German fuel stocks, enabling his men to reach the Marne and Meuse rivers when they would otherwise have been grounded, and he now authorized his men to hijack First Army supplies of petrol and ammunition by pretending to be from the First Army, and by getting his officers to divert First Army supply trucks to Third Army dumps. In October 1944 he admitted to his father-in-law: 'I've already stolen enough gas to put me in jail for life, but it's nowhere enough to keep us rolling'.[14] And when First Army officers complained, with good reason, that their supplies were being stolen, he is said to have replied:

> I'm sorry to learn that First Army has lost some of its gas, very sorry indeed ... None of my officers would masquerade as First Army officers. They wouldn't stoop to that, not even to get gas SHAEF stole from us.[15]

(Map 12)

On 3 September Bradley visited Patton and told him that his Army would be reinforced by four new divisions later in the month, but that in the meantime he was to begin his advance towards the Rhine on the 5th; his immediate objectives were the two main cities in the French Province of Lorraine – Metz and Nancy. Unfortunately for Georgie and his men, the many rivers and rolling, wooded hills facing them provided ideal terrain for the Germans defending the borders of their homeland; thus 'the conditions of breakout and pursuit, which had carried it [the Third Army] across the soft underbelly of Normandy, no longer existed in Lorraine'.[16] And to add to Patton's problems of terrain and lack of fuel and ammunition, Hitler had decided to build up his forces in the Saar sector with the aim of rolling up the Third Army from the south.[17] Lorraine was not only unsuitable for the rapid armoured thrusts so favoured by Patton, but his Army was to face more than a dozen unexpected German counter-attacks that would turn the fighting into 'a ghastly war of attrition'.

MARKET GARDEN and the Lorraine Campaign

The details of operation MARKET GARDEN and the campaign in Lorraine need not concern us. Those interested should in the first case, read Martin Middlebrook's *Arnhem 1944 – The Airborne Battle*, Cornelius Ryan's *A Bridge Too Far*, and this author's book *Sons of the Reich*, and in the second, Hugh M Cole's *The Lorraine Campaign* and Chester Wilmot's *The Struggle for Europe*. It is sufficient for our purpose to know that by the time both attacks were launched the Germans had made, 'one of the most remarkable military recoveries in history'.[18] This recovery was aided by the announcement by the Allies of the Morganthau plan which had as its aim the post-war destruction of German industry and the setting up of a bucolic economy that would prevent Germany from ever going to war again. Needless to say, Joseph Goebbels made the most of this great propaganda opportunity to motivate the German people as a whole and Hitler's armed forces in particular. As a result, both Monty's MARKET GARDEN and Patton's Lorraine campaign ended in failure. In the first case the Siegfried Line was never outflanked, the salient achieved in Holland led nowhere and was to prove extremely costly in the coming months, the Second British Army was never positioned for an attack along the north flank of the Ruhr and it cost 17,000 men. In the second, it took the Third Army over three months and 51,208 battle and 42,932 non-battle casualties to advance just fifty miles and capture the province of Lorraine; and even then the Siegfried Line had not been breached. In fact Patton's troops were still facing the toughest part of that Line where the maze of bunkers and forts would ensure that any further progress would be exceedingly difficult and painfully slow.

> The optimistic prediction by higher headquarters that Patton's troops would reach the Rhine by mid-December had been quietly forgotten. The Third Army commander himself had gradually abandoned hope of a quick breakthrough to the Rhine.[19]

With the war still in progress, it was inevitable that MARKET GARDEN would be presented to the British and American people as a victory. Churchill described it as 'a decided victory' and Montgomery claimed it was 90% successful since 90% of the ground specified in the original order had been taken. To this latter claim, Prince Bernhard of the Netherlands is said to have replied: 'My country can never again afford the luxury of a Montgomery success'. Monty admitted later that: 'The airborne forces at Arnhem were dropped too far away from the vital objective – the bridge . . . I take the blame for this mistake'.[20] But he also went on to criticize the Americans, Bradley and Patton of course, for the failure of the operation:

There is no doubt in my mind that Eisenhower always wanted to give priority to the northern thrust and to scale down the southern one. He ordered this to be done and he thought that it was being done. It was not being done. We now know from Bradley's book (*A Soldier's Story*), page 412, that in the middle of September, there was parity of logistics between the First and Third American Armies.

This was true. The official US historian wrote later that the day before Patton began his advance into Lorraine: 'the gasoline drought [in Third Army] started to break . . . and by 10 September the period of critical shortage had ended'.[21] Thus:

While Third Army was attacking in Lorraine with eight divisions, the critical supply situation in the north curtailed First Army's assault on the Siegfried Line and halted Second [British] Army on the Meuse–Escaut canal [Map 13].[22]

In his complaint about the lack of logistical support, Monty quoted Chester Wilmot's *Struggle for Europe*:

If he [Eisenhower] had kept Patton halted on the Meuse, and had given full logistic support to Dempsey and Hodges after the capture of Brussels, the operations in Holland could have been an overwhelming triumph, for First US Army could have mounted a formidable diversion, if not a successful offensive, at Aachen, and Second British Army could have attacked sooner, on a wider front and in much greater strength.

He did not, however, quote Wilmot's next paragraph which reads:

The [Second British Army's] week's delay on the Dutch frontier gave Model [Army Group B] and Student [First German Parachute Army] the opportunity of reorganizing and strengthening the defences of Holland . . . The strength of the German forces in the MARKET GARDEN area was more than doubled.[23]

The week's delay referred to was allegedly caused by problems of re-supply and was, at the very least, condoned by Montgomery. It is interesting though that Brian Horrocks, the commander of the Corps charged with breaking through to the airborne troops at Arnhem, had this to say about the delay:

I believe that if we had taken the chance and carried straight on with our advance instead of halting in Brussels the whole course of the war in Europe might have been changed. On 3rd September we still had 100 miles of petrol per vehicle, and one further day's supply within reach . . . To my mind 4th September was the key date in the battle for the Rhine. Had we been able to advance that day we could have smashed through . . . and advanced northwards with little or nothing to stop us. We might even have succeeded in bouncing a crossing over the Rhine. But we halted . . . When we were allowed to advance on 7th September, the situation had worsened drastically . . . Within three days, instead of being on a fifty-mile front . . . the Corps was concentrated on a five-mile front engaged in a tough battle.[24]

Monty ended his assessment by saying that: 'if the operation had been properly backed from its inception . . . it would have succeeded *in spite* of my mistakes . . . I remain MARKET GARDEN's unrepentant advocate'.[25] For others it was an operation, 'which showed most clearly why Montgomery was dangerously unsure in some aspects of offensive warfare'.[26]

George Patton's frustration at being unable to break through into Germany resulted in him blaming everybody except himself. Bradley wrote later that the Third Army commander:

slugged his way forward . . . to the Saar river, crossed it, but was stopped dead at the Siegfried Line. His failure to break through deeper into Germany infuriated him . . . In his frustration, he raged at me, Ike and Monty.[27]

Patton even cabled the War Department saying he hoped that: 'in the final settlement of the war, you insist that the Germans retain Lorraine, because I can imagine no greater burden than to be the owner of this nasty country'. And of course he exaggerated the adverse circumstances in which he found himself: 'We were fighting, with inadequate means, against equal or superior forces'.[28] He would never accept that his policy of attacking on too wide a frontage, instead of concentrating his forces, was one of the causes of his failure to break through.

Lorraine became Patton's bloodiest and least successful campaign . . . Patton and his corps commanders bore responsibility for failing to better employ their divisions. Often they were launched without adequate support or in tasks well beyond their capability. As a postwar US Army study concludes: 'Patton failed to concentrate Third Army's resources.'[29]

And of course he blamed the weather:

One of the unfortunate things about this campaign was that it had been planned [by him] when the weather was good and the country dry. Therefore the operations were envisaged as of a blitz nature. When it actually came off, we were in the middle of the greatest flood for eighty years.[30]

Perhaps the greatest criticism of Patton and his field commanders at this time came, not from anyone on the Allied side, but from the commander of the German Army Group G, General Hermann Balck. After pointing out that his own troops were, 'motley and badly equipped', he attributed the failure of the Third Army to breach the Siegfried Line to the: 'bad and timid leadership of the Americans'.[31]

The greatest success of the campaign was the fall of Metz on 22 November, which: 'was achieved only after overcoming the fanatical resistance of a German officer cadet school'.[32] Patton entered the city in triumph with sirens screaming and awarded dozens of medals to those who had taken part in its capture. He told the men of the Division that had borne the brunt of the fighting (the 5th Infantry): 'I am very proud of you. Your country is very proud of you. You are magnificent fighting men. Your deeds in the battle of Metz will fill the pages of history for a thousand years'.[33]

Despite all the setbacks, however, Patton remained as determined as ever to reach the Rhine before Christmas and shortly after taking Metz he directed his staff to start planning a major new offensive; it was to commence on 19 December.

Non-Operational Matters

It is time now to look at some of the non-operational aspects of our subjects' lives during the period September to mid-December 1944.

Patton

Taking George Patton first, we find him, as he put it in his book, *War As I Knew It*, 'touring France with an Army'. He was constantly on the move, visiting his Corps and Divisions and making sure his men were aware of his presence. Following the exhilarating advance across France and despite the rising casualty and sickness rate,[34] his popularity was immense. And he did not forget his French soldiers; on 18 September he decorated the commander of the French 2nd Armoured Division, Jacques Leclerc, with a Silver Star and gave him six more Silver Stars and twenty-five Bronze Stars to, 'spread among the soldiers'. But it was not all work – for a little light relief he appears to have again enjoyed the company of Jean Gordon. She arrived in France with the Red Cross in early September

215

and Everett Hughes for one believed the affair was renewed.[35] On the other hand, Jean's supervizor, Betty South, insisted Jean was in fact in love with a captain in the 4th Armored Division and that whilst: 'she adored General Patton . . . [it was] strictly a father-daughter relationship'.[36]

(Map 3)

During September Georgie found time to re-visit some of the WWI battlefields, including Verdun and its famous Fort Douaumont. Of the latter he wrote: 'This is a magnificent, though futile, monument to heroism . . . To me Douaumont epitomizes the folly of defensive warfare'.[37] And near Essey:

> I went over the same places I had lived in and attacked twenty-six years and four days before. Some of the landmarks were very clear, but a wall behind which I had lain while directing an attack was made of cement, whereas in my memory it had been stone. Possibly they had built a new one.[38]

On 26 September Patton and two of his staff officers had lunch in the Hôtel de France in Chaumont, where he and 'Black Jack' Pershing had done the same in the fall of 1917. 'The same people were running the hotel – only one generation younger . . . After lunch we visited General Pershing's house in town and also the barracks which had housed our HQ for two years'. Later that day they visited another house where Pershing had lived in 1918 and where Georgie had acted as an ADC to the Prince of Wales, later King Edward VIII, and where he claimed to have taught the Prince 'to shoot craps'. Farther on they came to Bourg where Patton's Tank Brigade Headquarters had been located in 1918. To his delight a local citizen arranged: 'a triumphal procession of all the village armed with pitchforks, scythes and rakes, and we proceeded to rediscover my old haunts, including my office and my billet in the château of Madame de Vaux'.[39]

(Map 12)

Despite the problems of the Lorraine campaign, Patton also found time to socialise and take time off from his military duties. In October he was invited by Ike, along with his fellow Army and Corps commanders, to lunch with King George VI at the First Army Headquarters east of Liège, and he is known to have visited Paris on more than one occasion, sometimes it is said with Jean Gordon. He stayed at the Ritz and enjoyed the Folies-Bergère and it seems Jean was also with him when, as part of his 59th birthday celebrations, Marlene Dietrich and her troupe provided the entertainment at his Headquarters in Nancy.

On the whole Patton welcomed visitors to Lucky Forward, although in the case of a Russian delegation he avoided them by 'going to the front' and leaving them with an intelligence map that 'showed exactly nothing'.[40] But the US ambassador to the Soviet Union, Averell Harriman, was a different matter. Patton took him on a visit to the 4th Armored Division where they: 'crossed the Saar river and spat on the far bank'. Afterwards he decorated a lieutenant who, in command of a Sherman, had 'put out five German Panther tanks'. But as usual Georgie could not help bragging. He claimed that Harriman told him that the Chief of Staff of the Russian Army had stated: 'The Red Army could not have conceived and certainly could not have executed the advance made by the Third Army across France'![41]

Montgomery

(Map 13)

Monty was also able to see, if not visit, some of the battlefields he had known in WWI. His Tac HQ moved on 4 September, after the usual church parade, from the Château Dangu to the Château Saulty near Arras, crossing the Somme on its way (Map 1). No one liked it at Saulty and another move soon followed into the beautiful grounds of the Château d'Everberg between Brussels and Louvain. Monty knew the place well as it had been the Headquarters of his 3rd Division immediately before the retreat to Dunkirk in 1940. During his time there, Monty wrote to his son David, telling him of a courtesy visit to the Burgermeister of Brussels. 'He received me in great state with officials in brilliant uniforms . . . then I heard the Queen wanted to see me; I was out in my corduroys and grey sweater, so went to the Palace like that!'.[42] Five days later he wrote again, saying that James Gunn's portrait of him was finished and that it was: 'completely the cat's whiskers; it will have to be shown in the [Royal] Academy next year, and will undoubtedly be *the picture of the year*'.[43]

On 21 September Monty wanted to get nearer to the MARKET GARDEN fighting and he ordered Tac HQ to move to the Belgian military training area at Hechtel. It had been taken over by the Germans during the war and they had been defending the area only eleven days previously. However, by the time MARKET GARDEN ended on the 26th, with only 2,300 of the 12,000 airborne soldiers who had landed in the Arnhem area coming back across the lower Rhine, Tac HQ had moved again. This time it was located in a park near the public swimming baths in Eindhoven and it was there that Monty received the commander of the British troops at Arnhem, Major General Roy Urquhart – an officer who had been with him from Alamein to Tunis and then on to Sicily and Italy. Monty questioned him sympathetically but in depth and then asked him to stay the night in the caravan normally reserved for the King or Churchill. The following morning Monty gave Urquhart a very moving, hand-written message which was later typed up and issued to the press. In it he expressed his admiration:

> for the magnificent fighting spirit that your Division displayed in battle . . . there can be few episodes more glorious than the epic of Arnhem, and those that follow after will find it hard to live up to the standards you have set.

Some critics have suggested that this was merely Monty engaging in a public relations exercise, but Urquhart certainly did not think so and later mentioned the warmth of understanding shown by Monty at their meeting in Eindhoven. And there is further evidence of the genuineness of Monty's feelings in the letter he wrote to Brooke dated 28 September; in it he asked the CIGS to ensure that the Arnhem survivors were properly looked after and even suggested that Brooke himself should go down and, 'see them all and give them a good pat on the back'. He also asked that medals should be set aside for some of those who had become prisoners of the Germans – over 6,500 of them.

The failure of MARKET GARDEN and the damp and cold in Holland in the autumn of 1944 did little for the morale of those serving in Tac HQ. Monty himself became pessimistic, realising that there was no hope of ending the war that year. He sent Kit Dawnay home to Phyllis Reynolds with his summer clothes and a request for winter woollens. King George VI paid a six-day visit commencing on 11 October during which he visited units, carried out award ceremonies and, as we have heard, lunched with senior American officers including Eisenhower and George Patton at Hodges' First Army Headquarters near Liège. Apparently Monty did not stay up later than 9.30 p.m. – even for the King!

Monty, like Patton, spent most of his time during the autumn visiting his commanders, formations and units, and there is little doubt that his no-nonsense approach, openness and obvious pride in his men made a very favourable and lasting impression on virtually everyone under his command.

Then, for a few days in late October/early November, Monty joined his Main Headquarters in the Residence Palace in Brussels. He wrote to David on 3 November:

> I have, for the moment, left my caravans and am living in a house, a very palatial residence, full of lovely furniture. I expect the natural repercussions will be that when I return to my caravans I shall catch a colossal cold.

On 7 November Monty returned to London to receive his Field Marshal's baton from the King, have his dentures repaired yet again and to have discussions with Brooke about the course of the war; he predicted that unless the Allies concentrated their forces and set up a better system of command and control, the fighting would go on for most of 1945. During the brief visit he also found time to visit his son at Winchester College.

On 10 November Monty returned to Belgium to be greeted by a V-1 flying bomb that:

> exploded fifty yards away from my house in Brussels . . . all the glass in my windows was broken and I got covered in debris, but no harm was done. I am leaving Brussels tomorrow for the country!![44]

Tac HQ had by then moved to Zonhoven in the Flemish part of Belgium, where it took over the local schools and some houses. Monty took up residence in the Villa Mommen, 'a typically Breughelesque home . . . of simple but appalling taste, with only one bath, set back a short distance from the main road'.[45] A P Herbert recalled that: 'the heating system did not work . . . and Monty's room was always full of the rumble of tanks and guns and lorries. Doodle-bugs [V-1s] roared over now and then'. And Paul Odgers said: 'It was an awful place. The flat, dreary, water-logged fields brought depression of the spirit, which the single redbrick village street did nothing to relieve'.[46] Despite the depressing atmosphere Monty did his best to improve morale amongst his junior officers: 'Evenings in the mess were always jolly affairs. Monty would discreetly turn a blind eye to the escapades of his officers with mistresses in Brussels. But it was still, largely, a monastic, closed society'.[47] Tac HQ was destined to remain in Zonhoven for over three dreary months.

Final Decisions on Strategy

On 7 December Eisenhower summoned Monty and Bradley to a conference in Maastricht at which he reviewed the current situation and then asked for their ideas about the future. When asked for his views, Monty inevitably put forward his case for an attack on the Ruhr to be carried out *north* of the Ardennes (Map 12) by fifty divisions, more than half of which would be American. This thrust would of course be under his command. Ike disagreed and said he believed the right wing of Bradley's Army Group (basically Patton's Third Army) should develop a strong thrust on the axis Frankfurt–Kassel (Map 12). Monty was devastated. Ike's plan was the very antithesis of everything he believed in – the forthcoming Allied offensive was to be made on *two* fronts. Even worse, 'Bradley's 12th Army Group was disposed in two main concentrations, each deployed for attack. In between was a gap of some 100 miles, held by VIII American Corps of [just] four divisions'.[48] He wrote to Brooke that evening:

> Eisenhower and Bradley have their eyes firmly on Frankfurt and the route thence to Kassel. We shall split our forces, and our strength, and we shall fail . . . The whole thing is really rather a tragedy. I think now that if we want the war to end within any reasonable period you will have to get Eisenhower's hand taken off the land battle. I regret to say that in my opinion he just doesn't know what he is doing. And you will have to see that Bradley's influence is curbed.[49]

Monty was of course unaware that Ike had no choice other than to acquiesce in Bradley's demand for an independent thrust south of the Ardennes. The latter had told Ike that: 'if he put the Twelfth Army Group under Marshal Montgomery, he would of necessity have to relieve me of command, because it would be an indication that I had failed as a separate Army Group commander'.[50] In doing this, Bradley was fully aware that Marshall and American public opinion would never condone his removal from command.

On 12 December Monty, having cleared his proposal with Eisenhower, wrote to the Reynolds telling them that he planned to spend Christmas in England – his first for three years. He would fly over on the 23rd and be with them and David for Christmas Eve. 'All well here; dogs, canaries, goldfish, ADCs etc. Love to you all, Monty.' Then, on the evening of the 15th, he signalled Brooke that he did: 'not propose to send any more evening situation reports until the war becomes more exciting'. The following day he flew to Eindhoven to play golf with Dai Rees, a professional golfer currently serving as a driver for Air Vice-Marshal Sir Harry Broadhurst. That same afternoon Bradley arrived in Versailles (Map 12) to stay the night with Eisenhower at the Trianon Palace Hotel and soon after his arrival they sat down with Bedell Smith and Everett Hughes to play bridge; away to the south in Nancy, George Patton had little to do but think about his forthcoming 19 December offensive. None of them was aware that they were about to be engulfed in Hitler's latest counter-offensive, an offensive far larger and more serious than Mortain. It became know as the Battle of the Bulge.

NOTES

1 Montgomery, *Memoirs*, p. 271.
2 Ibid, p. 270.
3 Ibid, p. 273.
4 Eisenhower, *Crusade in Europe*, pp. 225–9.
5 A few days earlier Ike had badly wrenched his knee when getting out of his aircraft.

6   D'Este, *A Genius for War*, p. 650.
7   Montgomery, op. cit., pp. 275–6.
8   No major port east of the Seine had been captured, the British supply lines stretched 300 miles, all the way back to Bayeux, and those of the Americans ran even farther, 400 miles, through Paris to the Cotentin Peninsula. There were sufficient stocks of all commodities already ashore in Normandy but the problem remained of getting them to the forward units in the quantities needed. The first supply train reached Paris from the Normandy bridgehead on 30 August, but the bulk of the supplies still had to be transported by road.
9   Montgomery, op. cit., p. 276.
10 Ibid, p. 277.
11 1st British, 82nd and 101st US Airborne Divs & the 1st Polish Indep Parachute Bde Group.
12 D'Este, op. cit., p. 648.
13 Ryan, *A Bridge Too Far*, p. 78.
14 D'Este, op, cit., p. 914, Note 19.
15 Quoted in D'Este's *A Genius for War*, p. 651.
16 Ibid, p. 671. In order to fully understand the difficulties faced by Patton's troops, one really needs to drive from Saverne in the Vognes mountains to Nancy and then to Metz and Saarbrücken.
17 Army Group G was allocated three Pz and Pz-Gren Divs, plus four indep Pz Bdes, some 600 tanks, for this operation.
18 Horrocks, *A Full Life*, p. 232.
19 Cole, *The Lorraine Campaign*, p. 520.
20 Montgomery, op. cit., p. 297.
21 Cole, op. cit., p. 52.
22 Wilmot, op. cit., p. 531.
23 Ibid, pp. 531–2.
24 Horrocks, op. cit., p. 205–6.
25 Montgomery, op. cit., pp. 296–8.
26 Chalfont, *Montgomery of Alamein*, p. 253.
27 Bradley, *A General's Life*, p. 342.
28 Patton, *War As I Knew It*, p. 134.
29 D'Este, op. cit., p. 669.
30 Patton, op cit., p. 168.
31 Quoted from Whiting's *Patton*, p. 83.
32 Shulman, *Defeat in the West*, p. 247.
33 D'Este, op. cit., p. 669.
34 According to Patton, *War As I Knew It*, the Third Army had suffered 38,006 battle and 18,537 non-battle casualties by 15 Oct; these figures had risen to 39,428 and 24,386 respectively by 7 Nov.
35 D'Este, op. cit., p. 744. Everett Hughes, a close friend of Patton from West Point days, was now a major general logistician serving on Eisenhower's staff in Paris.
36 Ibid.
37 Patton, op. cit., p. 127.
38 Ibid, p. 128.
39 Ibid, pp. 134–5.
40 Ibid, p. 127.
41 Ibid, p. 171.
42 Horne, *The Lonely Leader*, p. 290.
43 Ibid.
44 Letter to David dated 10 Nov 44.

45 Horne, op. cit., p. 295.
46 Ibid.
47 Ibid, p. 296.
48 Montgomery, op. cit., p. 306. It has to be pointed out, however, that this statement was made fourteen years later with the benefit of hindsight.
49 Montgomery Papers, M 537.
50 Bradley Papers, Memo for the Record dated 13 Dec 44.

CHAPTER XXII

The Battle of the Bulge

Background

By the autumn of 1944 it was obvious to the German High Command, and even to Adolf Hitler, that in the long term it would be impossible to conduct a successful defence of the Greater German Reich on three fronts – in the West, the East and in Italy. The Führer resolved therefore to deliver a massive blow on one of the two most important fronts, designed to render that particular enemy incapable of serious offensive action for a considerable period. This, he reasoned, would give him strategic freedom and provide the forces necessary to deliver other decisive blows and, most importantly, buy time for the perfection of his new 'Victory' weapons.

The sheer scale of the Eastern Front militated against an attack in that direction. This factor, coupled with the threat to the Ruhr and Hitler's low opinion of the fighting capabilities of both the American and British Armies, turned his eyes again to the Western Front. Once that front was stabilized, he believed he would have sufficient forces to resist the inevitable Soviet winter offensive. The fact that he was committing Germany's last reserves in men and resources gave the operation an air of finality – even Hitler predicted that the outcome of this offensive would bring life or death for the German nation. Nevertheless, in his eyes this desperate gamble, which invited disaster in the East, was the only course of action that might bring about his own survival and that of his Nazi regime.

(Map 12)

On 16 September 1944 Hitler revealed his basic plan and strategic goals to a small inner circle. Despite objections, particularly from the two senior field commanders involved – von Rundstedt and Model – the final plan was basically unchanged when it was issued in late November. Originally code-named WACHT AM RHEIN, but later changed to HERBSTNEBEL

(AUTUMN MIST), the plan called for three Armies under Model's Army Group 'B' to break through the weak American front in the Ardennes and Luxembourg and then, with the main weight on the right flank, cross the Meuse south of Liège and exploit to the great port of Antwerp. This would cut off Monty's 21st Army Group, hopefully causing mass surrenders and deprive the Allies of their most important port. Indeed, Hitler saw it as the basis of another 'Dunkirk', with a loss to the Allies of some twenty to thirty divisions. He even believed it might destroy the British and Canadian Armies once and for all. The reality, however, was that Hitler's plan was 'based on a gross over-estimate of his own strength and an even grosser under-estimate of Allied strength and particularly of the American capacity to recover'.[1] He also failed to appreciate that fuel and other serious shortages in logistic support for his attacking armies would largely negate the advantages of a surprise attack.

Operation AUTUMN MIST began at 0535 hours on 16 December with a barrage by over 1,900 guns and rocket launchers. Three German Armies, the Sixth Panzer under Sepp Dietrich, the Fifth Panzer under Hasso von Manteuffel and the Seventh under Erich Brandenberger, with a total of seven Panzer, two Parachute and eleven Volks-Grenadier Divisions, were unleashed on a ninety-mile front against the five infantry Divisions of Troy Middleton's VIII US Corps, part of Courtney Hodges' First Army. The Germans had some 200,000 men, 700 tanks and armoured assault guns against the Americans' 83,000 men and just over 400 tanks and tank destroyers. The bulk of Bradley's 12th Army Group Divisions were deployed to the north and south of the Ardennes – sixteen of them to the north on a forty-mile front north of Monshau, and ten of them (Patton's Third Army) to the south on a sixty-mile front facing the Saar and, as we have heard, preparing to attack.

Eisenhower and Bradley received their first news of the German offensive during a game of bridge in Versailles on the afternoon of the 16th. Bradley was not overly concerned, believing it was probably an attempt to 'spoil' the forthcoming American offensive, particularly Patton's thrust towards the Saar, but Ike took it more seriously and suggested that it might be an idea to transfer two armoured divisions to Hodges' First Army 'just in case' – the 10th from Patton's Third Army and the 7th from Simpson's Ninth US Army in Holland. Bradley agreed and gave the necessary orders and then he and Eisenhower, with Bedell Smith and Everett Hughes 'cracked a bottle of champagne to mark Ike's fifth star . . . played five rubbers of bridge, [and] got to bed about twelve'.[2]

(Map 14)

It is important to understand the difficulties imposed on both sides by the terrain and weather in this campaign. Since 1970 the author has spent many weeks in the Ardennes and has come to know many parts of it better than the area of England in which he lives. It is a hilly, heavily forested area, broken by steep and twisting valleys, many of them filled by streams and rivers which often become raging torrents in the winter. Most of the roads in 1944 had to pass through narrow, awkward defiles where they crossed these rivers and their condition was generally poor. Furthermore, in trying to advance west and north-west, the Germans found themselves advancing against the grain of the country and were forced, in the most part, to take roads and tracks that followed the winding river valleys or ran across high ridges and through forests. To add to their problems, the autumn of 1944 was one of the wettest on record and most of the low-lying roads and virtually all the forest tracks had been turned into rivers of mud.

Although the winter of 1944 was the worst for thirty-eight years, there was very little snow when the offensive began; even so, temperatures fell to below zero every night and early morning mists shrouded the valleys and forests. Readers should also be aware that in 1944, unlike today, freezing weather averaged 112 days a year at Stavelot in the northern part of the combat area and 145 days a year at Bastogne, in the centre.[3] However, on 18 December a thaw set in which made off-road foot, and even tank movement extremely difficult, and by the 22nd the troops were facing a mixture of mud, snow, blizzards, fog and rain. In the north the Sixth Panzer Army was bogged down by the rain and mud, in the south the Fifth Panzer Army was hampered by fog and snow and back in the high Eifel in Germany, the supply roads were blocked by almost continuous snow. Another major change followed on the 23rd when cold, dry winds from the east stripped the German armies of their immunity to air attack.

> But this was not the whole story. Snow began to drift in the Eifel hills, bringing traffic on the main supply roads west of the Rhine [Map 12] almost to a standstill. Horse-drawn snowploughs were few and ineffective, hastily erected snow fences were torn down by troops scrounging for firewood, there was no gravel available, and a large number of the engineer construction battalions had been taken west for employment as infantry. By the time power snowploughs reached the Eifel the American [and British] fighter-bombers were strafing and bombing every large vehicle that moved.[4]

Readers interested in the details of this battle, the largest ever fought by the US Army, should read the US Official History by Hugh M Cole, or Jean Paul Pallud's *The Battle of the Bulge, Then and Now*. For the purposes of this book it is sufficient for us to know that although the Germans took 25,000 American soldiers prisoner and destroyed 300 tanks in the first five days, the greatest depth of the German penetration, achieved on the tenth day of the attack, was about sixty miles as the crow flies and that by then the average width of the German salient had been reduced to thirty miles and that its tip, facing the Meuse, measured no more than five miles across. As Chester Wilmot put it, by 26 December: 'the spearhead of Manteuffel's Fifth Panzer Army lay broken in the snow. The Germans had looked upon the Meuse for the last time'.[5]

By the end of January 1945 the 'Bulge' had been eliminated. The cost to both sides was roughly the same – about 80,000[6] men and 700 tanks. There was, however, a vital difference – the Germans had reached the limits of their strength, the Americans had not. Far from being 'America's greatest defeat since Pearl Harbor', as one well known historian has described it,[7] the last German offensive in the west saw the German reserves exhausted and the end of Hitler's chance of saving himself and the Third Reich.

Having set the scene, let us look now at Patton's and Monty's participation in the Battle of the Bulge.

Patton

(Map 12)

George Patton's first knowledge of the German offensive came when he was called by Bradley's Chief of staff on the night of the 16th and told to detach his 10th Armored Division to Middleton's VIII Corps:

> As the loss of this Division would seriously affect the chances of my breaking through [into the Saarland], I protested very strongly, saying ... that to move the 10th Armored to the north would be playing into the hands of the Germans. General Bradley admitted my logic, but said that the situation was such that it could not be discussed over the telephone.[8]

The next day Patton directed the commander of his XII Corps, Major General Manton Eddy, to get his:

> 4th Armored [Division] engaged, because I felt that, if we did not, it too might be moved north by higher authority. The fact that I did this shows how little I appreciated the seriousness of the attack on that date.[9]

At 1030 hours on the 18th Patton was told to report to Bradley at his Headquarters in the Administration Building of the Luxembourg State Railways in Luxembourg City. On arrival he was briefed on the overall situation and the extent of the German penetration, such as it was known, and asked what he could do to help the First Army. He replied that he could halt the attack of his 4th Armored Division (see above) and concentrate it by midnight, have another Division[10] set out for Luxembourg the following morning and a third[11] alerted to move in twenty-four hours. It was clear of course that the planned Saar offensive was now out of the question and although clearly disappointed, Georgie was obviously not too upset for he is said to have exclaimed: 'What the Hell, we'll still be killing Krauts!'.[12]

At 2300 hours that night Patton was told to meet Eisenhower in Verdun the following morning. Convinced now that he was going to be ordered to go to the relief of the First Army, and certainly unaware that Monty had been urging Ike to order him to do so (see later in Monty's message to Brooke on the evening of the 18th), Patton called an immediate staff meeting and directed his officers to plan three possible axes to the north in the following order of priority: from Diekirch, due north; from the Arlon area to Bastogne; and from the vicinity of Neufchâteau, 'against the left nose of the enemy salient'.

Eisenhower's Verdun meeting was attended by Tedder (his Deputy), Bedell Smith (his Chief of Staff), Bradley, Patton of course and Devers, the commander of the 6th US Army Group.[13] Monty did not attend, but sent Freddie de Guingand instead. This was construed by the others as a calculated insult to Ike and indeed to themselves, but as far as Monty was concerned it was an all-American battle and, knowing that he was less than popular with the American generals, he believed it prudent to stay away.

Ike opened the meeting by saying that the: 'present situation is to be regarded as one of opportunity for us and not of disaster'. Patton butted in at once with: 'Hell, let's have the guts to let the sons of bitches go all the way to Paris. Then we'll really cut 'em up and chew 'em up'.[14] But Eisenhower would have none of this and made it clear that the Meuse river was his stop line and that there was to be no retreat beyond it.

Ike then told Patton that he wanted him to move up to Luxembourg: 'and take command of the battle'. When asked when he could do it, Patton replied: 'As soon as you're through with me'.

> [Ike] also said he would like me to make a strong attack with at least six divisions. I told him I would make a strong attack with three divisions . . . by the 22nd, but that I could not attack with more than that until some days later, and that if I waited, I would lose surprise. When I said I could attack on the 22nd, it created a ripple of excitement. Some people thought I was boasting and others seemed to be pleased.[15]

Patton's ADC, Charles Codman, recorded:

Within an hour everything had been thrashed out – the divisions to be employed, objectives, new Army boundaries, the amount of our own front to be taken over by [Devers's] 6th Army Group, and other matters – and virtually all of them settled on General Patton's terms.[16]

Those terms included the stipulation that the Seventh Army (from southern France) should take over most of the Third Army's sector in the Saar in order to release two of Patton's Corps for the drive north, and the need for Troy Middleton's decimated VIII Corps (from the First Army) to come under Georgie's command. Furthermore, Patton was not boasting – immediately after the meeting he telephoned 'Hap' Gay and told him to move the Third Army Headquarters from Nancy to Luxembourg and to get two Divisions moving towards Arlon and another towards Luxembourg.[17] That they all achieved this within twenty-four hours is a superb example of military organization and flexibility, especially when one takes into account the icy conditions and limited hours of daylight available in December. The ninety-degree turn demanded of the Third Army inevitably caused enormous administrative problems – as well as having to continue supplying the units left behind in the south of the Army's sector, new supply points had to be established to support the drive to the north, and to resupply the battered VIII Corps which had lost most of its equipment in the German onslaught. The extent of those problems can be gauged by the fact that at one time stocks of 105mm and larger calibre artillery shells, light and medium tanks, bazookas, mortars and 30-calibre machine-guns were all virtually exhausted. The fact that these problems were overcome and that two complete Corps were able to turn north and take offensive action can only be attributed to brilliant staff work and American ingenuity.

After spending the night of the 19th at Thionville with his XX Corps and ordering a fourth Division[18] 'pulled out of action and started on Luxembourg', Patton arrived at Bradley's Headquarters in Luxembourg City the following morning to find that his superior had not only detached part of the 4th Armored Division to a position south-west of Bastogne (Map 14), but had also halted one of his two Infantry Divisions[19] in Luxembourg. He immediately countermanded these orders. He was then told that Monty was to be given operational command of the First and Ninth[20] US Armies:

owing to the fact that telephonic communications between Bradley and these armies were difficult . . . It appeared to me at the time that Bradley was being sidetracked, either because of lack of confidence in him, or as the only way Eisenhower could prevent Montgomery from 'regrouping' . . . General Bradley took what was practically a demotion in a most soldierly manner, nor did he at any time during the subsequent campaign inject himself into the operations of the Third Army, as he might well have done, since that was the only unit he had to command.[21]

Patton then drove to Arlon where he met Troy Middleton and learned of his Corps' severe mauling during the first four days of the offensive; he then spent the rest of the day visiting four of his Divisions[22] (all in different Corps), telling them exactly what he expected of them and:

> telephoning to get up self-propelled tank destroyer battalions, divisional tank battalions, hospitals, ammunition, bridging materials, etc., and I directed the two armored Divisions and the 4th Infantry Division to cannibalise their anti-tank gun units and turn them into riflemen because all three Divisions [due to take part in the drive north] were excessively short.[23]

On the 21st Patton received a number of calls from 'various higher echelons' expressing concern that his forthcoming attack, with only three divisions, would not be strong enough to ensure success; but he maintained his position that it was better to advance as planned rather than wait and lose the element of surprise. Anyway, he felt sure that he would have at least two, if not three more Divisions to reinforce his thrust by the 23rd or 24th at the latest.[24] He also met the staffs of three of his four Corps and found 'everyone felt full of doubt except myself. It has always been my unfortunate role to be the ray of sunshine and the backslapper before action'.[25]

Patton had said he would begin his attack at 0400 hours on the 22nd and this gave Major General John Milliken's III Corps[26] only forty-eight hours to move more than 100 miles over icy, unfamiliar roads in snow and fog. Nevertheless, before dawn on the 22nd eighty-eight battalions or 1,056 guns were in position to support the advance[27] and the attack was launched only two hours late – at 0600 hours.

(Map 14)

Readers who would like to read a relatively simple account of the Third Army's advance in December and January are recommended to read Jean Pean Pallud's *The Battle of the Bulge, Then and Now*, pages 367–81 and 469–79. It is sufficient for the purposes of this book to know that within seven days of the beginning of the German offensive, two Corps had been assembled along the south flank of the German penetration and that at about 1645 hours on the 26th the siege at Bastogne was lifted. Patton himself entered the town on the 30th and by the beginning of January he had six Divisions attacking with the object of widening the salient thereby established and driving it deeper into the southern flank of the German 'Bulge'. 'This thorn in the enemy's side thus became a knife and . . . Patton turned the knife in the wound.'[28] At 0905 hours on 16 January the leading elements of his Third Army met up with their counterparts in the First Army at Houffalize – the latter, part of Monty's 21st Army Group, had begun their advance south on the 3rd – and by 26 January the 'Bulge' had to all intents and purposes been eliminated. It was a great achievement:

> However, the opportunity for a mass envelopment of the German forces by the two Armies had slipped away with the slow progress of the advance on the southern flank [Patton] and with the lateness – unavoidable or not – of the attack from the north [Montgomery]. The delays imposed by the skill and determination of the [German] grenadiers had enabled the bulk of the threatened units to escape the trap.[29]

With the benefit of hindsight, it is clear that Patton's suggestion of letting 'the sons of bitches go all the way to Paris', a view shared incidentally by Brian Horrocks, the commander of XXX British Corps, was, from a purely military point of view, a sound one in that it would almost certainly have resulted in the destruction of the bulk of the German forces involved in AUTUMN MIST; however, this was not obvious at the time and it clearly ignored the political realities of the situation.

Despite the Third Army's spectacular success in turning ninety degrees and then advancing over 100 miles in extremely difficult conditions, Patton's generalship during this period has not been without its critics. Some have pointed out that the heaviest fighting in the Bastogne sector took place *after*, rather than *during*, the relief of the town and that the Third Army's initial fighting, 'though important, was conducted against four mediocre infantry divisions of Branderberger's Seventh Army'.[30] Furthermore, that his aggressiveness and his failure, as in Lorraine, to concentrate his strength on a narrow front, resulted in many unnecessary casualties. Patton made no secret of his determination to succeed, regardless of cost:

> I had to use the whip on both Middleton and [the untried] Millikin [VIII and III Corps commanders] today. They are too cautious. I know their men are tired, but so are the Germans.[31]

And when his initial attempts to advance the eleven miles from Bastogne to Houffalize stalled or failed, he was far from sympathetic. He described the 11th Armored Division as: 'very green and took unnecessary casualties to no effect' and the 17th Airborne Division as being 'hysterical' in reporting its losses.[32] As Carlo D'Este, the renowned American military historian, makes clear in his biography, the Third Army commander:

committed two green divisions into battle without adequate reconnaissance, and seems to have launched a task force[33] at night in order
to claim Houffalize for the Third Army before the First Army . . . a
ploy reminiscent of the race for Messina.[34]

But despite these criticisms it is this author's view that few, if any,
commanders could have manoeuvred an Army as Patton did and drive it
so successfully in such difficult conditions. That said, the Battle of the
Bulge cost his Army 27,860 battle casualties and 22,770 non-battle
casualties.[35] For those who wish to understand more fully the physical
difficulties facing Patton's Divisions during their advances into the
'Bulge', they should drive, preferably in a snowy December, from Metz to
Thionville and then on to Arlon, Martelange, Assenois, Bastogne and
Houffalize, and from Luxembourg to Heiderscheid and then over the Sûre
to Wiltz and Clervaux.

Before we leave Patton in the Bulge however, let us look for a moment
at some of his more personal activities. Determined to be seen by as many
of his men as possible, he spent little time in his Headquarters in the
Fondation Pescatore (an old people's home) in Luxembourg City and was
usually to be found visiting units in an open armoured jeep wearing his
steel helmet and a winter parka or an overcoat, with one ivory-handled
pistol strapped to his waist and another tucked into his waistband. He
always sat ramrod stiff, usually with his arms folded and rarely wore a
smile. 'I spent five or six hours almost every day in an open car . . . I never
had a cold, and my face, though sometimes slightly blistered, did not hurt
me much'.[36]

Patton was always concerned about the welfare of his soldiers, even to
the extent of personally commissioning a French factory to manufacture
10,000 white camouflage smocks per week to make up for the US Army's
failure to provide these important items.[37] He also gave orders that every
man was to have turkey on Christmas Day – if only in sandwiches.
Needless to say, his opinion of army mess sergeants was similar to that of
most of his soldiers. They 'couldn't qualify as goddam manure mixers.
They take the best food Uncle Sam can buy and bugger it all up'.[38]

> Christmas Day dawned clear and cold; lovely weather for killing
> Germans, although the thought seemed somewhat at variance with
> the spirit of the day. I left early in the morning with the purpose of
> visiting all the divisions in combat . . . the 4th Armored, the 26th, the
> 80th, the 5th and elements of the 4th Infantry and 10th Armored
> Divisions . . . Late that night we had a quiet Christmas dinner at
> General Bradley's mess.[39]

On 30 January Patton:

drove to Bastogne through the corridor, passing quite close to the Germans ... I decorated with the Distinguished Service Cross Brigadier General McAuliffe, who commanded the 101st during the fight . . . [and] then drove around so the soldiers could see us and they were quite delighted.[40]

And two days later, in his first General Order of 1945, he told his men:

From the bloody corridor at Avranches, to Brest, thence across France to the Saar, over the Saar into Germany, and now on to Bastogne, your record has been one of continuous victory. Not only have you invariably defeated a cunning and ruthless enemy, but you have overcome by your indomitable fortitude every aspect of terrain and weather. Neither heat nor dust nor floods nor snow have stayed your progress. The speed and brilliancy of your achievements are unsurpassed in military history. Recently I had the honor of receiving at the hands of the 12th Army Group, Lieutenant General Omar N. Bradley, a second Oak Leaf Cluster to the DSM. This award was bestowed on me, not for what I have done, but because of what you have achieved. From the bottom of my heart I thank you.[41]

Patton was often generous in his praise of his commanders, staff and men and on occasions he could be self-effacing. When a war correspondent asked him about his Army's amazing ninety-degree turn to the north he said:

Yes, we broke all records moving up here. It was all done by the three of us . . . me, my chauffeur, and my Chief of Staff. All I did was to tell my divisional commanders where they'd got to be tomorrow. Then I let the others do it. To tell you the truth, I didn't have anything much to do with it. All you need is confidence and good soldiers . . . I'll put our goddam, bitching, belching, bellyaching GIs up against any troops in the world. The Americans are sons of bitches of soldiers – thanks to their grandmothers! . . . Yes, the American is a hell of a fine soldier.[42]

But Patton was not popular outside his own Army. The praise heaped on Georgie and the Third Army in the American press following the relief of Bastogne and the suggestion that they had won the Battle of the Bulge almost unaided, seriously irritated Hodges and the men of the First Army. The author has met many members of the First Army and indeed counts a number as close friends and he has yet to hear a really good word spoken about Patton. And even Georgie himself admitted in a letter to a friend: 'Fortunately for my sanity, and possibly for my self-esteem, I do not see all the bullshit which is written in the home town papers about me'.[43]

Perhaps the best description of Patton at this time is provided in an interview he gave with Bill Mauldin, the famous cartoonist and war correspondent. His cartoons of *'Willie and Joe'* which appeared in the *Stars and Stripes* drove Georgie to distraction, even causing him to threaten that: 'if that little son of a bitch sets foot in Third Army I'll throw his ass in jail'. Nevertheless, he did grant him an interview and Mauldin gave this picture of our prima donna:

> His hair was silver, his face was pink, his collar and shoulders glittered with more stars than I could count, his fingers sparkled with rings ... His face was rugged, with an odd, strangely shapeless outline; his eyes were pale, almost colorless, with a choleric bulge. His small, compressed mouth was sharply downturned at the corners, with a lower lip which suggested a pouting child as much as a no-nonsense martinet ... Beside him, lying in a big chair, was *Willie*, the bull terrier. If ever a dog was suited to master this one was. *Willie* had his beloved boss's expression and lacked only the ribbons and stars. I stood in that door staring at the four meanest eyes I'd ever seen.[44]

Now it is time to turn to 'the little fart', as Patton called him, and look at Monty's part in the Battle of the Bulge. Sadly: 'By the end of the battle, both Patton and Bradley were thoroughly soured on Montgomery, and where previously there had been a measure of mutual respect for the British general, there now existed only contempt'.[45]

Montgomery

(Map 13)

Monty first heard about a German attack in the Ardennes sector during the late morning of 16 December whilst playing golf in Eindhoven. He immediately flew back to Zonhoven and sent out his entire team of liaison officers (LOs) to find out exactly what was happening. As a result, and despite the fact that he had heard nothing from Eisenhower or Bradley, he was able to give the CIGS in London some details of the German offensive in his nightly report on the 17th.

(Map 14)

The following day, again after hearing nothing from Ike or Bradley, or from the Headquarters of Hodges' First US Army, which was hardly surprising since it was in a state of chaos having evacuated Spa in a panic,

Monty sent his LOs out again. As a consequence he was able to signal Brooke that night:

> I have had to send down to the HQ of [two American] Corps to ascertain the picture. The main enemy thrust has now penetrated some 20 miles ... There is much confusion in the area of V and VIII Corps ... I have been urging for two days that the whole southern front should close down and become defensive under Patch [commander Seventh US Army] and that Patton's Army should be moved northward to put in a strong attack on the axis Prüm–Bonn ... I have heard tonight that Ike has now agreed to do this.[46]

Also on 18 December, he:

> was forced to consider the possible effects of the enemy's thrust upon the dispositions of 21 Army Group ... I therefore ordered the concentration for the Rhineland battle to stop and had plans prepared for switching British divisions ... to the west of the Meuse ... [Furthermore by the 19th] the situation remained unpleasantly vague and I undertook emergency measures to get reconnaissance troops down to the line of the Meuse and to assist in forming effective cover parties for the Meuse bridges ... I could see little to prevent German armoured cars and reconnaissance elements bouncing the Meuse and advancing on Brussels [Map 12]; during the night therefore hastily formed road block detachments were posted round the capital ... [That night] Eisenhower instructed me to take command on the following day [at 1030 hours] of the American Armies north of the German salient [this amounted to two-thirds of Bradley's troops].[47]

The reasons for giving Monty command of all troops north of a line drawn from Givet through Houffalize to Prüm were quite clear: one, the Germans had split the American front and there was no longer any direct contact between Bradley's Headquarters in Luxembourg City and Hodges' in its new location near Liège;[48] and two, Monty was the only commander with any available reserves[49] and an organization capable of dealing with the crisis. He was already moving the four Divisions of XXX Corps to a position between the Meuse and Brussels on his own initiative. Bedell Smith had suggested the command change as early as the 19th and on the 20th Eisenhower agreed. He then telephoned Bradley and after what was clearly a very heated conversation, ended his call with the words: 'Well, Brad, those are my orders'.[50]

This decision:

> to pass the US First and Ninth Armies to British command must have

been hard to make, since both Eisenhower and [Bedell] Smith were acutely conscious of the smouldering animosity toward the British in general and Montgomery in particular which existed in the 12th Army Group and Third Army, not to mention the chronic anti-British sentiment which might be anticipated from some circles in Washington.[51]

But the reorganization did not come a moment too soon:

The battle was already getting out of hand. Except on the northern and southern shoulders of the Bulge there was no coherent front, and the operations of First US Army had developed into a series of individual delaying actions.[52]

Monty wasted no time. After ordering his staff to drape the bonnet of his Rolls Royce with the largest Union Jack they could find, and to provide him with eight motor-cycle outriders, he set off for the First Army Headquarters at Chaudfontaine, near Liège. Arriving there within one and a half hours of taking command, 'The Field Marshal strode into Hodges' HQ like Christ come to cleanse the temple'. And unlike Hodges, who had little idea of the overall picture, Monty was, thanks to his LOs, well briefed and looked, according to de Guingand, 'supremely cheerful and confident'.[53] Chester Wilmot has suggested that there was:

something more than confidence in his manner . . . In the hour of triumph after Normandy the Americans . . . had spurned his leadership . . . Now in defeat they had turned to him . . . to extricate them from a predicament which, he believed, would never have developed if he had been left in command of the ground forces. That afternoon Montgomery did not endear himself to his American audience, for his confident tone seemed to carry a note of censure.[54]

His first suggestion, that the Americans should shorten their current line, withdraw from some exposed positions on the northern shoulder and assemble a counter-attack force much farther west, in the area of Marche, was greeted with dismay. In the end Monty did not press the point. He knew that by the evening of the following day, the 21st, the Meuse bridges at Namur, Dinant and Givet would be firmly help by his own troops and that his XXX Corps would be correctly positioned west of the river to deal with anything unforeseen. In other words, he was 'balanced'; as long as the Germans could not advance north-west he was content and he was certainly not going to be hurried into attacking south to link up with Patton's Third Army thrust towards Bastogne.

Nevertheless, Monty finally got his way and was able to 'tidy up the battlefield'. Eisenhower had authorized: 'the newly assigned commander of all Allied forces north of the German salient . . . to give up such ground as was necessary in order to assemble sufficient strength for a decisive counter-attack',[55] and on the 24th Monty gave orders for the First Army to pull back from its very exposed positions between Trois Ponts and Vielsalm and establish a firm, defensive front farther west, firmly blocking any German advance in the direction of Namur. There has been a lot of post-war controversy about this decision, but at the time it was clearly necessary and had the concurrence of most of the senior American commanders concerned, including Eisenhower, Ridgway (commander XVIII US Airborne Corps) and Gavin (commander of the 82nd US Airborne Division). The latter wrote in his book, *On to Berlin*:

> Obviously, in the situation confronting the XVIII Corps, a withdrawal was very much in order. It shortened the section allocated to the 82nd by about 50 per cent, thus enabling us to do much better on the defensive. The new defensive position was far superior in terms of fields of fire and cover for the defenders than the old position. Finally, we would be in a much better position to launch a counter-attack when the moment for that came, and we knew it was inevitable.

On Christmas Day Bradley flew up to see Monty at Zonhoven. Having spent the previous five days visiting American as well as British headquarters and units (in his Rolls Royce and as usual without a helmet), it was the latter's first day back in his Headquarters since assuming command of the First and Ninth US Armies. It is not clear whether it was because it was Christmas or because of Bradley's visit, but Monty chose to wear his tailored battle-dress, covered with his many medal ribbons, and highly polished shoes – rather than his usual fur-lined boots, baggy corduroy trousers, grey turtle-neck pullover and numerous sweaters. Bradley arrived in a bad mood. After a wretched journey and a lunch of consisting of an apple and a pear eaten *en route*, he was incensed to find that Monty had not even sent a car to meet him – Bradley's ADC had to borrow one at the airfield. And he was clearly irritated to find, according to the same ADC, that: 'the officers there had celebrated Christmas, smoked pipes over port in a lower room where all Monty's Christmas cards were tacked to a wall in exhibition'.[56]

The meeting between the two Army Group commanders lasted about half an hour and Bradley left no record of their conversation. It is widely believed, however, that he was given a severe mauling and certainly Monty's own account of what was said would support that premise. He claimed that he briefed Bradley on the situation and explained that a lack of strength precluded any immediate counter-offensive in his sector.

I was absolutely frank with Bradley . . . I then said it was entirely our fault; we had gone much too far with our right; we had tried to develop two thrusts at the same time, and neither had been strong enough to gain decisive results. The enemy saw his chance and took it. Now we were in a proper muddle.[57]

This was of course Monty rubbing salt into the American wound; he was telling them that he, rather than Ike, Bradley and Patton, had been right all along. That he did so is all the more surprising since Brooke had warned him only four days previously that: 'Any remarks you make are bound to come to Eisenhower's ears'. The conversation clearly went from bad to worse when Bradley said: 'he had not seen Eisenhower recently and did not know [what Ike proposed to do next] . . . I said it was quite clear that neither of us could do anything without more troops'.[58] Monty went on to claim that Bradley 'agreed entirely with all I said', but it is clear that the meeting, far from ending in agreement, marked the beginning of the end of their relationship.

On 28 December Eisenhower travelled to Hasselt (Map 12) in his heavily guarded and armoured train for his first meeting with Monty since the 7th. Once again, in accordance with his principle that senior commanders must always go *forward* to see their subordinates, Monty had refused to travel to Versailles to see the Supreme Commander. The meeting was held in private. That evening Monty told Brooke:

> He [Ike] wanted to discuss first the details of the present tactical battle in the penetration area. I said that the forces were coming in from all sides and that control of this battle should be vested in one man. He agreed and he accepted my views on the correct action to be taken by 12 Army Group and he sent an order to Bradley to take that action . . . I then said it was vital to decide now on the master plan for the future conduct of the war so that all concerned could equate their present action with the future plan. In making this plan he [Eisenhower] must satisfy two basic conditions. First. All available offensive power must be allocated to the northern front. Second. One man must have the powers of operational control and coordination of the whole northern thrust.[59]

Monty claims he again offered to serve under Bradley if that was necessary to achieve the second point, but that Ike told him he had no intention of giving Bradley such a command. This is certainly not what Ike later told his own staff, but be that as it may, Monty was certainly left with the impression that Ike had agreed his 'master-plan' and that he was to be the commander of the single thrust to the Ruhr. He cabled Brooke:

He ... clearly realises that the present trouble would not have occurred if he had accepted British advice and not that of American generals. There will be no trouble over the first basic condition. I am taking steps to ensure he does not run out over the second.

Those 'steps' were to land Monty in deep trouble. On the 29th he sent off a confirmatory letter of what he thought he and Ike had agreed. It was written in the most arrogant terms. Part of it read:

I would say that your directive will assign tasks and objectives to the two army groups, allot boundaries, and so on ... one commander must have the power to direct and control the operations; you cannot possibly do it yourself, and so you would have to nominate someone else ... Any loosely worded statement will be quite useless ... if you merely use the word 'coordination' it will not work.[60]

This was Monty in the role of a Staff College instructor counselling a student and Eisenhower, not surprisingly, was infuriated by the tone of the letter. Unfortunately for Monty his letter arrived at SHAEF Headquarters at the same time as news that he had still not authorized the counter-offensive in the north to begin on 1 January (as understood by Ike and mentioned to the SHAEF staff on his return from Hasselt). A telegraph from General Marshall to Eisenhower also arrived on the same day, saying that the British press were proposing: 'a British Deputy Commander for all your ground forces and implying that you have undertaken too much of a task yourself ... Under no circumstances make any concessions of any kind whatsoever'.[61] This gave Ike the backing he needed and a cable was drafted to the Combined Chiefs of Staff saying that Monty was predicting failure unless given command of the whole Allied thrust to the Ruhr and that, 'it was impossible for the two of them to carry on working together'. Fortunately for Monty, Freddie de Guingand, realising that his Chief's letter was likely to upset Eisenhower, had flown to Versailles in an attempt to put matters right. Ike agreed to let him try and on arrival back at Zonhoven he warned Monty that the draft cable to the Combined Chiefs of Staff amounted to a demand for Monty to resign and that if he did not retract his demands and apologise, he would almost certainly be sacked and replaced by Alexander. De Guingand recalled: 'I felt very sorry for my Chief, for he now looked completely nonplussed ... it was as if a cloak of loneliness had descended on him ... What shall I do, Freddie? he asked'.[62] His Chief of Staff had already prepared a draft message and without further ado Monty agreed to sign it. It ended: 'Very distressed that my letter may have upset you and I would ask you to tear it up. Your very devoted subordinate, Monty'.[63] On 1 January Ike replied:

I received your very fine telegram this morning. I truly appreciate the understanding attitude it indicates. With the earnest hope that the year 1945 will be the most successful for you of your entire career, as ever, Ike.[64]

A major crisis had been averted – but only just.

Chester Wilmot brilliantly summarized Monty's contribution to the winning of the Battle of the Bulge in his book *The Struggle for Europe*:

> When Montgomery took command, the Germans still had a very good chance of reaching the Meuse in force, but this was soon eliminated by his strong and patient handling of the chaotic situation he had inherited. Bradley, Patton and other generals thought that he was too patient and that his policy was unduly cautious. It may well be that Montgomery under-estimated the toughness and resilience of the American troops and did not appreciate their remarkable capacity to take up the offensive immediately after suffering a severe reverse ... Montgomery's contribution was that he converted a series of individual actions into a coherent battle fought in accordance with a clear plan ... It was his refusal to make piecemeal and premature counter-attacks that enable the Americans to accumulate the reserves which thwarted the German attempts to penetrate and outflank this front.[65]

Readers who wish to study exactly what happened in the northern half of the 'Bulge' during the period 16 December 1944 to 25 January 1945 are recommended to read Jean Paul Pallud's *The Battle of the Bulge, Then and Now*, and this author's books, *The Devil's Adjutant*, *Men of Steel* and *Sons of the Reich*.

Unfortunately for Monty his achievements in the Ardennes were almost wholly negated by remarks he made at a press conference on 7 January 1945, a conference held whilst the fighting was still going on and American lives were still being lost. One would have thought Monty might have learned his lesson after the showdown with Eisenhower but, seemingly insensitive to his wider audience and apparently determined to give the British Army some of the limelight, Monty was even more arrogant than usual. To the embarrassment of some of the British officers present he wore a parachute red beret (Monty had never parachuted and was therefore not entitled to wear the coveted beret) and he delivered his remarks in a condescending matter. These are some of his most controversial statements:

> As soon as I saw what was happening, I took certain steps to ensure that if the Germans got to the Meuse they would certainly not get over

that river. And I carried out certain movements so as to provide balanced dispositions to meet the threatened danger ... I was thinking ahead.

Then the situation began to deteriorate. But the whole Allied team rallied to meet the danger; national considerations were thrown over board [including Bradley as many Americans saw it!]; General Eisenhower placed me in command of the whole northern front.

I employed the whole available power of the British Group of Armies; this power was brought into play very gradually and in such a way that it would not interfere with the American lines of communication. Finally it was put into battle with a bang and today British divisions are fighting hard on the right flank of First US Army. You have thus the picture of British troops fighting on both sides of American forces who have suffered a hard blow. This is a fine Allied picture.

The battle has been most interesting; I think possibly one of the most interesting and tricky battles I have ever handled.

The battle has some similarity to the battle that began on 31 August 1942 when Rommel made his last bid to capture Egypt and was 'seen off' by the Eighth Army.[66]

Needless to say many Americans took great offence at his description of the biggest battle the US Army had ever fought as 'interesting and tricky', and saw some of his statements as a claim that he and the British Army had saved the situation. 'Lightning Joe' Collins, the commander of VII US Corps and a man greatly admired by Monty, was outraged: 'Monty got under my skin by downgrading the American troops ... only one British division participated in the fighting.[67] It left a sour note'.[68] It made no difference that Monty told the correspondents that the German offensive had been halted *before* any British units were committed, or that the Germans had been beaten by: 'the good fighting qualities of the American soldier and the teamwork of the Allies'. Or that he went on to say:

I have now formed a very great affection and admiration for the American soldier. I salute the brave fighting men of America ... Let me tell you that the captain of our team is Eisenhower. I am absolutely devoted to Ike ... It grieves me to see uncomplimentary articles about him in the British Press.

But despite these glowing compliments the damage was done, and then further aggravated by the fact that in both his speech and the written statement issued afterwards, Monty even failed to mention Bradley. Commenting later, Eisenhower said: 'I doubt that Montgomery ever came to realise how deeply resentful some American commanders were. They believed he had belittled them – and they were not slow to voice reciprocal scorn and contempt'.[69] Bradley of course never forgave Monty and although, in the interests of Allied unity, he acknowledged Monty's 'notable contribution' at his own press conference two days later, he did not hold back after the war in his book, *A Soldier's Story*.

Monty acknowledged later that the press conference had been a mistake and that his own attitude was at fault:

> I should never have held that Press conference. So great was the feeling against me on the part of the American generals, that whatever I said was bound to be wrong. I should therefore have said nothing ... Whatever I said (and I was misreported) the general impression I gave was one of tremendous confidence. In contradistinction to the rather crestfallen American command, I appeared, to the sensitive, to be triumphant – not over the Germans but over the Americans.[70]

That said, he remained as convinced as ever that he, and he alone, had been right all along:

> In the battle of the Ardennes the Allies got a real 'bloody nose', the Americans had nearly 80,000 casualties, and it would never have happened if we had fought the campaign properly after the great victory in Normandy, or had even ensured tactical balance in the disposition of the land forces as the winter campaign developed. Furthermore, because of this unnecessary battle we lost some six weeks in time – with all that entailed in political consequences as the end of the war drew nearer.[71]

Nevertheless, Monty realised it was time to try to make amends and so on 12 January he wrote to Bradley congratulating the First US Army and expressing his admiration for:

> the operations that have been conducted on the southern side [of the 'Bulge']; if you had not held on firmly to Bastogne the whole situation might have become very awkward. My kind regards to you and to George Patton.

However, it is clear from a letter to Phyllis Reynolds that by this time Monty was getting very tired – hardly surprising when one considers the pressures he had been under and the responsibilities he had been bearing since D-Day – indeed, since August 1942. The following day he wrote:

> There seems to have been a great 'flutter' in the press over my talk to war correspondents here on 7 Jan . . . Life is very busy at present as I have a very large parish to look after, with over two million men . . . I long to get home for a day or two; I am getting rather exhausted and could do with a few days rest.

On 17 January, however, the day after the meeting of the First and Third US Armies at Houffalize and the day Hodges' First Army reverted to Bradley's command, Monty's spirits received a boost. It came in a letter from the commander of the XVIII US Airborne Corps, Major General Matt Ridgway:

> It has been an honored privilege and a very great personal pleasure to have served, even so briefly, under your distinguished leadership. To the gifted professional guidance you at once gave me, was added your own consummate courtesy and consideration. I am deeply grateful for both. My warm and sincere good wishes will follow you and with them the hope of again serving with you in pursuit of a common goal.[72]

It seems that at least one American general liked and respected him.

NOTES
1 Wilmot, *The Struggle for Europe*, p. 608.
2 Diary of Bradley's ADC, Maj Chester B Hansen.
3 Cole, *US Army in World War II: the European Theater of Operations, The Ardennes, Battle of the Bulge*, p. 47.
4 Wilmot, op. cit., p. 649.
5 Ibid, p. 602.
6 Exact American casualty figures are impossible to ascertain. According to Eisenhower's personnel officer (Merriam, *The Battle of the Ardennes*, p. 199), American losses totalled 70,890, of whom 8,607 were killed, 41,139 wounded and 21,144 missing. SHAEF records (Wilmot, op.cit., p. 664, Note 2) give figures of 8,407 killed, 46,170 wounded, 20,905 missing, for a total of 75,482. Most post-war reports give a total figure of around 81,000, with 19,000 killed. In the case of the Germans: 'No official casualty figures have ever been computed. However, the German High Command's own estimate of losses in the Bulge is 81,834, with 12,652 killed' – D'Este, *A Genius for War*, p. 699, Note 71. On the other hand, Milton Shulman gives a figure, 'in the neighbourhood of 120,000', including 'about 50,000 prisoners-of-war' – *Defeat in the West*, p. 275.
7 Nigel Hamilton, *Monty The Field Marshal 1944–1976*, p. 179. He goes on to claim that the initial success of the German attack was due to the fact that it followed Monty's tactics at Alamein with infantry paving the way for an

armoured second wave. It is the author's view that if the attack, certainly in the north, had been led by tanks rather than infantry, it would have been much more successful.

8   Patton, *War As I Knew It*, p. 179.
9   Ibid, p. 180.
10 80 Inf Div.
11 26 Inf Div.
12 D'Este, op. cit., p. 678.
13 Comprising the Seventh US and First French Armies from southern France.
14 D'Este, op. cit., p. 679.
15 Patton, op. cit., p. 180.
16 D'Este, op. cit., p. 681.
17 Gay had become Patton's Chief of Staff for a second and final time when Gaffey was given the 4th Armd Div in Nov 44.
18 5 Inf Div.
19 80 Inf Div.
20 Positioned in Holland between the First US and Second British Armies.
21 Patton, op. cit., p. 186.
22 9 & 10 Armd & 4 & 80 Inf Divs.
23 Patton, op. cit., p. 187.
24 10 Armd & 4 & 5 Inf Divs of XII Corps.
25 Patton, op. cit., p. 188.
26 4 Armd & 26 & 80 Inf Divs.
27 Patton, op. cit., p. 189.
28 Wilmot, op. cit., p. 607.
29 Pallud, *The Battle of the Bulge Then and Now*, pp. 458–9.
30 Merriam, op. cit., p 210.
31 Diary dated 9 Jan 45.
32 The Patton Papers.
33 Task Force Green of 11 Armd Div.
34 D'Este, op. cit., pp. 699–700.
35 Patton, op. cit., pp. 192 & 217.
36 Ibid, p. 228.
37 Winter overshoes & parkas were nonexistent & there was not even white paint to camouflage tanks – D'Este, op. cit., p. 689.
38 D'Este, op. cit., p. 691.
39 Patton, op. cit., p. 192.
40 Ibid, p. 198.
41 Ibid, p. 199.
42 D'Este, op. cit., pp. 689–90.
43 Ibid, p. 701.
44 Ibid, p. 693.
45 Ibid, p. 697.
46 Montgomery Papers, M 381.
47 Montgomery, *Normandy to the Baltic*, pp. 353–4.
48 The chain of repeater stations, necessary for directional radio links, was broken on 23 Dec and the cable telephone link was cut on the same day.
49 The 82nd & 101st Airborne Divs had already been deployed; an armd div was disembarking at Le Havre & two more airborne divs were in the UK, but they could not be brought into action in time to affect the crisis.
50 Bradley, *A General's Life*, p. 363.
51 Cole, op. cit., p. 424.

52 Wilmot, op. cit., p. 591.
53 Ibid, p. 592.
54 Ibid, pp. 592–3.
55 Cole, op. cit., p. 411.
56 Diary of Bradley's ADC, Maj Chester B Hansen.
57 M 393, Montgomery Papers.
58 Ibid.
59 M 402, Montgomery Papers.
60 M 540, Montgomery Papers.
61 Diary of Harry C Butcher.
62 De Guingand, *Generals at War.*
63 M 406 dated 31 Dec 44, Montgomery Papers.
64 Montgomery, *Memoirs*, p. 320.
65 Wilmot, op. cit., p. 610.
66 Montgomery, op. cit., pp. 311–12.
67 This is not true. 6 Airborne, 53 & 51 Inf Divs & 29 Armd Bde were engaged on Collins' right flank.
68 Horne, *The Lonely Leader*, p. 310.
69 Eisenhower, *Crusade in Europe*, p. 356.
70 Montgomery, op. cit. p. 314.
71 Ibid, p. 315.
72 Letter dated 17 Jan 45 in Montgomery Papers.

CHAPTER XXIII

Into Germany

(Map 15)

Background

Author's Note

No attempt will be made in this or subsequent chapters to explain the political background to the military campaign in Europe in the period February to May 1945. Readers interested in the Yalta Conference and the decisions on the partition of post-war Germany should consult the books listed in the Bibliography by Chester Wilmot, Carlo D'Este and Nigel Hamilton.

By the beginning of February 1945 it should have been clear to Hitler that there was no longer any hope of a split between the Western Allies and the Soviet Union and that there was no possibility of producing sufficient V-weapons to prevent an Allied victory. His armies were almost exhausted.

With most of Poland in Soviet hands and the Ruhr in ruins from Allied air attacks, the replenishment of fuel, ammunition and weapon stocks had almost come to a halt and coal and steel production had been reduced to a fifth of what it had been only six months earlier. On the eastern front the Soviet winter offensive had reached a line less than 100 miles from Berlin and although in the west the Siegfried Line (Map 13) was still basically intact and the Rhine had yet to be crossed, it was clear that with American divisions arriving in Europe at the rate of one a week, it was only a matter of time before the Third Reich collapsed in chaos and disaster. But still Hitler refused to consider surrender.

The success and speed of the Soviet advance had in fact presented the Western Allies with a serious problem – unless they broke through to the North German Plain within a few weeks, Stalin would almost certainly seize control of virtually the whole of Germany, including its Baltic and North Sea ports.

On 31 December 1944 Eisenhower wrote a letter to Monty in his own handwriting, enclosing his outline plan for the first phase of the advance into Germany. In it he said:

> The plan concentrates everything for the destruction of the enemy north of [the line] Prüm–Bonn, and gives to you and Bradley each a specific task. The plan also provides for great strength north of the Ruhr when the Rhine is crossed . . . In the matter of command I do not agree that one Army Group Commander should fight his own battle and give orders to another Army Group Commander . . . I know your loyalty as a soldier and your readiness to devote yourself to assigned tasks. For my part I would deplore the development of such an unbridgeable group of convictions between us that we would have to present our differences to the Combined Chiefs of Staff.[1]

This sounded like an ultimatum from the Supreme Commander, but in fact the plan was much to Monty's liking. It called firstly for the destruction of the German forces west of the Rhine, following which Monty was to make the main drive to the North German Plain, north of the Ruhr, whilst Bradley made a complementary, but secondary, attack from the Mainz–Frankfurt area, north-east to Kassel. The overall objective of the plan was to effect 'a massive double development of the Ruhr to be followed by a great thrust to join up with the Russians'.[2] After studying it Monty came to the conclusion that:

> It did all I wanted except in the realm of operational control, and because of Marshall's telegram that subject was closed. It put the weight in the north and gave [me] the Ninth American Army. It gave me power of decision in the event of disagreement with Bradley on

the boundary between 12 and 21 Army Groups. In fact, I had been given very nearly all that I had been asking for since August.[3]

He replied: 'You can rely on me and all under my command to go all out one hundred per cent to implement your plan'.[4]

Eisenhower's plan for the Rhineland campaign, which was to precede the thrust into Germany proper, saw Monty's 21st Army Group, with the Ninth US Army under command, seizing the west bank of the Rhine from Nijmegen to Düsseldorf. During this phase Bradley's 12th Army Group was to maintain an aggressive defence. Then, while Monty prepared to cross the lower Rhine, Bradley was to secure the river from Düsseldorf to Cologne, following which George Patton's Third Army would 'take up the ball' and thrust eastwards from Prüm to Koblenz. At the same time the Third and Seventh US Armies would be responsible for securing crossing places over the Rhine between Mainz and Karlsruhe for the forces destined to carry out the thrust south of the Ruhr.

Needless to say Bradley was far from happy to see Monty being given not only the main role, but also a complete US Army. With two-thirds of the Allied Expeditionary Force now made up of American troops he wanted, not surprisingly, the main effort to be made by American troops under American command – indeed, he envisaged all four US Armies driving into central Germany with the British, Canadian and French Armies being relegated to flank protection. When Eisenhower rejected this plan, however, he told his Army commanders that the whole plan had been instigated by Monty and imposed upon the Supreme Commander by the Combined Chiefs of Staff.

Montgomery

Even before the Rhineland campaign began, Monty upset the Americans yet again. In his initial planning directive to the 21st Army Group for the crossings of the Maas and Roer rivers, issued on 21 January, he laid down that Dempsey's Second British Army would command *all* the assault forces, including one of the Ninth US Army's Corps. This left General Simpson, the Ninth Army commander, with nothing to do in the operation and was construed by the Americans, not unreasonably, as a clear attempt by Monty to gain a 'British' victory. He was forced to amend his directive – the US Corps would report to its own Army commander, who would in turn report to Monty.

On 7 February Monty moved his Tac HQ from Zonhoven to Geldrop, five miles east of Eindhoven (Map 13), in preparation for the first phase of the renewed offensive. The British and Canadians were to attack south-east from the Nijmegen area (Operation VERITABLE), and forty-eight hours later Simpson's Ninth US Army was to attack across the Roer in a north-east direction (Operation GRENADE). The overall aim was to envelop and destroy the Germans west of the Rhine.

VERITABLE opened on 8 February with 1,034 guns firing more than half a million shells in a barrage lasting five and a half hours. The British and Canadian advance involving 50,000 men and 500 tanks was successful, but it was seriously slowed down by quagmire conditions in the area of the Reichswald between the Maas and Rhine rivers. In the south the American attack had to be delayed when the Germans destroyed the discharge valves on the Roer dams, ensuring the river remained in flood for two more weeks. It was eventually launched on 23 February and by 11 March the whole of Monty's 21st Army Group was lined up on the left bank of the Rhine from Nijmegen to Düsseldorf. The campaign, although successful, was costly – the British and Canadians suffered 15,000 casualties and the Americans 7,300.

At this point controversy resurfaced. The US Ninth Army had broken through to the Rhine between Düsseldorf and Duisburg and, believing the Germans had not had time to man the east bank in any strength, its commander suggested that he should attempt a 'bounce' crossing. Knowing that such a crossing would lead directly into the industrial complex of the Ruhr, something that Eisenhower had expressly forbidden, Monty would have none of it. Simpson was told to wait for a set piece crossing of the Rhine as laid down in the original plans. Inevitably the Americans saw this as just another example of Monty depriving them of an opportunity to get across the river first and that under British command they would never be allowed to use their initiative and 'Frontier' spirit.

On 10 March Monty ordered his Tac HQ to move again – this time to Venlo only twenty-eight miles from the Rhine. Whilst it did so he flew back to Ypres (Map 4) to an award ceremony. One of the recipients wrote later that on arrival Monty paid more attention to a crowd of Belgians waiting outside the theatre where the awards were being made than he did to the guard of honour, and that the first thing he did in the theatre was to adjust a bank of flood lights. Everyone was photographed and given a copy of their personal photograph signed by Monty. 'He was a great showman, but why not? He was a morale-booster and I think a great general as well', wrote one award winner.[5]

That night Monty wrote to Phyllis Reynolds:

> I am busy getting ready for the next battle. The Rhine is *some* river, but we shall get over it. I move out tomorrow into the fields, and from now on will have a caravan–tent life. It will be cold at first, after a house with central heating . . . I shall take great care not to get cold.

He also took the opportunity to send home with the Director of Military Operations who had been visiting him, photographs and press cuttings of and about himself, a wristwatch and a cake for his son and a photograph of James Gunn's painting of himself!

Eight days later Monty wrote to his son David:

> We are now up on the Rhine; it is a pretty large affair – 500 yards wide; but we shall go over it at the right time and place; when we are ready. My canaries find it a bit chilly, living in a caravan; and I fancy the goldfish also notice the change.[6]

On 17 March Tac HQ moved again – over the Maas to a riding stable in a pine forest near Straelen, eight miles north-east of Venlo and two miles inside Germany. After nearly five years Monty was back on German soil and it was here that he approved the plans for his last great set piece operation of the war – the Rhine crossing; he had scheduled it for the 23rd. It was a typical Montgomery operation designed to ensure success and minimize casualties. Operation PLUNDER involved a quarter of a million men from thirty divisions and three Armies, including nearly 50,000 British and American engineers. 3,300 guns were concentrated on a twenty-five-mile front and a total of 7,000 air sorties were flown before, during and immediately after the crossing, dropping 50,000 tons of bombs. But as usual Monty merely laid down the general outline of the operation; he was perfectly happy to let each of his Army commanders plan their particular contribution and the various staffs get on with the details. On 9 March he called his first planning conference:

> It was a most informal little affair, held out in the open air, with just General Dempsey of the Second Army, General Crerar of the Canadian Army, and General Simpson of the Ninth US Army. Monty had given them the outline of his plans before, and he wanted them to say what they proposed to do. No staff officers were in attendance. Each of the generals had his own very clear plans which, subject to one or two quite minor amendments made by Monty, were completely accepted. The whole conference could have taken no longer than two hours.[7]

This was of course Monty again playing the role of a Staff College instructor – a role he never really gave up from the time he left Camberley in 1929.

Whilst his Tac HQ moved to Straelen on the 17th, Monty set off on a tour of the Canadian units that had been recently transferred from Italy in order to 'increase the weight of Imperial forces on the Western Front'.[8] He had made a promise to the Secretary of State for War that he would do this and once again Monty was to be seen standing on the bonnet of his jeep addressing groups of up to 5,000 men.

Before the opening of Operation PLUNDER, Monty issued another special message to his troops. The final part of it read:

> Having crossed the Rhine, we will crack about in the plains of Northern Germany, chasing the enemy from pillar to post. Over the Rhine, then let us go. And good hunting to you all on the other side. 'May the Lord Mighty in battle' give us victory in this our latest undertaking, as He has done in all our battles since we landed in Normandy on D-Day.[9]

On 18 March Eisenhower sent a secret letter to Monty, Bradley and Devers (commander 6th Army Group). It stated that if Monty's planned advance north of the Ruhr succeeded, the resultant thrust was to be subdivided into two, with the 21st and 12th Army Groups operating alongside each other.[10] Devers was to take command of the remainder of the Allied forces south of the Ruhr. Monty was aghast, but decided to keep quiet – at least for the moment. However, to the acting CIGS in London he wrote:

> Actually of course the whole thing is complete nonsense; the employment of two Army Groups round the *north* of the Ruhr is not only unsound tactically, it is quite impossible administratively. One man must be in general command north of the Ruhr.[11]

Inevitably Monty could not keep quiet for long and on 21 March when the SHAEF Chief of Operations, Jock Whiteley, visited him, he gave him his views 'in no uncertain voice'. He proposed that Bradley should encircle the Ruhr from the south and then strike north-east, 'joining me east of the Ruhr'. To his surprise Monty heard nothing for two days. Ike was trying to relax at the Villa Sous le Vent, a spacious mansion near Cannes on the French Riviera. According to his Chief of Staff, Bedell Smith, and his driver, Kay Summersby, he was exhausted and badly needed the break.[12] Omar Bradley was also invited – 'to be sure that he and Bradley understood each other completely'.[13]

On the 23rd, just before the arrival of Churchill and Brooke to witness the beginning of Operation PLUNDER, Monty heard, to his jubilation, that Bradley was 'very pleased' with the idea of a double envelopment of the Ruhr and that Ike had approved the gist of 'Whiteley's new plan'.

Much to Monty's irritation, Winston Churchill had insisted on being present for the Rhine crossing. 'I didn't want him but he was determined to come; so I have invited him in order to keep the peace', he wrote to the Secretary of State for War. The Prime Minister arrived with the CIGS on the 23rd and from the safety of an armoured car watched as nearly 17,000 men of the 6th British and 17th American Airborne Divisions landed beyond the river on the morning of the 24th (Operation VARSITY). Despite heavy casualties in the two airborne Divisions, PLUNDER was, hardly surprisingly, overwhelmingly successful.

Whilst Churchill and Brooke watched the airborne landings, Monty drove south to Rheinberg, ten miles north-west of Duisburg, to see the US Corps commander responsible for the river crossings in that sector. Eisenhower and Simpson, the Ninth US Army commander, were also there and Monty was able to have a private meeting with the Supreme Commander at which Ike confirmed that he was agreeable to an envelopment of the Ruhr from the north *and* the south. Monty was delighted and they agreed to meet again the following day at Simpson's Headquarters to sort out the details with Bradley. Churchill and Brooke would also be present. Unwittingly, and for good military reasons, Monty had played straight into Ike's and Bradley's hands – by refusing to accept two Army Groups north of the Ruhr, he had endorsed their 'broad front' strategy.

The meeting on the 25th appears to have ended with both sides believing their strategies had won the day. Thanks to Monty's suggestion that Bradley should attack south of Duisburg and meet up with his Army Group, which still included Simpson's Ninth US Army, on the east side of the Ruhr, Eisenhower and Bradley believed their 'broad front' strategy had won the day. Monty on the other hand, thought that his strategy of a single main thrust into Northern Germany was intact. What he did not know was that Bradley had been pressing the Supreme Commander to return Simpson's Ninth Army to him so that he could share in the glory of crossing the Rhine and advancing into Northern Germany, nor that Ike was now completely fed up with the constant niggling of his two Army Group commanders. Eisenhower had already written to Marshall on the 12th saying that he was getting 'tired of trying to arrange the blankets smoothly over several prima donnas in the same bed',[14] and he now decided to act. Some time between the Rheinberg meeting and the afternoon of the 28th Ike resolved to return Simpson's Ninth US Army to Bradley's command and more importantly, to move the main weight of the offensive into Germany from the north to the centre.[15] Berlin was to be left to the Russians and the objectives of a new main offensive would be Dresden and Leipzig. It has been suggested, and indeed it is quite possible, that a report that Hitler and the Nazis were planning to make a final stand in the Bavarian mountains, some sort of 'National Redoubt', was behind Eisenhower's decision. Certainly the presence of six of the seven SS Panzer Divisions in the Danube valley in the southern part of the Eastern Front and well away from Berlin added to the suspicion that Hitler and his Nazi regime were planning to withdraw into some sort of mountain stronghold. A SHAEF Intelligence Summary dated 11 March stated:

The main trend of German defence policy does seem directed primarily to the safeguarding of the Alpine Zone. This area is, by the very nature of the terrain, practically impenetrable . . . The evidence indicates that considerable numbers of SS and specially chosen units are being systematically withdrawn to Austria . . . and that some of the most important ministries . . . are already established in the Redoubt area.

Whatever the reason for Eisenhower's decision, it led in the end, and to Monty's chagrin, to thirty-one American divisions being directed south-east towards the so-called National Redoubt, leaving only eight on the direct route to Berlin.

When Churchill left on the 26th, after pissing in the Rhine[16] (he had already pissed on the Siegfried Line on 3 March near Jülich, thirty miles west of Cologne, in the presence of Brooke and Simpson[17]), he wrote in Monty's autograph book:

The Rhine and all its fortress lines lie behind the 21st Group of Armies . . . A beaten army not long ago master in Europe retreats before its pursuers. The goal is not long to be denied to those who have come so far and fought so well under proud and faithful leadership.[18]

That evening Monty, believing that 'there was not very much in front of me', decided to 'make for the Elbe' and the following morning he issued the appropriate orders to his Army commanders. He was fully aware that his order to 'drive hard for the line of the Elbe' was in direct contravention of Eisenhower's directive, issued immediately after their meeting at Rheinberg, which laid down that the Ruhr was to be surrounded and mopped up before any advance farther east was made, but 'there are moments in war when you take risks and act boldly; and use the doctrine of the blind optic'.[19]

Monty's orders, issued formally on the 27th, directed Dempsey's Second British Army to drive for Hamburg and Simpson's Ninth US Army for Magdeburg. They were to 'move their armoured and mobile forces forward at once and get through to the Elbe with the utmost speed and drive'.[20] Immediately after issuing these orders, and believing that Ike would be delighted, he communicated his intentions to SHAEF, giving the inter-Army boundaries he had laid down, and stating that after crossing the Rhine his own Tac HQ would 'move to Wesel, Münster, Wiedenbrück, Herford, Hannover – thence by autobahn to Berlin, I hope'.

Eisenhower did not see Monty's message until the following day. He replied, in a message marked 'For Field Marshal Montgomery's eyes only':

I agree in general with your plans up to the point of gaining contact with Bradley east of the Ruhr. However, thereafter my present plans [are] being coordinated with Stalin . . . As soon as you have joined hands with Bradley . . . Ninth United States Army will revert to Bradley's command. Bradley will be responsible for mopping up and occupying the Ruhr and with the minimum delay will deliver his main thrust on the axis Erfurt–Leipzig–Dresden to join hands with the Russians. The mission of your Army Group will be to protect Bradley's northern flank.[21]

Monty was dumbfounded. He wrote to the Director of Military Operations in London: '[On 28 March] I received the blow from Ike in which he disagrees with my plan and removes Ninth Army from me; a very good counter-attack!! All very dirty work, I fear'.[22]

In fact Ike's decision to cable Stalin with his new plan, specifying that: 'For my forces the best axis on which to effect this junction [the link up with the Red Army] would be Erfurt–Leipzig–Dresden', was even more astonishing than Monty realised – he had done so without being asked and without first showing his plan to the Combined Chiefs of Staff!

But still Monty would not give up; in the vain hope that Eisenhower would change his mind, he signalled on the 29th:

I note . . . that you intend to change the command set-up. If you feel this is necessary I pray you do not do so until we reach the Elbe as such action would not help the great movement which is now beginning to develop.[23]

It was to no avail. On the 31st, to rub salt into the wound, Eisenhower signalled:

You will note that in none of this do I mention Berlin. That place has become, so far as I am concerned, nothing but a geographical location, and I have never been interested in these. My purpose is to destroy the enemy's forces and his powers to resist.[24]

Again Monty could hardly believe his eyes. He recalled Ike's letter to him of 15 September in which he had written: 'Clearly, Berlin is the main prize. There is no doubt whatsoever, in my mind, that we should concentrate all our energies and resources on a rapid thrust to Berlin'.[25]

But there was nothing that Monty, Brooke, or even Churchill, who never forgave Eisenhower, could do about the Supreme Commander's decision. On 9 April Monty wrote coldly to Eisenhower: 'It is quite clear to me what you want. I will crack along on the northern flank one hundred percent and will do all I can to draw the enemy forces away from *the main effort* (author's emphasis) being made by Bradley'.[26] He wrote later:

> It was useless for me to pursue the matter further. We had had so much argument already on great issues; anyhow it was now almost too late ... Berlin was lost to us when we failed to make a sound operational plan in August 1944, after the victory in Normandy. The Americans could not understand that it was of little avail to win the war strategically if we lost it politically.[27]

Interestingly, Bradley wrote after the war: 'As [American] soldiers we looked naively on the British inclination to complicate the war with political foresight and non-military objectives'.[28] And George Patton's conversation with Ike on the subject of Berlin is equally interesting. When told by Ike that Berlin had 'no tactical or strategic value and would place upon the American forces the burden of caring for thousands and thousands of Germans, displaced persons and Allied prisoners of war', Patton replied, 'I don't see how you figure that out. We had better take Berlin, and quick – and on to the Oder!'. He went on to point out that Simpson's Ninth Army could take the capital in forty-eight hours, but Ike replied: 'Well, who would want it?'. Patton did not apparently reply at once, but placed his hands on his friend's shoulders and said: 'I think history will answer that question for you'.[29] It seems our two prima donnas were in complete agreement on the subject of Berlin.

Monty was of course bitterly disappointed with Eisenhower's decision – after five years of war he was to be denied the prize he believed was rightfully his. He dictated a 'note for the record':

> The Field Marshal considered it was useless to continue to argue with the American generals as to what the correct strategy should be. They were unable to see his point of view, and were in any case determined to finish off the war in their own way.[30]

Patton

Readers will not be surprised to learn that George Patton was furious when he was told that his Army was to adopt a posture of 'aggressive defence', whilst Monty's Army Group launched a major offensive. 'We felt it was ignoble for the American armies to finish the war on the defensive'.[31] On 4 February he wrote to his wife Beatrice telling her that if she heard he was on the defensive: 'It was not the enemy who put me there. I don't see much future for me in this war. There are too many safety first people running it'.

Patton was certainly not going to be defeated by the 'safety first people' and he chose to view the order to adopt a posture of aggressive defence as meaning that he could 'keep moving towards the Rhine with a low profile'.[32] He told his staff that the Third Army was going to carry out an 'armoured reconnaissance', but that it would be done with seven *divisions* (author's emphasis), and that the initial objectives were Prüm, Bitburg and the vital city of Trier on the Moselle. Furthermore he told his commanders to make sure that their units were always fully committed so that they could not be removed from his command and placed in Eisenhower's new theatre reserve. 'Reserve against what? . . . Certainly at this point in the war no reserve was needed – simply violent attacks everywhere with everything', he wrote in his diary.[33]

On 5 February Patton was summoned to Bastogne (Map 14) to meet Eisenhower and Bradley. He fully expected to receive a direct order to halt his Army, but to his great relief the summons turned out to be nothing more serious than a photo call. He noted, however, that Ike: 'never mentioned the Bastogne offensive, although this was the first time I had seen him since 19 December, when he seemed much pleased to have me at the critical point'.[34]

On 10 February Bradley telephoned Patton to tell him that Ike was transferring divisions from the 12th Army Group to Simpson's Ninth US Army, now part of Monty's Army Group. Georgie replied that as the oldest and most experienced serving general in the theatre he was damned if he would release any of his divisions, or go on to the defensive, and that he would resign rather than comply with such orders. He clearly had no intention of really resigning, but he withdrew his threat anyway when Bradley suggested that he owed too much to his troops to even consider it. Nevertheless, in early February he lost the 17th Airborne and 95th Infantry Divisions to Simpson and Monty – as readers are already aware, the 17th was to suffer badly in Monty's Operation VARSITY.

The area in which the Third Army was operating during February 1945, the Eifel, is hilly, heavily forested and bisected by three fast-flowing rivers, which at that time were swollen by the snow and rains of the worst winter for thirty-eight years. As a result the Third Army's campaign was similar to that it had endured in Lorraine (Map 12), but carried out in much worse weather conditions. Patton wrote later that: 'The crossing of . . . these rivers was a magnificent feat of arms'.[35] The campaign, carried out in appalling conditions, cost a total of 42,217 battle casualties and a staggering 20,790 non-battle casualties,[36] but it was eventually successful and by 1 March Patton's troops had captured Prüm and Bitburg; Trier fell a day later. SHAEF had estimated that it would take four Divisions to take the former Roman fortress of Trier, but Georgie was able to send a message saying: 'Have taken Trier with two divisions. Do you want me to give it back?'.[37]

During the sluggish campaign in the Eifel, Patton took his first real leave for two and a half years. He spent it in Paris, where he almost certainly met Jean Gordon again, and where he certainly visited the Folies-Bergère and was allegedly invited by the manager's wife to make it his home whenever he was in the French capital. He wrote in his diary: 'I can imagine no more restless place than the Folies, full of about one hundred practically naked women'. He also enjoyed a day's shooting with Bedell-Smith in the game reserve formerly used by the kings of France, but had to be evacuated with a violent case of ptomaine poisoning which he thought was due to someone trying to kill him![38]

On 5 March Hodges' First Army finally went over to the attack; Cologne fell on the 6th, and to everyone's amazement by 1600 hours on the 7th a bridge had been secured over the Rhine roughly halfway between Cologne and Koblenz – the Ludendorff railway bridge at Remagen.[39] 'We were quite happy over it, but just a little envious', wrote Patton later.[40] American bravery and initiative had ensured that the bridge, although prepared for demolition, was secured intact; but the euphoria soon disappeared the following day when, sadly for Bradley and Hodges, Eisenhower gave orders that in order to provide the necessary number of divisions to Simpson's Ninth Army for Monty's northern push, no more than four were to be committed at Remagen, and that for the time being at least the bridgehead was to be held but not developed. This in fact also made sense tactically since beyond the bridge, for about twelve miles, were heavily forested mountains, crossed by poor roads making further advance against any kind of determined resistance extremely difficult. Even so by the 17th, when the bridge finally collapsed (it had been damaged when some of the demolitions had gone off on the 7th), there were six American divisions in a bridgehead ten miles deep and thirty miles wide.

On 5 March, as Hodges launched his attack, Patton finally obtained Eisenhower's authority to advance into the rest of the Rheinland Palatinate. Bradley told him to: 'take the Rhine on the run'[41] and on 6 March, just two days after the Remagen bridge fell to the First Army, Georgie's 4th Armored Division reached the river north of Koblenz; it had advanced fifty-five miles in less than forty-eight hours. On the 13th Patton ordered his divisions across the Moselle and through the Hunsrück, a mountainous area to the east of Trier thought by SHAEF to be too difficult for armour; nevertheless, by the 22nd he had eight divisions on the Rhine from Koblenz to Ludwigshafen.

> He used his armour and armoured infantry almost as if they were cavalry, making deep probes ... Ever since getting Bradley's permission to cross near Mainz, he had been flying from headquarters to headquarters like a wild man – begging, coaxing, demanding and threatening. He wanted speed and more speed.[42]

Patton's campaign west of the Rhine was over. Chester Wilmot compared it to his 'end run south of the bocage. Once again the German left flank was broken and turned and, as in France, there were no reserves to restore the line'.[43] The Palatinate campaign had cost another 7,287 casualties,[44] but the Third Army engineers were ready and Patton, desperate to cross the great river before Monty, agreed with Eddy that they should make a feint at Mainz and cross at once at Oppenheim. By daylight on the 23rd six battalions were over the river for a loss of only twenty-eight men killed and wounded, whilst other infantry and engineer units had crossed just to the north, at Nierstein, without opposition. Patton telephoned Bradley: 'Brad, don't tell anyone but I'm across . . . there are so few Krauts around there they don't know it yet. So don't make any announcement. We'll keep it secret until we see how it goes'. However, the 'Krauts' soon became aware of the crossings and after heavy Luftwaffe raids on the Third Army pontoon bridges during the day, Patton called Bradley again that evening: 'For God's sake tell the world we're across . . . I want the world to know Third Army made it before Monty'.[45] In fact 'the world' already knew; at Bradley's Headquarters that morning, Georgie's representative had announced that the Third Army had crossed the Rhine at 2200 hours on 22 March, 'without benefit of aerial bombing, ground smoke, artillery preparation and airborne assistance' – clearly a dig at Montgomery who, readers will recall, was using all these assets at that very moment to assist his crossing of the river. Unfortunately, a further crossing by men of the US 87th Division five miles south of Koblenz, at Rhens, on the 24th, and another by the 89th on the 25th at St Goar, fifteen miles farther south, were more costly – in the first case twenty per cent of the attacking Battalion was lost to artillery and mortar fire before it even got in the river and in the second, 277 men were lost – a third of the unit. 'It was rather prophetic, I thought,' wrote Patton later, 'that we should cross at St Goar, near the legendary site of the Lorelei –one of the sacred spots of German mythology'![46]

On the day his first troops crossed the Rhine, Patton issued his 'General Order Number 70' to the Third Army and to 'Our comrades of the XIX Tactical Air Command':

In the period from January 29 to March 22, 1945, you have wrested 6,484 square miles of territory from the enemy. You have taken 3,072 cities, towns, and villages, including among the former: Trier, Coblenz, Bingen, Worms, Mainz, Kaiserslautern and Ludwigshafen. You have captured 140,112 enemy soldiers and have killed or wounded an additional 99,000, thereby eliminating practically all of the German 7th and 1st Armies. History records no greater achievement in so limited a time . . . The world rings with your praises; better still General Marshall, General Eisenhower, and

General Bradley have all personally commended you. The highest honor I have ever attained is that of having my name coupled with yours in these great events . . .

The following day George Patton crossed the Rhine on a pontoon bridge at Oppenheim. Halfway across he undid his trousers: 'to take a piss in the Rhine. I have been looking forward to this for a long time', he wrote in his diary. Another report says that he added: 'I didn't even piss this morning when I got up so I would have a really full load. Yes, sir, the pause that refreshes'.[47] He had not only beaten Monty across the famous river, he had peed in it two days before Winston Churchill! On arrival on the eastern bank he deliberately stubbed his toe and 'fell, picking up a handful of German soil, in emulation of . . . William the Conqueror',[48] who allegedly did the same thing on arriving on the shore of England in 1066. That evening, presumably for Eisenhower's benefit, Georgie wrote on the day's official report to SHAEF in his own hand: 'Today I pissed in the Rhine'.

Patton often complained about the press correspondents who tried to follow his every move, but he was more than happy to use them when it suited him. The day after crossing the Rhine he agreed to let the *Life* magazine photographer, Margaret Bourke-White take pictures of him, but only in profile from the left side. 'Don't show my jowls and don't show the creases in my neck. Stop taking pictures of my teeth . . . This is the only angle at which the little hair I have will show', he complained.[49] Like Monty he was acutely aware of his appearance and the importance of showing himself off in the best possible light to the people at home.

On 23 March, after gaining his first bridgeheads over the Rhine, Patton had written to his wife: 'I am scared by my good luck. This operation is stupendous'. But alas, his luck was about to run out, at least temporarily, in what became known as 'The Hammelburg Raid'.

Readers may recall that Patton's son-in-law, Lieutenant Colonel John Waters, had been captured in North Africa in February 1943. It seems that Georgie learned on, or shortly before, 23 March that Waters was being held in a German PW camp, Oflag XIIIB, three miles south of Hammelburg and some sixty miles east of Frankfurt. How he found out remains a mystery. The camp in fact held some 1,230 Americans and about 3,000 Serbian officers, former members of the Royal Yugoslav Army.

On 25 March, the day Monty, Churchill and Brooke met Eisenhower at Rheinberg, Brigadier General William Hoge, the new commander of the 4th Armored Division, received an order from his Corps commander, Manton Eddy, telling him to mount a special Task Force (TF) to liberate Oflag XIIIB, and on the same day, Patton's general factotum and bodyguard and a former sergeant in Patton's Headquarters in WWI, Major Al Stiller, arrived at Hoge's Headquarters and announced that he had been ordered by Patton to accompany the TF. Not surprisingly, both

Eddy and Hoge were unhappy with the idea of a raid some forty miles behind enemy lines and expressed their concerns. This brought Patton to XII Corps on the 26th and he ended up giving Hoge a direct order over the telephone, 'to cross the Main river and get over to Hammelburg'. Apparently it was at this point that Hoge turned to Stiller, who had been listening, and was told that Patton's son-in-law was one of the prisoners in the camp.[50]

The TF organized for the raid came from Lieutenant Colonel Creighton Abrams' CCB of the 4th Armored Division. Its commander was a young captain named Abraham Baum and it comprised sixteen tanks, twenty-seven half-tracks, three 105mm SP guns and a total of 294 officers and men, including Al Stiller. Quite how the TF was meant to carry back some 1,200 released American prisoners remains a mystery – the total seating capacity of the vehicles was well under 500! Be that as it may, the basic plan was relatively simple. CCB would cross the Main river and make a hole in the German defences, following which TF Baum would drive flat out for the camp. It was hoped that the raiding party would be safely back in US lines in under twenty-four hours.

The details of the raid on Oflag XIIIB need not concern us. Those interested should read John Toland's very dramatic and detailed account in his book, *The Last 100 Days*. Sufficient for us to know that TF Baum set out at 1900 hours on the 26th and by first light on the 28th it had ceased to exist. Although the American prisoners were freed for a time, the raid ended up in chaos. Nine members of TF Baum were killed, thirty-two wounded, including Baum himself, and sixteen were never seen again. Every vehicle was lost and most of the prisoners and the raiding party ended up back in the camp, including the reason for the raid, John Waters, who was badly wounded. He was still in Oflag XIIIB when a unit of the 14th Armored Division, part of the Seventh Army, reached the camp on 5 April. His life had been saved by a Serbian doctor. Patton sent his personal doctor, Charles Odom, to look after him and arranged for him to be air-lifted to Frankfurt – this preferential treatment apparently causing resentment amongst some of the other wounded. On 5 April Georgie wrote to Beatrice:

> I feel terrible. I tried hard to save him and may be the cause of his death. Al Stiller was in the column and I fear he is dead. I don't know what you and B [his daughter] will think. Don't tell her yet . . . We have liberated a lot of PW camps but not the one I wanted.

Stiller was eventually found unharmed in another PW camp at Moosburg in southern Germany on 1 May.

Officially the Hammelburg raid never happened. When Patton visited Baum in hospital to award him a DSC, he told him he had done 'one

257

helluva job'. Baum replied that he could not believe the General would send his men on a mission like that to rescue one man. Patton allegedly replied: 'That's right, Abe, I wouldn't'. After Patton left his ADC told Baum the raid had been classified Top Secret and that he was to use discretion when discussing it. Baum interpreted this to mean that his TF would get no recognition and that he and his men had been 'screwed again'.[51]

Needless to say, Patton blamed everybody except himself for the failure of the Hammelburg raid, including Bradley, Eddy and Hoge. In his 5 April letter to Beatrice he wrote: 'My first thought was to send a combat command but I was talked out of it by Omar and others'. He went even further in his diary where he claimed that he sent only two companies instead of a complete Combat Command, 'on account of strenuous objections of General Bradley'.[52] This accusation however, seems to have been contradicted by Bradley who wrote later: 'It was a story that began as a wild goose chase and ended in tragedy. I did not rebuke him for it. Failure itself was George's own worst reprimand'.[53] In his own book, *War As I Knew It*, Patton certainly blamed Eddy and Hoge: 'I intended to send one combat command of the 4th Armored, but, unfortunately, was talked out of it by Eddy and Hoge'.[54] Readers will judge for themselves the likelihood of this happening! But for all Patton's subsequent claims that he had no knowledge of Waters' presence in Oflag XIIIB until nine days after the raid, and that it had only been launched to divert German attention and ease his Army's advance, those most closely involved at the top level – Hoge, Abrams, Baum and Stiller – all believed that the raid had been launched for one reason only and that was to rescue Patton's son-in-law. They remained silent at the time to protect their Army commander and it was long after the war, in 1967, before one of them, Creighton Abrams, stated openly that the raid had been launched solely because Waters was in the camp.[55] And it is quite clear from Patton's letters to his wife that this was true. Three days before the raid he wrote: 'We are headed right for John's place and may get there before he is moved, he had better escape or he will end up in Bavaria', and on the day of the raid he wrote again:

Last night I sent an armored column to a place 40 miles east of Frankfurt where John and some 900 PW are said to be. I have been as nervous as a cat all day as everyone but me thought it was too great a risk; I hope it works. Al Stiller went along. If I lose the column it will possibly be a new incident but I won't.

The Hammelburg raid was another potentially disastrous point in George Patton's career, but Roosevelt's untimely death on 12 April diverted the attention of his superiors and, perhaps more importantly, the press. As Patton put it so delicately in his diary two days later: 'With the President's death you could execute buggery in the streets and get no further than the fourth page!'. Once again Georgie had survived.

NOTES

1 Montgomery, *Memoirs*, pp. 320–1.
2 Eisenhower, *Report*, p. 100.
3 Montgomery, op. cit., p. 322.
4 Ibid.
5 Delaforce, *Marching to the Sound of Gunfire*, p. 198.
6 Horne, *The Lonely Leader*, p. 313.
7 Hamilton, *Monty The Field Marshal 1944–1976*, p. 409, Note 1.
8 Montgomery, *Normandy to the Baltic*, p. 373.
9 Montgomery, *Memoirs*, p. 329.
10 Hamilton, op. cit., pp. 415–16, Note 1.
11 Letter dated 20 Mar 45, Montgomery Papers.
12 Eisenhower, David, *Eisenhower at War 1943–1945*, p. 725.
13 Ibid, p. 724.
14 Hamilton, op. cit., p. 412, Note 1.
15 Possibly at a lunch with Bradley in Reims on the 28th; however, according to David Eisenhower in *Eisenhower at War 1943–1945*, pp. 726–30, these decisions originated during the discussions between Ike and Bradley in the South of France before 23 Mar.
16 Horne, op. cit., p. 317.
17 D'Este, *A Genius for War*, p. 713. Brooke wrote later: ' I shall never forget the childish grin of intense satisfaction that spread all over his face as he looked down at the critical moment'.
18 Montgomery, op. cit., p. 330.
19 27 & 28 Mar 45, Montgomery Papers.
20 M 562.
21 Hamilton, op. cit., pp. 442–3, Note 1.
22 M 569 dated 8 Apr 45.
23 M 562/1 dated 29 Mar 45, Montgomery Papers.
24 Montgomery, op. cit., p. 331.
25 Ibid.
26 Ibid, p. 321.
27 Montgomery, op. cit., pp. 331–2.
28 Bradley, op. cit., pp. 535–6.
29 D'Este, *Eisenhower, Allied Supreme Commander*, p. 688.
30 Horne, op. cit., p. 321.
31 Patton, *War As I Knew It*, p. 223.
32 Diary dated 2 Feb 45.
33 Ibid.
34 Patton, op. cit., p. 224.
35 Ibid, pp. 225–6.
36 Ibid, p. 224.
37 D'Este, *A Genius for War*, p. 708.
38 Diary dated 17 Feb 45.
39 Captured by A Coy, 27 Armd Inf Bn, 9 Armd Div.
40 Patton, op. cit., p. 240.
41 Bradley, *A Soldier's Story*, p. 319.

42   Toland, *The Last 100 Days*, pp. 255–6.
43   Wilmot, *The Struggle for Europe*, p. 681.
44   2,792 were non-battle casualties.
45   Bradley, *A General's Life*, p. 412.
46   Patton, op. cit., p. 259.
47   Province, *Patton's Third Army*, p. 226.
48   Patton, op. cit., p. 259.
49   D'Este, op. cit., p. 725.
50   Toland, op. cit., p. 287.
51   Ibid, p. 718.
52   Diary dated 31 Mar 45.
53   Bradley, *A Soldier's Story*, pp. 542–3.
54   Page 260.
55   D'Este, op. cit., p. 717.

CHAPTER XXIV

Triumph and Disappointment

(Map 16)

Background

By the time Simpson's Ninth US Army was returned to Bradley's 12th Army Group on 4 April, it had captured Münster, reached the Weser river north-east of Herford and linked up (on 1 April) with Hodges' First US Army near Lippstadt, thus completing the encirclement of a third of a million German troops in the Ruhr. As Monty put it, its operations had been, 'characterized by great dash and speed'.[1] So had those of the First US Army. On 28 March 'Lightning Joe' Collins' VII Corps covered fifty-five miles to the German tank training area near Paderborn. Known as 'the cradle of the Panzer Divisions', Sennelager,[2] centred twelve miles north of Paderborn, was home to the instructors, specialists, officer cadets and trainee crews of the Panzerwaffe and for three days they 'put theory into practice, manning the guns and armour they had so often used on exercises. They fought with vigour and determination, for the ground they were defending was sacred to the Wehrmacht'.[3] Nevertheless, Sennelager and Paderborn fell to the Americans on 1 April.

Meanwhile by the 5th, Dempsey's Second British Army, on Simpson's left flank, had cleared the Rheine airfield complex, thirty miles north of Münster, after heavy fighting; then, in accordance with Monty's order 'to drive hard for the line of the river Elbe so as to gain quick possession of the plains of Northern Germany', had advanced through Osnabrück to Stolzenau on the Weser. At the same time Crerar's First Canadian Army, with the 1st Polish Armoured Division under command, had begun its unenviable task of dealing with the Germans in Western Holland.

The advances of both Dempsey's and Simpson's Armies had to some extent been delayed by:

> the difficulty of negotiating passages through the towns which had been bombed with unnecessary severity. In their enthusiasm to make sure of sealing off the battlefield the Allied Air Forces had put down on most of the interdiction targets three times the tonnage the army had asked for, and by doing so had aided the German rearguards.[4]

Farther south George Patton's Third Army had captured Frankfurt and advanced some sixty miles beyond the Rhine in roughly the same period. By the end of March it had reached a line running from near Kassel to a point well east of Würzburg.

Events moved so rapidly during April and May 1945 that for the purposes of this book and in the interests of simplicity, it is best to merely summarize them:

10 April – **Second British Army** reached Celle and established bridgeheads over the Aller river. The Ninth US Army took Hannover.

11 April – **Third US Army**, after an advance of another 100 miles, reached a line running from near Erfurt south to Coburg.

12 April – **Third US Army** took Erfurt. Ninth US Army crossed the Elbe and took Brunswick.

13 April – First US Army tanks reached the Elbe at Magdeburg. The Red Army captured Vienna.

16 April – The Red Army broke through the German defences on the Oder, but had not yet entered what was to be the Soviet Zone of Occupation of post-war Germany; the Americans, on the other hand, were already 100 miles inside that Zone.

18 April – **Second British Army** took Lüneburg. The Ruhr Pocket was finally eliminated by eighteen divisions of the First and Ninth US Armies.

19 April – **Second British Army** reached the Elbe at Lauenburg, less than thirty miles from Hamburg. First US Army captured Leipzig. The **Third US Army** began its drive south-east towards the 'National Redoubt'.

20 April – Seventh US Army took Nuremberg.

21 April – The Red Army entered the eastern suburbs of Berlin and was approaching Dresden. Eisenhower advised the Soviet High Command that, apart from the British advancing to the Baltic near Lübeck, he would halt the American and British Armies on the Elbe and at the western frontier of Czechoslovakia.

22 April – **Third US Army** started its drive down the Danube valley.

23 April – **Second British Army** reached the outskirts of Hamburg.

24 April – Heinreich Himmler, C-in-C German Home Army and Head of the SS, met Count Bernadotte, Head of the Swedish Red Cross, in Lübeck and advised him that he was ready to surrender unconditionally to the American and British Governments while continuing the war in the east. The offer was rejected.

25 April – The Red Army completed its encirclement of Berlin and elements of the First US and 5th Soviet Guards Armies met on the Elbe at Torgau, thirty-five miles east of Leipzig.

26 April – Bremen surrendered to **Second British and First Canadian Armies**. **Third US Army** took Regensburg and established bridgeheads over the Danube.

28 April – Seventh US Army reached the Austrian border.

29 April – **Second British Army** crossed the Elbe near Hamburg.

30 April – Hitler committed suicide. Seventh US Army cleared Munich. **Third US Army** liberated 110,000 PWs in the Moosburg area, thirty-five miles north-east of Munich.

1 May – **Third US Army** reached the Austrian border at Braunau, seventy miles east of Munich.

2 May – **Second British Army** took Lübeck on the Baltic, sealing off the Danish Peninsula. The Red Army completed its capture of Berlin.

3 May – Hamburg was surrendered to the **Second British Army**. Field Marshal Keitel sent a delegation to **Monty's Headquarters** on Lüneburg Heath to open negotiations for surrender. **Third US Army** crossed the Inn river, while the Seventh US Army captured Innsbrück and reached the Brenner Pass thirty-five miles to its south.

4 May – Representatives of the German High Command signed an armistice at **Monty's Headquarters**, providing for the surrender, as from the morning of the 5th, of all German forces in North-West Germany, Denmark and Holland – and at Dunkirk (Map 4), which readers may be surprised to know remained in German hands until the 11th. The **Third US Army** crossed the Czech border, while the Seventh US Army took Salzburg and Berchtesgaden and linked up at the Brenner Pass with the Fifth US Army advancing from Italy.

6 May – Eisenhower ordered the **Third Army** advance into Czechoslovakia and Austria halted.

7 May – The unconditional surrender of all German forces on all fronts took place at Eisenhower's Headquarters at Reims (Map 12) in the presence of representatives of the United States, Great Britain, the Soviet Union and France. Hostilities were to cease at one minute past midnight on the 8th. Ninth US Army abandoned its bridgehead over the Elbe.

So now let us get back to the parts played by Monty and Patton during these momentous days – George Patton first.

Patton

On 27 March Patton moved his Headquarters from Luxembourg City to Oberstein, twenty miles east of Kassel. It was its first move for fourteen weeks, but at last he was commanding from German soil and in that period his Army had fought its way through nearly 300 miles of German territory.

Georgie continued to 'beg, coax, demand and threaten' his commanders in his desire to drive ever deeper into Hitler's Reich:

> I felt, and the Corps commanders, I think, agreed with me, that there was nothing in front of the Third Army which it, or any of its three Corps, could not easily overcome. We were, therefore, opposed to stopping but, in order to occupy the new boundaries as prescribed by higher authority [Eisenhower], we practically had to stop, or at least slow down, in order to perform, for the first time in the history of the Third Army, the act of regrouping. Even while doing this, however, we pushed along several miles each day.[5]

And just as Monty had allowed his Army commanders to make their own plans for Operation PLUNDER, so Patton 'decided to let the three [Corps commanders] settle this [the new boundaries] themselves'.[6]

On 6 April Patton received his first news of his son-in-law, John Waters. Late that evening Lieutenant General Sandy Patch, the commander of the Seventh US Army, called to say that one of his Divisions had recaptured Oflag XIIIB at Hammelburg and that amongst the seventy or so American prisoners still there was Waters, critically wounded. Two days later Patton visited him in hospital and pinned on him the Silver Star and Oak Leaf Cluster, awards he had earned in North Africa.

Patton was constantly on the move, visiting his commanders and troops and attending meetings with other Army commanders and his superiors, and during his travels during April he noticed several things that displeased him. One was that his:

> Army was going to hell on uniform. During the extremely cold weather it had been permissible, and even necessary, to permit certain variations, but with the approach of summer I got out another uniform order.

Another thing he noticed was:

263

great carelessness in leaving gasoline cans along the road, so issued an order that the Assistant Quartermaster General of the Third Army was personally to drive along the road, followed by two trucks, and pick up all the cans he found.

Georgie also found:

that practically every enlisted member of the medical Corps had captured a civilian automobile or motorcycle, with the result that we were wasting gasoline at a magnificent rate and cluttering up the road . . . We therefore issued an order for the sequestration of these vehicles.[7]

On 10 April Patton's Intelligence staff warned him that as well as radio broadcasts by the Germans that they were setting up a partisan movement, the so-called 'Werewolves', they might well try to land a small glider-borne force near 'Lucky Forward' with the mission of killing him. His reaction was typical: 'I never put much faith in this rumor, but did take my carbine to my truck every night'.[8]

On the 12th Patton had two unusual experiences – one exciting and one distressing. Five days earlier Manton Eddy had told him that one of his XII Corps units had discovered a number of sealed vaults two thousand feet deep in a salt mine at Merkers, sixty miles west of Erfurt. When Eddy went on to say he had no idea what was in the vaults, Patton allegedly responded: 'General Eddy. You blow open that fuckin' vault and see what's in it'.[9] He did, and found the entire German bullion reserve – 4,500 bars of gold with an estimated value of more than fifty-seven million dollars – millions of Reichmarks and dollar bills, paintings by great masters such as Titian and Van Dyck, some of which Patton thought were worth 'about $2.50, and were of the type normally seen in bars in America',[10] and many other treasures. Eisenhower, Bradley and Patton visited the mine on 12 April. As they were lowered down the mineshaft, Georgie, according to his ADC, said: 'If that clothesline [the elevator cable] should part, promotions in the US Army would be considerably stimulated'. To which Ike replied: 'OK, George, that's enough! No more cracks until we are above ground again'.

Afterwards the three commanders went on to the recently liberated concentration camp at Ohrdruf, less than thirty miles west of Erfurt, where, inevitably the scenes shocked and disgusted them. 'It was the most appalling sight imaginable', Patton wrote later.[11]

That night Eisenhower and Bradley spent the night at 'Lucky Forward'. After dinner Ike told Patton privately that in the near future he planned to halt the First and Ninth US Armies on the Elbe and direct his Third Army south-eastwards towards Czechoslovakia. He then went on to explain his views on Berlin (see previous chapter). Patton was shocked; and there was more bad news to come – as Georgie was getting ready for bed he turned on the radio and heard a BBC announcer report the death of President Roosevelt. He immediately informed Ike and Bradley and:

> We had quite a discussion as to what might happen. It seemed very unfortunate to us that at so critical a period in our history we should have to change horse. Actually, subsequent events demonstrated that it made no difference at all.[12]

But life had its lighter moments too. On the 14th Georgie flew back to Mainz to witness the opening of a railway bridge across the Rhine built by Army engineers. When he was asked to open it by cutting the red tape 'in lieu of a red ribbon', and was offered a pair of scissors, his 'romantic instinct prompted' him 'to ask for a bayonet with which I cut the tape'.[13] He then mounted a flat car and was pulled across the bridge.

The following day Patton visited the Buchenwald death camp, ten miles to the east of Erfurt and only three miles from the famous town of Weimar, where he 'could not stomach the sights he saw ... [and] went off to a corner thoroughly sick'.[14] As a result he gave orders that the inhabitants of Weimar were to be made to walk through the camp and see for themselves the results of the bestiality of their fellow countrymen.

On 16 April Bradley gave Patton the order he had been expecting since his conversation with Ike on the 12th. His Army was to change the direction of its advance from east to south-east and move towards the so-called Nazi 'National Redoubt'. This meant it would be moving parallel to the Czechoslovakian border. Patton did not believe in the 'National Redoubt' any more than he believed in the so-called 'Werewolf' movement, but he gave the necessary orders and then, on the 17th, flew to Paris for a twenty-four hour break. On arrival he visited his son-in-law, John Waters, in hospital and found him much improved and being prepared for evacuation to the States. According to his lifelong friend, Everett Hughes, Georgie stayed in the George V hotel and they had dinner together and drank 'until the weesome hours'; however, there have been suggestions that he in fact spent the night with Jean Gordon.

At breakfast on the 18th Patton learned from the *Stars and Stripes* newspaper that he and Hodges had been promoted to the rank of full general. He wrote later: 'While I was, of course, glad to get the rank, the fact that I was not in the initial group [Bradley and Devers] and was therefore an "also ran" removed some of the pleasure'.[15] At the time though, he was thrilled to find that when he arrived at Orly airport to fly back to Germany, his ADC, Charles Codman, had not only found four-star collar insignias for him to wear, but that his plane had a four-star pennant flying outside and a four-star general's flag and a bottle of four-star cognac inside.

The Third Army's final offensive began on 19 April. By then it had:

> developed a system known as the 'Third Army War Memorial Project' by which we always fired a few salvoes into every town we approached, before even asking for surrender. The object of this was to let the inhabitants have something to show future generations of Germans by way of proof that the Third Army had passed that way.[16]

The beautiful city of Passau in Austria was one of the last victims of Patton's 'War Memorial Project' – it was bombarded for thirty-six hours before his men entered the smouldering ruins.

On the 20th Patton flew to XII Corps to say goodbye to his great friend Manton Eddy who was being evacuated with very high blood pressure, first to Paris and then, like Waters, on to the States. On his return journey Georgie had a very narrow escape from death himself. In order to cover the long distances involved in commanding his Army and attending conferences with his superiors, he had, since arriving in Normandy, often flown to his destinations in a Cub light aircraft. Usually a reasonably safe way to travel, this was not so on this particular day. Georgie:

> noticed some tracers coming by the right side of our plane which, at the same instant, dove for the ground, very nearly colliding with a plane that looked like a Spitfire. This plane made a second pass, again firing and missing . . . On the third pass, our attacker came in so fast and we were so close to the ground that he was unable to pull out of his dive and crashed, to our great satisfaction.[17]

It turned out that the pilot of the Spitfire was a Polish officer serving with the RAF; he had presumably mistaken the Cub for a German Storch. A second life-threatening incident occurred on 3 May when an ox-cart 'came out of a side street so that the pole missed us [in a jeep] by about an inch'.[18] Patton is alleged to have exclaimed: 'God, what a fate that would have been. To have gone through all the war I've seen and been killed by an ox'.[19]

By 26 April Patton's Headquarters was located seventy-five miles north-west of Regensburg. His leading units had entered the city that day after having 'had quite a fight, but, after breaking the crust there, the rest of the advance was simply a road march'.[20] The Third Army was thus poised to move into either Czechoslovakia or Austria. Both the American and British Chiefs of Staff had agreed that Czechoslovakia was a political prize that should be denied to Stalin, but Eisenhower, ever fearful of a major 'blue on blue' incident with the Red Army, said he did not believe Patton could get to Prague before the Soviets and ordered a halt at the border some 100 miles south-west of the capital. Bradley, and of course

Georgie, believed Prague could have been liberated within twenty-four hours. On 2 May, with 'Lucky Forward' now at Regensburg, Patton was told that the Seventh US Army was to take over responsibility for reducing the 'National Redoubt' and that his Army was to halt. His Headquarters had moved nineteen times since arriving in Normandy and covered 1,225 miles (Monty's Tac HQ had moved twenty-seven times and covered 1,100 miles). Two days later, at 1930 hours on the 4th, Ike finally agreed that Georgie's Army could cross the Czech border – but he was to halt again at Pilzen (today Plzen), fifty-five miles from Prague. At this time the Third Army was, according to Patton, at its greatest strength in the war – eighteen divisions of just over 540,000 men.[21] On the 6th Bradley telephoned Patton; he was worried that Georgie, having heard of an uprising in Prague against the Germans, might ignore the order to halt. 'You hear me, George, goddamnit, *halt!*',[22] he yelled. Patton wrote later: 'I was very much chagrined, because I felt, and still feel, that we should have gone on to the Moldau river [in Prague] and, if the Russians didn't like it, let them go to hell'.[23] Monty took the same view; in 1958 he wrote:

> As regards Prague, the Third American Army was halted on the western frontier of Czechoslovakia . . . for reasons which I have never understood. When finally allowed to cross the frontier in early May, Bradley states in *A Soldier's Story*, page 549, that it was ordered not to advance . . . [farther], 'because Czechoslovakia had already been earmarked for liberation by the Red Army.'[24]

Patton was also ordered to halt his advance south-eastwards in the Danube valley. 'We were to stand fast where we were until the Russians made contact with us.'[25] Then early on the morning of the 7th, Bradley called him and told him the Germans had surrendered: 'It takes effect at midnight, May 8th. We're to hold in place everywhere up and down the line. There's no sense in taking any more casualties now'.

On the same day, together with the Under Secretary of War, Robert Patterson, who was staying with him, Patton flew to a village near the Austro/German border about 100 miles east of Munich, to see a group of Lipizzaner stallions from the Spanish Riding School of Vienna; they had been handed over to one of his units for safe keeping from the Russians. Although Georgie agreed that: 'These horses will be wards of the US Army until they can be returned to the new Austria', his private view of the whole event, expressed in his dairy, is interesting and, in view of his love of horses and riding ability, perhaps surprising:

> It struck me as rather strange that, in the middle of a world at war, some twenty young and middle-aged men in great physical condition, together with about thirty grooms, had spent their entire

time teaching a group of horses to wiggle their butts and raise their feet in consonance with certain signals from the heels and reins. Much as I like horses, this seemed to me wasted energy. On the other hand, ... to me the high-schooling of horses is certainly more interesting than either painting or music.

At his normal morning briefing on the 8th, exactly two and a half years since he had landed in Morocco, Patton told his staff this would be the last such meeting in Europe. 'I think most of them realised I was hoping to have some more briefings in Asia.'[26]

The day after the fighting officially ended, Patton issued his General Order Number 98 which outlined the Third Army's successes and claimed that it had 'advanced farther in less time than any other army in history' – just over 1,300 miles in 281 days. He had of course, either conveniently forgotten, or purposely ignored, the fact that Monty's Eighth Army had advanced some 1,850 miles from Alamein to Tunis in 201 days! He went on to claim that his Army had killed or wounded at least half a million Germans and captured another 956,000; though in view of his first claim one has to question the accuracy of these figures and indeed those quoted in his book *War As I Knew It*.[27] The General Order ended:

> During the course of this war I have received promotion and decorations far above and beyond my individual merit. You won them; I as your representative wear them. The one honor which is mine and mine alone is that of having commanded such an incomparable group of Americans, the record of whose fortitude, audacity, and valor will endure as long as history lasts.[28]

Patton's postscript to the war in Europe was written later:

> I can say this, that throughout the campaign in Europe I know of no error I made except that of failing to send a Combat Command to take Hammelburg. Otherwise, my operations were, to me, strictly satis-factory. In every case, practically throughout the campaign, I was under wraps from the High Command. This may have been a good thing, as perhaps I am too impetuous. However, I do not believe I was and feel that had I been permitted to go all out, the war would have ended sooner and more lives would have been saved. Particularly I think this statement applies to the time when, in the early days of September, we were halted, owing to the desire, or necessity, on the part of General Eisenhower in backing Montgomery's move to the north. At that time there is no question of doubt but that we could have gone through and across the Rhine within ten days. This would have saved a great many thousand men.[29]

The conceit evident in this statement is of course typical of Patton, and his claim that he could have crossed the Rhine within ten days in early September 1944 is certainly open to question; moreover it is clear that neither of his direct superiors believed it possible.

Montgomery

Eisenhower's main intention with regard to Monty's Army Group at this stage of the war was clear: 'having lined up on the Elbe . . . the 21st Army Group should advance to the Baltic and thus cut off Schleswig-Holstein and Denmark'.[30] And in order to achieve it he was again given American troops to help him – Ridgway's XVIII Airborne Corps. But it is clear that the Second British Army's advance from the Rhine to the Elbe and then on to the Baltic was very much more difficult than that of Patton's Third Army from the Rhine to the Danube and Czech frontier. Monty had this to say about it:

> The resistance . . . was lightest on the right flank . . . Elsewhere it varied; in some areas the enemy succeeded in delaying our progress with hastily formed battle groups. Despite the general disintegration of his forces, however, the German skill in using demolitions to impede the pursuit was as marked as ever . . . The area between the Rhine and Elbe was intersected by innumerable waterways . . . over 500 bridges had to be constructed in the course of the advance.[31]

Another impediment to a rapid advance was the destruction caused by the carpet-bombing of virtually all the large cities in northern Germany. The sergeant responsible for the security of Tac HQ, Norman Kirby, described Münster as a 'chaotic labyrinth where our tyres and tank tracks crunched and pulverized the carved stone faces and limbs of medieval statues'.[32]

Monty described his tactics as follows:

> In order to speed up the rate of advance, divisions operated in great depth on narrow thrust lines; enemy areas of resistance were by-passed by armoured spearheads and were later attacked from the flank or rear by other troops coming up behind.[33]

But a more down-to-earth description is given by one of his LOs, Major Peter Earle. When he asked one of the divisional commanders 'why he was getting on so slowly', he was told in no uncertain terms that that particular 'thrust line' had already suffered 350 casualties in a six-mile advance and 'that all roads were blocked and covered [by fire], and all bridges blown'.[34]

Monty again:

> As we moved eastwards, the Prime Minister and Eisenhower both
> became anxious lest I might not be able to 'head off' the Russians from
> getting into Schleswig-Holstein, and then occupying Denmark. Both
> sent me messages about it. I fear I got somewhat irritated and my
> replies possibly showed it! To Eisenhower I replied on 27 April that I
> was very well aware what had to be done, but he must understand
> that when he had removed the Ninth American Army from my
> command . . . the tempo of operations slowed down automatically on
> the northern flank. In the end we beat the Russians to it. We reached
> the Baltic at . . . Lübeck on 2 May and thus sealed off the Danish
> peninsula with about six hours to spare, before the Russians arrived
> . . . On 2 and 3 May the prisoners taken by Second Army totalled
> nearly half a million.[35]

Readers will have noted that the removal of Simpson's Ninth US Army
still clearly rankled with Monty. They should also note that the distance
covered by both the Second British and Third US Armies from their Rhine
crossing sites to their final objectives – the Baltic and Pilsen and the
Danube respectively, was the same – approximately 300 miles, and that
they covered it in the same time frame – 23 March to the first week in May.
  It should not be forgotten that Monty was also responsible for the
operations of the First Canadian Army[36] which was tasked with
neutralizing the German presence in Holland. This had been virtually
achieved by 18 April when successful thrusts to the Zuider Zee and the
North Sea isolated the enemy. Monty, conscious as always of the need to
avoid military and civilian casualties, particularly at this late stage in the
war, instructed:

> First Canadian Army to halt its offensive operations against 'Fortress
> Holland' . . . until the German garrison capitulated. Although the
> enemy was completely cut off from any hope of relief or
> reinforcement, he was strongly entrenched behind a formidable
> barrier of artificial floods . . . The reduction of western Holland might
> also have caused even greater suffering to the civilian population,
> already reduced to desperate straits by lack of food and the ruthless
> inundation of their land.[37]

On 4 April Monty moved his Tac HQ forward to a windswept site, ten
miles west of Münster, where the tents were 'entirely submerged in thick
white clay, mud and water'. But he was having a job to keep up with his
advancing troops and within two days it was moved again into 'a badly
bombed and filthy' ex-Luftwaffe camp at Rheine where the pervading

smell was of 'decay and death'.[38] Four days later Tac moved yet again, to a spot fifteen miles east of Osnabrück, described by Sergeant Kirby as 'the most idyllic resting place in our whole odyssey'.[39] It was the Schloss Ostenwalde and Monty and his staff moved into its sumptuous accommodation. He was heard to declare: 'This is where I am going to live when we have won the war'. Sadly, but perhaps understandably, everyone, according to Peter Earle, soon got 'busy furnishing themselves with towels, linen and silk nightdresses, etc.'.[40] Earle was Monty's newest LO, having only become one on 7 April after being a staff officer in London.

Monty seems to have had plenty of time to write personal letters during this period. He wrote (on paper captured from the commander of the German VI Corps based in Münster), to his son three times in eight days; in the first he told him: 'the battle here goes very well, we are capturing enormous numbers of German soldiers; mostly very young, the ages varying from fourteen to eighteen'. In the second he chastised David for 'playing the fool a great deal and wasting your time', and in the third he advised him that: 'it takes a proper chap to run straight down the course'.[41] Then on 16 April he sent him pictures of Rommel and Kesselring for hanging on the walls of the Reynolds' school and a cake, chocolates and sweets for himself. He added that: 'Here it is very cold. My HQ is now not far from Bremen and we get the cold east winds blowing down from the Baltic'.

Monty also took the time to supervize group photographs of himself with his LOs, directing every shot in detail. There was also time to enjoy good dinners at Schloss Ostenwalde. Peter Earle described one such dinner during which Monty not only discussed the principles of war, but also his decorations, saying that he had put the British ones on the top row and the foreign ones on the bottom. He had, however, left the top row uncompleted 'in case he was given any more'. Surprisingly, Earle summed up his master as 'a bounder' – surprising, since there is no evidence that this author can find of Monty ever being dishonest. Earle went on, however, to say that Monty was 'a complete egoist, a very kind man, very thoughtful to his subordinates, a lucid tactician, a great commander'.[42] Few, even those Americans who came to dislike him intensely, would disagree with that.

To the intense disappointment of everyone, perhaps even including Monty himself, Tac HQ moved on again after only three days, first to a damp field, forty miles south-east of Bremen, and then on the 21st (the day Monty's adversary in Normandy and at Arnhem, Field Marshal Model, shot himself), to a farm near Soltau, only forty-five miles south of Hamburg.

On this same day Monty suffered his worst personal tragedy of the war. His youngest LO and the one who had been with him for nearly three years, since Alamein in fact, was killed. John Poston, a dashing cavalryman, had won two Military Crosses and was 'clearly the favourite among his young men, if not a kind of surrogate son'.[43] A typical example of Monty's fondness for him occurred shortly before his death. Poston had asked for leave in order to go home and ask a girl to marry him; Monty apparently not only told him to take his personal aeroplane, but to keep it in England until the girl accepted him, and then even went on, according to Poston, 'to tell me how I was to go about it and what I was to say'.[44]

The tragedy occurred when Poston and Peter Earle were sent on a joint mission to visit the Headquarters of the 11th Armoured Division and VIII Corps. They were required to get the latest information on a group of enemy known to be between Tac HQ and the VIII Corps Headquarters at Lüneburg. Earle dismissed his driver and took the wheel himself. All went well until the return journey when they came under German machine-gun fire. Earle drove the jeep straight at the machine-gun, crashing the vehicle and killing the firer, but Germans soldiers quickly surrounded them. Earle, who was wounded in the arm and thigh, wrote later:

> The Germans closed in on us. John was now some three yards on my right; as I was slowly getting to my feet, I heard John cry out in an urgent and desperate voice, 'N-No –stop – stop'. These were his last words and were spoken as a bayonet thrust above the heart killed him instantaneously.[45]

Peter Earle was captured and given treatment for his wounds in a German Field Hospital, but was released by British troops the following day. Monty was devastated when he heard the news. According to Bob Hunter, his personal doctor, no one could get a decision out of him for two days. He signalled Brooke asking him to inform Churchill who knew 'them all and takes a keen interest in their work', and went on to write Poston's obituary for *The Times* newspaper in which he declared: 'I was completely devoted to him'. On the 28th he wrote to Phyllis Reynolds:

> We have been rather sad here for the last few days as a former ADC (John Poston) was killed on the 21st ... He was buried by the Germans, but we found the place, dug it up, and gave him a very moving funeral at my HQ here yesterday afternoon.

Monty wept openly beside the grave – just as Patton had wept over the body of his ADC, Dick Jensen, in April 1943.

Tac HQ's location near Soltau was only sixteen miles north of the recently liberated concentration camp at Belsen and Monty visited it on the 29th. He was sickened and wrote to Phyllis Reynolds that night: 'You have actually to see the camp to realise fully the things that went on; the photographs [enclosed] were all taken by a photographer from my HQ'.

On 1 May Tac HQ moved to its final location – on Lüneburg Heath, thirty-five miles south-east of Hamburg. By then it had grown in size to some fifty officers, 600 soldiers and 200 vehicles. On the 3rd Monty wrote to David:

> I really think the German war is drawing to a close. We [the Allies] have taken one million prisoners in April, and the total since D-Day is now three million. Now that Hitler is dead I think we can expect large-scale surrenders on all sides ... I shall try and snatch a few days' leave, if I can; it has been an exhausting business. But I am very fit and well and the caravan life in the fields is very healthy. My present HQ is on a hill about 5 miles south-east of Lüneburg.

The same day a German delegation, headed by Admiral von Friedeburg, Chief of the German Naval Staff and including General Kinzel, Chief of Staff of the North-West Command, arrived under escort at Tac HQ at 1130 hours to negotiate the surrender of all German forces in the north, including those facing the Red Army north of Berlin. Monty met them under 'the Union Jack, which was flying proudly in the breeze'.[46] He was 'wearing a pair of corduroy trousers that had been washed so many times they were bleached white and had no crease; a grey turtle-neck sweater with a single American ribbon pinned to it', and his Royal Tank Corps beret with its two badges.[47] He asked them 'in a very sharp, austere voice': 'Who are you? ... I have never heard of you ... What do you want?'. Monty wrote later:

> Admiral Friedeburg then read me a letter from Field Marshal Keitel offering to surrender to me the three German armies withdrawing in front of the Russians ... I refused to consider this, saying these armies should surrender to the Russians ... Von Friedeburg said it was unthinkable to surrender to the Russians as they were savages ... I said the Germans should have thought of all these things before they began the war and particularly before they attacked the Russians in June 1941.[48]

Monty was now in his element. He demanded the surrender of all German forces to his north and west, including those in Holland, Schleswig-Holstein and Denmark. He then sent them away to think about this over lunch whilst he drew up a document summarising their discussions and his demands. The crunch-line said: 'Field Marshal Montgomery desires that all German forces in Holland, Friesland ... Schleswig-Holstein and Denmark lay down their arms and surrender unconditionally *to him*' (author's emphasis). Then, while Kinzel and another admiral remained at Tac HQ, von Friedeburg and a staff officer were sent back to Flensburg, near the Danish border, to see Keitel and Admiral Doenitz, who had succeeded Hitler as Führer of the Third Reich. They were to return by 1800 hours the next day, 4 May. Monty wrote later: 'I was certain von Friedeburg would return with full powers to sign'. Accordingly, he called a press conference for 1700 hours on the 4th, at which he explained what had gone on and what he hoped would happen at 1800 hours.

Monty dressed for the occasion, wearing a smart battledress with five rows of decorations. He was in boyish mood with the war correspondents. 'My intention is that they shall sign a piece of paper I have prepared. No doubt that if the piece of paper is signed, forces to be surrendered total over a million chaps. Not so bad, a million chaps! Good egg!'.[49] But when von Friedeburg returned Monty's mood changed to one of deadly seriousness. In 1958 he described what happened:

> The German delegation went across to the tent [wired for BBC recording instruments], watched by groups of soldiers, war correspondents, photographers, and others – all very excited. They knew it was the end of the war. I had the surrender document all ready ... The Germans stood up as I entered ... The Germans were clearly nervous and one of them took out a cigarette; he wanted to smoke to calm his nerves. I looked at him, and he put the cigarette away ... I read out in English the Instrument of Surrender ... I then called on each member of the German delegation by name to sign the document, which they did without any discussion. I then signed, on behalf of General Eisenhower ... I was asked to forward it [the original document] to Supreme Headquarters. Instead I sent photostat copies. The original is in my possession and I will never part with it; it is a historic document. I do not know what happened to the pen ['an ordinary army one that you could buy in a shop for two pence'] we all used; I suppose someone pinched it.[50]

In 1992 Monty's son tried to find a cairn constructed on Lüneburg Heath to commemorate the surrender, but all he found were 'broken fragments of a plinth inside the [current German Army] tank ranges'.[51]

Immediately after the Germans had signed the Instrument of Surrender, Monty gave orders that all offensive action was to cease at 0600 hours GMT the following day; he then sent a message to his senior commanders:

> At this historic moment I want to express to Army Commanders and to the Commander Lines of Communication my grateful thanks for the way they and their men have carried out the immense task that was given to them ... I must at once tell you all how well you have

done and how proud I am to command 21 Army Group. Please tell your commanders and troops that I thank them from the bottom of my heart.[52]

Meanwhile in Reims, Eisenhower waited for a phone call telling him of the German surrender. It came at precisely 1900 hours. Harry Butcher, his naval aide, and Kay Summersby, eavesdropped: 'Fine. Fine. That's fine, Monty.' Ike then said that if the Germans had the authority of Doenitz to stop all the fighting, to send them to Reims. Shortly afterwards Bedell Smith announced that a German delegation under Colonel General Jodl and von Friedeburg, was indeed being flown down to Ike's Headquarters the following morning.

That evening Monty signalled Brooke in London: 'I was persuaded to drink some champagne at dinner tonight'.

Of the four original members of the German delegation, only one survived the immediate post-war years – von Friedeburg and Kinzel committed suicide and the staff officer was killed in a motor accident shortly after the signing. Sadly, Monty's German-speaking Intelligence officer, Colonel Joe Ewart, who had interpreted during the surrender meetings and who had been with him since Alamein, also died – his jeep hit a mine. Again Monty was distressed.

Although the surrender on Monty's front was signed just after 1800 hours on 4 May, it was, to his intense annoyance, to be another fifty-five hours before it was signed at Eisenhower's Headquarters. This procrastination on the part of the Germans allowed many of their units on the eastern front, including some of those of the Waffen-SS, to escape to the west, away from the dreaded Red Army.

In Reims on 7 May, after signing the unconditional surrender of all German forces on all fronts, Alfred Jodl declared: 'With this signature the German people and the German armed forces are, for better or worse, delivered into the victor's hands ... In this hour I can only express the hope that the victor will treat them with generosity'. There was no reply.

Monty's VE Day message to his troops was very different from Patton's. In it, as well as thanking 'each one of you from the bottom of my heart', he made the following main points:

> I would ask you to remember those of our comrades who fell in the struggle. They gave their lives that others might have freedom and no man can do more than that. I believe that He would say to each one of them: 'Well done, thou good and faithful servant'.

> We who remain . . must remember to give praise and thankfulness where it is due: 'This is the Lord's doing, and it is marvellous in our eyes'.

In the early days of this war the British Empire stood alone . . . [but] let us never forget what we owe to our Russian and American allies . . .

We have won the German war. Let us now win the peace.[53]

But if Monty and Patton differed in style in their messages to their troops, they were in complete accord on the menace from the Russians. As far as Monty was concerned: 'the oncoming Russians were more dangerous than the stricken Germans'.[54] Patton expressed his views on his eastern allies rather more forcibly at a press conference he gave on VE Day. Pointing to a map of central Europe he said:

> What the tin-soldier politicians in Washington and Paris have managed to do today is . . . to kick hell out of one bastard and at the same time forced us to help establish a second one as evil or more evil than the first . . . This day we have missed another date with our destiny, and this time we'll need Almighty God's constant help if we're to live in the same world with Stalin and his murdering cutthroats.[55]

Later that day in a farewell meeting with Cornelius Ryan and another correspondent, he confirmed his views on this subject: 'You cannot lay down with a diseased jackal. Neither can you do business with the Russians . . . I just couldn't stand being around and taking any lip from those S.O.B.'s'.[56]

NOTES

1   Montgomery, *Normandy to the Baltic*, p. 388.
2   The author, during his time with the British Army of the Rhine, spent many happy weeks training on the former Panzerwaffe manoeuvre area. He went there first as a platoon commander in 1950 and the last time as a brigade commander in 1976.
3   Wilmot, *The Struggle for Europe*, p. 684.
4   Ibid, p. 683.
5   Patton, *War As I Knew It*, p. 270.
6   Ibid.
7   Ibid, p. 274.
8   Ibid, p. 275.
9   D'Este, *A Genius for War*, p. 719, Note 53.
10 Patton, op.cit., p. 276.
11 Ibid.
12 Ibid, p. 278.
13 Ibid, pp. 279–80.
14 D'Este, op. cit., p. 720, Note 60.

15 Patton, op. cit., p. 288.
16 Ibid, p. 278.
17 Ibid, p. 290.
18 Ibid, p. 305.
19 D'Este, op. cit., p. 724, Note 76.
20 Patton, op. cit., p. 295.
21 Ibid, p. 306. However, Charles Province in *Patton's Third Army*, p. 294, claims that its greatest strength, 437,860 (102,140 men less than Patton's figure), was reached on 8 May.
22 D'Este, op. cit., p. 728.
23 Patton, op. cit., p. 309.
24 Montgomery, *Memoirs*, p. 332.
25 Patton, op. cit., p. 309.
26 Ibid, p. 312.
27 See also Note 21.
28 Province, *Patton's Third Army, A Daily Combat Diary*, p. 334.
29 Patton, op. cit., p. 313.
30 Ibid, p. 395.
31 Montgomery, *Normandy to the Baltic*, p. 389.
32 Horne, *The Lonely Leader*, p. 323. The author was stationed there in 1965; the entire city had been rebuilt and there were no signs of war damage.
33 Montgomery, *Memoirs*, pp. 332.
34 Horne, op. cit., pp. 325–6.
35 Montgomery, op.cit., pp. 332–3.
36 Including the 1st Polish Armd Div.
37 Montgomery, *Normandy to the Baltic*, p. 393. It has been estimated that 25,000 Dutch people died of starvation during the winter of 1944/45.
38 Horne, op. cit., p. 324.
39 Kirby, *1100 Miles with Monty*, p. 114.
40 Horne, op. cit., pp. 327–8.
41 Letters dated 8 & 10 Apr 45.
42 Horne, op. cit., p. 332.
43 Ibid. Readers should note that Monty's son, David, co-authored Alistair Horne's book, *The Lonely Leader*.
44 Ibid.
45 Ibid, p. 334.
46 Montgomery, *Memoirs*, p. 335.
47 Horne, op.cit., p. 336.
48 Montgomery, op. cit., p. 335.
49 Press dispatch by R W Thompson.
50 Montgomery, op. cit., pp. 338–9.
51 Horne, op. cit., p. 359.
52 Montgomery, op. cit., p. 341.
53 Ibid, pp. 341–2.
54 Ibid, p. 334.
55 D'Este, op. cit., pp. 733–4.
56 Ibid, p. 735.

CHAPTER XXV

Patton – May to December 1945

George Patton took no great pleasure in the events of VE Day. He already knew that despite his lobbying of many influential figures in Washington, he had no hope of being assigned to the Pacific theatre. As he put it to his III Corps commander, Major General James Van Fleet: 'There is already a star [MacArthur] in that theater and you can only have one star in a show'. He was also depressed because he knew there would be a rapid reduction in the strength of the US Army in Europe and he believed this was inviting disaster. On 7 May he had pleaded with the visiting Under Secretary of War, Robert Patterson:

> Let's keep our boots polished, bayonets sharpened and present a picture of force and strength to these people [the Russians]. This is the only language they understand and respect. If you fail to do this, then I would like to say to you that we have had a victory over the Germans and have disarmed them, but have lost the war.

When Patterson told him that he did not understand the 'big picture', but asked Georgie what he would do about the Russians, he allegedly replied that he would keep the US Army in Europe intact, delineate the border with the Soviets and if they did not withdraw behind it, 'push them back across it'.[1] And then in words that sound very familiar as this book is being written, he went on:

> We did not come over here to acquire jurisdiction over either the people or their countries. We came to give them back the right to govern themselves. We must either finish the job now – while we are here and ready – or later in less favorable circumstances.[2]

Needless to say such ideas were totally unacceptable to the politicians in Washington – and indeed to most of the American soldiers in Europe; all they wanted to do was go home.

Stories of Patton's encounters with the Russians are legendary and some may well be apocryphal. Nevertheless, three examples will be quoted. On 13 May he entertained and decorated the commander of the Soviet Fourth Guards Army at a luncheon in Linz in Austria. Georgie noted in his diary that after a bout of heavy whiskey drinking during and after the meal, the Russian 'went out cold', whilst he himself 'walked out under my own steam . . . They are a scurvy race and simply savages. We could beat hell out of them'. The following day he in turn was entertained by Marshal Tolbukhin, a Soviet Army Group commander, who tried to get him drunk and whom he described as 'a very inferior man who sweated profusely'. He admitted though that the Russian soldiers:

> put on a tremendous show ... [they] passed in review with a very good imitation of the goose step ... The officers with few exceptions gave the appearance of recently civilized Mongolian bandits.

But the most notorious incident allegedly happened towards the end of May when an English-speaking Russian brigadier-general arrived at Patton's Headquarters with a demand that some river boats on the Danube that had contained Germans who had surrendered to the Third Army should be returned to the Russians. Patton opened a drawer, pulled out a pistol, slammed it down on his desk and raged: 'Goddammit! Get this son-of-a-bitch out of here! Who in hell let him in? Don't let any more Russian bastards into this headquarters'. After the shaken Russian was escorted out, Georgie is said to have exclaimed: 'Sometimes you have to put on an act ... That's the last we'll hear from those bastards'. And apparently it was.

Three days after VE day Eisenhower called a conference of all his American Army commanders at which he told them that they were not to criticize publicly any of the campaigns that had won the war, and of the need for solidarity in the event that any of them were called before any Congressional Committees. Patton's version of what Ike said at this conference can be read in his diary. He records that the Supreme Commander:

> made a speech which had to me the symptoms of political aspirations, on cooperation with the British, Russians and the Chinese, but particularly with the British. It is my opinion that this talking cooperation is for the purpose of covering up probable criticism of strategic blunders which he unquestionably committed during the campaign. Whether or not these were his own or due to too much cooperation with the British I don't know. I am inclined to think he over-cooperated.

In mid-May Patton took a few days' leave in London where, according to his great friend Everett Hughes, he renewed his relationship with Jean Gordon.

(Map 16)

On his return to Bavaria, Patton, as Military Governor as well as commander Third US Army, moved into his new Headquarters – a former Waffen-SS officers' training school at Bad Tölz, thirty miles south of

Munich. Georgie renamed the barracks Flint Kaserne, after Colonel Paddy Flint, an old friend and one of his Regimental commanders who had been killed in Sicily. Patton's personal residence was a palatial house on a nearby lake named Tegernsee. It had a swimming pool, bowling alley and two boats, and had once been owned by Max Amann, the publisher of Hitler's *Mein Kampf*; it is also of interest that Himmler's wife had lived in another house on the lake, as had the wife of his adjutant, the infamous Waffen-SS Kampfgruppe commander, Jochen Peiper.[3]

At the beginning of June came the news that Patton had been dreading – he was to return to the States for a thirty-day 'goddamm bond-raising tour'. Again according to Everett Hughes, Georgie confided in him at a farewell dinner at the Ritz Hotel in London that because his wife Beatrice believed he was continuing his affair with Jean Gordon, he 'was scared to death of going back home to America'.[4] Hughes went on to claim that Jean had attended the farewell dinner and had left with him, but in tears knowing that Georgie was returning to the States and Beatrice the following day.

Patton's plane, escorted by a formation of fighters and B-17s, touched down at an airfield near Boston on 7 June, where an Honour Guard, a seventeen-gun salute and the Governor of Massachusetts greeted him. The American press had guaranteed him a hero's welcome. Rather surprisingly Patton chose to return the Governor's hat-doffing salute by removing his own helmet, complete with its four stars and the emblems of the Third and Seventh Armies and I Armored Corps. Then, with the formalities over, he was finally able to embrace Beatrice – it was their first hug in nearly three years. They were then driven through the suburbs of Boston to a ticker-tape reception in the city itself. The crowd along the twenty-five-mile route was estimated at a million; people wept and girls threw flowers. Then, before a crowd of between thirty and fifty thousand, he made a speech in which he said: 'My name is merely a hook to hang the honors on. This great ovation by Boston is not for Patton the general, but Patton as a symbol of the Third Army'.[5] The *Daily Record* had as its headlines the following day: 'FRENZIED HUB HAILS PATTON' and 'GEN PATTON IN TEARS AT HUB TRIBUTE'. This latter headline was due to Georgie breaking down in tears during a 'thank-you' speech at a state dinner held in his honour that night; he was completely overcome by the glowing tributes. Beatrice is said to have declared: 'I can hardly speak, I'm so overcome. This has been a proud and wonderful day'. But in fact Patton had put his foot in it again. During his first speech that morning he had told his audience that the fact that a soldier was killed in action often made him a fool rather than a hero. What exactly he meant is unclear, but needless to say this remark enraged those who had lost relatives in the war and telegrams and letters soon began to flood into the War Department demanding an apology. They did not get it.

The day after his return Patton and his wife flew to Denver and then on to Los Angeles and Pasadena. He made emotional speeches in all three places, with a hundred thousand people, including many Hollywood stars, turning out to hear him in the LA Coliseum. And so it went on throughout his leave – adulation from family, friends and the vast majority of the public. To his superiors though, George Patton remained, as in the past, a potential embarrassment – a missile that might go off track at any moment – a missile that needed to be kept under tight control. No doubt with this in mind Secretary of War Stimson did just that at a press conference in Washington on 14 June; Patton was left merely to add a few comments about the Germans and the Third Army.

Fortunately the official aim of Georgie's month-long leave was achieved – his enthusiastic oratory helped to sell millions of war bonds and he received a letter of thanks from the Treasury Secretary, Henry Morgenthau. His personal aims, however, in both his private and professional life, were not achieved. In the former he later confessed to Everett Hughes that Beatrice had given him 'hell' over Jean Gordon, and in the latter his renewed attempts to get an appointment in the Pacific had again failed. His name had been included in a list of six generals submitted by the War Department for consideration by MacArthur, but the Supreme Commander had rejected him out of hand. And even a plea to Harry Truman had failed to persuade the new President to intercede with Marshall and Stimson.

As well as the faux pas committed during his Boston speech, Patton's past indiscretions continued to dog him. During a visit to the Walter Reed Hospital in Washington, he rounded on the press reporters following him with the words: 'I'll bet you goddam buzzards are just following me to see if I'll slap another soldier, aren't you? You're all hoping I will!'. His daughter, who worked in the amputee ward as an occupational therapist, recalled later that when her father saw the soldiers there he burst into tears and exclaimed: 'Goddammit, if I had been a better general, most of you would not be here'. The men, who were not looking for sympathy, cheered him as he left.[6]

Patton is said to have predicted his own death to his daughters Ruth Ellen and Bee during a visit to the latter's home in Washington shortly before his return to Germany. He told them, whilst Beatrice was out of the room, that he believed his luck had run out.

In early July in Paris, Patton again confided in Everett Hughes that he was glad to be out of the States and back in Europe. This was despite the fact that an Army order banning dependants had prevented Beatrice accompanying him – even if she had wished to! Georgie's morale, however, was given a lift when his aircraft was given a fighter escort for its flight down to Bavaria and troops and tanks lined the route from the airfield to Bad Tölz. He wrote in his diary: 'It gave me a very warm feeling in my heart to be back among soldiers'.

Even so Patton was pessimistic about the future of Europe, reluctant to get involved in the complexities of military government and, perhaps more importantly, reluctant to purge the Nazis. In the case of Europe he was convinced it would soon become Communist and in the case of the Nazis he saw practical problems:

> My soldiers are fighting men and if I dismiss the sewer cleaners and the clerks my soldiers will have to take over those jobs. They'd have to run the telephone exchanges, the power facilities, the street cars, and that's not what soldiers are for.[7]

In short, provided a German had the right qualifications for a particular job, Patton was prepared to ignore his former Nazi background. This was of course completely contrary to the political direction he had received from Eisenhower for the denazification of the American zone of Germany. Furthermore, his problems were compounded by the fact that Washington was intent on demobilizing its warrior soldiers as quickly as possible, thus reducing his pool of skilled American manpower. But by his very nature and background Georgie was unsuited to his role as Military Governor – he was not interested in the details of rebuilding a country. He had little patience with the thousands of displaced persons (DPs), whom he described as 'too worthless to even cut wood to keep themselves warm', and 'his growing anti-Semitism coupled with despair of the fate of Germany'[8] led him to the depths of melancholia. He wrote in his diary:

> If we let Germany and the German people be completely dis-integrated and starved, they will certainly fall for Communism, and the fall of Germany for Communism will write the epitaph of democracy in the United States. The more I see of people, the more I regret I survived the war.

He even accused the US Treasury Secretary of 'Semitic revenge against Germany'.

On 16 July the Potsdam Conference convened and Patton, resplendent with twenty stars and ivory-handled pistols, was in Berlin to see Truman preside over the raising of the American flag in the US sector of the divided former German capital. The two men did not get on – Truman wrote in his diary: 'Don't see how a country can produce such men as Robert E Lee, John J Pershing, Eisenhower and Bradley and at the same time produce Custers, Pattons and MacArthurs'. Georgie did not enjoy his time there and on the 21st wrote to Beatrice:

We have destroyed what could have been a good race and we [are] about to replace them with Mongolian savages. Now the horrors of peace, pacifism and unions will have unlimited sway. I wish I were young enough to fight in the next one [war]. It would be real fun killing Mongols . . . It is hell to be old and passé and know it.

In his despondency Patton reverted to the things he liked and did best – overseeing the training and discipline of his Army, riding, hunting and reading – and for exercise he added a squash court to his residence. But the end of the war with Japan only added to his low morale; on 10 August he wrote in his diary:

Another war has ended and with it my usefulness to the world. It is for me personally another very sad thought. Now all that is left is to sit around and await the arrival of the undertaker and posthumous immortality.

Patton's biographer, Carlo D'Este, has suggested that his melancholy and increasingly extraordinary behaviour may have been due to brain damage caused by a series of head injuries caused by a lifetime of falls from horses and road accidents – the most serious being his accident in Hawaii in 1936 that resulted in a two-day blackout. He goes on to say, however, that we shall never know, for Beatrice refused to allow an autopsy on Patton's body despite a request from the Army.[9]

In September Patton returned to Berlin for a military review hosted by the legendary Marshal Zhukov. He had lost none of his quick wit or audacity. When his host pointed out a new, massive and very advanced Stalin IS-3 tank and mentioned that its cannon had a range of 17,000 metres, Georgie is said to have replied:

Indeed? Well, my dear Marshal Zhukov, let me tell you this, if any of my gunners started firing at your people before they had closed to less than 700 yards, I'd have them court-martialled for cowardice.

Despite Patton's indiscretions and lack of interest in his overall duties, in August 1945 Bavaria was judged by Secretary of War Stimson to be the best-governed area in the whole US European Theater of Operations (ETO), an opinion apparently shared by his Deputy. But any satisfaction Patton might have derived from this report was to be short-lived for in September things began to go badly wrong for him.

During the early part of the month he decided to visit some of the prison camps in his area holding hardened Nazis and former members of the Waffen-SS. Camp 24 at Auerbach, 100 miles north-east of Munich, held former members of the 1st (Leibstandarte) and 12th (Hitlerjugend) SS

Panzer Divisions and there had already been complaints by the senior German officer of 'unbearable treatment of seriously disabled comrades'. These had, however, been rejected and when references had been made to the Geneva Convention, the officer had been told: 'What do you mean Geneva Convention? You seem to have forgotten that you lost the war!'. However, Hubert Meyer, the ex-Chief of Staff of the Hitlerjugend, recalled that on the occasion of Patton's visit, things had been very different. After satisfying himself about the correctness of the complaints, Patton immediately ordered action to rectify the situation, and then went further and ordered that the starvation diet which was described by one former senior German officer as 'not enough to live on, but too much to die on', should be supplemented by American C-Rations.[10]

It was in Camp 8 near Garmisch-Partenkirchen, sixty miles south of Munich, on 8 September that an incident occurred that was to have severe implications for Patton's future career. After inspecting the American garrison responsible for administering and guarding the camp, he met the German commander of the PWs. He complained that some Germans were being interned there without justification as political prisoners. Patton is said to have told the American officers accompanying him that he thought it was: 'sheer madness to intern these people'. Not surprisingly one of the American officers, a Jew, reported the incident to Eisenhower's Head-quarters, now housed in the IG Farben building in Frankfurt and known as Headquarters US Forces European Theater (USFET).[11] The complaint landed on the desk of Ike's Civil Affairs officer, Brigadier-General Clarence Adcock. He briefed Bedell Smith who sent the report of the incident at Garmisch-Partenkirchen to Eisenhower who was on leave in the South of France, with a covering letter saying he thought Patton was out of control in Bavaria and that Ike ought to come back and take the matter in hand before any further damage was done.

Eisenhower returned and went to see Patton at Tegernsee on 16 September. They talked until three in the morning but there is no record of any discussion about Georgie's Military Governorship. They did, however, discuss Ike's successor. The former Supreme Commander was due to return home in November to take over from Marshall at the end of the year. When Patton heard that Ike's likely successor was to be his Deputy, General Joseph McNarney, he said he had no wish to serve under a man who had never heard a gun go off. The only jobs in which he was interested were Commandant of the Army War College or Commanding General of the Army Ground Forces. Ike told him they were both already filled. Georgie wrote in his diary: 'I guess there is nothing left for me but the undertaker'.

Eisenhower returned to Bavaria a week later following reports of bad conditions in some of the DP camps there. The reports were true – Ike found not only appalling conditions but *German* guards, some of whom were former SS men. Patton tried to explain that the camp had been fine before the arrival of the present occupants who were 'pissing and crapping all over the place'. Despite being told to 'Shut up, George', he apparently went on to say that there was an empty village nearby which he was planning to turn into a concentration camp for 'these goddamm Jews'. Eisenhower's response is unrecorded.

By now Bedell Smith, Adcock and others had come to the conclusion that Patton was mentally unbalanced. Adcock's civilian deputy, Walter Dorn, was a history professor on leave from Ohio State University; of German origin, he was determined to rid Germany of all vestiges of Nazism. When Patton eventually met him on 28 September he described him as a 'smooth, smart-ass academic type'. Academic or not, Dorn soon focused his attention on the success or otherwise of the denazification programme in Bavaria. He discovered that the German organization set up by a Colonel Keegan, on behalf of Patton, to administer Bavaria, was riddled with former Nazis. Patton had taken so little interest in the new Administration that he did not even recall meeting its Minister President, a Dr Fritz Schaeffer.

As a result of Dorn's discoveries and the PW Camp 8 incident, he and Adcock, presumably with Bedell Smith's agreement, arranged for a psychiatrist, disguised as a supply officer, to be posted to Patton's Headquarters to study his behaviour – and, unbelievably, for Georgie's phones to be tapped and his residence bugged. It is not clear if, or what the psychiatrist reported, but needless to say it was not long before the wire-tappers heard their subject expressing violently anti-Russian views and even suggesting that ex-members of the Wehrmacht should be rearmed and used to help the US Army force the Red Army 'back into Russia'. In one conversation with Ike's Deputy, McNarney, he allegedly went as far as to say: 'In ten days I can have enough incidents happen to have us at war with those sons of bitches and make it look like their fault'.[12]

Readers interested in the full details of Patton's final demise as the commander of Third US Army and Governor of Bavaria should read the relevant books listed in this Bibliography. Certainly there were allegations of Nazi conspiracies and of orchestrated attempts by a group of newspaper correspondents to 'get' Patton, but these need not concern us. All that really matters is that Patton held two disastrous press conferences within a month. At the first, in Frankfurt on 27 August, he 'spoke out against the Russians and signed a letter proposing the release of some Nazi internees'.[13] This apparently so angered Eisenhower that he is said to have demanded that Patton should carry out the denazification programme as ordered, 'instead of mollycoddling the goddamn Nazis'.[14] But Georgie was not going to change; two days later he wrote in his diary: 'the Germans are the only decent people left in Europe. If it's a choice between them and the Russians, I prefer the Germans'.

Worse was to follow – on 22 September Patton agreed to answer questions from reporters after his normal morning briefing at Bad Tölz. When asked why Nazis were being retained in governmental positions in Bavaria, he replied:

> I despise and abhor Nazis and Hitlerism as much as anyone. My record on that is clear and unchallengeable. It is to be found on battlefields from Morocco to Bad Tölz ... Now, more than half the Germans were Nazis[15] and we would be in a hell of a fix if we removed all Nazi party members from office. The way I see it, this Nazi question is very much like a Democrat and Republican election fight. To get things done in Bavaria, after the complete dis-organization and disruption of four years of war, we had to compromise with the devil a little. We had no alternative but to turn to the people who knew what to do and how to do it. So, for the time being we are compromising with the devil ... I don't like the Nazis any more than you do. I despise them. In the past three years I did my utmost to kill as many of them as possible. Now we are using them for lack of anyone better until we can get better people.[16]

Needless to say the press 'ran' with this story, particularly the Democrat/Republican analogy. When it became clear to Eisenhower that the press reports were basically accurate he was aghast and ordered Patton to report to him in Frankfurt. The weather was too bad to fly and when Georgie arrived on the 28th, after a seven-hour car journey in heavy rain, he was uncharacteristically dressed in an ordinary khaki jacket and 'GI' trousers – his normal cavalry breeches, swagger stick and pistols had been left behind. Patton knew he was in trouble. During their two hour meeting Eisenhower was 'more excited than I have ever seen him', remembered Patton in his diary. At one stage the officer responsible for USFET Civil Affairs, Clarence Adcock, was summoned and he brought Professor Dorn into the room with him. The latter then skilfully and ruthlessly demon-strated that the Fritz Schaeffer Administration in Bavaria was full of former Nazis. When they were alone again Patton suggested that he should 'be simply relieved', but Ike said 'he did not intend to do that and had had no pressure from the States to that effect. I then said that I should be allowed to continue the command of the Third Army and the govern-ment of Bavaria'.[17] But Eisenhower's mind was made up. Georgie was offered command of the Fifteenth Army – an Army in name only since its sole mission was to prepare a history of the war in Europe! The only alternative was resignation. Surprisingly, at least to this author, he accepted the job with the Fifteenth Army, explaining this away in his diary by writing that in resigning: 'I would save my self respect at the expense of my reputation but ... would become a martyr too soon'. He went on in his diary to justify his acceptance of the Fifteenth Army command as follows:

> I was reluctant, in fact unwilling, to be party to the destruction of Germany under the pretence of denazification . . . I believe Germany should not be destroyed, but rather rebuilt as a buffer against the real danger which is Bolshevism from Russia.

Eisenhower ended the meeting by telling Patton that he felt he should get back to Bad Tölz as quickly as possible and that his personal train was ready to take him at 1900 hours. Georgie's diary entry ended with the words: 'I took the train'.

The following day Bedell Smith phoned Patton and read a letter to him from Eisenhower. It told him he was to assume his new appointment on 8 October. When this was announced on the 2nd, many of the newspaper headlines, including that in the *Stars and Stripes*, read: 'PATTON FIRED'. Some papers were sympathetic; the *New York Times* leader wrote:

> Patton has passed from current controversy into history. There he will have an honored place . . . He was obviously in a post which he was unsuited by temperament, training or experience to fill. It was a mistake to suppose a free-swinging fighter could acquire overnight the capacities of a wise administrator. His removal by General Eisenhower was an acknowledgement of that mistake . . . For all his showmanship he was a scientific soldier, a thorough military student . . . He reaped no laurels from the peace, but those he won in war will remain green for a long time.

Patton's letter to Beatrice, written the day after his meeting with Ike, indicates the turmoil in his mind: 'The noise against me is the only means by which Jews and Communists are attempting and with good success to implement a further dismemberment of Germany'. He ended it by saying that he had no wish to be 'executioner to the best race in Europe'.

With regard to the fateful 22 September press conference he wrote later:

> This conference cost me the command of the Third Army, or rather, of a group of soldiers, mostly recruits, who then rejoiced in that historic name, but I was intentionally direct, because I believed that it was then time for people to know what was going on. My language was not particularly politic, but I have yet to find where politic language produces successful government . . . My chief interest in establishing order in Germany was to prevent Germany from going communistic. I am afraid that our foolish and utterly stupid policy . . . will certainly cause them to join the Russians and thereby ensure a

communistic state throughout Western Europe. It is rather sad for me to think that my last opportunity for earning my pay has passed. At least, I have done my best as God gave me the chance.[18]

Patton handed over command of his beloved Third Army to another cavalryman, General Lucian Truscott, as ordered on 7 October. It was a wet day and the ceremony was held, rather inappropriately, inside a gymnasium. Georgie made a short farewell speech which began with the words 'All good things must come to an end', and ended ' Goodbye and God bless you'. A band then played 'Auld Lang Syne', the Third Army flag was handed over and Patton left to the music of the Third Army march and 'For he's a jolly good fellow'. After a luncheon in his honour, he left in the Third Army train for his new Headquarters in Bad Nauheim, twenty miles north of Frankfurt.

One of Patton's last acts before handing over command was to award a Silver Star to his driver of more than four years' standing, Master Sergeant John Mims. The award of a Silver Star to Mims, who was returning to the States for demobilization, is surprising in that this medal was meant to be awarded: 'for gallantry in action . . . not warranting the award of a Medal of Honor or Distinguished Service Cross'. Clearly, as a general's driver, even Patton's, Mims had never been in direct contact with the enemy and therefore could hardly have been gallant *in action*. One could perhaps be forgiven for suspecting that Georgie saw this as an award to himself – the Silver Star was after all conspicuous by its absence amongst his many decorations. This suspicion is reinforced by a comment in a letter to Beatrice dated 24 November:

> I finally after a fight of three years got the DSM for all my people, ten in all. I think it is amusing that no one tries to get any [medals] for me. I got nothing for Tunisia, nothing for Sicily and nothing for the Bulge. Brad and Courtney [Hodges] were both decorated for their failures in this operation.

Patton arrived at his new Headquarters in the early hours of 8 October. He was met by the officer temporarily 'holding the fort' – Major General Leven Allen, Bradley's former Chief of Staff. Georgie's opening words were: 'Well, you know damn well I didn't ask for this job, don't you?'

The Headquarters was in an old hotel in Bad Nauheim and Patton's arrival in the mess for lunch was greeted by some 100 officers standing to attention. In a highly successful attempt to 'break the ice', Patton's first words were: 'There are occasions when I can truthfully say that I am not as much of a son-of-a-bitch as I may think I am. This is one of them'. Allen wrote later: 'The relieved staff roared with surprised delight. From then on it was as wholeheartedly for him as the Third Army staff had been'.[19]

But Patton was not really interested in an Army without weapons or a combat mission and consisting mainly of historians and an administrative staff. He announced that he intended to return to the States by March 1946 at the latest and that he expected all the necessary reports about the European campaign to be finished by then. Even so, he took little serious interest in the work other than to ensure, according to Eisenhower's son John, a lieutenant on the Fifteenth Army staff, that 'Patton's Army was mentioned about three times as often as any other in the theater' – even though John Eisenhower himself 'felt that the First Army had contributed more to victory than had the Third'.[20] Few unbiased military historians would disagree with that view!

So what did Patton do with his time? He toured France collecting, according to his ADC, enough certificates of honorary citzenship from cities like Avranches, Rennes and Chartres, 'to paper the walls of a room', and he had lunch with the unanimously elected President of the provisional French government, Charles de Gaulle and dinner with the Chief of Staff of the French Army. Most of his time, however, was spent preparing his book *War As I Knew It*, at the end of which he included his *Reflections and Suggestions* on soldiers, tactics, 'Battle Tricks', command and other miscellaneous military subjects. Part of the Introduction by Douglas Southall Freeman, to *War As I Knew It*, which was published in November 1947, reads:

> He undertook this small book after the close of hostilities and he drew heavily from [his] diary for detail. Some pages of the narrative are almost verbatim the text of the diary, with personal references toned down or eliminated.

Although perhaps mentally satisfying, such activities did little for Patton's morale and he soon became moody and tense. 'Hap' Gay, still his loyal friend and Chief of Staff, and other members of his staff noticed that he became withdrawn, often taking long drives by himself, having little to say during meals and going home early. One staff officer wrote later: 'It was obvious he was undergoing deep and gnawing turmoil'.[21]

Sometime in October Patton resolved to: 'quit outright, not retire . . . For the years that are left to me I am determined to be free to live as I want and say what I want to'.[22] This inevitably worried Gay who surmised, almost certainly correctly, that Patton planned to speak out against Eisenhower's handling of the campaign in Europe and against other senior officers, like Bedell Smith, Hodges and even Bradley. Gay counselled Georgie to consult Beatrice and other family members before taking such a drastic step, but it seems his mind was made up.

On 11 November, Patton's 60th birthday, he was thrilled to find his staff had arranged a surprise party. It took the form of a gala evening in the ballroom of the Spa Hotel in Bad Nauheim and Georgie found himself once again surrounded by friends and the centre of attention. And then, two weeks later he was again thrilled to receive an invitation to go to Sweden to address the Swedish-American Society. However, the trip, which involved travelling on a special train once used by Hindenburg, turned out to be much more than just a speaking engagement. Patton was greeted by the Chief of Staff of the Army and eight former members of the 1912 Pentathlon team and was later received by the King and the Crown Prince. He also breakfasted with Count Bernadotte and was able to enjoy a specially staged ice carnival and hockey game in the Olympic Stadium. The highlight, perhaps, was a re-enactment of the 1912 Olympic pistol competition – Georgie came second, '13 points better than I made in 1912'.

The Swedish trip was the last highlight of Patton's life. His last diary entry dated 3 December describes a luncheon hosted by Bedell Smith for Eisenhower's successor, McNarney. His bitterness is very evident:

> General Clay [Ike's deputy] . . . and General McNarney have never commanded anything, including their own self-respect . . . The whole luncheon party reminded me of a meeting of the Rotary Club in Hawaii where everyone slaps everyone else's back while looking for an appropriate place to thrust the knife. I admit I am guilty of this practice, although at the moment I have no appropriate weapon.

Two days later Patton wrote his last letter to his wife in which he said he was coming home for Christmas. 'I have a month's leave but don't intend to go back to Europe. If I get a really good job I will stay, otherwise I will retire.' The plan was to fly to London and then sail from Southampton on the USS *Augusta*. Readers will recall that the *Augusta* had been the flagship of the Western Task Force in the invasion of Morocco.

On the evening of 8 December 'Hap' Gay suggested to Patton that they should spend the following day pheasant shooting in an area known to be rich in game about 100 miles south-west of the Headquarters. Georgie accepted with enthusiasm. He could think of no better way to spend his last Sunday in Europe than hunting with an old and trusted friend.

Patton and Gay left Bad Nauheim at about 0900 hours on 9 December in Georgie's 1939 Model 75 Cadillac driven by a Private First Class Horace Woodring. A jeep driven by Tech/Sergeant Joe Spruce followed, carrying the guns and a gun dog. The exact details of the traffic accident that led directly to Patton's death need not concern us. They can be found in Carlo D'Este's *A Genius for War*. All we need to know is that at about 1145 hours, in the north-east suburbs of Mannheim (Map 15), an oncoming two-and-a-half-ton US Army truck swung across the path of Patton's Cadillac in an attempt to turn into a Quartermaster depot. Woodring was unable to stop in time and the two vehicles collided at a ninety-degree angle, with the right front bumper of the truck smashing the radiator and bumper of the Cadillac. Neither driver was injured and Gay received only slight bruises. Patton on the other hand, although conscious, was bleeding profusely from head wounds received when he was thrown forwards against the steel frame of the glass partition separating the front and rear seats and then backwards again into his seat. There were of course, no seat belts in those days and whereas Gay and Woodring, having seen the oncoming truck, had braced themselves for the impact, Patton who had been looking out of the side window had not. He knew he was seriously injured and apparently murmured: 'I think I'm paralysed' and later: 'This is a helluva way to die'.

The ambulance which eventually arrived at the scene with two medical officers took Patton to the 130th Station Hospital in Heidelberg, fifteen miles away, where he was admitted at 1245 hours. He was paralysed from the neck down and suffering from severe traumatic shock; his pulse rate was 45 and he had a blood pressure reading of 86/60. As well as blood covering his face and scalp from cuts that had gone through to the bone, he was diagnosed as having: 'a fracture of the third cervical vertebra, with a posterior dislocation of the fourth cervical vertebra'.[23] Whether or not the spinal cord had been transected or merely traumatized remained a matter of conjecture.

Patton was put in a crude and extremely painful form of traction that evening and the US Army Surgeon General in Washington recommended that a British neurosurgeon, Brigadier Hugh Cairns, and an orthopaedic surgeon were brought in to assist. A plane was sent to London to fetch them and after they arrived on the morning of the 10th, they:

> advised some changes that turned out to be an equally dreadful new method of traction . . . A metal fish hook was inserted just below the bony process beneath Patton's eyes. Each hook was then attached to a tensile strut, or tong, to maintain constant tension. Whether or not due to this makeshift device, Patton's condition did begin to stabilize, though he stoically endured almost unbearable pain. After several days the tissue surrounding the hooks began to die. Finally, after nine days of agony, the tongs were mercifully removed and traction was maintained by encasing Patton's neck and shoulders in a special plaster jacket.[24]

Beatrice and an American neurosurgeon, Colonel Geoffrey Spurling, flew in from the States on the 11th. Patton's medical records for that day read: 'Prognosis for recovery increasingly grave'. Spurling and the other doctors knew that it was impossible to operate to relieve the pressure on his badly damaged spinal cord to eliminate the paralysis. Patton too seems to have known that his injuries were irreversible, if not terminal; his first words to his wife were: 'I'm afraid, Bea, this may be the last time we see each other'.

George Patton died peacefully at 1755 hours on 21 December. The previous afternoon it had been necessary to give him oxygen to restore his breathing and X-rays revealed that a small pulmonary embolism had obstructed his upper right lung. Beatrice spent most of the final afternoon with him, but left to have supper when he fell asleep at about 1715 hours. A doctor summoned her at about 1800 hours, but it was too late – another embolism had struck his left lung.

Patton's body, draped with his personal four-star flag, lay in state for two days in the Villa Reiner, a nineteenth century mansion overlooking Heidelberg and the Neckar river. Beatrice initially wanted him flown home for burial at West Point, but was persuaded that this would be totally inappropriate since no American soldier had, up to that time, been sent home for burial. She was then given a choice of three large US military cemeteries in Europe and chose the one at Hamm, three miles east of Luxembourg City (Map 15). On the 22nd, the day the *Stars and Stripes* carried the headline: 'PATTON DIES', she drove to Bad Nauheim to oversee her husband's effects being prepared for shipment back to their home in Massachusetts. His beloved dog, *Willie*, was to follow later. Tributes were already beginning to flow in and would eventually include messages from President Truman, British Prime Minister Attlee and the French National Assembly.

On the afternoon of the 23rd Patton's coffin was taken on an Army half-track to the Protestant Christ Church in Heidelberg for a short Episcopalian service conducted by two Army chaplains during which there were no eulogies. It was escorted by a platoon of the 15th Cavalry, the unit in which Patton had begun his career in 1910. Bedell Smith did not attend the service, which is hardly surprising since Patton carried his dislike for both him and Eisenhower to his grave. Only two months before he had told Ike: 'I cannot eat at the same table with *Beetle* Smith', and before he died he told Beatrice that he did not want either of them to attend his funeral. Patton could never forgive Ike for removing him from command of the Third Army.

Following the service, the coffin, accompanied of course by Beatrice who was supported by Patton's old friend General Geoffrey Keyes, was taken to Heidelberg station along a route lined by some 6,000 US soldiers. At 1630 hours it began its journey to Luxembourg where it arrived at 0400 hours on the 24th. The train stopped six times during the journey to allow honour guards, bands and mourners, despite the freezing weather and heavy rain, to pay homage.

The route from Luxembourg City station to the US cemetery was lined by troops from the United States, Belgium, France and Luxembourg and the cortège was followed by Prince Felix of Luxembourg, two French, one Italian and numerous American generals, including of course 'Hap' Gay and Lucien Truscott.

George Patton was buried at 0930 hours on 24 December amongst other American soldiers, many of whom had died whilst under his command.[25] The ceremony lasted twenty-five minutes.

> In the final minute of the ceremony Master Sergeant William G Meeks, the Negro . . . who had served Patton faithfully as his orderly [since April 1942] . . . presented the general's widow with the flag that had draped the coffin. There were tears in Meek's eyes. His face was screwed up with the strain. He bowed slowly and handed the flag to Mrs. Patton. Then he saluted stiffly . . . Meeks turned away, a 12-man firing squad raised its rifles and a three-round volley of salutes echoed into the Luxembourg hills. The bugler played the soft, sad notes of 'Taps'.[26]

Needless to say, rumours soon began to circulate, as in the case of Diana, Princess of Wales, that the road accident that had led to the victim's death was no accident. In both cases there was, and in the latter case there still is as this book is being written, even talk of a conspiracy. With regard to Patton, his biographer, Carlo D'Este, sums up this idea succinctly:

> Those who suggest that Patton was somehow murdered have failed to provide the slightest evidence of how anyone could have planned such a caper or ensured that Patton's Cadillac would be momentarily stopped for the passage of a train at the crossing just down the street from the scene of the accident. Other than a handful of men on his personal staff, no one even knew where Patton would be, what route he would follow, or what time he would arrive at his destination.[27]

Eighteen days after Patton's death Jean Gordon, who had returned home to the States a month earlier, committed suicide by putting her head in a gas oven. She was 30 years old. Beatrice Patton died, aged 67, of an aneurysm whilst out riding in 1953 and, although forbidden by Army regulations, their daughter Ruth Ellen secretly sprinkled her ashes on Patton's grave in 1957.[28]

NOTES

1   D'Este, *A Genius for War*, pp. 735–6.
2   Ibid.
3   See *The Devil's Adjutant – Jochen Peiper, Panzer Leader* by this author.

4   D'Este, op. cit., p. 745.
5   Ibid, p. 746.
6   Ibid, p. 749.
7   Ibid, p. 758, Note 91.
8   Ibid, p. 755.
9   Ibid, p. 756.
10 Meyer, *The History of the 12th SS Panzer Division Hitlerjugend*, p. 329.
11 SHAEF had been disbanded on 14 Jul 45.
12 Farago, *The Last Days of Patton*, p. 207.
13 D'Este, op. cit., p. 764.
14 Farago, op. cit., p. 146.
15 Some estimates have put the figure much higher – at 70%.
16 D'Este, op. cit., pp. 765–6.
17 Diary entry for 29 Sep 45.
18 Patton, *War As I Knew It*, p. 366.
19 D'Este, op. cit., p. 778, quoting Allen's book *The Day Patton Quit*.
20 Ibid, p. 779, quoting John Eisenhower's book *Strictly Personal*.
21 Ibid.
22 Ibid, p. 780.
23 Patton's medical records.
24 D'Este, op. cit., p. 789.
25 Due to so many people visiting his grave and damaging the area around it, Patton's body was eventually reburied on its own at the front of the cemetery. In 1946 Winston Churchill paid his respects at the site, but no American President has ever done so.
26 United Press report.
27 D'Este, op. cit., p. 787. The driver of the truck that collided with Patton's car, T/5 Robert Thompson, was later exonerated of any fault, even though Gay and Woodring stated that he had never indicated his intention to turn left. 'According to [Ladislas] Farago's meticulous investigation, Thompson was out joyriding after a night of boozing with his buddies, and had no business even being on the road that Sunday morning.' – D'Este, op. cit., pp. 786 & 785.
28 Ibid, p. 808.

CHAPTER XXVI

Montgomery – May to December 1945

In a book of this nature it is unnecessary to go into the details of exactly how Monty went about running the British zone of Germany immediately after VE Day, or the complex problems facing the western Allies as a whole in their dealings with the Russians. Similarly, the details of the final withdrawal of the four Armies into the four agreed Zones of Germany and Berlin and the Potsdam Conference of July 1945 need not concern us. Those interested should consult Nigel Hamilton's *Monty: The Field Marshal 1944–1976*. Instead we will give an outline of Monty's actions as Military Governor, or 'Dictator' as some commentators have called him, and concentrate instead on the more personal aspects of his life at this time.

Following Church parade on the first Sunday after the German surrender, Monty addressed the personnel of his Tac HQ on Lüneburg Heath:

> You will probably think, now that the war is over, that Tac will cease to function and that you can all go home. That is far from the case. Far from it . . . Fighting Germans is easy compared with the job of dealing with the politicians, or statesmen as I believe they are called.[1]

He was in fact, like George Patton, already fearful that a defeated and devastated Germany might turn, as Russia had during WWI, to revolution and communism.

Monty described his problems as follows:

> In the area occupied by 21 Army Group there were appalling civilian problems to be solved. Over one million civilian refugees had fled into the area before the advancing Russians. About one million German wounded were in hospital in the area, with no medical supplies. Over one and a half million unwounded German fighting men had surrendered to 21 Army Group on the 5th May, and were now prisoners of war, with all that entailed. Food would shortly be exhausted. The transport and communication services had ceased to function, and industry and agriculture were largely at a standstill. The population had to be fed, housed and kept free of disease. It was going to be a race against time whether this could be achieved before the winter began; if by that time the population was not fed, and housed, famine and disease would run riot through Germany . . . I had suddenly become responsible for the government and well-being of about twenty million Germans.[2]

Monty also shared Patton's view on the Russians:

> From their behaviour it soon became clear that the Russians, though a fine fighting race, were in fact barbarous Asiatics who had never enjoyed a civilisation comparable to that of the rest of Europe . . . Their behaviour, especially in their treatment of women, was abhorrent to us.[3]

The difference, however, was that Monty kept his views to himself.

A further point of agreement between our two prima donnas was the manner in which former German soldiers, whether they had been members of the Nazi party or not, could and should be used. Monty decreed that prisoners:

> were to be documented and checked over. They were then to be demobilized and directed back to their civil vocations, as and when they were needed and work became available – the farmers, the miners, the post office workers, the civil servants, etc., etc.[4]

In fact Monty went much further than Patton and used the former Wehrmacht organization itself to provide the framework for organizing the civilian population. The basis of his plan:

> was to work through the German command organization in the first instance, and to issue my orders regarding the disposal of German forces to Field Marshal Busch, the German C-in-C in NW Europe . . . German army boundaries were to be altered to coincide with British boundaries.[5]

In his *Memoirs*, written in 1958, Monty goes on to make the surprising statement that: 'I had also been given a "stand still" order regarding the destruction of German weapons and equipment, in case they might be needed by the *Western* (author's emphasis) Allies for any reason'.[6] He does not say where this 'stand still' order came from, but it almost certainly originated at the very top, Churchill, who like Monty was concerned with the threat of the Red Army on the borders of Western Europe.

Monty had been chosen by the British Chiefs of Staff to be the 'Gauleiter for the British Occupied Zone [of Germany]'[7] as early as 10 April, but Churchill, to Monty's intense annoyance, had refused to ratify the appointment. This matter was still unresolved when the Germans surrendered and Monty decided he could not do his job properly without the authority of his political masters. He therefore decided to fly to London to try to get Churchill to make a decision. He signalled Eisenhower on 8 May asking for permission to return to England, citing the need for a short leave as his reason, and wrote to Phyllis Reynolds on the 9th telling her he hoped to stay in England for ten days, but asking her not to 'tell any of my family I am coming home'. Five days later he took off for London.

The period between the German surrender and his return to London was not an easy time for Monty. Just a few days after John Poston's burial another of his favourite LOs, Major Charles Sweeny, died as the result of a road accident. He had been with Monty since Dunkirk, had earned a Military Cross and had only recently married. Again Monty was extremely upset and again he wrote an obituary for *The Times*: 'Charles was an orphan and possibly it was that fact which drew us close together

... as if I was his father ... I loved this gallant Irish boy and his memory will remain with me for all time'.

Monty's duties as de facto Military Governor were also weighing heavily upon him. As he saw it, in the absence of any real political direction from London he had no option other than to get on with the job; and being a professional soldier rather than a politician, he started giving orders. The day after VE Day he announced his plans for the disposition of his forces. Two divisions and an armoured brigade were to be sent home and the remainder moved into four occupation areas; and in typical Monty fashion, one division was to be held in reserve for unforeseen eventualities! At the same 'Orders Group' he forbade fraternisation, gave strict instructions concerning the treatment of prisoners and civilians, and said that all looters, regardless of rank, would be court-martialled. Like Patton, he also said that all looted vehicles were to be handed in.

Monty had already entertained his Russian opposite number, Marshal Rokossovsky, to lunch on 7 May and on the 10th he was invited for a 'return match'. Unlike Patton who, readers may recall, had found his opposite number 'a very inferior man who sweated profusely', Monty found his man 'an imposing figure, tall, very good looking, and well dressed; I understand he was a bachelor and very much admired by ladies'. Some idea of his character can be gauged by the fact that when he was told that Monty did not drink, smoke or like women, he apparently exclaimed: 'What the devil does he do all day?'[8]

The following day Monty found it necessary to send for the German he had appointed as head of the German command organization, Field Marshal Busch. He wrote later:

> The German military leaders, having been saved from the Russians, were only too willing to be friends with the British and to do whatever was wanted. But in return for this co-operative attitude they expected to be treated as allies of the British against the Russians, and in some cases my orders had been queried and delay had occurred in carrying them out ... [I] told him that this attitude was entirely unacceptable ... If he did not carry out his orders promptly and efficiently, I would remove him from his command ... He was to understand that the German Army had been utterly defeated in the field and must now accept the consequences of that defeat. After this I had no more trouble with Busch or with any other German commander.[9]

When Monty arrived in London on 14 May he found the Prime Minister was more concerned with a forthcoming General Election than he was about the situation in Germany, and it was not until the 16th that Monty discovered that Churchill had in fact never had any objection to his becoming C-in-C British Forces of Occupation and the British member of the Allied Control Commission in Germany. All Winston had wanted was for a civilian to be his deputy. In the end, after various political manoeuvres, it was agreed, to the satisfaction of both Churchill and Monty, that the CIGS's Deputy, Lieutenant General Ronald Weeks, would get the job. The announcement of the two appointments was made on 22 May, the day Monty flew down to Winchester to give, according to his son, 'a very impressive' lecture to the school. It was the first time he had seen David since VE Day.

The following day, back in London, Monty summoned the heads of the British civil divisions of the Control Commission to outline the problems in the British Zone of Germany and to tell them how 'our combined brains and much sheer hard work' would sort them out. It was vintage Monty – in what amounted to a military 'Orders Group', he told them he was convinced 'that we shall not begin to make real progress until we are all together' – in other words that they should move out from London at once! He ended:

> My personal HQ is now on Lüneburg Heath; a historic site!! I move it on 3 June to Ostenwalde Schloss; this is east of Osnabrück and about 15 miles from Main HQ 21 Army Group at Bad Oeynhausen [fifteen miles north-west of Herford (Map 16)]. I [will] live there alone, with my personal staff [his Military and Personal Assistants, both majors, and two ADCs] and my small set-up for command e.g., signals, cipher, liaison, etc, etc. The only other member of my personal HQ is my Deputy, or Chief of Staff, i.e., General Weeks. It is to this place that I shall ask you to come to see me.[10]

'Having given orders about the deployment in Germany of the British [civilian] element of the Control Commission',[11] Monty returned to his Tac HQ via Paris where he had been invited to open a British Military Exhibition and be decorated by de Gaulle with the Grande Croix of the Legion of Honour. Huge crowds turned out to greet him and in the evening they formed again outside the British Embassy where he was staying.

> I went out on the balcony to thank them. I made a very short speech in English; but the crowd still kept cheering and showed no signs of dispersing; so I made a second appearance on the balcony and said: 'Allez-vous en'. That finished it! There were shouts of laughter and they all went away, seemingly quite happy.[12]

Monty was now without question the Supremo in the British Zone of Germany and having come to the conclusion that 'his' Germans were becoming restive and anxious about their future, he issued what amounted to an 'Order of the Day' to 'The Population of the British Area in Germany'. It was dated 30 May. In it he laid down how he was going to 'establish a simple and orderly life' for them, how 'the German people will work under my orders to provide the necessities of life for the community' and how those who had committed war crimes would be dealt with 'in the proper fashion'. He ended by saying that: 'The population will be told what to do. I shall expect it to be done willingly and efficiently'.[13] Perhaps not surprisingly, this message and others issued on 10 June and 25 July,

> were viewed with some mistrust in Whitehall. Was I becoming a military dictator who would seize power? . . . But I stuck to my guns and refused to be 'seen off' by my political masters; so long as I was responsible I was determined to use my own methods.[14]

Despite Monty's statement to his staff that they would not be able to go home until the post-war problems of Germany had been sorted out, it was not long before his team of wartime LOs began to break up – Ray Bondurant of course returned to the US Army and Trumbull Warren to Canada – and with the arrival of new officers the atmosphere at his Head-quarters inevitably changed. 'Comments from the newcomers tended to be more critical, less reverential now the war was over . . . Some of the more junior officers were shocked by the gusto with which Monty would criticize, and encourage criticism of, other senior commanders.' Johnny Henderson recalled later though that Monty would not tolerate criticism of his own battles, and the most decorated of all the LOs, now his Personal Assistant, Richard O'Brien, with a DSO and two MCs, remembered it to be 'a strange set-up'. Like Patton, '[Monty] wanted to be kept away from the detail – and the starving Germans of course! . . . It was so remote, and there we were, this privileged corps, playing tennis on a summer's afternoon, and calm reigned'.[15] Needless to say, no women were allowed in the Headquarters and Monty saw few people of his own age group.

The most extraordinary aspect of the running of Headquarters 21 Army Group during this period was Monty's remoteness. He left virtually all Control Commission business in Berlin to his Deputy, Ronald Weeks and later Sir Brian Robertson, and the administration of the British Zone of Germany to his Corps and Divisional commanders and his Civil Affairs officers. He never went to Bad Oeynhausen; rather, anyone wanting to see him, including even his Chief of Staff, had to make an appointment and then drive to Schloss Ostenwalde. Richard O'Brien recalled: 'We were remote. People came and went at Tac HQ. They were summoned to the "presence" – it was almost like Berchtesgaden!'[16]

Freddie de Guingand had been Monty's Chief of Staff from Alamein to Lüneburg Heath, but it had taken a lot out of him and Monty soon sent him on sick leave. He wrote a letter of gratitude to him on 31 May which ended: 'have a good rest. And then, later on, together we will conquer fresh fields'.[17] But amazingly, when de Guingand, who had been doing a lieutenant general's job, albeit as an acting major general, for over a year and a half, was required, under Army regulations, to revert to his substantive rank of colonel, Monty did nothing to help him. De Guingand appealed to him, but Monty would have none of it. According to his biographer, Nigel Hamilton, it was only when *Eisenhower* protested in person to the British Secretary of State for War, that de Guingand's rank of major general was restored.[18]

Monty's stay at Schloss Ostenwalde was not quite as peaceful as he intended. A lake just outside his bedroom was home to thousands of frogs and their croaking at night drove him mad. German prisoners were ordered to collect them and dump them in a pond several miles away, but the offending amphibians marched back again after a few days. In 1975 the Bürgermeister of the local town (Melle) told the author[19] that the locals, including the owners of the Schloss, were amused and delighted that the famous commander had lost this final battle on German soil.

On 5 June Monty, as one of the four Allied C-in-Cs, flew to Berlin to sign a document recognizing the joint responsibility of their governments for Germany. Marshal Zhukov, the Russian C-in-C, failed to greet his western counterparts at Templehof airfield, no food was available in their villas and when Monty found no programme provided for the visit, he threatened to fly home. This did the trick and at the ensuing meeting with Zhukov he and Eisenhower were told that Stalin had conferred on them the 'Order of Victory', the highest Soviet order and one never before given to a foreigner. Monty was thrilled since the emblem was 'of great intrinsic value, being in the form of a five-pointed star beautifully set with rubies and diamonds'. After some discussion it was agreed that the award ceremony would take place, not in Berlin, but in Eisenhower's office in Frankfurt on the 10th.

At the conclusion of the meeting Monty sent an amazingly frank letter to Eisenhower which shows his character in a slightly different light. Written in his own hand and dated 7 June, it said:

> Now that we have all signed in Berlin I suppose we shall soon begin to run our own affairs. I would like, before this happens, to say what a privilege and an honour it has been to serve under you. I owe much to your wise guidance and kindly forbearance. I know my own faults very well and I do not suppose I am an easy subordinate; I like to go my own way. But you have kept me on the rails in difficult and stormy times, and have taught me much. For this I am very grateful. And I thank you for all you have done for me.[20]

Between Berlin and Frankfurt, Monty flew to Antwerp to receive the Freedom and valuable 'Golden Dagger' of the City. In fact he was now being showered with honours. As early as 13 May he had been decorated by the Danes and given the Freedom of Copenhagen and the following month he was made a Knight Grand Cross of the Order of the Bath in King George VI's Birthday Honours List. Later in the year he was made a Chief Commander of the American Legion of Merit – how that must have irritated George Patton – and presented with the Polish Order of Virtuti Militari. Meanwhile, in Antwerp, the Belgians, in their usual generous manner, provided a lavish luncheon of many courses after which Monty felt so ill that he asked for the rest of the programme to be cut short. He was driven to the airfield for the return flight, 'through streets lined with cheering citizens – with myself sitting on the floor of the car being violently sick'.[21]

Monty flew down to Frankfurt on 10 June to receive his Russian award from Zhukov and was surprised and thrilled to receive the American DSM from Ike before the main ceremony. He was also surprised that following a fly-past by 1,700 American and British war planes, put on to impress the Russians, there was a lavish lunch during which the Americans 'produced a coloured cabaret show, with swing music and elaborate dancing by Negro women who were naked above the waist line ... It was a day which revealed undeniably the wealth and power of the United States'.[22]

By 12 June Monty had decided that he could start to relax his rule of complete non-fraternisation with the Germans. Nevertheless, even as late as September 1945, it was still forbidden for soldiers to be billeted with Germans or for them to marry Germans. SHAEF, readers will recall, was disbanded in the middle of July, but Eisenhower remained as C-in C US Forces and Military Governor of the US Zone and Monty positioned a small liaison headquarters in Frankfurt in order to ensure that his policy was 'in step' with that of his old master. In fact he held the view that it had been a mistake to split western Germany into three zones: 'Eisenhower should have been left in overall control of the western half of Germany; we would then have confronted the Russians with a united front'.[23]

As early as 9 July Monty had indicated that he was already thinking of his next appointment – in fact there is no doubt that he saw himself as Brooke's successor as CIGS. He wrote to Brooke on that day:

> The shape and fashion of the post-war army must now be considered, and this can be done properly only by those who have fought in command of units and formations in battle and who understand clearly what weapons and equipment are needed, and why; and how each article fits into the tactical picture. You will probably tell me to mind my own business, and get on with my job,

and that it is nothing to do with me. But so long as you will read this letter, I do not mind.[24]

The Potsdam Conference between Churchill, Truman and Stalin opened on 17 July and Monty was required to fly up to Berlin to greet Churchill. He wrote later:

> Very hot here . . . No one knows anything about the problem; the PM has been electioneering for weeks and has read nothing; Eden has been sick; there is no agreed Agenda; everyone is reading Foreign Office briefs madly. A curious show!![25]

The conference had to be adjourned on 25 July so that Churchill could fly home to hear the results of the General Election and, to the amazement of the Americans and Russians, he did not return. He had lost the election to the Labour (Socialist) party and Clement Attlee, the new Prime Minister, came back to Potsdam with a new delegation. Monty was to develop a high regard for Attlee and 'was much impressed' by Ernest Bevin, the new Foreign Secretary. He took a very different view, however, of two Socialist Members of Parliament who visited the British Zone later that month. They stayed the first night with him at Schloss Ostenwalde, before beginning their tour of army units, but after only one day Monty received reports that they had asked officers to leave meetings so that they could talk to the soldiers alone. He 'was extremely angry and at once issued an order . . . forbidding such action'. As the man 'responsible for discipline in the armed forces in Germany . . . I was not going to have it undermined by wandering Members of Parliament'.[26]

In early August David Montgomery flew out to Germany in his father's Dakota for a ten-day holiday. It was a very happy time for both of them; particularly David, for although Monty had forbidden him to go on holiday with one of his LOs, Major Carol Mather, during the Easter holidays – because he was likely to 'develop bad habits and drink and smoke'[27] – on this occasion he agreed that David could go sailing with Mather in the Baltic in a requisitioned German yacht.[28]

On 22 August, shortly after David returned to England, Monty was very nearly killed in an air crash. During a flight to visit the Canadian 3rd Infantry Division on the North Sea coast, the engine of his light aircraft cut out and the plane crash-landed. The pilot and ADC were unhurt, but Monty was severely shaken and suffered two broken vertebrae as well as serious bruising. Clearly in considerable pain, he still managed to carry out an investiture and make a speech before insisting, to the amazement of the Canadians, that he be flown back to his Headquarters. He took the view that 'no one had ever crashed twice in the same day' and that it was safer than going by road. The consultant surgeon to 21 Army Group was called in that evening and gave Monty the choice of being in plaster and hobbling about as best he could, or of bed rest and physiotherapy for ten days. Monty chose the latter, but refused female nurses saying he would have no women at the Schloss. In the end though, he had to put up with a female physiotherapist. Three days after the accident, whilst he was still bed-ridden, Monty's beloved 21st Army Group ceased to exist – his troops became the British Army of the Rhine.

Monty's energy in the last half of 1945, despite an attack of tonsillitis in July and the injuries sustained in the air crash, was amazing. In addition to the official meetings and conferences already described, he travelled to Oxford, Cambridge and Belfast to be awarded Honorary Doctorates of Law, and in just six days in October he received the Freedoms of Warwick, Canterbury, Manchester and Maidenhead – all day-long affairs. Yet Monty still found time to visit his troops in Germany, attend sports meetings and hold investitures, and to carry on a copious correspondence with virtually anyone who wrote to him including charities, football clubs and even the author who, as a schoolboy, wrote to him for his autograph.[29] Fortunately, between his visits in the United Kingdom, Monty was able to spend a number of weekends relaxing at the Reynolds' preparatory school in Hindhead.[30] He had of course no home of his own at this time and seems to have had little or no compunction in using theirs as a base.

One of the more bizarre incidents of this period occurred on 25 September when Monty was invited to Newport in Wales to receive the Freedom of that city and to attend a banquet in his honour being given on behalf of the whole population of Wales. He had prepared a speech, which was distributed to the press before the banquet, extolling the part played by the 53rd Welsh Division in the war, and all seemed set for a very happy occasion. Things went badly wrong however, when the Mayor of Newport announced that the Council had invited Monty's mother over from Ireland for the occasion.[31] Monty is said to have turned white with anger at this news and exclaimed: 'I won't have her here. If she comes, I go!'[32] In the end it was agreed that her place-name would be removed from the top table and she would sit in a far corner of the room. Even more surprising, Monty refused to speak to her before, during, or after the meal. In fact it was the last time he saw her alive – and he did not attend her funeral. 'But it was not just Maud who was punished. His justly proud brothers and sisters all experienced similar snubs'.[33]

As early as 6 August Monty had been told that he would probably succeed Brooke as CIGS, but that no date had been fixed for the handover. As it turned out Brooke was persuaded to remain in post until the spring of 1946. Monty hid his disappointment by telling his Military Assistant, Lieutenant Colonel 'Kit' Dawnay, that he had:

told the Prime Minister and the CIGS that I consider it would be most unwise to move me from Germany until the Battle of the Winter has been won. The CIGS will stay on till the Spring; it is his idea that I should succeed him, and he has told the Prime Minister this.[34]

In fact Brooke was very uncertain about Monty as a successor. He noted in his diary on 26 August that Monty was: 'very efficient from an Army point of view but very unpopular with a large proportion of the Army'. He was of course referring to officers rather than soldiers in this respect. The campaigns in the Middle East and particularly in Europe had demonstrated only too clearly to Brooke how difficult it was for Monty to work as part of a team and he foresaw great difficulties in Monty's future dealings with the government – particularly a socialist one determined to spend money on health, education and welfare rather than on defence. Brooke's problem was that there was virtually no one else he could recommend to Attlee as his successor. Alexander was Governor General of Canada, Wavell was too old and Auckinleck's career had mainly been in the Indian rather than the British Army, and anyway both were fully occupied with the problem of India; and Slim, despite his brilliant campaign in the Far East, was largely unknown. 'As the nation's most popular general, Field Marshal Montgomery gravitated almost inevitably to the job of CIGS.'[35]

Whilst George Patton's body lay in state in Heidelberg and arrangements were being made for his burial in Luxembourg, Monty flew home to spend Christmas at Hindhead with David and the Reynolds. It was the first Christmas Monty had spent with his son since 1937 and he was in high spirits. He kept it to himself, but he already knew that on New Year's Day he would become a viscount, thus outranking his father (Knight Grand Cross of the Order of St Michael and St George) and his grandfather Sir Robert Montgomery, and although not yet confirmed, he knew that he was almost certain to take over from Brooke as CIGS the following June. His highest ambitions would thus be fulfilled.

When Monty returned to Germany his staff asked him what title he was going to take as a viscount. 'What do you think of Montgomery of Alamein?' he asked. They tried to look surprised; in fact they had seen him practising that signature for weeks on a blotting pad![36] His official title therefore, as he soon informed the Reynolds, was to be: 'Field Marshal The Viscount Montgomery of Alamein, GCB, DSO'.

Our comparison of the lives of Monty and Patton is therefore ended. However, for readers interested in the remaining thirty years of Monty's life, a brief résumé is given in the Appendix. Sadly, as often happens in the case of famous men, the passing years saw a graduation erosion of his hard-won wartime reputation. Full details can be found in Nigel Hamilton's biography, Volume 3 and Brian Montgomery's *A Field Marshal in the Family*.

NOTES

1   Horne, *The Lonely Leader*, p. 340.
2   Montgomery, *Memoirs*, p. 356 & p. 359.
3   Ibid, p. 356.
4   Ibid, p. 358.
5   Ibid, pp. 357–8.
6   Ibid, p. 359.
7   Alanbrooke diary; he added 'May heaven help him with that job!!'.
8   Montgomery, op. cit., pp. 359–60.
9   Ibid, p. 367.
10 Montgomery Papers.
11 Montgomery, op. cit., p. 364.
12 Ibid, p. 366.
13 Ibid, p. 368.
14 Ibid, p. 367.
15 Horne, op. cit., pp. 341–2.
16 Hamilton, *Monty: The Field Marshal 1944–1976*, p. 584.
17 De Guingand Papers, IWM.
18 Hamilton, op. cit., p. 563.
19 At that time a Brigade commander & commander of nearby Osnabrück Garrison.
20 Eisenhower Papers, Eisenhower Library, Abilene, Kansas.
21 Montgomery, op. cit., p. 363.
22 Ibid, p. 362.
23 Ibid, p. 389.
24 M 588 dated 7 Jul 45.
25 Letter to Simpson dated 16 Jul 45.
26 Montgomery, op. cit., p. 408.
27 Letter to the Reynolds dated 7 Apr 45.
28 David Montgomery to the author, 25 Feb 2004.
29 He also wrote to, and received autographs from, Eisenhower, 'Bomber' Harris, Bertram Ramsay, Guy Gibson VC and James Doolittle. Churchill did not reply.
30 Amesbury Preparatory School.
31 According to Brian Montgomery, *A Field Marshal in the Family*, p. 321, their mother wrote to the Council *asking* for an invitation.
32 Horne, op. cit., p. 346.
33 Ibid, pp. 346–7.
34 Hamilton, op. cit., pp. 581–2.
35 Chalfont, *Montgomery of Alamein*, p. 279.
36 Hamilton, op. cit., p. 603.

Epilogue

Most readers will by now have made up their own minds about Monty and Patton as both men and generals and this author will make only a few points in summary. Clearly they were both great soldiers and remarkable men who seized their moment in history. Inevitably such men have their admirers and detractors, but it is hoped that this book will help readers to make an unbiased assessment of their characters and capabilities. One thing is certain – both Monty and Patton would have found it extremely difficult, if not impossible, to adapt to our current way of life with its emphasis on multiculturalism and materialism and its lack of self-discipline, and in fairness they should be judged by the standards and ethics of their own time, not ours.

Let us look at them first as men and as gentlemen. In the case of Monty it is clear that on the whole he was courteous and considerate (except in relation to his own family), but not always polite or respectful. His egotism was astounding and was well summed up by his brother in his book *A Field Marshal in the Family*, pages 320–1:

> Increasingly during his official life ... my brother developed an absolute fixation not to allow any person, no matter who it might be, and including members of his own family, to appear as though he or she should have the main credit (on occasions it would be any credit) for the achievements attributed to himself.

Patton was rarely courteous, considerate or respectful. He too was clearly an egoist. Monty, as a result of his upbringing, never used bad language and hated war; Patton on the other hand, has been well described as a foul-mouthed lover of war.

As generals they were as different as chalk and cheese. One an infantryman, the other a cavalryman, they displayed the basic charac-teristics of these two combat arms – Monty, for very good reasons, careful and meticulous; Patton dashing and devil-may-care. It has been said that Patton could never have planned the D-Day landings as Monty did, and that the latter could never have chased the Germans across France in the Patton manner. Few would disagree with this view – or with Churchill when he described Monty as austere, severe, accomplished and tireless – or with Omar Bradley who said of Patton: 'Some people may not approve of the kind of man Georgie was but he was one hellava soldier.'

Clearly both men found it hard to work in harness with others. They were both individualists with whom it was difficult to do business and it is clear that neither of them was cut out to be a coalition general. Patton was convinced that since America was providing most of the manpower and equipment for the European campaign, only Americans should be in charge and they should claim the glory. Monty, intensely proud of Great Britain and its Empire, completely failed to comprehend the inevitable outcome of this American dominance.

In writing this book the author feels he has come to know both men intimately and to understand their ambitions and frustrations; and he believes he would probably have acted and reacted in the same way that they did on many (but hopefully not all!), of the occasions described. One thing is certain – he would never have felt completely comfortable in the company of either of them. They were certainly not *nice* people – but then, generals in war are not meant to be *nice*.

The final tributes to these two great men should perhaps come from their Supreme Commander. Eisenhower said of Monty: 'I don't know if we could have done it without him. It was his sort of battle. Whatever they say about him, he got us there'. And of George Patton he said: 'His presence gave me the certainty that the boldest plan would be even more daringly executed. It is no exaggeration to say that Patton's name struck terror at the heart of the enemy'.

Finally, the author asked himself which of our prima donnas he would have preferred to serve under – regardless of rank. The answer was obvious – Monty. Why? Not just because the author is British and an ex-infantryman, but because Monty would have been much less likely to have 'cussed' him out and because he would have had a much better chance of surviving the war.

APPENDIX

Montgomery – 1946 to 1976

As well as the honours and awards already mentioned in this book, during his post-war career Monty was made a Knight of the Order of the Garter (Great Britain's highest Order of Chivalry), a Freeman of the City of London and forty-three other major cities and towns at home and abroad, a Freeman of three London Livery Companies and awarded honorary degrees at thirteen universities. In addition he received France's highest military decoration, the Médaille Militaire. During this period Monty found time to write ten books, the most successful of which was *Memoirs*. Published in 1958 and subsequently translated into fifteen languages, it earned him a six-figure sum – something very rare in those days.

The highlights of Monty's life can be summarized as follows:
1946
On 2 May he left Germany and in June visited Malta, Egypt, Palestine, Greece, Italy and India to assess the situations in those countries before becoming CIGS. He received cool receptions in Cairo, Jerusalem and Delhi.

26 June: Monty assumed the appointment of CIGS and during the next two years he visited all the countries of the British Commonwealth, most of the British colonies, the Soviet Union as the guest of Stalin, and the USA where he was the guest of Eisenhower and the US Army and met Truman in the White House. He also had several audiences with Pope Pius XII whom he held in high regard. However, his tenure as CIGS was not a happy period as it was marked by constant dissension between him and the government.

1947

In February Monty bought a rundown mill at Isington in Hampshire and eventually turned it into his home.

1948

20 September: Monty became Chairman of the Western Europe C-in-C's Committee (Britain, France, Belgium, Holland and Luxembourg). His tenure is best remembered for his clash with the French C-in-C, General de Lattre de Tassigny.

1 November: Monty relinquished the post of CIGS. His Deputy, Lieutenant General Gerald Templer, who later rose to the rank of Field Marshal and who was greatly admired by the author's generation, described Monty as 'the worst CIGS for fifty years'.

1949

Monty's mother died; he did not attend her funeral.

1951–8

2 April 1951 Monty was appointed Deputy Supreme Commander Europe (NATO), first to Eisenhower and subsequently to Ridgway (with whom he fell out and whose removal he engineered), Gruenther and Norstad. His responsibilities were chiefly in the field of training and readiness and since this involved a lot of travelling, Monty thoroughly enjoyed it. The post was outside the main decision-making machinery of NATO and this enabled Monty for once in his life, as Alun Chalfont put it in his book *Montgomery of Alamein*, to 'criticize without causing too much offence'.

1958

18 September: Monty completed fifty-one years service in khaki, but since field marshals are never retired from the British Army, he became unemployed, actually drawing 'the dole' for a limited period whilst still drawing his pay as a Field Marshal.

1959–67

Monty visited South Africa seven times, China (where he met Chairman Mao Tse Tung), Central America, the Soviet Union (where he met Khruschev), India (where he met Nehru) and Egypt (where he met Nasser), including the El Alamein battlefields. He often travelled to the continent of Europe, meeting amongst other heads of state, Marshal Tito, entertained frequently at Isington Mill and regularly attended important debates in the House of Lords. He also became a regular radio and television broadcaster.

1967

17 November was Monty's 80th birthday. During a celebratory dinner for him in London, there was a break-in at Isington Mill and he lost many precious items including his Field Marshal's baton.

1968

Monty published his last book, *A History of Warfare,* and retired, due to ill health, from public life.

1972

12 May: Monty unveiled a portrait of himself by Terrance Cuneo at the Staff College Camberley.

1976

Monty died on 24 March in his 89th year; his funeral was held on 1 April at St George's Chapel Windsor and he was buried in the graveyard of the Holy Cross church at Binstead, Hampshire.

Bibliography

This bibliography comprises the works used in this book or directly quoted. In the case of Montgomery, particular general use was made of Nigel Hamilton's three-volume biography, *The Lonely Leader* by Alistair Horne with David Montgomery, Brian Montgomery's *A Field Marshal in the Family*, Alun Chalfont's *Montgomery of Alamein* and Chester Wilmot's *The Struggle for Europe*. Permission to quote from Nigel Hamilton's biography was given by David Higham Associates of London. In the case of Patton, my main sources of information were Carlo D'Este's *A Genius for War* and George S Patton Jr's own book *War As I Knew It*. The Houghton Mifflin Co. of New York has asked that I make the following acknowledgement: 'Excerpts from *War As I Knew It* by General George S Patton. Copyright © 1947 by Beatrice Patton Walters, Ruth Patton Totten and George Smith Patton. Copyright © renewed 1975 by Major General George Patton, Ruth Patton Totten, John K Waters Jr and George P Waters. Reprinted by permission of Houghton Mifflin Co. All rights reserved'. George S Patton Jr's letters and notebooks, unless otherwise stated, are to be found in Box 6, The George S Patton Papers, Manuscript Division, Library of Congress, Washington, DC.

The following books were consulted or directly quoted:

Barnett, Correlli, *The Desert Generals*, Cassell & Co, 1983 and *Engage the Enemy More Closely*, Hodder & Stoughton, 1991.

Bennett, Ralph, *Ultra in the West, The Normandy Campaign, 1944–45*, Charles Scribner's Sons, New York.

Blumenson, Martin, *The Patton Papers, 1885–1940*, and *1940–1945*, Boston, Houghton Mifflin, 1972 and 1974 and *Patton, The Man Behind the Legend*, New York, Morrow, 1985

Bradley, Omar N, *A Soldier's Story*, Henry Holt, New York, 1951 and with Clay Blair, *A General's Life*, New York, Simon & Schuster, 1981.

Chalfont, Alun, *Montgomery of Alamein*, Weidenfeld & Nicolson, London, 1976.

Churchill, Winston, *The Hinge of Fate*, and *The Second World War, Vol VI: Triumph and Tragedy*, Reprint Society, London, 1954.

Cole, Hugh M, *The Lorraine Campaign*, 1950 and *The Ardennes, Battle of the Bulge*, 1965, US Army in World War II: the European Theater of Operations, Historical Division, Department of the Army, Washington, DC.

D'Este, Carlo, *A Genius for War*, HarperCollins Publishers, 1995, and *Eisenhower Allied Supreme Commander*, Weidenfeld & Nicolson, London, 2002.

De Guingand, F, *Operation Victory*, Hodder & Stoughton, London, 1947 and *Generals at War*, London, 1964.

Delaforce, Patrick, *Marching to the Sound of Gunfire*, Sutton Publishing, 2003.

Eisenhower, David, *Eisenhower at War 1943–1945*, Random House, New York, 1986.

Eisenhower, Dwight D, *Report by the Supreme Commander to the Combined Chiefs of Staff on the Operations in Europe of the Allied Expeditionary Force 6 June 1944 to 8 May 1945*, HMSO, London, 1946; *Crusade in Europe*, Doubleday, New York, 1948; *At Ease: Stories I Tell to My Friends*, Doubleday, New York,1967.

Ellis, John, *World War II Data Book*, Aurum Press, London, 1995

Ellis, L, *Victory in the West, Vol I, The Battle of Normandy*, HM Stationery Office, 1962.

Farago, Ladislas, *Patton: Ordeal and Triumph*, New York, Ivan Obolensky, 1963, and *The Last Days of Patton*, New York, McGraw-Hill, 1981.

Fergusson, Bernard, *The Watery Maze: The Story of Combined Operations*, London, 1961.

Galloway, Strome, *The General Who Never Was*, Belleville, Ontario, 1981.

Gavin, James, *On to Berlin*, Pen and Sword Books Ltd, London, 1978.

Hamilton, Nigel, *Monty: the Making of a General 1887–1942*, Hamish Hamilton, London,1981; *Monty: Master of the Battlefield 1942–1944*, Hamish Hamilton, London,1983; *Monty: The Field-Marshal 1944–1976*, Hamish Hamilton, London,1986; *The Full Monty*, Penguin Books, 2002.

Horne, Alastair and Montgomery, David, *The Lonely Leader*, Pan Books, 1995.

Horrocks, Sir Brian, *A Full Life*, Collins, London, 1960

Howe, George F, *Northwest Africa: Seizing the Initiative in the West*, Center of Military History, Pub 6–1, 1957.

James, M E C, *I Was Monty's Double*, London, 1954.

Kirby, Norman, *1100 Miles with Monty*, London, 1989.

Liddell Hart, B H, ed., *The Rommel Papers*, London, 1953.

Merriam, Robert E, *The Battle of the Ardennes*, Souvenir, Press, London, 1958.

Meyer, Hubert, *The History of the 12th SS Panzer Division Hitlerjugend*, J J Fedorowicz Publishing Inc., Canada, 1994.

Montgomery, Bernard, *El Alamein to the River Sangro; Normandy to the Baltic*, Barrie & Jenkins Ltd, London, 1973, *The Memoirs of Field Marshal the Viscount Montgomery*, Constable, London, 1958.

Montgomery, Brian, *A Field Marshal in the Family*, Constable, London, 1973.

Moorehead, Alan, *Montgomery*, Hamish Hamilton, London, 1946.

Nicolson, N, *Alex*, Weidenfeld & Nicolson, 1973.

Pallud, Jean Paul, *The Battle of the Bulge, Then and Now*, Battle of Britain Prints International Ltd, London, 1984.

Patton, George S Jr, *War As I Knew It*, Bantam Books, 1980.

Province, Charles M, *Patton's Third Army, A Daily Combat Diary*, Hippocrene Books, New York, 1992.

Ray, Cyril, *Algiers to Austria*, Eyre & Spottiswoode, London, 1952.

Reynolds, Michael, *Steel Inferno*, Spellmount, 1999 and *Eagles & Bulldogs in Normandy 1944*, Spellmount, 2003.

Runciman, Steven, *A Traveller's Alphabet*, Thames & Hudson, 1991.

Ryan, Cornelius, *A Bridge Too Far*, Coronet Books, London, 1974.

Shulman, Milton, *Defeat in the West*, Masquerade, 1995.

Smurthwaite, Nicholls & Washington, *Against All Odds: The British Army of 1939 –1940*, National Army Museum, London, 1989.

Stacey, Col., C P, *The Official History of the Canadian Army in the Second World War, Vol III, The Victory Campaign*, Queen's Printer, Ottawa, Canada, 1960.

Toland, John, *The Last 100 Days*, Arthur Barker, London, 1965.

Whiting, Charles, *Patton*, Ballantine, New York, 1970 and *Patton's Last Battle*, Spellmount, UK, 2002.

Wilmot, Chester, *The Struggle for Europe*, Collins, London, 1952.

Index

FORMATIONS & UNITS

PLACES

319

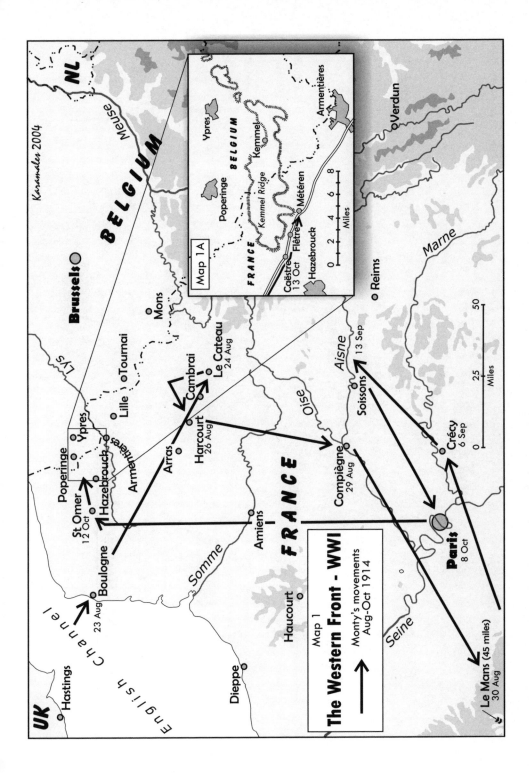

Karander 2004

UK

Hastings

English Channel

Dieppe

Boulogne
23 Aug

St Omer
12 Oct

Hazebrouck

Poperinge

Ypres

Lille

Tournai

Mons

Armentières

Arras

Harcourt
26 Aug

Amiens

Haucourt

BELGIUM

Meuse

LYS

Brussels

Cambrai

Le Cateau
24 Aug

FRANCE

Somme

Seine

Oise

Compiègne
29 Aug

Soissons

Aisne
13 Sep

Reims

Verdun

Marne

Crécy
6 Sep

Paris
8 Oct

Le Mans (45 miles)
30 Aug

Map 1
The Western Front - WWI

Monty's movements
Aug-Oct 1914

0   25   50
Miles

Map 1A

Ypres

Kemmel

BELGIUM

Poperinge

Kemmel Ridge

FRANCE

Caëstre
13 Oct   Flêtre

Hazebrouck

Météren

Armentières

0   2   4   6   8
Miles

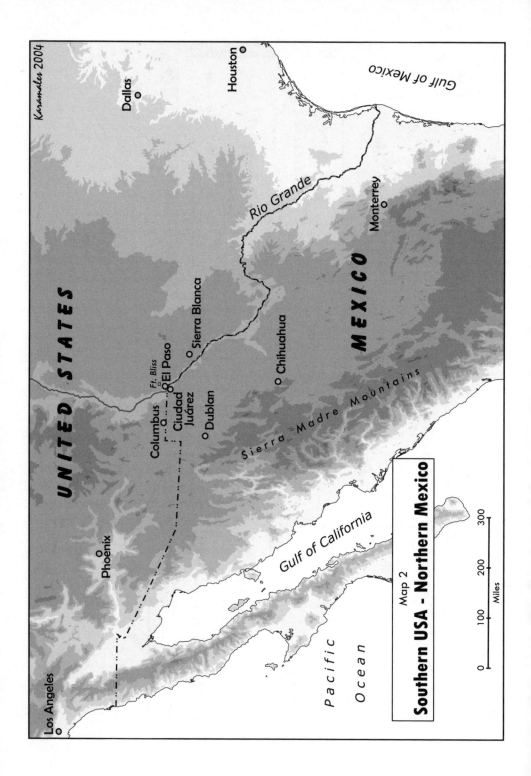

Map 2
Southern USA - Northern Mexico

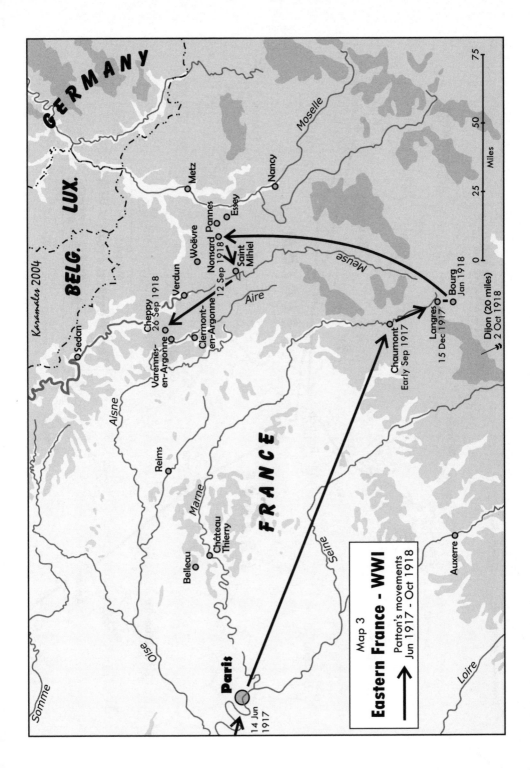

GERMANY

BELG.

LUX.

Kanander 2004

Moselle

Metz

Nancy

Woëvre

Nonsard Pannes

Essey

Saint
Mihiel

12 Sep 1918

Meuse

Bourg
Jan 1918

Sedan

Verdun

Cheppy
26 Sep 1918

Aire

Dijon (20 miles)
2 Oct 1918

Varennes-
en-Argonne

Clermont-
en-Argonne

Chaumont
Early Sep 1917

Langres
15 Dec 1917

Aisne

Reims

FRANCE

Marne

Belleau

Château
Thierry

Seine

Auxerre

Paris

Oise

14 Jun
1917

Map 3

Eastern France - WWI

Patton's movements
Jun 1917 - Oct 1918

Somme

Loire

75

50

Miles

25

0

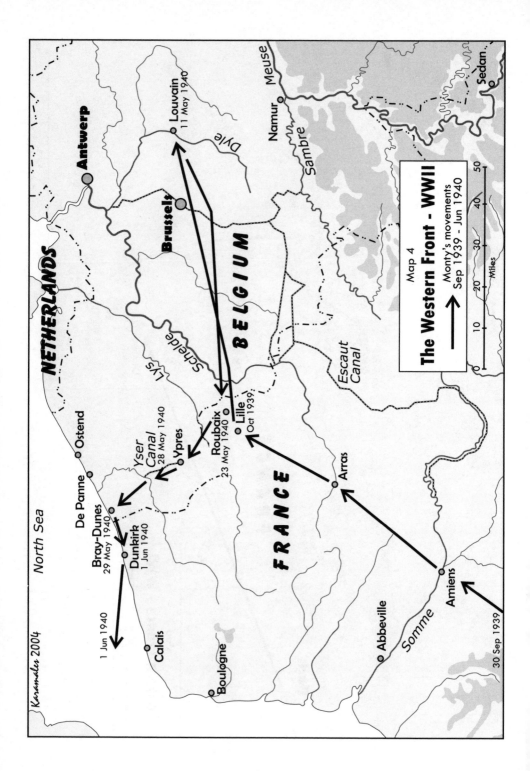

Map 4
The Western Front - WWII
Monty's movements
Sep 1939 - Jun 1940

Miles
0   10   20   30   40   50

NETHERLANDS

North Sea

BELGIUM

FRANCE

Antwerp

Brussels

Louvain
11 May 1940

Namur

Meuse

Sambre

Sedan

Dyle

Ostend

De Panne

Bray-Dunes
29 May 1940

Dunkirk
1 Jun 1940

Calais

Boulogne

Yser
Canal
28 May 1940

Ypres

Scheldt

Lys

Roubaix
23 May 1940

Lille
Oct 1939

Escaut
Canal

Arras

Abbeville

Somme

Amiens

30 Sep 1939

1 Jun 1940

Karambles 2004

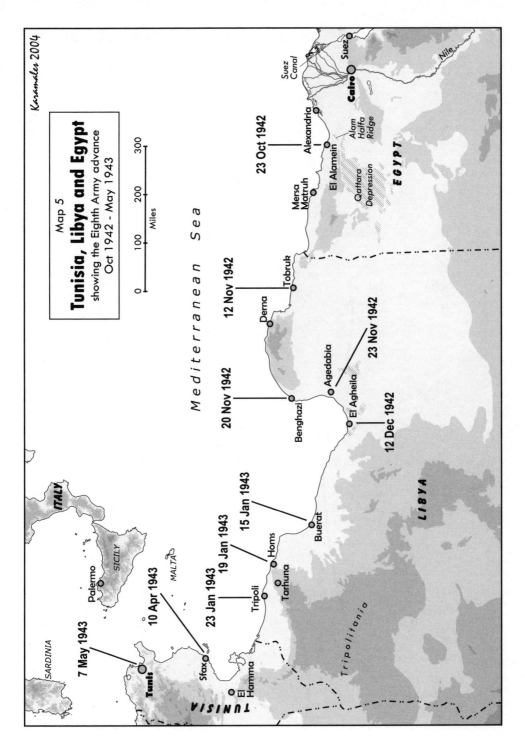

Map 5

Tunisia, Libya and Egypt

showing the Eighth Army advance
Oct 1942 - May 1943

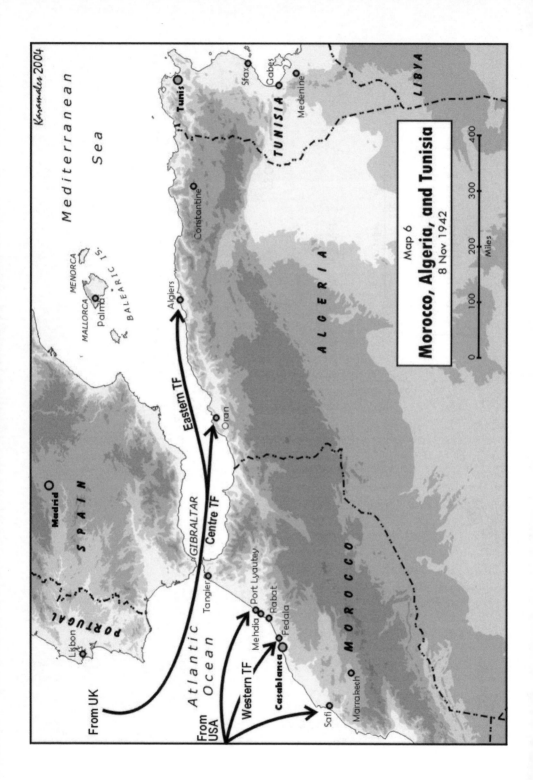

Map 6
Morocco, Algeria, and Tunisia
8 Nov 1942

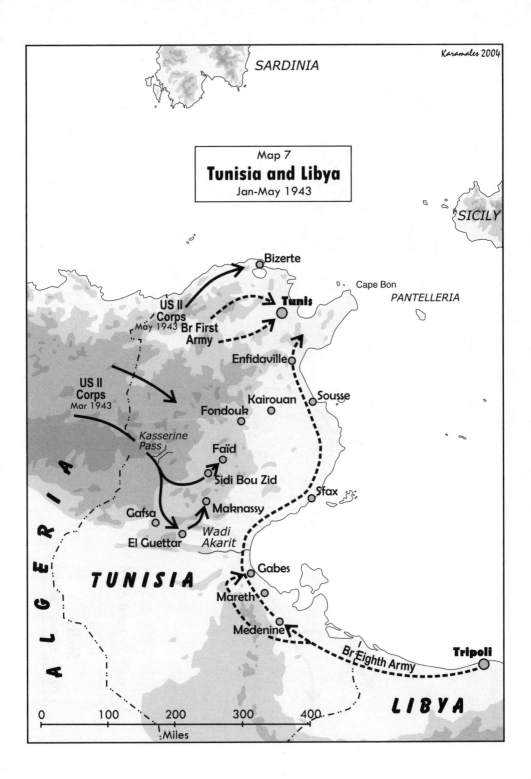

Karamales 2004

SARDINIA

Map 7
Tunisia and Libya
Jan-May 1943

SICILY

Bizerte

US II
Corps
May 1943
Br First
Army

Tunis

Cape Bon

PANTELLERIA

Enfidaville

US II
Corps
Mar 1943

Kairouan

Sousse

Fondouk

*Kasserine
Pass*

Faïd

Sidi Bou Zid

Sfax

Gafsa

Maknassy

El Guettar

*Wadi
Akarit*

TUNISIA

Gabes

Mareth

A L G E R I A

Medenine

Br Eighth Army

Tripoli

L I B Y A

0   100   200   300   400
Miles

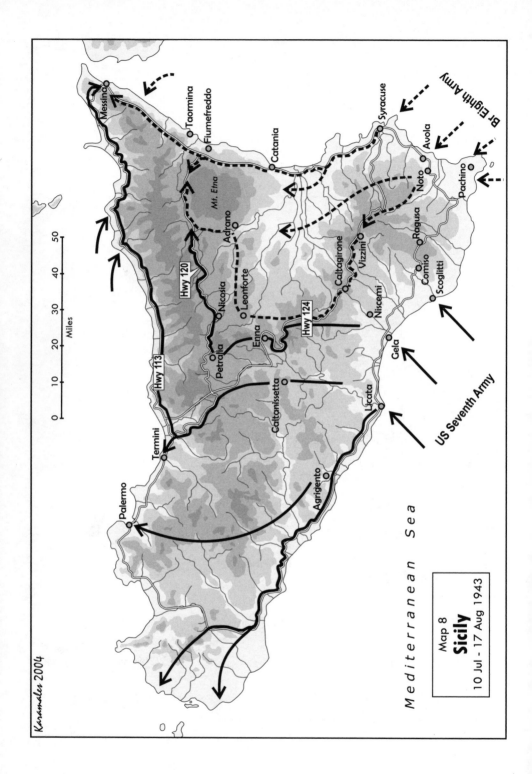

Kursander 2004

Mediterranean Sea

Map 8
Sicily
10 Jul - 17 Aug 1943

Br Eighth Army

US Seventh Army

Messina
Taormina
Fiumefreddo
Catania
Mt. Etna
Adrano
Nicosia
Leonforte
Caltagirone
Vizzini
Ragusa
Comiso
Scoglitti
Niscemi
Enna
Petralia
Caltanissetta
Gela
Licata
Agrigento
Termini
Palermo
Syracuse
Avola
Noto
Pachino

Hwy 120
Hwy 113
Hwy 124

Miles
0   10   20   30   40   50

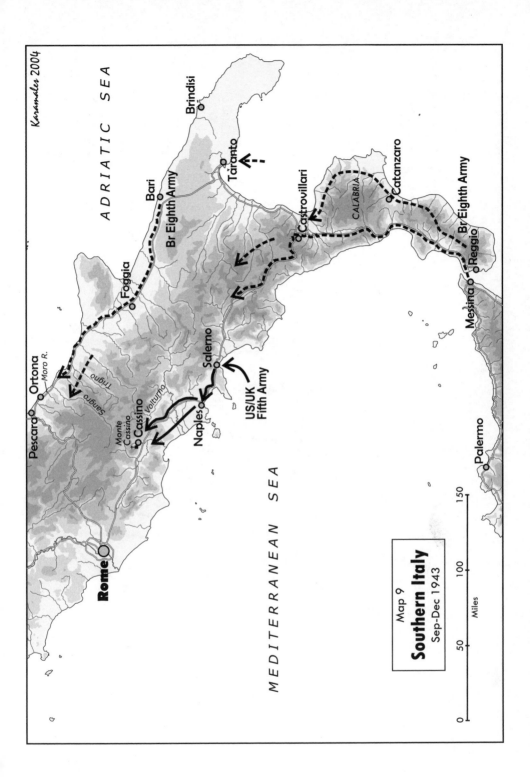

Kanmaler 2004

ADRIATIC SEA

Brindisi

Táranto

Bari

Br Eighth Army

Foggia

Castrovillari

Catanzaro

CALABRIA

Br Eighth Army

Reggio

Messina

Pescara
Ortona
Moro R.
Sangro
Trigno

Salerno

US/UK
Fifth Army

Monte
Cassino
Cassino

Volturno

Naples

Rome

MEDITERRANEAN SEA

Palermo

Map 9
Southern Italy
Sep–Dec 1943

0   50   100   150
Miles

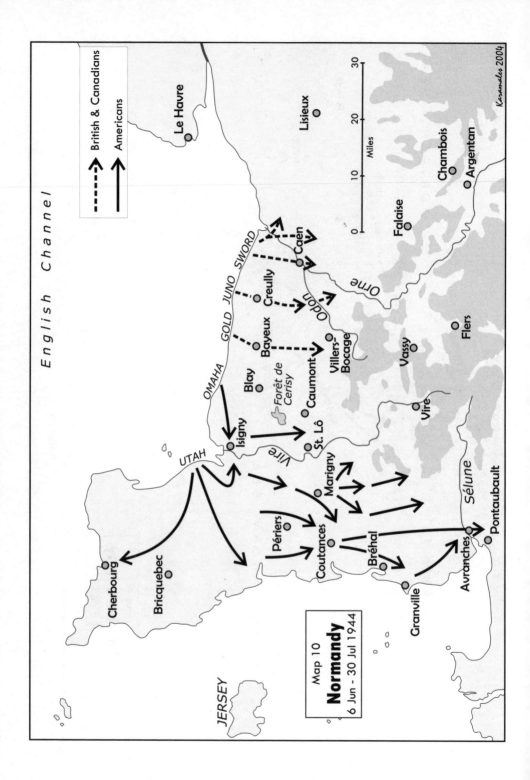

English Channel

Le Havre

British & Canadians

Americans

Lisieux

Chambois

Argentan

Falaise

Flers

Orne

Caen

SWORD
JUNO
GOLD
OMAHA

Creully

Odon

Bayeux

Villers-
Bocage

Vassy

Blay

Forêt de
Cerisy

Caumont

Vire

St. Lô

Isigny

Vire

UTAH

Marigny

Cherbourg

Bricquebec

Périers

Coutances

Bréhal

Granville

Avranches

Pontaubault

Sélune

JERSEY

Map 10
Normandy
6 Jun – 30 Jul 1944

Kerendes 2004

Miles

0   10   20   30

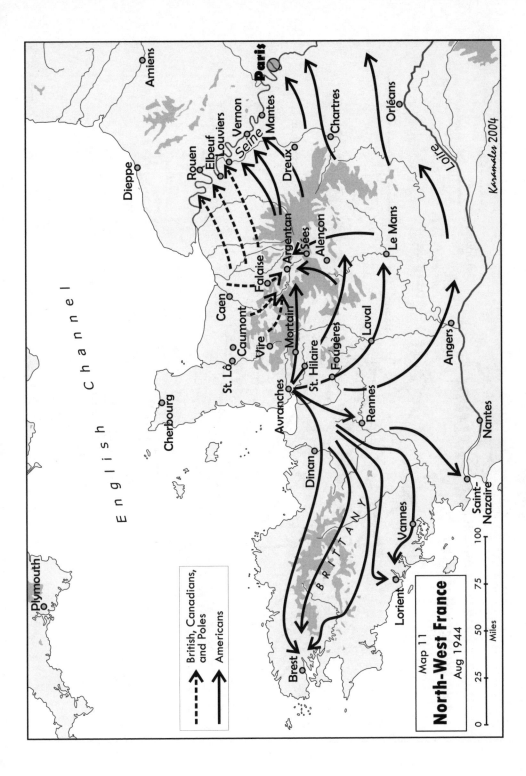

English Channel

Plymouth
Amiens
Dieppe
Cherbourg
Rouen
Elbeuf
Louviers
Vernon
Mantes
Paris
Chartres
Orléans
Seine
Loire
Dreux
Argentan
Sées
Alençon
Le Mans
Falaise
Caen
Caumont
Vire
Mortain
St. Lô
St. Hilaire
Fougères
Laval
Angers
Avranches
Rennes
Nantes
Dinan
Saint-Nazaire
BRITTANY
Vannes
Lorient
Brest

Karamdes 2004

British, Canadians,
and Poles
Americans

Map 11
North-West France
Aug 1944

0   25   50   75   100
Miles

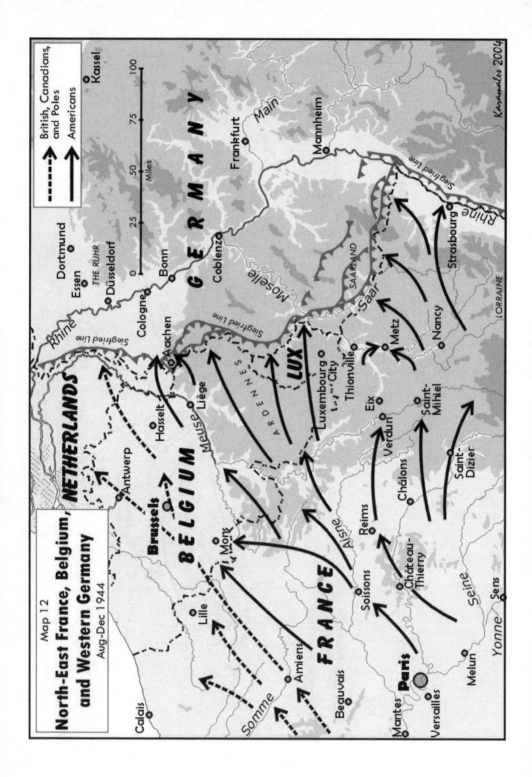

Map 12

North-East France, Belgium, and Western Germany

Aug–Dec 1944

British, Canadians, and Poles

Americans

Karunder 2004

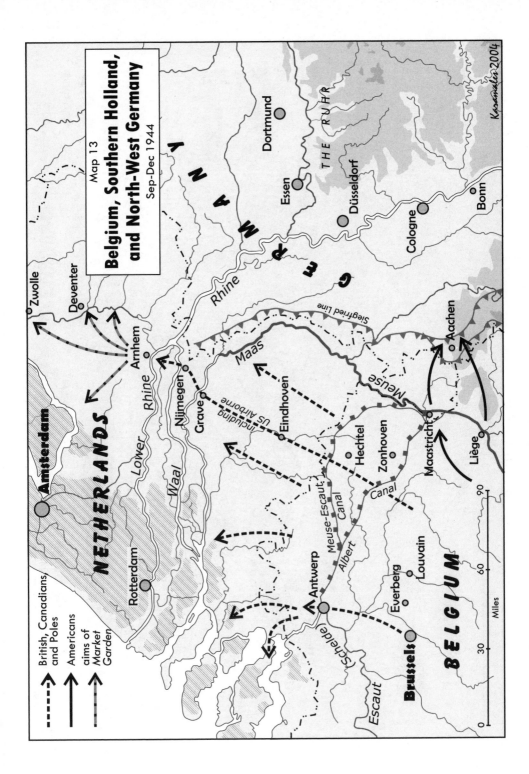

Map 13

Belgium, Southern Holland, and North-West Germany

Sep-Dec 1944

Kaminski 2004

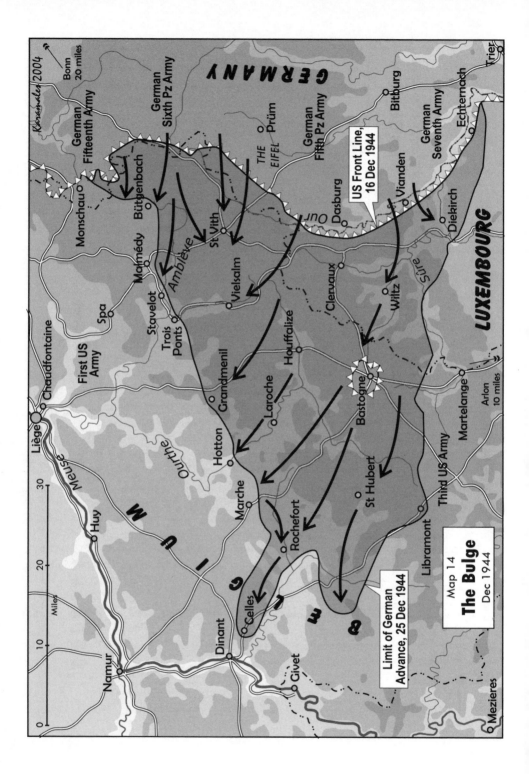

Kiremder 2004

Bonn
20 miles

GERMANY

German
Fifteenth Army

German
Sixth Pz Army

Prüm

THE EIFEL

German
Fifth Pz Army

Dasburg

Bitburg

German
Seventh Army

Echternach

Monschau

Bütgenbach

St Vith

Our

US Front Line,
16 Dec 1944

Vianden

Diekirch

Malmédy

Amblève

Vielsalm

Clervaux

Wiltz

Sûre

LUXEMBOURG

Spa

Stavelot

Trois
Ponts

Grandmenil

Houffalize

Bastogne

First US
Army

Chaudfontaine

Laroche

Liège

Meuse

Ourthe

Hotton

Marche

St Hubert

Martelange

Third US Army

Arlon
10 miles

Huy

30

A R D E N N E S

Rochefort

Libramont

20

Celles

Dinant

Givet

Limit of German
Advance, 25 Dec 1944

Map 14

The Bulge
Dec 1944

Namur

10

Miles

0

Mezieres

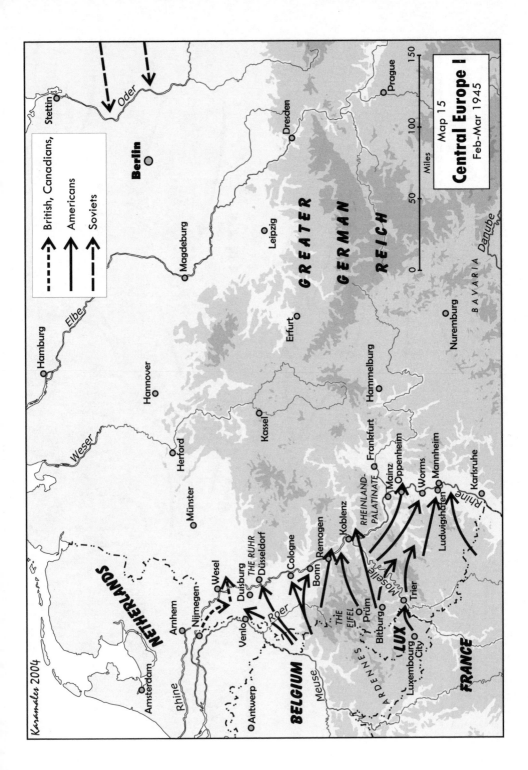

Karamales 2004

NETHERLANDS

BELGIUM

LUX

FRANCE

BAVARIA

GREATER

GERMAN

REICH

THE EIFEL

RHEINLAND-PALATINATE

ARDENNES

THE RUHR

Amsterdam

Antwerp

Arnhem

Nijmegen

Venlo

Wesel

Duisburg

Düsseldorf

Cologne

Bonn

Remagen

Koblenz

Prüm

Bitburg

Trier

Luxembourg City

Ludwigshafen

Mannheim

Worms

Oppenheim

Mainz

Frankfurt

Hammelburg

Karlsruhe

Nuremburg

Kassel

Erfurt

Herford

Münster

Hannover

Hamburg

Magdeburg

Leipzig

Dresden

Prague

Berlin

Stettin

Rhine

Meuse

Roer

Moselle

Rhine

Weser

Elbe

Oder

Danube

British, Canadians,

Americans

Soviets

Map 15
Central Europe I
Feb–Mar 1945

0   50   100   150

Miles

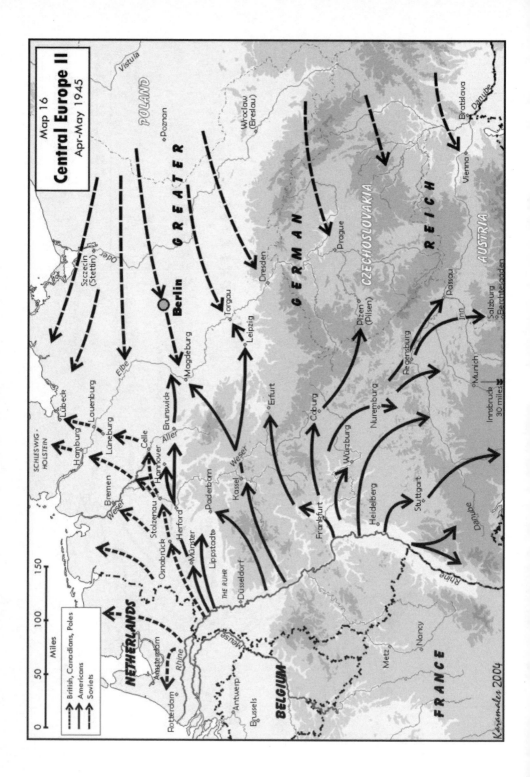

Map 16
Central Europe II
Apr-May 1945

British, Canadians, Poles
Americans
Soviets

Miles
0   50   100   150

GREATER GERMAN REICH

POLAND

CZECHOSLOVAKIA

AUSTRIA

NETHERLANDS

BELGIUM

FRANCE

SCHLESWIG-HOLSTEIN

THE RUHR

Vistula

Poznan

Wrocław (Breslau)

Szczecin (Stettin)

Oder

Berlin

Magdeburg

Elbe

Torgau

Leipzig

Dresden

Prague

Plzen (Pilsen)

Bratislava

Danube

Vienna

Salzburg
Berchtesgaden

Passau

Inn

Munich

Innsbruck
30 miles

Regensburg

Nuremburg

Coburg

Erfurt

Würzburg

Heidelberg

Stuttgart

Danube

Rhine

Frankfurt

Kassel

Weser

Paderborn

Aller

Brunswick

Hannover

Celle

Lüneburg

Hamburg

Lübeck

Lauenburg

Bremen

Weser

Stolzenau

Osnabrück

Herford

Münster

Lippstadt

Düsseldorf

Rhine

Meuse

Amsterdam

Rotterdam

Antwerp

Brussels

Metz

Nancy

Karamales 2004